LUTHER'S WORKS

American Edition

VOLUME 50

LUTHER'S WORKS

VOLUME 50

Letters

III

EDITED AND TRANSLATED BY

GOTTFRIED G. KRODEL

GENERAL EDITOR

HELMUT T. LEHMANN

FORTRESS PRESS / PHILADELPHIA

Library of Congress Catalogue Number 74–76934

ISBN 0–8006–0350–8

4033H74   Printed in the United States of America   1–350

GENERAL EDITORS' PREFACE

The first editions of Luther's collected works appeared in the sixteenth century, and so did the first efforts to make him "speak English." In America serious attempts in these directions were made for the first time in the nineteenth century. The Saint Louis edition of Luther was the first endeavor on American soil to publish a collected edition of his works, and the Henkel Press in Newmarket, Virginia, was the first to publish some of Luther's writings in an English translation. During the first decade of the twentieth century, J. N. Lenker produced translations of Luther's sermons and commentaries in thirteen volumes. A few years later the first of the six volumes in the Philadelphia (or Holman) edition of the *Works of Martin Luther* appeared. But a growing recognition of the need for more of Luther's works in English has resulted in this American edition of Luther's works.

The edition is intended primarily for the reader whose knowledge of late medieval Latin and sixteenth-century German is too small to permit him to work with Luther in the original languages. Those who can will continue to read Luther in his original words as these have been assembled in the monumental Weimar edition (*D. Martin Luthers Werke.* Kritische Gesamtausgabe, Weimar, 1883–). Its texts and helps have formed a basis for this edition, though in certain places we have felt constrained to depart from its readings and findings. We have tried throughout to translate Luther as he thought translating should be done. That is, we have striven for faithfulness on the basis of the best lexicographical materials available. But where literal accuracy and clarity have conflicted, it is clarity that we have preferred, so that sometimes paraphrase seemed more faithful than literal fidelity. We have proceeded in a similar way in the matter of Bible versions, translating Luther's translations. Where this could be done by the use of an existing English version—King James, Douay, or Revised Standard—we have done so. Where it could not, we have supplied our own. To indicate this in each specific instance would have been pedantic; to adopt a uniform procedure would have been artificial—especially in view of Luther's own inconsistency in this regard. In each volume the translator will be responsible primarily for matters of text and language, while the responsibility of the editor will extend principally to the historical and theological matters reflected in the introductions and notes.

Although the edition as planned will include fifty-five volumes, Luther's writings are not being translated in their entirety. Nor should they be. As he was the first to insist, much of what he wrote and said was not that important. Thus the edition is a selection of works that have proven their importance for the faith, life, and history of the Christian church. The first thirty volumes contain Luther's expositions of various biblical books, while the remaining volumes include what are usually called his "Reformation writings" and other occasional pieces. The final volume of the set will be an index volume; in addition to an index of quotations, proper names, and topics, and a list of corrections and changes, it will contain a glossary of many of the technical terms that recur in Luther's works and that cannot be defined each time they appear. Obviously Luther cannot be forced into any neat set of rubrics. He can provide his reader with bits of autobiography or with political observations as he expounds a psalm, and he can speak tenderly about the meaning of the faith in the midst of polemics against his opponents. It is the hope of publishers, editors, and translators that through this edition the message of Luther's faith will speak more clearly to the modern church.

J.P.
H.T.L.

CONTENTS

ADB   *—Allgemeine Deutsche Biographie*, edited by Historische Kommission bei der Königlichen Akademie der Wissenschaften, Munich (Leipzig, 1875–1912).

ARG   *—Archiv für Reformationsgeschichte.*

C.R.   *—Corpus Reformatorum*, edited by C. G. Bretschneider *et al.* (Halle/Saale, 1834–   ).

C.T.   *—Concilium Tridentinum*, edited by Görres-Gesellschaft (Freiburg, 1901–   ).

DNB   *—The Dictionary of National Biography*, edited by L. Stephen *et al.* (London, 1937–1938).

DRTA.JR   *—Deutsche Reichstagsakten unter Kaiser Karl V.*, edited by Historische Kommission bei der Bayerischen Akademie der Wissenschaften (Gotha, 1893–   ; reprint: Göttingen, 1962–   ).

EHD 5   *—English Historical Documents*, Vol. 5: 1485–1558, edited by C. H. Williams (New York, 1967).

LCC   *—Library of Christian Classics.* J. T. McNeill and H. P. van Dusen, General Editors (Philadelphia, 1953–1969).

LJB   *—Lutherjahrbuch.*

L.P.   *—Calendar of Letters and Papers, Foreign and Domestic, Henry VIII*, edited by J. S. Brewer, J. Gairdner, R. H. Brodie (London, 1864–1932).

LThK   *—Lexikon für Theologie und Kirche*, edited by J. Höfer and K. Rahner (2nd ed., Freiburg, 1957–1967).

LW   *—American Edition of Luther's Works* (Philadelphia and St. Louis, 1955–   ).

NB I.Abt.   *—Nuntiaturberichte aus Deutschland. I.* Abteilung: 1533–1559, edited by K. Preussisches historisches Institut in Rom and Deutsches historisches Institut in Rom (Gotha, Berlin, Tübingen, 1892–1959).

NB I.Abt.,E.1—*Nuntiaturberichte aus Deutschland.* I. Abteilung: 1533–1559. Ergänzungsband 1: 1530–1531, edited by G. Müller (Tübingen, 1963).

NCE —*New Catholic Encyclopedia,* edited by The Catholic University of America (New York, 1967).

NDB —*Neue Deutsche Biographie,* edited by Historische Kommission bei der Bayerischen Akademie der Wissenschaften (Berlin, 1953–   ).

S-J —*Luther's Correspondence,* 2 vols., edited by P. Smith and C. M. Jacobs (Philadelphia, 1913–1918).

St. L. —*D. Martin Luthers sämmtliche Schriften,* 23 vols. in 25, edited by J. G. Walch (2nd ed., St. Louis, 1880–1910).

UASA —*Urkunden und Akten zur Geschichte von Martin Luthers Schmalkaldischen Artikeln* (1536–1574), edited by H. Volz (Berlin, 1957).

WA —*D. Martin Luthers Werke. Kritische Gesamtausgabe* (Weimar, 1883–   ).

WA, Br —*D. Martin Luthers Werke,* Briefwechsel (Weimar, 1930–1970).

WA, DB —*D. Martin Luthers Werke.* Deutsche Bibel (Weimar, 1906–1961).

WA, RN —*Revisionsnachtrag* to Individual Volumes of the Four Series of WA.

WA, TR —*D. Martin Luthers Werke.* Tischreden (Weimar, 1912–1921).

Witt.Art. —*Die Wittenberger Artikel von 1536,* edited by G. Mentz (Leipzig, 1905).

ZKG —*Zeitschrift für Kirchengeschichte.*

INTRODUCTION TO VOLUME 50

Volume 50 of the American Edition of *Luther's Works* is the third and final volume of letters in this series; it presents 89 letters[1] written by Luther in the period from January, 1531, to February 14, 1546, a date four days prior to Luther's death.

For the Empire the period covered by the letters set forth in volume 50 was a time dominated by the Nürnberg Truce of 1532, which (at least for the time being) conceded to the Reformation a legal opportunity to exist, and by the efforts of Emperor Charles V to defeat the Turks and the French and to find a solution to the Reformation issues. He first sought a peaceful solution by means of compromises, religious colloquies, and a general council; later he sought a military solution by means of war against the Protestants. For the Protestants of the Empire this period was a time of consolidation, expansion, and international contacts, especially with England, but also a time marked by setbacks stemming from political ineptitude and personal failure. For the papacy and the papal church in the Empire this period was a time of loss of territory, souls, and resources to the Protestants, but it was also a time of inventory, of reconsideration of the essentials and marginals of the Roman church, and of preparing for battle with Protestantism. These years saw both the papacy's participation in the Smalcaldic War against the Protestants in the Empire and the opening of the Council of Trent on December 13, 1545. For Luther this period was

---

[1] Throughout *LW* 48–50 the letters are numbered continuously; in *LW* 48 the numbers run from 1 to 119, and in *LW* 49 from 120 to 236; *LW* 50 continues this numbering system with letters running from 237 to 325. For the organization of the text of *LW* 50, see *LW* 48, xiii ff. In *LW* 50 a special problem was to find English equivalents for the various units of measurement that occur rather frequently in these letters. Since there was great variety in the units of measurement in the Germany of Luther's day—in some cases there was a difference even from one town to the next—it is extremely difficult to convert these measurements accurately into metric equivalents. The information given in Grimm's *Deutsches Wörterbuch* and the conversion tables found in the *Brockhaus* encyclopedia and in F. W. Clarke, *Weights, Measures, and Money* (New York, 1877) were consulted in arriving at approximate metric and decimal equivalents. However, the units of measurement that Luther used were often rather obscure, and little information is available on them.

a time of peace; it is not that Luther was free of controversies with enemies on his right and his left—in fact, Luther wrote some of his most polemical writings during this period—but rather that the Nürnberg Truce enabled Luther to live in comparative peace and to remain within the legal and political order of the Empire to the end of his life.

The period in Luther's life covered by the letters of the present volume is often called that of the "old" Luther; it is contrasted to the period of the "young" Luther, and is often characterized as a period of lack of intellectual dynamics, of dogmatism, of growing egocentricity, of cantankerousness, of ecclesiastical and bourgeois "establishment-mindedness." And in all these labels there is a grain of truth. In the portrait of an older person we discover lines and wrinkles which we have not seen in the portrait of that same person at an earlier age, or which we perhaps simply did not want to see. Consequently it seems wiser to make a little less noise about the "old" Luther than is made in certain circles, especially since in contrast to the "young" Luther our knowledge of the "old" Luther is still sketchy at best.[2]

Since Letters I and II had covered only the first five volumes of WA, Br, Letters III had to cover the letters in the remaining six volumes of WA, Br. Thus, the problem of selection was increased simply because of the abundance of letters. There were two further difficulties. First, many—perhaps the majority—of the letters in WA, Br 6 through 11 deal less with events in Luther's life than with day-by-day matters in the life of the evangelical churches or congregations of the Empire. These matters[3] lack the excitement of the events of the 1520s, and are probably of interest only to the specialist—and he too may soon be bored. Second, tighter restrictions as to time and space available for volume 50 made necessary a revision of the original selection of letters to be presented; in this

---

[2] For a discussion of the "old" Luther, see G. Ritter, *Luther: His Life and Work* (New York, 1963), pp. 175 f., 202 f., 206 f. How little Luther's life after 1532 is known can be seen from a glance at the standard biographies. Except for Köstlin-Kawerau (see p. xix, n. 20), all the major biographies, esp. the more popular ones, spend less (sometimes considerably less) than a third of their space on describing these last fourteen years, while they spend over two-thirds of their space on the first fourteen years (1517/18 to 1532) of Luther's public activities.

[3] E.g., matters pertaining to marriage laws, to congregations seeking a pastor, or pastors seeking congregations, or to aid for people, esp. students.

process almost all those letters dealing with the Eucharistic controversy and its settlement by the Wittenberg Concord of 1536, with Luther's controversy with the Law Faculty of Wittenberg's University, and with the bigamy case of Philip of Hesse had to be eliminated. The letters which were finally incorporated in volume 50 concentrate on three major topics:

(1) Luther the person: all of the extant letters written by Luther to his wife, all the letters from the journey to Eisleben where Luther died in the early morning hours of February 18, 1546, and as many letters as possible that deal with Luther's family and home, especially his children, have been included. That this last category does not even approach completeness is obvious.

(2) The contacts which Luther, his University, and his territorial government had with England during this period.

(3) The council for which Luther had called as early as 1518, which was finally opened a little over two months prior to his death, and which had directions totally different from those envisioned by him.

These principles of selection may of course be questioned. But it seemed natural to this editor, working in an ecumenically-minded age, to concentrate on the council; and to emphasize Luther's contacts with England in an edition of Luther's letters designed for an English-speaking audience should need no justification.

According to John of Salisbury, Bernard of Chartres compared the scholars of his day to dwarfs borne aloft on the shoulders of giants. This comparison is also applicable to the selection and editing of Luther's letters presented in volumes 48 through 50 of the American Edition of *Luther's Works*: this work, too, rests on the shoulders of those who in the past have edited and translated Luther's letters and of those who have aided this present editor in his task. To name them individually or to dedicate these three volumes to some of them would not be in keeping with the editorial principles of the American Edition of *Luther's Works*. Yet scholarly integrity requires the acknowledgment of the dwarf status of this editor, and at the very least requires the acknowledgment of the work of Hans Volz, to whom international Luther research owes so much. If in a few instances this present editor was able to suggest or present new insights into the texts, then this was possible only because he had available the results of the works of the giants. If all three volumes of letters in the American Edition of *Luther's Works* can contribute to making Luther less a saintly church father or a demon-filled monk and more of a real person to the reader, if they can in any way encourage and stimulate the reader to dig more deeply into the subject matter, then these three volumes will fulfill their function, and will be worth the time and labor put into them.

G.G.K.

Bibliographical Note

It would have been impossible to produce the present volume without the work done by Ernst Ludwig Enders and his successors,[1] by Otto Clemen,[2] Hans Volz, Eike Wolgast,[3] and Hanns Rückert,[4] scholars who have dedicated their energies to editing Luther's letters either totally or in selection.[5] In the preparation of the translation of and commentary to the letters presented below the common technical aids have been used.[6]

The general history which is reflected in the letters of this volume is portrayed and analyzed in Ranke's history of the Reformation[7] (still the unsurpassed masterpiece for this period), in the

---

[1] E. L. Enders et al., Dr. Martin Luther's Briefwechsel (19 vols.; Frankfurt, Leipzig, 1884–1932); hereinafter cited as: Enders, Briefwechsel.

[2] He was the editor of WA, Br 1–11.

[3] Volz and Wolgast are the editors of WA, Br 12–14.

[4] Rückert, Luthers Briefe. Luthers Werke in Auswahl, Vol. 6; general editor: O. Clemen (2nd ed.; Berlin, 1955); hereinafter cited as: Rückert, LB. Rückert gives his notes to the number of the line of the text. In order to facilitate the citing in the present volume, the line numbers of Rückert have been treated as footnote numbers.

[5] For selections from Luther's letters in English, see LW 48, xiv, n. 5; T. G. Tappert (ed.), Luther: Letters of Spiritual Counsel. LCC 18 (Philadelphia, 1955); hereinafter cited as: LCC 18.

[6] To the bibliographical tools cited in LW 48, xviii, n. 5, have to be added the bibliographical reports published annually in LJB; and Bibliographie de la Réforme: 1450–1648 (Leiden, 1960–   ); Bibliographie internationale de l'Humanisme et de la Renaissance (Geneva, 1966–   ). The following technical aids were used for the preparation of the translation and the commentary: C. Lewis, C. Short, A Latin Dictionary (Oxford, 1958); hereinafter cited as: Lewis and Short.—C. du Cange, Glossarium mediae et infimae Latinitatis (7 vols.; Paris, 1840–1850); hereinafter cited as: Du Cange.—A. Götze et al. (eds.), Trübners Deutsches Wörterbuch (8 vols.; Berlin, 1939–1957); hereinafter cited as: Trübner.—A. Götze (ed.), Frühneuhochdeutsches Glossar (5th. ed.; Berlin, 1956); hereinafter cited as: Götze.—P. Dietz (ed.), Wörterbuch zu Dr. Martin Luthers Deutsches Schriften (Leipzig, 1870); hereinafter cited as: Dietz.—F. L. Cross (ed.), The Oxford Dictionary of the Christian Church (New York, 1958); hereinafter cited as: O.D.C.C.—M. Cary et al. (eds.), The Oxford Classical Dictionary (Oxford, 1949); hereinafter cited as: O.C.D.—E. Haberkern, J. F. Wallach (eds.), Hilfswörterbuch für Historiker: Mittelalter und Neuzeit (2nd ed.; Bern, Munich, 1964); hereinafter cited as: Hilfswörterbuch.—E. Brinckmeier, Glossarium Diplomaticum (2 vols.; Gotha, 1856–1863; reprint: Aalen, 1967).—B. Altaner, Patrology (New York, 1960).—K. Aland, Hilfsbuch zum Lutherstudium (3rd ed.; Witten, 1970).—G. S. Robbert, "A Checklist of Luther's Writings in English," Concordia Theological Monthly 36 (1965), 772 ff. and 40 (1970), 214 ff.—G. Buchwald, Luther-Kalendarium (Leipzig, 1929); hereinafter cited as: Buchwald, L.K.—See also p. XIII, n. 1.

[7] L. von Ranke, Deutsche Geschichte im Zeitalter der Reformation, critical edition by P. Joachimsen (6 parts in 3 vols.; Meersburg, Leipzig, 1933); herein-

second volume of the *New Cambridge Modern History,* which is edited by Geoffrey R. Elton,[8] and in the Reformation history by Franz Lau and Ernst Bizer.[9] This history is documented in the collections prepared by Beresford J. Kidd[10] and Hans Hillerbrand.[11] Emil Sehling began to collect all the evangelical church ordinances of the sixteenth century into a monumental corpus, and this task is now being carried on by the Institute for Evangelical Ecclesiastical Law in Göttingen.[12] Otto Winckelmann[13] and Ekkehart Fabian[14] have analyzed the early history of the Smalcaldic League; Walther Köhler[15] and Hermann Sasse[16] have presented the history of the Eucharistic controversy; and Friedrich Prüser[17] has shown the ups and downs in the negotiations between the Smalcaldic League and Henry VIII of England. Charles V, the great political counterpoint to the evangelicals, is the subject of Karl Brandi's well written and researched biography which breaks much new ground.[18] The plans of Charles V for dealing with the German Protestants did not always match those of the papacy. In this connection the idea of settling the issues raised by the Reformation by means of a general council of the church was of major importance.

after cited as: Ranke. Since this Joachimsen edition presents the documentary apparatus it is the only edition which has been used in this present volume. S. Austin has published an abridged English version of Ranke (London, 1905).

[8] *The Reformation: 1520–1559* (Cambridge, 1962); hereinafter cited as: Elton.

[9] *A History of the Reformation in Germany to 1555* (London, 1969); hereinafter cited as: Lau-Bizer.

[10] *Documents Illustrative of the Continental Reformation* (Oxford, 1911; reprint: Oxford, 1967); hereinafter cited as: Kidd.

[11] *The Reformation: A Narrative History Related by Contemporary Observers and Participants* (New York, Evanston, 1964); hereinafter cited as: Hillerbrand.

[12] *Die evangelischen Kirchenordnungen des XVI. Jahrhunderts* (Leipzig, Tübingen, 1902–   ); hereinafter cited as: Sehling.

[13] *Der Schmalkaldische Bund und der Nürnberger Religionsfriede* (Strassburg, 1892); hereinafter cited as: Winckelmann.

[14] *Die Entstehung des Schmalkaldischen Bundes und seiner Verfassung* (Tübingen, 1956 [1st ed.]; 1962 [2nd ed.]); hereinafter cited as: Fabian, *ESBV.*

[15] *Zwingli und Luther,* 1 (Leipzig, 1924), 2 (Gütersloh, 1953); hereinafter cited as: Köhler 1 and 2.

[16] *This is my Body. Luther's Contention for the Real Presence in the Sacrament of the Altar* (Minneapolis, 1959); hereinafter cited as: Sasse.

[17] *England und die Schmalkaldener: 1535–1540* (Leipzig, 1929); hereinafter cited as: Prüser.

[18] *Kaiser Karl V. Werden und Schicksal einer Persönlichkeit und eines Weltreiches.* Vol. 1: Text (5th ed.; Munich, 1959). Vol. 2: Quellen und Erörterungen (2nd ed.; Munich, 1967). Reprint: Darmstadt, 1959–1967. This reprint is hereinafter cited as: Brandi 1 and 2. Because of the documentary apparatus only this edition has been used in this present volume. An English version was published in London, 1939.

After much negotiating a council was finally opened on December 13, 1545. Hubert Jedin[19] presented the prelude of this event, and his work is a necessary companion volume for many of the letters presented below.

Julius Köstlin,[20] Roland Bainton,[21] and Ernest Schwiebert[22] have made the life and work of Luther the topic of profound studies which supply the details necessary to place the presented letters into the background of Luther's life. During much of the time covered in the present volume, Luther was dean of Wittenberg's Theological Faculty; in this position he was involved in many academic disputations of which the texts have been edited by Paul Drews.[23] The documents and events related to the last days of Luther's life, and to his death, have been presented by Jakob Strieder[24] and Christof Schubart.[25]

The lives and letters of some of the men[26] with whom Luther either worked or corresponded are valuable sources of information concerning the background of some of the following letters. A selection from the works of Luther's co-worker Melanchthon is now available in a modern edition.[27] Clyde Manschreck[28] has presented

---

[19] *A History of the Council of Trent*, 1 (London, 1957), hereinafter cited as: Jedin.

[20] G. Kawerau (ed.), *Martin Luther. Sein Leben und seine Schriften* (5th ed., 2 vols.; Berlin, 1903); hereinafter cited as: Köstlin-Kawerau.

[21] *Here I Stand. A Life of Martin Luther* (Nashville, 1950); hereinafter cited as: Bainton.

[22] *Luther and His Times. The Reformation From a New Perspective* (St. Louis, 1950); hereinafter cited as: Schwiebert.

[23] *Disputationen Dr. Martin Luthers in d. J. 1535–1545 an der Universität Wittenberg gehalten* (Göttingen, 1895); hereinafter cited as: Drews.

[24] *Authentische Berichte über Luthers letzte Lebensstunden* (Bonn, 1912); hereinafter cited as: Strieder.

[25] *Die Berichte über Luther's Tod und Begräbnis* (Weimer, 1917); hereinafter cited as: Schubart.

[26] For Melanchthon's correspondence, see *C. R.* 1–10.—For Zwingli's correspondence, see *C. R. Zwingli Werke*, 7–11.—G. Kawerau (ed.), *Der Briefwechsel des Justus Jonas* (2 vols.; Halle, 1884–1885; reprint: Hildesheim, 1964); hereinafter cited as: Kawerau, *Jonas Briefwechsel.*—O. Vogt (ed.), *Dr. Johannes Bugenhagens Briefwechsel* (Stettin, 1888; reprint with additions: Hildesheim, 1966).—J. V. Pollet, *Martin Bucer, Études sur la Correspondance* (2 vols.; Paris, 1958–1962); hereinafter cited as: Pollet.—M. Lenz (ed.), *Briefwechsel Landgraf Philipps des Grossmüthigen von Hessen mit Bucer* (3 vols.; Stuttgart, 1880–1891; reprint: Hildesheim, 1965); hereinafter cited as: Lenz, *BPB.*

[27] R. Stupperich *et al.* (eds.), *Melanchthons Werke in Auswahl* (Gütersloh, 1951–   ); hereinafter cited as: *Melanchthon:* Studienausgabe. For a selection of Melanchthon's works in English, see *LW* 48, xiv, n. 18.

[28] *Melanchthon. The Quiet Reformer* (New York, Nashville, 1958); hereinafter cited as: Manschreck.

a biography of Melanchthon, while Irmgard Höss[29] has made available a biography of Spalatin, and Bernhard Klaus[30] has published a biography of Dietrich.

The works of Erasmus of Rotterdam are cited according to the early eighteenth century Clericus edition,[31] while the correspondence of Erasmus has been made available by Percy S. Allen[32] in a masterful modern edition.

The history of the University of Wittenberg, Luther's base of operation, is reflected in the official papers,[33] from which much information on persons and events contemporary with Luther can be gained.

Many of the letters presented in volume 50 deal with the relationship of Luther, of Wittenberg University, and of Luther's territorial sovereign, Elector John Frederick, to England. In addition to Prüser's work mentioned above, the works by Gordon Rupp,[34] William Clebsch,[35] Gustave Constant,[36] and Neelak Tjernagel[37] provide the necessary materials for placing these letters into their proper context.

---

[29] *Georg Spalatin: 1484–1545. Ein Leben in der Zeit des Humanismus und der Reformation* (Weimar, 1956); hereinafter cited as: Höss, *Spalatin.*

[30] *Veit Dietrich: Leben und Werk* (Nürnberg, 1958); hereinafter cited as: Klaus.

[31] *Desiderii Erasmi opera omnia* (10 vols.; Leyden, 1703–1706); hereinafter cited as: Clericus.

[32] P. S. Allen *et al., Opus epistolarum Desiderii Erasmi Roterodami* (12 vols.; Oxford, 1906–1958).

[33] W. Friedensburg (ed.), *Urkundenbuch der Universität Wittenberg,* Part 1: 1502–1611 (Magdeburg, 1926); hereinafter cited as: *Urkundenbuch.*—W. Friedensburg, *Geschichte der Universität Wittenberg* (Halle, 1917); hereinafter cited as: Friedensburg, *GUW.* See also *LW* 48, xviii, n. 10.

[34] *Studies in the Making of the English Protestant Tradition* (Cambridge, 1947); hereinafter cited as: Rupp, *Tradition.*

[35] *England's Earliest Protestants: 1520–1535* (New Haven, 1964); hereinafter cited as: Clebsch.

[36] *The Reformation in England* (New York, 1935); hereinafter cited as: Constant.

[37] *Henry VIII and the Lutherans* (St. Louis, 1965); hereinafter cited as: Tjernagel.

Note on Scriptural References

In quoting Scripture, Luther cites only chapter, not verse, since at Luther's time chapters were not yet customarily divided into verses. In the present translation Luther's own citations have been retained —except in the case of the Psalms—and supplemented or corrected as need be in brackets to conform to the versification in the RSV. If there is a major difference between the text offered by the RSV and the text offered by the Luther Bible, or some other version, then the version which comes closest to the passage cited by Luther has been added in parentheses.

Citations from the Psalms present a special problem. In the Vulgate—and in the modern Roman Catholic English versions based upon it—the Psalms are numbered differently than in the AV and RSV, though in both cases the total number of Psalms is 150. The difference parallels that between the Septuagint and the Hebrew text in that for the greater part of the Psalter the numeration of the former is one behind that of the latter; only for Psalms 1–8 and 148–150 is the numeration identical. Further confusion arises from the fact that in modern Latin and German Bibles—following Hebrew precedent—the title or introductory statement attached to many of the Psalms is frequently given a verse number, a practice not followed in the RSV. In the present volume Luther's Psalm citations, if they were correct in terms of the Vulgate of his time, have been altered directly in the process of translation to conform to the chapter numbers of the RSV. The reference to the Vulgate or to Luther's Bible found occasionally in the parentheses suggests only that the quoted text is closer to the Vulgate translation or to Luther's translation than to the RSV.

LUTHER'S WORKS

VOLUME 50

237

To Elector John[1]
[Wittenberg, about January 16, 1531]

One of the problems facing the evangelicals was the dissension on the Lord's Supper. Consequently they responded to the Imperial Summons for the Diet of Augsburg[2] as three independent parties, each one highly suspicious of the others. There were the Lutherans who rallied around the Augsburg Confession; there was Zwingli and the Zürich city council which, on July 8, 1530, handed in to the Imperial government a confession of faith;[3] and between these two parties stood some of the upper German cities led by Strassburg, which, on July 9, 1530, handed in to the Imperial government the Tetrapolitana.[4] As early as the end of September, 1530, Martin Bucer[5] took the initiative and conferred with Luther at the Coburg in an attempt to bring about the unification of German Protestantism. Encouraged by the results of this conference, Bucer went on a fact-finding mission[6] through the upper German cities, and ended this trip with a visit to Zwingli in Zürich, and to Oecolampadius in Basel. Upon his return to Strassburg on October 17,[7]

---

[1] The letter is available only in printed form. In all witnesses the address, the date, and the signature are missing, obviously because the original was not a brief, or a formal letter, but only a hastily written *Zettel* (note), as Elector John called it; see note 15. One may suggest January 16 as the approximate date of this note in view of Elector John's January 17 letter to Landgrave Philip (see note 15). Wittenberg can be established as the place from which Luther wrote this letter (and all the following letters for which this city has been supplied as place of the letter's origin) on the basis of Buchwald, *LK*, and other material.

[2] See *LW* 49, 280 f.

[3] For the text of Zwingli's *Fidei ratio*, see *Huldrici Zwinglii Opera*, ed. M. Schuler *et al.*, 4 (Zürich, 1841), 3 ff.; for an analysis, see *Zwingliana* 5 (1929–33), 242 ff.

[4] On the *Tetrapolitana*, see W. Gussman, *Quellen und Forschungen zur Geschichte des Augsburgischen Glaubensbekenntnisses* 1¹ (Leipzig, 1911), 21 ff.

[5] See *LW* 48, 247, n. 13. He was at the Coburg on September 26 and 27; see *WA*, Br 5, 658, n. 2; 12, 134, n. 4a. For Bucer's report to the Strassburg delegates to the Diet of Augsburg, see *Politische Correspondenz der Stadt Strassburg im Zeitalter der Reformation* 1, ed. H. Virck (Strassburg, 1882), 512 ff. For the discussions at the Coburg, see Köhler 2, 233 ff.

[6] For details, see Köhler 2, 241 ff.; Pollet 1, 55 ff. Luther wrote on November 7 that, provided Bucer did not try to deceive him, there was hope that unity could be achieved; *WA*, Br 5, 678.

[7] See Köhler 2, 243. On October 21 Luther's Strassburg friend of many years, Nicholas Gerbel (see *LW* 48, 317 f.), wrote Luther a long letter expressing his joy over the rapprochement between Bucer and Luther; *WA*, Br 5, 656 ff.

Bucer drafted a document[8] which was to demonstrate that Luther and Zwingli were really in agreement on the Lord's Supper, and that the whole controversy was more a matter of terminology than of substantial disagreement. This document was approved by the evangelical clergy of Strassburg on November 9,[9] and was sent to Oecolampadius, and by him to Zwingli. The latter categorically rejected it.[10] Bucer now revised his document[11] in the hope that it would be, if not accepted by Zwingli, then at least tolerated by him, and forwarded this new version to Luther and to Landgrave Philip,[12] apparently on January 1, 1531.[13] On January 10 Landgrave Philip, following Bucer's request,[14] sent this document to Elector John, and urged him to enjoin Luther from engaging in polemics against the Zwinglians. The Elector delayed the return of the Landgrave's messenger and forwarded the document to Luther, requesting Luther's opinion on it by return mail. On January 17 the Elector forwarded to the Landgrave a copy of a Zettel (note), sent to him by Luther, which contained Luther's opinion on Bucer's document.[15] It is generally assumed that letter No. 237 is this note. While Luther rejoices that he and Bucer have found agreement, he insists that before the matter can be finally settled and unity proclaimed, the following points have to be clarified: (a) Do the Zwinglians really teach about Christ's real presence in the Lord's Supper as Bucer says they do? (b) What is Bucer's position, and what is the Zwinglians' position on the manducatio oralis impiorum? In view of his discussions with Bucer at the Coburg concerning this last issue Luther expresses hope that it can be settled to his satisfaction, and without too much difficulty.

On Elector John, see LW 48, 269, n. 8.

Text in German: WA, Br 6, 20–21.

---

[8] Text: C. R. Zwingli Werke, 11, No. 1134; for an analysis, see Köhler 2, 243 ff. As early as 1528 Bucer had published the Dialogus, in which he tried to establish that, with good will, Luther and Zwingli could actually agree on the Lord's Supper. See LW 49, 200 f. For Bucer's theology of the Lord's Supper, see Sasse pp. 303 ff.
[9] See Köhler 2, 247.
[10] See Köhler 2, 248.
[11] Text: ARG 16 (1919), 221 ff.
[12] See LW 49, 124, n. 18.
[13] So according to Köhler 2, 252, n. 7. See also Lenz, BPB 1, No. 7.
[14] See Köhler 2, 252.
[15] For the Elector's letter to Landgrave Philip, see Urkunden aus der Reformationszeit, ed. C. G. Neudecker (Kassel, 1836), 164 ff.

First, Martin Bucer indicates that the other party[16] agrees with us regarding the sacrament: that is, they believe, as we do, that the true body and blood of our Lord are present in the sacrament and with the Words [of Institution] are distributed as food of souls, or as strengthening for the Christian faith. We are pleased to receive this news, and we rejoice in our hearts hearing it.

Second, however, Bucer alone confesses this and presents his own opinion, as if the others, too, teach likewise.[17] Yet, we are of course well aware—and books and actions plainly document it—that Zwingli and Oecolampadius have intensely fought against this teaching[18] and have maintained as the central point that Christ is able to be corporeally present [only] in heaven, at only one place, and not in the sacrament. At this point, therefore, it is necessary first of all to be certain whether the others, too, teach as Bucer in good hope thinks they do, and whether they also publicly teach this among the people and act accordingly. Otherwise the unification might be put on a poor foundation, and matters might afterwards become worse. As I, Doctor Luther, have diligently stressed to Bucer at the Coburg,[19] one must start such unification from a solid, clear foundation, or forget about it.

Third, in addition to this corporeal presence of Christ for souls, which Bucer affirms here, I have discussed with him also that type of corporeal presence by which both believers and unbelievers orally receive Christ's true body and blood under bread and wine. In this connection he made statements[20] over which I heartily rejoiced. In this document, however, nothing is said about this issue. Yet we think that if they go so far as to say that Christ's body is

---

[16] "Other party," "others," "they" refers in this letter to Zwingli and Oecolampadius and their followers, and also to Bucer and his followers.

[17] Even though Luther at this point did not know that Zwingli had rejected Bucer's document (see Introduction), he was well aware of Bucer's eagerness to bring about unity, an eagerness which might, as Luther correctly sensed, simply wishfully assume agreement, where in reality no agreement existed. This explains Luther's demands in the following lines. Luther assumed that the document presented *only* Bucer's opinion, but he was only partially correct in this assumption. For Bucer had made clear in the document itself, and also in his correspondence with Zwingli, that the document was a confession of the faith of the Strassburg preachers; see *C. R. Zwingli Werke* 11, 237, 302, n. 8.

[18] This is a reference to the past literary controversy on the Lord's Supper which had been fought so bitterly; see *LW* 49, Index, *s.v.* Lord's Supper, controversy of.

[19] See note 5.

[20] See Bucer's report, cited in note 5.

corporeally distributed and present to the soul, it should not be difficult [for them] to affirm that Christ's body is also present to the mouth, or to the body, or in the bread and given to the mouth.

If now God would abundantly give grace (which we wish from our hearts) that they also would be one with us on this issue, and together with us affirm and teach this, then unity among us would indeed be a reality, and a great work and miracle of God would be completed.

238

To Martin Bucer
Wittenberg, January 22, 1531

In this letter Luther once more discusses the document mentioned in letter No. 237.[1] He expresses his joy that the matter has progressed to the point that he and Bucer can agree on Christ's presence in the Lord's Supper. The condition which for Luther has to be fulfilled before unity could be proclaimed, however, is the securing of Christ's real presence in the Lord's Supper. This could be accomplished only by affirming that in the Lord's Supper Christ's true body and blood are distributed to the believer and also the unbeliever. If Bucer cannot join in this affirmation—and Luther envisions this as a real possibility—then unity could not be established, argues Luther, and this for two reasons: (a) Luther's own conscience demands affirmation of the confession that Christ's body and blood are offered to believers and unbelievers alike; and (b) a minister's responsibility for the faith of the communicants permits no yielding at this point, since unity means altar fellowship. To establish altar fellowship before agreement on the manducatio oralis impiorum[2] *had been reached would mean that communicants*

---

[1] Luther's letter is an answer to Bucer's no-longer extant January 1 letter, with which the Strassburg Reformer forwarded this document to Luther. For the reconstruction of the content of Bucer's letter, see Lenz, *BPB* 1, 28 ff.; *WA*, Br 6, 24 (where the Bucer letter is mistakenly dated January 5 or 6); Köhler 2, 256 f.
[2] As will be clear from Luther's statements in the second paragraph of the letter, at this point the issue was not so much the *manducatio oralis impiorum*, i.e., the

could receive something other than what they believed they were
receiving. Luther pleads with Bucer to interpret his stand not as a
matter of stubbornness, but as a matter pertaining to conscience
and faith. This plea is underscored by Luther's statement that unity
among the evangelicals is a matter highly desirable, even necessary,
for the promotion of the gospel. In conclusion Luther assures Bucer
of his continuous prayers for Christ's guidance and grace that unity
may indeed come.

On Martin Bucer, see LW 48, 247,.n. 13.
Text in Latin: WA, Br 6, 25–26.[3]

To the venerable Mr. Martin Bucer,[4] a minister of God's Word
in the church at Strassburg,
my superior[5]

Grace and peace in Christ. We have read the small confession[6]
which you, my Bucer, have sent, and we approve of it. We give
thanks to God that we agree at least, as you write, insofar as we
both confess that the body and blood of Christ are truly present in
the Lord's Supper, and that together with the Words [of Institu-
tion] they are distributed as food of the soul. I am amazed, however, that you think that Zwingli and Oecolampadius also share this
opinion or position. But now let me speak to you.

If, then, we confess that the body of Christ is truly distributed[7]
to the soul as food, and if there is no reason for us not to say that
the body of Christ is also distributed in this way to the unbelieving
soul, although the unbelieving soul does not receive it—just as the
light of the sun is offered equally to the seeing and to the blind—I

---

eating of Christ's true body and blood by the unbeliever, but rather the *oblatio*
corporis Christi, i.e., the *distribution* of Christ's true body and blood to the unbeliever along with the Eucharistic elements. The important issue for Luther
was that in the Lord's Supper Christ was present independent of the faith of the
communicant.

3 Pollet 1, 146 f., collated for his text of this letter two manuscript copies which
were not used by Enders (*Briefwechsel* 8, 349 ff.), whose text is the basis for
the *WA*, Br text.

4 Literally: "To the venerable man, Mr. Martin Bucer."

5 Or: "elder."

6 Literally: "booklet of confession." See letter No. 237, Introduction.

7 Or according to one of the Pollet manuscript copies: "If, then, we truly confess
that the body of Christ is distributed."

am wondering why it bothers you people to confess also that the body of Christ is offered, together with the bread, externally to the mouth of the believer and unbeliever alike; for through the concession that the body of Christ is distributed to individual souls it is, of course, necessarily granted that the body is present and can be distributed in many places at the same time. If this thought has not yet matured among you people, however, then I think this matter should be postponed and further divine grace should be awaited. I am unable to abandon this position, and if, as you write, you do not think that this position is demanded by Christ's words, my conscience nevertheless holds that it is required. Therefore I am unable to confess with you that total unity exists between us, if I do not wish to harm my conscience, [or] rather, if I do not wish to sow among us the seed of far worse turmoil for our congregations, and of more dreadful future dissension among us. [This would be the result,] if we had created unity among us in this way. I ask you, therefore, for the sake of conscience and peace in your congregations and in ours, not to let it go so far that we stir up more disturbances and scandals through this remedy for schism, but to entrust this matter to God. In the meantime let us be guardians of whatever peace and agreement thus far has been established, as we declare that the body of the Lord is truly present and distributed inwardly to the believing soul. For you people can easily understand that, if unity were established between us, some of your people would commune in our congregations,[8] and also some of ours in your congregations. Those who would commune with a different faith and with a different attitude of conscience would necessarily on both sides receive something different from that which they believe [they are receiving]. Thus it would be unavoidable that through the ministry [of the sacrament] and[9] our consciences either their faith would be made a mockery through hidden deceit and lies[10] if the communicants were unaware of this difference, or, if they were aware of the difference, then their faith would be destroyed through a public sacrilege. You can see how devout and Christian this would be. For this reason let us select rather the lesser of two evils, if one

---

[8] Literally: "would commune with us [i.e., at our altars]."
[9] The translation here is based on the text made available by Pollet.
[10] See note 9.

of the two must be endured at all. Let us therefore rather put up with this smaller disagreement, together with a limited peace, lest through our efforts to cure this evil we may stir up real tragedies of more serious discord and unbearable uproar.

I wish you would believe that, as I have told you at the Coburg,[11] I want to settle our discord even though I might have to live three times to accomplish it, because I have seen how necessary your fellowship is for us, and how the gospel was and still is disadvantaged [by our discord]. I have become so much aware of this that I am convinced that all the gates of hell,[12] the whole papacy, all of Turkey, the whole world, all the flesh, and whatever evils there are could not have harmed the gospel at all, if we had only been of one mind. But what am I to do with something which cannot be accomplished? If you wish to be fair, then you will attribute the fact that I shun this unity not to stubbornness, but to the urging of my conscience and to the force of my faith. Since our discussion at the Coburg I have great hope, but this hope is not yet unwavering.

May the Lord Jesus enlighten us, and may he make us perfectly of one mind; for this I pray, for this I sigh, for this I long. Farewell in the Lord.

Wittenberg, January 22, 1531   MARTIN LUTHER

239

To Lazarus Spengler
[Wittenberg,] February 15, 1531

In the alliance negotiations of the evangelicals which followed the 1529 Diet of Speyer the right of armed resistance to the emperor had been questioned.[1] The Nürnberg city council categorically rejected the existence of any such right.[2] In the aftermath of the Diet

---

[11] See p. 3, n. 5.
[12] Matt. 16:18 (Vulgate; Luther Bible).
[1] See *LW* 49, Index, *s.v.* Resistance, armed, to the emperor.
[2] See *LW* 49, 272.

of Augsburg[3] a meeting of the evangelicals was held during the last days of December, 1530, in Smalcald for the purpose of creating a defense alliance. The Nürnberg delegation to this meeting was pushed into a corner by the Electoral Saxon delegation, which cited the short note Luther had written on this issue in October of 1530.[4] The Saxons presented this document in such a way that Luther appeared to have changed his position on the resistance issue fundamentally, and to have endorsed wholeheartedly armed resistance to the emperor. Lazarus Spengler, Nürnberg's chancellor,[5] immediately contacted Luther through Wenceslas Link[6] and asked for clarification.[7] Shortly thereafter, on February 3, 1531, Spengler contacted Luther once more, this time through Veit Dietrich.[8] In his reply, letter No. 239, Luther first makes clear that he is not at all aware of having changed his position on the resistance issue. He goes on to state that during a meeting at Torgau he had endorsed armed resistance to the emperor, provided that the situation were as the legal experts had then presented it to him. If indeed this were the case, then, Luther states, there would be no reason for not endorsing armed resistance to the emperor;[9] since thus far the legal experts had not proven their arguments, however, Luther refuses to make any final decision on this matter.

On Lazarus Spengler, see LW 48, 184.

Text in German with portions in Latin: WA, Br 6, 36–37.[10]

To the excellent Mr. Lazarus Spengler,
chancellor[11] of the Nürnberg city council,[12]
my friend and brother

---

[3] See also *LW* 49, 423 f., 429 ff.

[4] On this meeting at Smalcald, see Fabian, *ESBV* (2nd ed.), pp. 151 ff. Spengler hinted in his February 3 letter to Dietrich (see note 8) how the Electoral Saxon delegation had behaved. For Luther's note, see *LW* 49, 431 ff.

[5] On Spengler's title, see *LW* 49, 97, n. 6.

[6] See *LW* 48, 169 f.

[7] While Link's letter to Luther is not extant, Luther's reply, dated January 15, 1531, is extant; see *WA*, Br 6, 16 f.

[8] See *LW* 49, 282, n. 13; Klaus, pp. 85 ff., 114 f. For Spengler's letter, see M. Mayer, *Spengleriana* (Nürnberg, 1830), p. 78.

[9] For "emperor," see *LW* 49, 430, n. 14.

[10] The letter is available only in printed form; one edition claims that its text is taken from the autograph.

[11] See note 5.

[12] Literally: "by the Nürnbergers from the most secret letters."

Grace and peace. Prudent, dear Sir and Friend! Master[13] Veit[14] has informed me of Your Honor's concern, that Your Honor is troubled by the arguments[15] of our friends who boast as if we had recanted the earlier brief[16] [which stated] that one is not to resist the emperor.

I am certainly not aware of any such recantation. At Torgau,[17] however, it did happen that our friends heatedly debated with us on this matter. Some of them even intended to decide and do what seemed right to them without consulting us. This we had to allow to happen.[18] Since we finally insisted, however, that the legal dictum, "One may fight force with force,"[19] would not be sufficient [to justify resistance to the emperor], as we had also argued[20] earlier in the brief,[21] etc., our friends produced the following: the Imperial law permits armed resistance to the governing authority in case of flagrant injustice. At this point we said that we did not know whether the law states this. If the emperor has bound[22] himself in such a way, then we will let him be bound—but it would be their responsibility.[23] Since we teach:[24] "Render to Caesar the things that are Caesar's,"[25] and since it is the emperor's [law] that one is to resist him in case of flagrant injustice, it would not be up to us either to alter or to improve[26] the emperor's law. And so the matter rested on this syllogism: Whatever the emperor or the Imperial law has ordained has to be observed; the law, however, ordains resisting the emperor in such a case;[27] therefore one has to resist [the em-

---

13 I.e., Master of Arts.
14 Veit Dietrich; see note 8.
15 Literally: "that you [i.e., plural, and with an upper case first letter which suggests the formal way of addressing a person] are loaded down by the talk of."
16 Dated March 6, 1530; LW 49, No. 204.
17 See LW 49, 431.
18 Luther's statement is confirmed by Melanchthon's letters, January 1, 1531, and February 16, 1531, to Camerarius in Nürnberg; C.R. 2, Nos. 955, 957.
19 See LW 49, 276 f.
20 Literally: "as we had also refuted earlier."
21 See note 16.
22 Literally: "The emperor has entrapped and bound himself in this way."
23 Literally: "and they should see to it."
24 Literally: "For since our teaching says."
25 Matt. 22:21.
26 The text reads meistern, i.e., to master. The word can be used in the sense of schulmeistern, i.e., to teach, correct, improve, or discipline as a schoolmaster would do.
27 I.e., in case of flagrant injustice on the emperor's part.

peror], etc. Until now we have taught the major premise, [that is,] that one is to obey the sword in matters of state. We have, however, neither affirmed the minor premise, nor do we know [whether it is correct]. Therefore I would draw no conclusion; but we referred the whole matter back to the legal experts, that they might handle it. We do not wish, however, to settle [this issue], or counsel, impel, or urge anyone to do anything other than this major premise: the emperor is to be obeyed. If [the legal experts] could prove the minor premise, and this is not our task,[28] then we, who have taught the major premise, cannot deny the conclusion. And then one would resist the emperor not on the basis of that dictum of natural and divine law[29] "One may fight force with force," and of the others which we have discussed, but on the basis of a new law which goes beyond natural law—[that is,] on the basis of the law of state and the Imperial law, by which the emperor has renounced his law[30]— [for] we cannot undermine the use and efficacy of a law of state and of the Imperial law. Thus we theologians have maintained our earlier position,[31] have postponed a decision on that new [legal opinion], and are awaiting the proof of the legal experts, which we have not yet seen.

Veit[32] will report the rest.[33] Hurriedly,

February 15, 1531   MARTIN LUTHER

---

[28] Luther wrote: "*De quo* [i.e., either the whole previous sentence, or 'minor premise'] *nihil ad nos.*" This could mean either that the producing of the proof for the minor premise is not "our" task, or responsibility (or concern), or that concerning the proof of the minor premise nothing has come to "us." In the first case Luther would establish the responsibility of the legal experts in this matter, while in the second case he would state that until now this proof has either not yet been produced, or has not been seen by him. In the latter case Luther would then already state here what he repeats at the end of the letter.
[29] See Exod. 21:24.
[30] "His law," i.e., the law on the basis of which the emperor demands obedience.
[31] As expressed in *LW* 49, No. 204.
[32] See note 8.
[33] Dietrich's letter is not extant.

240

To Wenceslas Link[1]
Wittenberg, May 12, 1531

In connection with the sacrament of baptism, the evangelical church was confronted with the custom of the papal church of conditionally baptizing children.[2] This conditional baptism was used for foundlings, or if parents or midwives were not certain whether an emergency baptism had been correctly performed, or in any case in which one did not know whether a person had been correctly baptized or baptized at all. In these cases the priest was to use the regular liturgy of baptism but was to say: "I do not baptize you again, but if you have not yet been baptized, then I baptize you in the name of the Father, and of the Son, and of the Holy Spirit, Amen."[3]

Letter No. 240 is Luther's opinion on this practice. The letter is a reply to an inquiry made by Link[4] in Nürnberg. Here, in connection with the work on the Brandenburg-Nürnberg Church Ordinance,[5] *a controversy on the practice of conditional baptism had developed.[6] On the one side stood Link and others who either openly rejected the practice or did not wish to adopt a precise statement on it; on the other side stood Andrew Osiander[7] who advocated the retention of the practice.*

Luther categorically rejects the practice of conditional baptism,[8] and then develops a detailed argumentation for his position.

---

[1] The letter is extant only in manuscript copies, and in the common editions of Luther's works. For the sometimes quite extensive textual variations offered by some of the witnesses, see Enders, *Briefwechsel* 9, 12 f. The translation is based on the text of the WA, Br edition with one exception; see note 18. In all the witnesses collated by Enders, the address is missing. The content and background of the letter, however, substantiate the addressee.
[2] On the practice and history of conditional baptism with special reference to the Reformation, see *LJB* 25 (1958), 110 ff.; *Zeitschrift für Bayerische Kirchengeschichte* 35 (1966), 138 ff.
[3] See *LJB* 25 (1958), 119.
[4] Link's letter to Luther is no longer extant.
[5] Sehling 11, 116 ff., 140 ff.
[6] On this controversy, see the references cited in note 2, and *ARG* 62 (1971), 193 ff.
[7] See *LW* 49, 238, n. 26.
[8] This presents a change in Luther's attitude to this practice, for on May 13,

His main reason is that conditional baptism turns the sacrament of baptism into a matter of uncertainty, while baptism is and should be the most certain assurance of a man's salvation. Concluding his argumentation, Luther briefly discusses Numbers 5:19–20, a passage which Osiander had used to substantiate his position. In the last paragraph of the letter Luther thanks Link for some oranges; he also inquires whether Link had intended him to have a small washbasin and a two-arm candelabrum, both of which had arrived with the oranges.

On Wenceslas Link, see LW 48, 169 f.

Text in Latin: WA, Br 6, 96–97.

Grace and Peace

Regarding the question of conditional baptism, which you have presented to me in your recent letter, my Wenceslas, I have consulted with Master[9] Philip,[10] and after carefully considering the issue, we arrived at the following decision: Conditional baptism must be abolished in the church. In case one either doubts[11] or

---

1530, he had written to Osiander: "Regarding your question, my Osiander, concerning the baptism of infants who have not yet [completely] come from the womb, I shall willingly tell you my opinion without prejudicing your own opinion. I have forbidden our midwives at Wittenberg to baptize an infant that has not yet been [completely] born. For some used to baptize a child [*foetum*] when hardly the crown of the head had appeared. But why then do they not likewise baptize over the mother's abdomen, or rather baptize the mother's abdomen itself, so that one may assume the fruit of the womb has been baptized? I have ordered that one assist a laboring woman with prayer. The baptism administered by a midwife, by which she baptizes an already completely born infant endangered by weakness, I consider to be valid. Yet the infant should nevertheless be [later] brought into church so that one may publicly pray over the child, and that the baptism may be publicly approved by the laying on of the minister's hands, or be confirmed through the testimony of the congregation. I cannot reject a conditional baptism of a totally born infant, however, if there is doubt of the certainty of the privately administered baptism." See WA, Br 6, 98, as this text has been corrected in *Zeitschrift* (see note 2), 150 ff. Gottfried Seebass has convincingly demonstrated (*ibid.*) that the date given to this letter in WA, Br 6 is wrong; see also WA, Br 14, xxvii f. Luther's change of heart can be explained by his apparent desire to eliminate all possible casuistry, and to make baptism a matter of certainty for the faith.
[9] I.e., Master of Arts.
[10] Philip Melanchthon; see LW 48, 77, n. 3. See also Melanchthon's letter to Camerarius in Nürnberg, dated about mid-May, 1531; C.R. 2, No. 983.
[11] This would be the case with an emergency baptism.

simply doesn't know[12] that a person has been baptized, one is simply to baptize unconditionally, and as if that person never had been baptized.

These are the reasons [for our position]: A conditional baptism accomplishes nothing; it neither denies nor affirms anything; it neither gives nor takes away anything. Suppose someone is baptized conditionally;[13] this person is afterwards forced to say: I am now as ignorant and uncertain whether I am baptized as I was before, and so are all who have baptized me. For if the first baptism was a valid one (a fact which has to be unknown, whether I like it or not), then the second baptism is nothing (because it is a conditional one). If the first baptism was not a valid one (and again, I am unable to know this), then the second baptism also is nothing because it is a matter of uncertainty and has to be considered a matter of uncertainty, so long as the first baptism is a matter of uncertainty. Because of the condition attached to the first baptism,[14] which has been a matter of uncertainty, the validity of the second baptism, too, remains forever a matter of uncertainty.

It is better now that baptism be a matter of certainty, at least for the baptizers themselves, who afterwards could testify before the congregation.[15] Therefore, in this case[16] one sins more safely by rebaptizing, if one sins at all (which we don't believe), than by giving an uncertain baptism;[17] this would definitely be wrong, because such a baptism is not a matter of certainty, but is something uncertain. Under these circumstances we then have a true and certain baptizing versus an uncertain baptizing. In this way we do not,

---

[12] This would be the case with a foundling.

[13] I.e., he is baptized on the condition that he has not been baptized before.

[14] I.e., that the first baptism was administered improperly, or that there was no first baptism at all.

[15] The text reads *ecclesiae*. For "congregation," see *LW*, 49, 61, n. 9.

[16] I.e., if the baptizer, e.g., a midwife, can testify that the (first) emergency baptism was not administered correctly. Then the "second" baptism would not be a second baptism, as the Anabaptists argue (see in the text, below), but would be a valid first baptism, and thus a matter of certainy, since Luther considers an incorrectly administered baptism to be no baptism at all. If no one can testify concerning the original baptism, as in the case of a foundling, then one would also not be wrong by baptizing without a condition, even though one might thus inadvertently rebaptize. To the contrary, one would be on safe grounds because one would commend the past to God (see in the text, below), and would administer an unconditional baptism, which in turn is something certain.

[17] I.e., a conditionally administered second baptism.

however, thereby become raging Anabaptists. For they, as you know, publicly condemn the first certain baptism and do not want to call it a baptism [at all]. We, however, wish to leave that which is uncertain to its own fate, commend it to God's judgment, and administer a certain baptism. We believe we thus act correctly and safely.

Further, should someone baptize with a different formula, as you write,[18] for instance, "In the name of the Father, and of the Son, and of St. Michael," etc., then we are certain that this is no baptism at all, not even a conditional one.

Regarding the principle[19] of condition in the law concerning jealousy,[20] that is another argument.[21] For law and gospel are different matters. The gospel is God's promise, which must be a matter of certainty. The law deals with our things and works, can be observed or not observed, and can easily be made subject to a condition. And finally, the law also reveals the hearts of men to us who know nothing. But the promise simply bestows upon us things of God, whether we know it or not, even though we definitely know that men are in need of God's things, while we do not know with certainty, however, whether men have sinned against the law.[22]

Since I am busy, I am writing this without order and in a hurry. Please sort it out and collect from this jungle[23] the better thoughts.

I thank you for the oranges which you have presented to us. A small washbasin, together with a two-arm candelabrum, was en-

---

[18] On the basis of some witnesses one could also translate: "formula, as foolish people do." The translation is here based on the variants offered in Enders, *Briefwechsel* 9, 12.

[19] Literally: "law."

[20] Num. 5:11–31, esp. verses 19, 20.

[21] Osiander had made the following argument, as summarized in *Zeitschrift* (see note 2), 146, 150: "In the Bible certain consequences are frequently made dependent upon one unknown presupposition, according to which in each case only one consequence actually could occur, as in Numbers 5:11–31, especially verse 19 f. . . . " Consequently, according to Osiander, by using the formula for conditional baptism, only one of the two possibilities could occur, that is, either the conditional baptism is valid, or it is not valid. "Since Luther assumed in the following that he was able to refute Osiander's reference to Numbers 5:19 f. by citing the difference between gospel and law . . . then Link apparently had not written quite clearly [to Luther] that Osiander did not wish to tie a condition to the promise [i.e., the gospel], but wished only to illustrate that in using the conditional mode of speaking, indeed, only one consequence could actually occur."

[22] I.e., because "we" do not know the hearts of men.

[23] Literally: "from that forest of my ignorance [or: clumsiness]."

closed [with your last shipment]. I do not know whether you have given them [to us, since] you said nothing about it.

Farewell, and pray for me.

Wittenberg, May 12, 1531   Yours, MARTIN LUTHER

241

To Mrs. Margaret Luther[1]
[Wittenberg,] May 20, 1531

Having been informed by his brother James that their mother is seriously ill, Luther writes this letter of spiritual counsel to her. Luther impresses upon his mother that her present illness is a sign of God's gracious chastisement, which is slight if compared with Christ's suffering. Taking John 16:33, and I Corinthians 15:54 f., as point of departure, Luther introduces the theme of Christ's victory over death and the devil, a victory which is pledged to the faithful through Word and sacraments, and which has to be affirmed especially now in the hour of illness, because it is the devil's purpose to make this victory uncertain. Consequently Luther encourages his mother to see in this illness an opportunity for gratefulness to God for his act of salvation in Christ, and for the fact that God has rescued her from the papistic darkness and brought her to the light of the gospel. In closing, Luther commends his mother to God's grace, and assures her of the prayers of his whole family.

On Margaret Luther, see LW 48, 329 f.[2]

Text in German: WA, Br 6, 103–106.

---

[1] The letter is extant in manuscript copies, in some special editions, and in the common editions of Luther's works. The address is missing in most witnesses, obviously because the addressee was established in the title. The content of the letter corroborates this title. Within a short time of being written, copies of the letter circulated widely among Luther's friends. In the summer of 1532, e.g., Veit Dietrich (see *LW* 49, 282, n. 13) sent a copy of this letter, together with a copy of *LW* 49, No. 203, to Spengler in Nürnberg (see *LW* 48, 184), who in turn had both letters copied prior to returning them to Dietrich. Spengler gave his copies to one of his Nürnberg friends who was seriously ill, and who shortly afterwards died. See *WA, Br* 6, No. 1820, Introduction; Enders, *Briefwechsel* 9, 16, n. 1. For the following translation, the translation furnished by Theodore G. Tappert (*LCC* 18, 33 ff.) has been consulted.

[2] Luther's mother died on June 30, 1531. To the references for Luther's parents cited in *LW* 48, 329 f., should be added the materials cited in *WA, Br* 5, No. 1820, Introduction, and in *WA, Br* 13, 195, addition to *WA, Br* 6, 103.

Grace and peace in Christ Jesus,
our Lord and Savior, Amen

My dearly beloved[3] Mother! I have received my brother James's[4] letter concerning your illness. Of course this grieves me deeply, especially because I cannot be with you in person, as I certainly would like to be. Yet I am coming to you personally through this letter, and I, together with all the members of my family, shall certainly not be absent from you in spirit.

I trust that you have long since been abundantly instructed, without any help from me, that (God be praised) you have taken [God's] comforting Word into [your heart], and that you are adequately provided with preachers and comforters. Nevertheless I shall do my part too and, according to my duty, acknowledge myself to be your child, and you to be my mother, as our common God and creator has made us and bound us to each other with mutual ties, so that I shall in this way increase the number of your comforters.

First, dear Mother, by God's grace you well know by now that this sickness of yours is [God's] fatherly, gracious chastisement.[5] It is a quite small chastisement in comparison with that which he inflicts upon the godless, and sometimes even his own dear children, when one person is beheaded, another burned, a third drowned, and so on.[6] And so all of us must sing: "For Thy sake we are being daily killed and regarded as sheep to be slaughtered."[7] This sickness therefore should not distress or depress you. On the contrary, you should accept it with thankfulness as being sent by God's grace; [you should] recognize how slight a suffering it is—even if it be a sickness unto death—compared with the sufferings of his own dear Son, our Lord Jesus Christ, who did not have to suffer on behalf of himself, as we have to do, but who suffered for us and for our sins.

---

[3] Literally: "Beloved from the heart [or: heartily beloved]." See also *LW* 49, 312, 323.

[4] James Luther; see *LW* 49, 268, n. 4. The letter is not extant.

[5] See Heb. 12:6, 11; Rev. 3:19.

[6] This is perhaps a reference to the persecutions suffered by some of the evangelicals.

[7] Ps. 44:22; Rom. 8:36.

Second, dear Mother, you also know the true center and foundation of your salvation from whom you are to seek comfort in this and all troubles, namely, Jesus Christ, the cornerstone.[8] He will not waver or fail us, nor allow us to sink or perish, for he is the Savior and is called the Savior of all poor sinners, and of all who are caught in tribulation and death, and rely on him, and call on his name.

[Christ] says: "Be of good cheer; I have overcome the world."[9] If he has overcome the world, surely he has also overcome the sovereign of this world[10] with all his power. But what else is [the devil's] power but death, by which he has made us subject to himself, [and] held us captives on account of our sin? But now that death and sin are overcome, we may joyfully and cheerfully listen to the sweet words: "Be of good cheer; I have overcome the world." We certainly are not to doubt that these words are indeed true. More than that, we are commanded to accept this comfort with joy and thanksgiving. Whoever would be unwilling to be comforted by these words would do the greatest injustice and dishonor to the dear Comforter, as if it were not true that he bids us to be of good cheer, or as if it were not true that he has overcome the world. [If we acted thus,] we would only restore within ourselves the tyranny of the vanquished devil, sin, and death, and oppose the dear Savior. From this may God preserve us.

Let us therefore now rejoice with all assurance and gladness, and should any thought of sin or death frighten us, let us in opposition to this lift up our hearts and say: "Behold, dear soul, what are you doing? Dear death, dear sin, how is it that you are alive and terrify me? Do you not know that you have been overcome? Do you, death, not know that you are quite dead? Do you not know the One who says of you: 'I have overcome the world?' It does not behoove me either to listen to your terrifying suggestions, or heed them. Rather [I should listen] to the comforting words of my Savior: 'Be of good cheer, be of good cheer; I have overcome the world.' He is the victor, the true hero, who gives and appropriates to me his victory with this word: 'Be of good cheer!' I shall

---

8 See I Pet. 2:6; Isa. 28:16.
9 John 16:33.
10 See John 12:31.

cling to him, and to his words and comfort I shall hold fast; regardless whether I remain here or go yonder, I shall live by [this word, for] he does not lie to me. You would like to deceive me with your terrors, and with your lying thoughts you would like to tear me away from such a victor and savior. But they are lies, as surely as it is true that he has overcome you and commanded us to be comforted.

"Saint Paul also boasts likewise and defies the terrors of death: 'Death is swallowed up in victory. O death, where is thy victory? O hell, where is thy sting?'[11] Like a wooden image of death, you can terrify and challenge, but you have no power to strangle. For your victory, sting, and power have been swallowed up in Christ's victory. You can show your teeth, but you cannot devour, for God has given us the victory over you through Christ Jesus our Lord, to whom be praise and thanks. Amen."

By such words and thoughts, and by none other, let your heart be moved, dear Mother. Above all be thankful that God has brought you to such knowledge and not allowed you to remain caught in papistic error, by which we were taught to rely on our own works and the holiness of the monks, and to consider this only comfort of ours, our Savior, not as a comforter but as a severe judge and tyrant,[12] so that we had to flee from him to Mary and the saints, and not expect of him any grace or comfort. But now we know it differently, [we know] about the unfathomable goodness and mercy of our heavenly Father: that Jesus Christ is our mediator,[13] our throne of grace,[14] and our bishop[15] before God in heaven, who daily intercedes for us and reconciles all who believe in him alone, and who call upon him;[16] that he is not a judge, nor cruel, except for those who do not believe in him, or who reject his comfort and grace; [and] that he is not the man who accuses and threatens us, but rather the man who reconciles us [with God], and intercedes for us with his own death and blood shed for us so that we should not

---

[11] See I Cor. 15:54 f.
[12] For the medieval understanding of Christ as a judge (rather than a mediator), see Bainton, pp. 28 ff.
[13] I Tim. 2:5.
[14] Rom. 3:25 (Luther Bible); Heb. 4:16.
[15] I Pet. 2:25 (Luther Bible).
[16] Rom. 8:34; I Tim. 4:10; Heb. 7:25.

fear him, but approach him with all assurance and call him dear Savior, sweet Comforter, faithful bishop of our souls, etc.

To such knowledge (I say) God has graciously called you. You possess God's seal and letter of this [calling], namely, the gospel you hear preached, baptism, and the sacrament of the altar,[17] so that you should have no trouble or danger. Only be of good cheer and thank [God] joyfully for such great grace! For he who has begun [his work] in you will also graciously complete it,[18] since we are unable to help ourselves in such matters. We are unable to accomplish anything against sin, death, and the devil by our own works. Therefore, another appears for us and in our stead who definitely can do better; he gives us his victory, and commands us to accept it and not to doubt it. He says: "Be of good cheer; I have overcome the world"; and again: "I live, and you will live also, and no one will take your joy from you."[19]

The Father and God of all consolation[20] grant you, through his holy Word and Spirit, a steadfast, joyful, and grateful faith blessedly to overcome this and all other trouble, and finally to taste and experience that what he himself says is true: "Be of good cheer; I have overcome the world." And with this I commend your body and soul to his mercy. Amen.

All your children and my Katie pray for you; some weep, others say at dinner: "Grandmother is very sick." God's grace be with us all. Amen.

May 20, 1531   Your loving son,
                                                       MARTIN LUTHER

---

[17] Literally: "the gospel, baptism, and sacrament, which you hear being preached."
[18] Phil. 1:6.
[19] John 14:19; 16:22.
[20] Rom. 15:5 (Luther Bible).

242

To Gregory Brück[1]
[Wittenberg, end of May, 1531]

As a result of the negotiations among the evangelicals, the Smal-
caldic League was organized at the end of December 1530.[2]
Though a defense alliance, it was sufficient reason for the propapal
Estates of the Empire to worry. Consequently the Archbishop of
Mainz and the Count Palatine (who already during the Diet of
Augsburg had been opposed to any forceful action against the
evangelicals)[3] began negotiations to bring about a compromise be-
tween the Emperor[4] on the one side, and the Elector of Saxony[5]
and the Landgrave of Hesse[6] (the leaders of the Smalcaldic
League) on the other side. Asked for his opinion, Luther urges
negotiating in good faith on the basis of the materials which had
been prepared for earlier negotiations. Luther justifies his position
with the saying: "Gain a night, gain a year."

On Gregory Brück, see LW 49, 51 f.

Text in German: WA, Br 6, 108.

My dear Mr. Chancellor: I am of the opinion that the negotiations
proposed by the Cardinal of Mainz[7] should not be rejected.[8] On
the basis of prior negotiations[9] it can easily be established at which

---

[1] The extant autograph does not give an address. While Luther could also
have addressed Christian Beyer as chancellor (see *LW* 49, 349, n. 8), it seems
that this note was addressed to Brück. At least this note was in Brück's possession, since on the reverse side Brück wrote in his own handwriting that this was
"Doctor Martin's" first brief concerning the peace negotiations with the Archbishop of Mainz and the Count Palatine; see *WA*, Br 6, No. 1822, Introduction.
The approximate date of this note can be established on the basis of the legation
sent by the Archbishop of Mainz to the Elector of Saxony. This legation was
dispatched on May 26. See Winckelmann, pp. 111 ff.
[2] See Fabian, *ESBV* (2nd ed.), pp. 151 ff.; Kidd, No. 124.
[3] See *LW* 49, 416, n. 5.
[4] Charles V; see *LW* 48, 175 f.; 49, 423 f., 435, n. 10.
[5] John of Saxony; see *LW* 48, 269, n. 8.
[6] Philip of Hesse; see *LW* 49, 124, n. 18.
[7] Cardinal Albrecht of Brandenburg, archbishop of Mainz; see *LW* 48, 44 f.
[8] Literally: "I maintain that the proposed dealing of the Cardinal of Mainz not
be rejected."
[9] I.e., the negotiations in Augsburg; see *LW* 49, 403 ff. In connection with the
new negotiations, the Wittenberg theologians did nevertheless draw up a new

points one may or may not give in.[10] If one could work for peace, and a decision on our case could be postponed,[11] then one should certainly accept this [proposal], according to the saying: "Gain a night, gain a year"; [or,] "Another day, another way,"[12] etc.

MARTIN LUTHER

243

To Elector John
[Wittenberg,] June 16, 1531

The following letter shows Luther as a concerned pastor and as a responsible member of the community. Luther informs the Elector of the scandalous behavior of John Metzsch, the Electoral captain in Wittenberg, who, notwithstanding brotherly admonition and privately enacted excommunication, continues to patronize prostitutes, and whom Luther plans to censure in public. Luther further brings to the Elector's attention the fact that portions of the Wittenberg city wall were torn down but not replaced, that this situation endangers the city, and that, in Luther's view, Metzsch is not fulfilling his responsibilities in connection with this matter. Luther warns the Elector that Metzsch's conduct may well cause some serious disturbances among the people.

On Elector John, see LW 48, 269, n. 8.

Text in German: WA, Br 6, 122–124.

To my Most Gracious Lord, Duke John, elector in Saxony:
Personal to His Electoral Grace

---

brief concerning the points which could or could not be negotiated. While this brief shows similarities to the material that had been drawn up in Augsburg, it also shows that the position of the evangelicals has become more precise and determined. Text: WA, Br 6, 109 ff.

[10] Literally: "it can easily be counselled what one may still grant or not."

[11] Literally: "peace, and that the affairs of our party be postponed."

[12] Literally: "Comes a day, comes advice." For both sayings, used several times by Luther, though not always verbatim, see WA, 51, 691, No. 196; 708, No. 321. Present-day German has the saying: *Kommt Zeit, kommt Rat*, i.e., when the time comes, the advice comes.

Grace and peace in Christ! Most Illustrious, Noble Sovereign, Most Gracious Lord! It is not for me to be concerned with the affairs of secular government, or to disparage Your Electoral Grace's officials, nor shall I. Since the general talk is so loud and widespread, however, and since I am of the opinion that Your Electoral Grace expects faithful and loving service of me—which, of course, I am abundantly obligated to perform—and since, should something later go wrong, I would not want to be blamed for having been silent to the disadvantage of Your Electoral Grace, [I am writing this letter].

Our captain,[1] Hans Metzsch,[2] has time and again been admonished by me, kindly but seriously, to stay away from harlotry and dealings with prostitutes. After a while it was impossible for me, as a preacher, to tolerate such scandalous behavior or to be silent about it. But he continues, and does it so openly that everyone's mouth and nose, ears and eyes are full of it. He also admitted to me in private that he could not be without women. Thereupon I informed him of my refusal to associate with him personally, and privately[3] I forbade him to come to the sacrament. Since he is so closely knit to the braids of prostitutes that he shows little fear of God with his conduct, and since from now on I will have to proceed against him also by means of public preaching and judgment, I ask with this letter for Your Electoral Grace's benevolent attitude [toward me]. Should Your Electoral Grace find out that I clash with Metzsch on this issue, then Your Electoral Grace may graciously remember this information I have given. For this scandal will be an obstacle to the preaching of the gospel,[4] and will give to others also occasion to do evil. Metzsch may be a good soldier, but I would not want him to defend me in an emergency since he does not have before his eyes God who has thus far miraculously protected us without striking a blow, and daily still preserves us.

Second, with this letter I also want to demonstrate my faithful-

---

[1] I.e., the Electoral captain, or bailiff, in charge of the security and the judiciary of the city and the surrounding district. See *Hilfswörterbuch, s.v.* Amtshauptmann.
[2] On Hans von Metzsch (who at that time was unmarried), and on Luther's relationship with him, see R. Götze, *Wie Luther Kirchenzucht übte* (Berlin, 1959), pp. 46 ff.
[3] I.e., not from the pulpit.
[4] Literally: "For such a scandal will close my mouth."

ness toward Your Electoral Grace. I also talked in a friendly way with Metzsch—and others—concerning the razing of the city wall.[5] But since I am told I am a man of the pen and do not understand such a matter, I leave it alone. Nevertheless, if things turn out differently than these contractors think, no one should be in a position to say that I have not warned Your Electoral Grace of this danger. For I know very well how concerned one has been until now with the gates of the city, so that the city would be properly locked. But now the city stands open day and night because [of a break in the wall] of more than one hundred paces, so that pigs and all kinds of animals[6] run into [town]; it is possible to see, walk, and shoot without any obstacle from the fields into the town square, and from the town square into the fields, because the wall is torn down to the foundation and nothing new has been built, or even surveyed, to replace it. If this is in good order, then it is fine with me, and Your Electoral Grace will accept this information of mine in a gracious attitude, and consider this matter further. My head is full of worry because there are many children[7] of important and good people here, and times are very dangerous. God might allow something to happen which we would have to deplore belatedly and in vain. Metzsch is headstrong,[8] and creates stout opposition toward himself. Therefore it is necessary for Your Electoral Grace to look into this situation, so that no dissatisfaction arises. For good people are patient, but too heavy a weight tears the bag, and a spark could easily start to glow among the impatient people who

---

[5] In the aftermath of the 1529 Diet of Speyer (see LW 49, 221 ff.), a program was begun to strengthen the fortifications of Wittenberg. For this purpose some houses and a section of the city wall were razed. Hans von Metzsch, who was in charge of this work, showed eagerness to get the work going, but lacked the ability, especially for negotiating with the people of Wittenberg; consequently the razing of houses and wall sections was begun before all legal details had been worked out, and before the proper building plans had been developed. As a result of several complaints, an Electoral commission came to Wittenberg for the purpose of settling matters properly. See WA, Br 5, No. 1548; 6, No. 1829; Götze, op. cit., pp. 48 ff.

[6] Literally: "pigs and all." Instead of "animals" Luther could also have thought of "undesirable" people.

[7] I.e., students.

[8] Literally: "He goes through with the head [i.e., through a wall]." Luther used this phrase several times; see WA, 30[II], 354; WA, TR 5, No. 5342a (p. 68); RN 32, 64 to 205, line 9 f. Present-day German has the saying: Mit dem Kopf durch die Wand gehen, i.e., to push one's head through the wall.

might get tired of Metzsch's stubbornness, cursing, and tyranny. Thank God this is a good, peaceful, and law-abiding town. Oppression and strongheadedness, however, could change people so that they might consider not respecting an official in spite of the fact that he is an official of their territorial lord.

Again I ask Your Electoral Grace to accept this letter as an expression of honest, humble faithfulness. I have been silent long enough so that I would by no means disparage anyone. But unless I am totally out of my mind, [Metzsch and the contractors] are doing with Your Electoral Grace's property and money as they please. Although Your Electoral Grace perhaps knows all of this, I wanted to demonstrate my services.

God strengthen and comfort Your Electoral Grace's heart against all the intrigues of the devil. Amen.

June 16, 1531   Your Electoral Grace's humbly dedicated

MARTIN LUTHER

244

To Michael Stifel[1]
[Wittenberg, June or July,][2] 1531

Luther announces that he, along with many cherry-loving boys, will soon visit Stifel's cherry garden.
On Michael Stifel, see LW 49, 140, 211, n. 6.
Text in Latin: WA, Br 6, 143.

Grace and Peace

Greetings, greetings, greetings, my Michael. I have nothing else to write to you. So that you might not complain, however, that I write nothing to you, I wanted at least to write to you this ["greeting"].

---

[1] This note is extant only in manuscript copies, and in the common editions of Luther's works. While no address is given in any of the extant witnesses, tradition has assumed that the "Michael" addressed in this letter was Michael Stifel.
[2] The approximate date of this letter can be deduced from the circumstances mentioned in the letter.

At the same time I wanted to inform you that shortly we, together with many cherry-loving boys, will come to you, God willing, and visit your cherries.

Farewell in the Lord.

1531   MARTIN LUTHER

245

To Robert Barnes[1]
[Wittenberg, September 3, 1531][2]

One of the events which shocked Europe in the first half of the sixteenth century was the divorce of Henry VIII from Catherine of Aragon.[3] *While the Roman Curia played politics and procrastinated in making a decision on Henry's request for an annulment of his marriage, Thomas Cranmer prepared the fatal blow to papal jurisdiction in England. In the late summer of 1529 he suggested to the King that the universities were the institutions which alone would be capable of giving an impartial verdict on the legitimacy and validity of the King's marriage. As a result of this suggestion the court contacted the major universities of Europe for opinions on the King's case. With very few exceptions the universities approved the planned annulment of the marriage.*[4]

---

[1] The address is supplied only in the (B) version of the text of this letter; see below, last paragraph of the Introduction. See also note 27.

[2] The date is supplied only in the (B) version of the text of this letter. Some witnesses give September 5 as the date of the letter. See also note 16.

[3] For some primary and secondary material, see *EHD* 5, 697 ff.; St. Ehses, *Römische Dokumente zur Geschichte der Ehescheidung Heinrichs VIII. von England. 1527–34* (Paderborn, 1893); N. Pocock, *Records of the Reformation: The Divorce* (2 vols.; Oxford, 1870); H. Thieme, *Die Ehescheidung Heinrichs VIII. und die europäischen Universitäten* (Karlsruhe, 1957); *English Historical Review* 11 (1896), 673 ff.; 19 (1904), 632 ff.; W. H. Dixon, *History of Two Queens: Catherine of Aragon, Anne Boleyn* (4 vols.; London, 1873); G. Mattingly, *Catherine of Aragon* (Boston, 1941); G. R. Elton, *Henry VIII* (London, 1962); E. Doernberg, *Henry VIII and Luther* (Stanford, 1961), pp. 63 ff.; Tjernagel, pp. 73 ff.; Constant, pp. 35 ff.

[4] See *WA*, Br 6, 176; Thieme, *op. cit., passim*; Doernberg, *op. cit.*, pp. 69 ff.; Tjernagel, pp. 85 f. The Universities of Alcala and Louvain opposed the annulment. Whether the University of Wittenberg was "willing" to take up the issue,

In order to strengthen his position, the King also sought out the opinions of the outstanding evangelical theologians on the Continent. To make the necessary contacts the court used Symon Grynaeus,[5] a Humanist from Basel, who visited England in spring of 1531 for the purpose of studying manuscripts, and who returned to Basel by mid-July. While Grynaeus' exact commission is unknown, he carried sufficient material with him so that Melanchthon, Bucer and the preachers of Strassburg, Zwingli, and others could issue briefs on this matter.[6] At the same time contacts were established between the English court and Landgrave Philip of Hesse,[7] who was to function as an intermediary between the court and Wittenberg University, especially Luther. By the time Philip contacted Luther,[8] Luther had already spoken[9] on the issue in a letter to Robert Barnes,[10] one of the English evangelical exiles.

Barnes, a former Augustinian and a Cambridge University Doctor of Divinity, had been the outstanding member of the evangelically-oriented White Horse Inn group of theologians.[11] He had

---

as Tjernagel, p. 85, suggests, has to remain open, just as the way Wittenberg *University* (in contrast to Luther alone) dealt with the issue has to remain open.

[5] On Symon Grynaeus, see *NDB* 7, 241 f.

[6] See *WA*, Br 6, 176; Pollet 2, 439 ff., 370 ff. It is not clear whether Grynaeus was to approach *only* the upper German Reformers for an opinion (because the King realized that Luther and his friends would not support his plan of annulment; so according to Tjernagel, pp. 87 f.), and then contacted Melanchthon on his own. Further, it is not clear in what relationship Melanchthon's brief (*C.R.* 2, Nos. 1000, 1001) stands to his letter to Grynaeus (*C.R.* 2, No. 1002), and to Luther's letter to Barnes.

[7] See *LW* 49, 124, n. 18. Did the English court contact the Landgrave in order to force him to take a stand because in 1530 William Tyndale had published in Marburg a book in support of Catherine of Aragon? See Tjernagel, p. 87. Further, did the court contact the Landgrave through Grynaeus? Or through Barnes? (So according to Doernberg, *op. cit.*, p. 85).

[8] *WA*, Br 6, Nos. 1867 (the Landgrave's letter to Wittenberg, dated about September 16, 1531), 1869 (Luther's reply to the Landgrave, dated September 22, 1531).

[9] It has to remain open whether Luther "volunteered his opinion," as Tjernagel, p. 88, suggests. In view of the lack of general information concerning the origin of Barnes's efforts to secure Luther's opinion regarding Henry's case, it is also dubious whether one may suggest, as Doernberg, *op. cit.*, p. 83, does, that the King "asked Luther for help" in this matter. Finally, the relationship between the activities of Grynaeus and Barnes needs to be clarified in more detail than has been done in the secondary literature.

[10] On Robert Barnes, see *DNB* 1, 1173; Rupp, *Tradition*, pp. 31 ff.; Clebsch, pp. 42 ff.

[11] See H. C. Porter, *Reformation and Reaction in Tudor Cambridge* (Cambridge, 1958), pp. 44 ff.

been tried for heresy and put under house arrest, but had been able to escape to the Continent. In the summer of 1530 he appeared in Wittenberg, and "early in September, 1531, Barnes became involved in" the matter of Henry's divorce[12]—how is not clear. Was Barnes contacted by Grynaeus? Or by the English court? The latter seems to be suggested by the fact that Thomas Cromwell was involved in arranging for Barnes's safe-conduct for the return to England.[13] Or was Barnes perhaps acting on his own initiative in an attempt either to bring about a rapprochement between Henry and Luther,[14] or to put himself into the good graces of the King? In any case, just as Grynaeus had done with his contacts, Barnes provided Luther with copies of the briefs issued by the universities.[15] Having obtained Luther's opinion on the matter, Barnes traveled via Magdeburg[16] and Lübeck to Antwerp, where in November of 1531 he published a supplication addressed to the King;[17] on the basis of this supplication Barnes hoped to be able to return to England. Under royal safe-conduct Barnes did indeed go to England in December of 1531, and delivered Luther's opinion on the marriage case. Obviously Luther's opinion, which was so contrary to all of the King's plans, did not endear Barnes to the King.

Luther categorically rejects the validity of the argument that the King has the duty or privilege to divorce the Queen. He substantiates this contention by discussing some of those arguments which had been presented in support of the divorce. He deals especially with the question of sin in marrying a deceased brother's wife. Concentrating on Leviticus 18:16, Luther points out that this passage does not establish the necessity of the divorce. Discussing the relationship of positive law to natural law and to divine law, Luther backs his stand against the divorce by arguing that matrimony is a matter of divine law, and that according to divine law matrimony is indissoluble. For divine law takes precedence over all statements of the positive law by which the King might have been

---

[12] See Clebsch, p. 51.
[13] See Tjernagel, pp. 122 ff.
[14] See *LW* 49, Index, *s.v.* Henry VIII, king of England.
[15] See note 4, and the second paragraph of the text of the letter.
[16] On September 4, 1531, Luther recommended Barnes to von Amsdorf in Magdeburg (see *LW* 48, 218); see *WA*, Br 6, 188.
[17] See Clebsch, pp. 51 f.; Tjernagel, pp. 59, 122 f.

forbidden to marry the wife of his deceased brother. If the King had done any wrong by marrying his deceased brother's wife, then he sinned at the most against positive law, as, for instance, set forth in the Canon Law. Luther doubts even this, because Pope Julius II had given his permission for the King to marry his deceased brother's wife; consequently the King was excused from obeying the positive law at this point. And further, two wrongs do not make one right. That is, even if the King had done wrong by marrying his deceased brother's wife, the divorce still would not remedy this situation; to the contrary, the divorce would be a more serious offense (because it would be contrary to divine law) than the alleged crime of the marriage to the deceased brother's wife (something which is forbidden only in the positive law of the pope).

Having delivered Luther's opinion to the court, Barnes considered it necessary to go once more into exile; in January of 1532 he was back on the Continent.[18] Apparently he functioned for some time as assistant to John Aepinus, the pastor of St. Peter's Church in Hamburg.[19] In 1533 he matriculated at Wittenberg University but never participated for any length of time in the life of the University. "From August, 1534, to January, 1535, Barnes returned to London to negotiate with Henry on behalf of the cities of Hamburg and Lübeck."[20] In May of 1535 he finally returned permanently to England, and in July of 1535 he attained the status of royal chaplain. Yet it was only for a short time that Barnes enjoyed the King's favor. He strongly opposed the Six Articles, "and for his stand against this policy Barnes was burned at Smithfield, July 30, 1540."[21]

Luther's letter to Barnes is extant in two versions, (A) and (B). The text of the (A) version provides the original text of this letter[22] (the one given by Luther to Barnes), and is the basis for the following translation. This version is extant in several sixteenth century manuscript copies, and in the common editions of Luther's works. One of the copies was written by Nicholas von Amsdorf, who was at that time a pastor in Magdeburg. It is safe to assume

[18] See Clebsch, pp. 52 f.; Tjernagel, pp. 90 f., 122 ff.
[19] See Tjernagel, pp. 127 f.; Clebsch, p. 54.
[20] See Clebsch, p. 54.
[21] See Clebsch, p. 55.
[22] See WA, Br 6, 177; W. W. Rockwell, *Die Doppelehe des Landgrafen Philipp von Hessen* (Marburg, 1904), p. 214, n. 1.

that he copied from the original when Barnes traveled from Wittenberg via Magdeburg and Lübeck to Antwerp.[23] *The text of the (B) version also originates with Luther, but is of secondary quality. Luther prepared this version—from memory or from notes—for Landgrave Philip of Hesse, to whom, on September 22, 1531, Luther promised to send a copy of his opinion concerning Henry's divorce.*[24] *A manuscript containing the text of this (B) version is deposited in the Marburg archive.*[25] *It is written in two different (unknown) handwritings, but corrected in Luther's own handwriting. This is the reason that St.L. and Enders*[26] *considered this (B) version to be the original one. In addition to this Marburg manuscript, the (B) version is extant in several sixteenth century manuscript copies, of which one was written by John Bugenhagen,*[27] *and in the common editions of Luther's works.*

Text in Latin: WA, Br 6, 178–182 (A); 183–188 (B).

Grace and Peace in the Lord

My Antony:[28] here you finally have also[29] my opinion on the case of the King of England, since you insist on it with such great perseverance.

To begin with, as I have said, I approve of the decision of the

---

[23] See above, and WA, Br 14, xxix, addition to WA, Br 6, 177. For some of the variant readings, see Enders, *Briefwechsel*, 9, 98 f.; none of these variants have any major bearing on the interpretation of the text. See also note 68.

[24] See note 8. In comparison with the (B) version, the (A) version is briefer and more to the point, but also more sketchy in some places; see also notes 63, 68.

[25] See WA, Br 6, 177; 13, 200, addition to WA, Br 6, 177.

[26] Enders, *Briefwechsel*, 9, 89, n. 2; St.L. 21a, 1688.

[27] On the Bugenhagen manuscript copy, see WA, Br 6, 177; WA, Br 13, 200, addition to WA, Br 6, 177. John Bugenhagen (see LW 48, 303, n. 44) apparently copied directly from the Marburg manuscript before it was dispatched, and, seeing Luther's own handwriting for the corrections, considered this manuscript to have been written by Luther. Therefore Bugenhagen added as address: "To his venerable brother in Christ, Mr. Antonius Anglus [see note 28], a Doctor of Theology, Martin Luther sends greetings in his own handwriting." Enders, *Briefwechsel* 9, 81, n. a. See also note 40.

[28] In the matriculation records of Wittenberg University Melanchthon wrote "Robertus Barns" on the margin, next to the recorded name "D.[octor] Antonius Anglus." See *Album Academiae Vitebergensis* 1, ed. C. E. Foerstemann (Leipzig, 1841), 149.

[29] I.e., in addition to the other opinions which were solicited in this matter. See Introduction.

faculty of Louvain,[30] especially regarding the latter question,[31] and the King may abide by it with a sufficiently safe conscience; in fact, he has to abide by it if he wants to be on the safe side. Under no circumstances will he be free to divorce the Queen to whom he is married, the wife of his deceased brother,[32] and thus make the mother as well as the daughter[33] into incestuous women. Even if the King might have sinned[34] by marrying the wife of his deceased brother, and even if the dispensation granted by the Roman pope might not have been valid[35] (I do not debate this now), nevertheless it would be a heavier and more dreadful sin [for the King] to divorce the woman he had married; and this especially for the reason that then the King, as well as the Queen and the Young Queen,[36] could be forever charged with, and considered as, being incestuous people. According to my opinion, therefore, those[37] who

---

[30] See note 4.

[31] To what specific question Luther is referring here could not be established.

[32] The brother to whom reference is made here and throughout the letter is Henry's brother Arthur. In November 1501, he was married to Catherine of Aragon. He died in 1502, apparently without having had marital relations with Catherine; at least this is what the Queen and her supporters continuously affirmed. See *EHD* 5, 710; *WA*, Br 6, 176.

[33] I.e., Mary Tudor, who was born on February 18, 1516.

[34] One argument in defense of the divorce was drawn from Lev. 18:16 and 20:21; these passages were interpreted as referring to the marriage of a living *and* of a deceased brother's wife. Since these passages were considered to be divine law, the King's marriage was considered to be a matter of sin, a fact which in turn ostensibly bothered the King's conscience. The divorce was considered to be the only way out of this dilemma. See *EHD* 5, 706 ff.; Doernberg, *op. cit.*, p. 83. As Luther's arguments here, and later (see p. 310), demonstrate, Luther took the King's scruples of conscience quite seriously, in fact, so seriously that he had doubts about the King's desire for an heir as motivation for the divorce. See also note 39.

[35] Since according to the Canon Law, which was based on Lev. 18:16 at this point, the marriage to a (deceased) brother's wife was prohibited, the pope had to grant a special dispensation for Henry not to abide by the Canon Law. On December 26, 1503, Pope Julius II issued the permission for Henry to marry Catherine of Aragon, the widow of Henry's brother Arthur. The advocates of the divorce argued that the papal dispensation was invalid because the pope had no right to excuse from obedience to a divine law, as set forth in Lev. 18:16. For the way in which the *Corpus Iuris Canonici* dealt with a marriage to a deceased brother's wife, see H. Feine, *Kirchliche Rechtsgeschichte: Die Katholische Kirche* (4th ed.; Köln-Graz, 1964), pp. 431 f.; *English Historical Review* 19 (1904), 632 ff.

[36] See note 33.

[37] "They," "the opponents," "sophists," "these people," "doctors of the opposition," refer throughout the letter to the advocates of the divorce, esp. the authors of those briefs with which Luther had become acquainted (see above). In the

urge the King to the divorce for this reason alone torture his conscience in vain. If he has sinned by marrying, then this sin is past, and like all other sins of the past is amended through repentance; but the marriage should not be torn apart for this reason, and such a heavy future sin ought not to be permitted. For how many marriages are there in the world which have been made through sinning? And yet they ought not and may not be put asunder. So much for this one reason.

Regarding the other reason—whether you are fabricating it, or whether it is true—that the King is searching for a son, an heir to the kingdom, but that the Queen gives birth only to girls,[38] etc., [I reply:] Who doesn't see that this is an even less valid argument? Who will assure the King either that this present Queen will not give birth to a boy (if age does not hinder it), or that the other Queen,[39] the one whom he is to marry, will give birth to boys? Nevertheless, even if it would be certain that the other Queen would give birth to boys, it still will not be permissible to divorce the former Queen, especially not as an incestuous woman, and thus equally to put the mark of incest forever on the [already born] offspring, that is, to punish them without any cause with this extremely heavy punishment. Before I would approve of such a divorce I would rather permit the King to marry still another woman and to have, according to the examples of the patriarchs and kings, two women or queens at the same time.[40]

(B) version much more than in the (A) version Luther presents his position in the form of a debate with those who advocate the divorce of the King.

[38] Catherine of Aragon had given birth to seven children, among them three boys; all the children, except for Mary (see note 33), died during infancy.

[39] I.e., Anne Boleyn. It cannot be established how much detailed knowledge—if any—Luther had about the relationship between Henry VIII and Anne Boleyn.

[40] This last sentence is missing in all witnesses of the (B) version of the text (that version which was to be sent to the Landgrave; see Introduction). Did Luther eliminate this sentence on purpose? Or did he simply forget it? In any case, Bugenhagen remembered this sentence, and consequently he added in his manuscript copy (see Introduction), in the last paragraph of the whole letter, a sentence which reads in translation: "She [i.e., the Queen] should rather permit the King to marry a second queen according to the example set by the patriarchs, who had many wives even prior to the law; but she herself should not agree to be excluded from the royal matrimony and from the title of queen of England." Enders, *Briefwechsel* 9, 88, n. u. The idea of solving Henry's problem by suggesting or approving bigamy seems to have originated with Melanchthon, who as early as August 23 in his brief discussed this issue in detail; *C.R.* 2, 526. The question whether this solution of the problem was original with the Wittenbergers,

The opponents bring forth, however, that it is contrary to divine law for a man to marry his deceased brother's wife; Leviticus 18 [:16]. To this I reply first of all: If they want to abide by the law of Moses, and also force us to live under the authority of this legislator, then what they will accomplish is that in this case the King will be held responsible not only for keeping the Queen to whom he is married, but also, if she had not [yet] been remarried to someone else, for marrying her by all means possible, and for begetting an offspring to his brother, since the deceased brother did not leave any children by this woman. This is clearly and definitely stated in Deuteronomy 25 [:5]. For if we are forced to observe one law of Moses, then by the same reason we also ought to be circumcised, and ought to observe the whole law, as Paul argues in Galatians 5 [:3]. Now, however, we are no longer under the law ·of Moses, but are subject in these matters to the laws of the state, just as, prior to Moses, Abraham and Nahor were. They married the daughters of their brother; this was a relationship which Moses afterwards prohibited.[41] And Jacob married two sisters,[42] also in opposition to Moses' law, who later prohibited such marriages for his people.[43] Therefore that law of Moses, which beforehand was not valid and which after Christ again ceased to be valid as positive law, does not bind the King, and does not demand the divorce. But that law of God and that statement of divine law[44] according to which matrimony is established as something which ought to be maintained forever, until death, binds the King. For the sake of this law, Christ abolished the letter of divorce handed down from Moses when he said: "From the beginning it was not so."[45]

---

or simply reflected Henry's own ideas, has to remain open. As Enders, *Briefwechsel* 9, 91, n. 15, points out, as early as 1528 Henry had asked the Curia whether under certain circumstances bigamy was permissible, and Rome was not at all opposed to giving an affirmative answer.

[41] In Gen. 11:29 it is reported that Abraham married Sarai, and his brother Nahor married Milcah, who was the daughter of Abraham's and Nahor's brother, Haran, and the sister of Haran's other daughter, Iscah. According to Clemen (*WA*, Br 6, 182, n. 7), Luther follows here the rabbinical tradition (which had been adopted by Jerome and other Christian scholars; see *WA*, Br 13, 200, addition to *WA*, Br 6, 182, n. 7) which identifies Iscah with Sarai, so that Abraham would have married a daughter of Haran, just as Nahor did.

[42] I.e., Leah and Rachel; Gen. 29:23, 28.

[43] Lev. 18:18.

[44] Gen. 2:24; Matt. 19:6.

[45] Matt. 19:8.

Therefore only this argument is left, that the King, if he has sinned by marrying his deceased brother's wife, has sinned against a man-made law, or a law of the state. If he would divorce the Queen, however, he would indeed sin against the divine law.[46] If the law of God is in conflict with the law of man, then the law of man has to yield, so that one does not sin against the law of God; the law of God does not have to yield so that one does not sin against the law of man. An offense against the law of man may either be quashed, or the need to obey this law may be nullified, so that we are not forced to sin against God's law or nullify the validity of God's law.[47]

This, however, is the situation regarding the divine law, namely, that the superior law nullifies the inferior one. For instance: It was a divine law to observe the Sabbath;[48] yet another divine law, that is, the law of circumcision,[49] nullified this law concerning the Sabbath, and permitted, even more, required circumcising exactly on the Sabbath (as often as the Sabbath was the eighth day after birth), as Christ himself argues in John 7 [:22]. Consequently the law concerning the Sabbath had to yield to the law concerning circumcision; one sinned against the law concerning the Sabbath, or rather the law concerning the Sabbath yielded, and in this case was nullified. Even more, on each Sabbath in the morning and in the evening sacrifices were made and all the works of the priests were performed in the Temple; and yet the priests were without guilt, as Jesus states in Matthew 12 [:5]. Even circumcision yielded to a new law of God by which the people were ordered to go out from Egypt;[50] during all the forty years that this new law was in effect, they did not circumcise, and did this without [committing] sin.[51] Further, it had been divine law that the Bread of the Presence

---

46 See note 44.
47 Indirectly Luther deals in this paragraph with the dispensation issued by the pope (see note 35). He considers the way in which the Canon Law interprets Lev. 18:16, and in which the Canon Law is used to challenge the validity of the King's marriage, to be in conflict with the divine and the natural law as expressed in Matt. 19:6 and Gen. 2:24. For Luther, therefore, the Canon Law (the man-made law) had to yield to the divine law, and the papal dispensation was not only valid but absolutely necessary.
48 Exod. 20:8.
49 Gen. 17:10 f.
50 See Exod. 3:17, 5:1, 6:13.
51 Josh. 5:5 ff.

ought to be eaten only by the priests.[52] And yet David, a layman, ate it without committing sin, as if he were ordered by another law of God, that is, the law to love one's neighbor who is in need.[53] There are many such examples in which one divine law nullifies another. What else are magistrates, and those who wield the sword and enforce the law by killing [or] imprisoning those who are guilty, [or] confiscating their property, doing other than nullifying these divine laws: "You shall not kill; you shall not steal"?[54] This is the same as if by another divine law these magistrates were ordered to kill, imprison, [or] punish those who are guilty. These actions would not be permitted unless the law, "You shall not kill," is nullified by another law. How much more in this case does that man-made law,[55] "You shall not marry your deceased brother's wife," have to yield to that former, superior law, "A man shall not abandon his wife, and the two shall be one flesh."[56] Even if this statement, "You shall not marry your deceased brother's wife," were a divine law, it would nevertheless have to yield and be nullified because of the law concerning matrimony, which is a superior law, as has been stated above concerning the examples which demonstrate just how often one divine law nullifies another one.

Let us nevertheless assume (which certainly is not true) that the law of Moses is still valid and binds us Gentiles when it states in Leviticus 18 [:16]: "You shall not uncover the nakedness of your brother's wife." What are the opponents making out of this text? The text, of course, speaks of a living brother, not a deceased one. Since the contradictory law in Deuteronomy 25 [:5] orders that a brother ought to marry his deceased brother's wife, it becomes clear that [Leviticus 18:16] deals with a living brother (who could have had one or perhaps several wives at the same time). So for instance John the Baptist, on the basis of this passage (as is known), charges Herod that he is not permitted to have the wife of his brother Philip, who was [still] living.[57] Therefore on

---

[52] Lev. 24:5 ff.; Exod. 25:23 ff.; Num. 4:7.
[53] I Sam. 21:6; Matt. 12:3 f.
[54] Exod. 20:13, 15.
[55] I.e., Lev. 18:16 as used in the Canon Law (see notes 35, 47), and by the advocates of the divorce.
[56] See note 44.
[57] See Mark 6:18. "Among the reasons cited by the advocates of the divorce

the basis of this passage the doctors of the opposition could accomplish nothing that is sound, even if the law of Moses [still] bound us Gentiles. How much less can they accomplish now since Moses' law does not bind us Gentiles![58]

You will reply: If someone continues this argumentation then he will end up teaching[59] that we also are not prevented by any law of God from marrying daughters, sisters, or mothers, since the law of Moses prohibits this, but the law of Moses now no longer binds us Gentiles. I answer that such marriages are prohibited and considered incestuous by natural law. This is sufficiently proven by the fact that in Scripture before, during, and after [the time in which] the law [of Moses was valid,] no example [for the permission of such marriages] can be found, and without example and law nothing may be undertaken. Precisely by this fact God has sufficiently demonstrated that he condemns such marriages. But there are laws and examples for marrying your deceased brother's wife.

The opponents argue that it follows from the law of Deuteronomy 25 [:5] that someone could marry, or would be obligated to marry his own daughter; so, for instance, if Othniel[60] at his death had left his wife Achsah, who was the daughter of his brother Caleb, then Caleb, as Othniel's brother, would have been obligated to marry his own daughter. Who does not see the evil effort in this argument to support an evil cause? [The opponents argue] as if they did not know, or ought not to know, that one law nullifies another whenever they contradict each other, as stated above. Therefore even if through the law of Deuteronomy 25 [:5] Caleb would have been obligated to marry his brother's wife, yet because this wife of his brother was his own daughter he was prohibited from marrying her by another, superior law, [and was ordered] to stay away from her. So the law of Deuteronomy 25 [:5] yields to

---

was also the testimony of John the Baptist against Herod, which, by citing Tertullian, *Adv. Marcion.* c. 34, was interpreted to mean that John designated each marriage with the wife of a brother to be sin, even if the latter had already died." So Enders, *Briefwechsel* 9, 91, n. 9.

[58] For this paragraph, see also Luther's arguments in his *Against the Heavenly Prophets* (*WA* 18, 67 ff.; *LW* 40, 84 ff.), and *LJB* 16 (1934), 51 ff.

[59] Literally: "You will say: In this way you will teach."

[60] Judg. 1:13 f.

the other law, that is, to the natural law, and simultaneously also to the Mosaic law of Leviticus 18 [:16]. Therefore it is impossible for the opponents to establish, by means of this law in Deuteronomy 25 [:5], the validity of that law in Leviticus 18 [:16], which deals with a living brother—or at least speaks ambiguously—and simply to condemn every marriage according to the law of Deuteronomy 25 [:5]. They do not see that by this condemnation they totally nullify the law concerning the marriage of a deceased brother's wife. Yet this law is confirmed through that noble example of Ruth, who cites this law[61] (even though Boaz was not her brother), and by the testimony of the Gospel of the Seven Brothers who were married to one and the same woman.[62] One may not quibble that in Ruth's case "brother" means "kinsman"; otherwise this same sophistry will also be valid in case of Leviticus 18 [:16]. And further, in Deuteronomy 25 [:5] the text itself does not permit this interpretation, since [in this passage] the word "brother" is so often repeated, and laws are given concerning "brothers who live together." This sophistry is insufficient to quiet consciences; therefore it also should not be permitted to disturb consciences.[63]

---

[61] Ruth 4:5, 10; it is, however, not Ruth who refers to this law, but Boaz.

[62] Matt. 22:23 ff.

[63] I.e., one cannot use Lev. 18:16 for "disturbing" the King's conscience (that he would consider his marriage sinful; see note 34), or for "justifying" the divorce. All the early witnesses except one end the text with this paragraph. The text of the following two paragraphs can be found only on the margin of a manuscript deposited in Jena. The manuscript itself, written by Michael Stifel (see *LW* 49, 140), presents the text of the letter up to this point; see *WA*, Br 14, 249, 252. The marginal text of the following two paragraphs, as well as of other portions of the letter, was written by George Rörer (see *LW* 49, 173, n. 17), one of the editors of the Wittenberg edition of Luther's works; see *WA*, Br 6, 182, n. 24; Enders, *Briefwechsel* 9, 99, n. q; *WA*, Br 13, 200, addition to *WA*, Br 6, 177, where the variant readings of Rörer's text for other portions of the letter are listed; on Rörer as collector and editor of Lutherana, see also *WA*, Br 14, 175 ff.; E. Wolgast, *Die Wittenberger Lutherausgabe* (Nieuwkoop, 1971), *passim*. One has to consider the two following paragraphs to be a part of Luther's letter to Barnes for the following reasons: (*a*) In the (B) version Luther deals also with the law concerning ceremonial matters; see *WA*, Br 6, 184, line 53 ff. (*b*) The Amsdorf manuscript copy of the (A) version of the text, that copy which is probably closest to the original (see above, the last paragraph of the Introduction), ends the text (after the equivalent for "disturb consciences") with a statement to the effect that it was apparently not Amsdorf's intention to copy the whole letter, and that therefore he added an "etc." See Ender's *Briefwechsel* 9, 99, n. q. I.e., the text as extant even in the Amsdorf copy is incomplete. Rörer therefore completed the text of Luther's letter as it is extant in all early witnesses. The source of Rörer's text cannot be established. Since Rörer put on the margin

But here the opponents say that the law of Deuteronomy 25 [:5] was a law concerning ceremonial matters, which ought to yield to the law of Leviticus 18 [:16], which was a law concerning morals, since ceremonial matters have ceased to be valid, but matters concerning morals have not ceased to be valid. To this I reply: Let those corrupt interpreters say whatever they wish without sound judgment; we contradict them [with the following argument]: The law of Deuteronomy 25 [:5] has certainly been a law concerning morals, because as a law of the state it was indeed instituted for the conservation of families, for the preservation of legacies, and for the begetting of heirs, that is, for the augmenting and strengthening of the common good, just as it certainly serves the common good and is moral to till the soil at this or that time, [and] in this or that way, so that the soil brings forth more fruit, since by using such a method goods are produced. At Moses' time there was no contradiction in the laws since both laws were valid, and were observed. Therefore both are abolished now. Consequently the opponents should stop insisting on the validity [only] of the law of Leviticus 18 [:16], or should maintain both laws as being valid.

At the risk of losing his salvation, and under the threat of eternal damnation, therefore, the King is to be held responsible for retaining the Queen to whom he is married. This is proven by the following argument: First of all, neither according to natural law nor according to divine law is it definitely prohibited to marry one's brother's wife, but only according to positive law. For, as I have said, the legislator Moses is dead and invalid for us. Matrimony is a matter of divine and of natural law. In cases where the divine and the positive laws contradict each other, the positive law must yield to the divine law. For this reason Christ, too, nullified the law of divorce given by Moses in order to establish the validity of the divine law concerning matrimony. If, therefore, the King of England has sinned by marrying his deceased brother's wife, then he

---

of the Stifel manuscript copy several variant readings which are unique and are not confirmed by any other witnesses, and show a tendency to shorten the text, perhaps even summarize it, one is safe in assuming that the two following paragraphs do not produce Luther's text verbatim, but rather Rörer's version of it. See also note 68.

has sinned against a man-made law, or a law of the state. If the emperor[64] and the pope, provided that the latter rules through his worldly tyranny,[65] have suspended their laws for the King, then the King has not sinned at all, because that same God who approves of the law of the state promulgated by the emperor also approves the emperor's suspension of the emperor's law. For God has given the emperor the authority to make and suspend laws, and that I might say so, the keys[66] of binding and freeing people in the territory which is subject to the emperor. If the King should divorce the Queen, however, he will most gravely sin against the divine law, which states: "What God has joined together, let no man put asunder."[67] "Man," that is, no man-made laws may separate those whom God has joined, either by ordinance or by permission, because God's joining, whether done through the law or through human action, stands higher than any man-made ordinance. Therefore if these laws now contradict each other, then one should be careful that the King of England does not observe a man-made law and sin against the divine law, but that he observe the divine law; he may be forgiven if he has sinned against a man-made law. Suppose now the divorce goes through, she is [still] the queen, and will be the queen of England,[68] and an injustice before God and man will have been done to her.

---

[64] Obviously Luther did not mean here that Henry VIII was subject to the laws promulgated by the emperor of the Holy Roman Empire; Luther apparently used "emperor" as a synonym for "any secular legislator."

[65] I.e., if the pope has any secular jurisdiction, either by right or concession. For Luther's understanding of the difference between the church's secular and spiritual jurisdiction, see *LW* 49, 382 ff.

[66] See Matt. 16:19.

[67] See note 44.

[68] Clemen (*WA*, Br 6, 182, n. 28) states that further deliberations on the issue are broken off here. This suggests that the (A) version of this letter, as extant in the Jena manuscript copy (i.e., Stifel's text and Rörer's addition; see note 63), is only a fragment. If one compares both versions, however, it becomes clear that the argument against the divorce itself is completed. Further, in the (A) version only the rather long-winded conclusion of the (B) version (see *WA*, Br 6, 187, line 186 ff.) is missing, which has little to do with the argument against the divorce, but deals with the way in which Luther wishes that his document be used, and with pastoral concern for the Queen. This raises the question of whether the conclusion in the (B) version was indeed a part of the letter (so that one would have to assume that a similar conclusion is now missing in the [A] version), or whether Luther had not told this conclusion to Barnes personally, but had added it to the (B) version for the Landgrave. The fact that in the (A) version the address, conclusion, and signature are missing, and that the argumentation in the (A) version appears to be compact, sometimes even

246

To Elector John
[Wittenberg, about February 12, 1532][1]

To promote religious peace in the Empire[2] the Archbishop of Mainz[3] and his staff drew up articles and in November of 1531 presented them to the Electoral Saxon government as basis for further discussions. On December 27 Chancellor Brück[4] met with the representative of the Archbishop of Mainz in Bitterfeld[5] for a discussion of these articles. Since the propapal Estates of the Empire were ready to grant peace and security to the evangelicals until such time as a general council of the church would decide all controversial issues, prospects for peace were good. Consequently on February 8 and 9 a second conference between Brück and a representative of the Archbishop took place in Bitterfeld.

Emperor Charles,[6] too, was willing to accept the articles on condition that Electoral Saxony and Hesse would abandon their opposition to the election of his brother, Ferdinand of Austria, as Roman king.[7] But this condition was categorically rejected by

---

sketchy, if compared with that in the (B) version, suggests that (A), as it is extant, was intended to be rather a summary of the discussion given by Luther to Barnes than a personal letter addressed to Barnes, and that for the (B) version Luther recast this material into the form of a letter.

[1] The approximate date of this letter can be established on the basis of the similar, sometimes even identical, statements Luther made in his February 12 letter to Duke John Frederick; *WA*, Br 6, No. 1904. The autograph of the letter is in private hands. The letter is extant in several manuscript copies, and in the common editions of Luther's works. The *WA*, Br edition reproduces the (in part quite substantial) variant readings of a sixteenth century copy of the letter which supposedly was made from the autograph. The *WA*, Br text is based on a manuscript copy which is deposited, together with other materials pertaining to the Smalcaldic League, in the Weimar archive; therefore this text has to be considered a chancellery copy.

[2] See letter No. 242.

[3] Cardinal Albrecht of Brandenburg, the archbishop of Mainz; see *LW* 48, 44 f. The following presentation is based on Winckelmann, pp. 175 ff.

[4] See *LW* 49, 51 f.

[5] Bitterfeld is located approximately twenty-five kilometers northeast of Halle/Saale.

[6] See *LW* 48, 175 f.

[7] In addition to the religious issue and the other matters to be decided by the Diet of Augsburg (see *LW* 49, 280 f.), Emperor Charles wanted to see a dynastic matter settled. Ever since his election in 1519, the Emperor's goal had been

Landgrave Philip of Hesse,[8] *who, in order to promote his own anti-Hapsburg plans, on February 1, 1532, wrote a letter to the Electoral prince, Duke John Frederick,*[9] *urging him not to abandon the protest against Ferdinand's election. One should procrastinate, suggested Philip, by saying that prior to accepting Ferdinand as king, we would have to see how Ferdinand would fulfill his royal obligations; once the Emperor had left the Empire then we could see what to do next. And Brück had, in fact, protested the Emperor's condition as early as the first meeting in Bitterfeld.*[10]

---

to preserve the Imperial office for the Hapsburg dynasty; see Brandi 1, 111 ff., 263 f. There had been instances in past German history when dynastic continuity was preserved by the election of a successor at a time when the incumbent of the German royal office (that is, the Roman king who was also emperor) was still alive. The two conditions necessary for such an arrangement were: (*a*) that the incumbent had been crowned emperor (a condition which in Charles's case had been fulfilled since February, 1530, when he finally had been crowned emperor; see *LW* 49, 280, n. 4), and (*b*) the actual election of the future Roman king by the Electors. (For the legalities concerning the election, see *Europe in the Late Middle Ages*, eds. J. R. Hale *et al.* [Evanston, 1965], pp. 217 ff., esp. 229 ff.; G. Barraclough, *The Origins of Modern Germany* [Oxford, 1946], pp. 282 ff., 320 ff., 355 ff.) Since Charles's son Philip was still a child, he wanted his brother Ferdinand (who had functioned as viceroy in Germany since 1521) elected Roman king. In the long drawn out negotiations at the Diet of Augsburg the Emperor reached agreement with all the Electors on November 13, 1530 (see Ranke 3[VI], 92 f.; Brandi 2, 219 f.), except for John of Saxony, who had left Augsburg on September 23; see *LW* 49, 422, n. 15, 423 f. Charles hoped to circumvent the necessity of negotiating with the "heretical" Elector of Saxony by simply excluding him from the election, or by admitting him but excluding him afterwards as an excommunicated heretic if he voted against Ferdinand; see Ranke 3[VI], 94 ff.; Brandi 1, 263; 2, 220. Notwithstanding the religious issue, the Electors, fully conscious of their power and responsibility to preserve the "liberties" of the German sovereigns (for the "liberties" of the German sovereigns, see *Reformatio und Confessio. Festschrift für D. Wilhelm Maurer*, ed. F. W. Kantzenbach and G. Müller [Berlin, 1965], pp. 98 ff.), insisted that Elector John be summoned for the election. While on November 13 the Imperial archchancellor, Cardinal Albrecht of Mainz, called the Electoral convention for December 29 to Cologne, Emperor Charles on the same day summoned Elector John to come to Cologne on December 21 for the purpose of conducting "important business" which demanded the presence of all Electors. Contrary to Luther's advice (see note 12), the Elector did not participate in the election, but protested the election. The majority of the evangelical Estates joined Elector John in this protest, and as a result, Ferdinand, who was elected anyhow, was not unanimously recognized as Roman king. It was not until 1534 that the evangelicals finally recognized Ferdinand as king.

[8] See *LW* 49, 124, n. 18.
[9] See *LW* 48, 181 f.
[10] At the end of February the Landgrave even sent a special envoy to the Electoral court in Torgau for the specific purpose of getting the Saxons to agree with his point of view. The Landgrave was not only unsuccessful but had to join

From the very beginning Luther was kept fully informed of these developments. Either prior to or after the first meeting at Bitterfeld, Brück used Melanchthon for obtaining Luther's opinion on the articles drafted by the Archbishop of Mainz. Luther gave his opinion in a discussion with Melanchthon, of which only Melanchthon's notes are extant.[11] *After the second meeting at Bitterfeld, Brück asked Luther to give a judgment on the articles, and to do it in the form of an official brief. The following letter to Elector John is this brief requested by Brück.*

Even though Luther is aware of the possibility that ambiguous passages might have been intentionally inserted into the articles, he urges his Sovereign to accept the articles as basis for negotiating in good faith, and thus have the opportunity to clarify whatever might be ambiguous in the articles. Regarding Ferdinand's election, Luther admonishes the Elector to abandon his opposition for the sake of peace.[12] *He interprets the situation as God's challenge to the evangelicals to give up their rights by abandoning their opposition to Ferdinand's kingship, and to accept the offered peace as a gift of God, who might wish to spread the gospel through this peace. Not to abandon this opposition would in the long run certainly mean war. In this connection Luther warns the Elector to be careful of political alliances, which are a sign of dependence upon human*

Electoral Saxony in establishing the next conference on this matter. A meeting with the representatives of the propapal Estates was planned for the end of April in Schweinfurt. See Fabian, *ESBV* (1st ed.), pp. 94 ff.

[11] *WA*, Br 6, 265.

[12] Luther had spoken on this issue as early as December 12, 1530, in a brief for the Elector, requested by Chancellor Brück; *WA*, Br 5, No. 1761. His judgment was that Elector John ought to participate in the election and cast an affirmative vote. Luther gave two reasons for his suggestion: (*a*) By participating in the election the Elector exercises his office; since the papists are plotting to take this office away from Elector John, or are using the confirmation of the fief and of the Electoral office to pressure the Elector in matters of faith (see *LW* 49, 374, n. 3), their plots would thus be nullified, because they themselves are requesting Elector John to exercise his office and would thereby acknowledge that he rightly holds this office. (*b*) Not to participate in the election could be to play directly into the hands of the papists, who might take the Electoral voice away from Elector John, give it to someone else, and do so with what would appear to be a just reason. This transfer of the Electoral voice certainly would mean war, for which Elector John could justly be held responsible. There is, therefore, no need now to refuse participation in the election and thus risk being responsible for the turmoil that might result from any such transferring of the Electoral voice. And further, the future stands in God's hands.

*planning, and which will falter and fail, because God alone guides
and protects the work of the gospel.*
  On Elector John, see LW 48, 269, n. 8.
  Text in German: WA, Br 6, 260–261.

To the Most Serene, Noble Sovereign and Lord,
Sir John, duke in Saxony, archmarshal and elector
of the Holy Roman Empire, landgrave in Thuringia
and margrave in Meissen, my Most Gracious Lord

Grace and peace in Christ our Lord! Most Serene, Noble Elector,
Most Gracious Lord! As he had once done previously, Doctor
Brück, Your Electoral Grace's chancellor, has now again presented
to me the articles[13] which are to be the basis for the negotiations
between the two Electors,[14] etc., and Your Electoral Grace for the
purpose of establishing a treaty or peace between His Imperial
Majesty and Your Electoral Grace. In behalf of Your Electoral
Grace, [Doctor Brück] has requested my judgment on these articles, etc.

  It is my humble judgment that these articles can be tolerated
and ought to be accepted. Even if some of them should still be
ambiguous or could be suspected [of being a trap], yet I think
that when the negotiations [actually] come about all matters could
be made clear and definite. Indeed (as far as I can see) it seems to
me that in these articles are expressed the honest intention and
opinion of both Electors; for they have succeeded in receiving from
the Emperor such a far-reaching and unencumbered order to negotiate, and they have used Count Palatine Frederick for this mission.[15] With all this they demonstrate that they have been and still
are seriously concerned with this matter.

  Since the matter has now progressed to the stage that nothing

---

13 See Introduction, and note 11.
14 I.e., the Archbishop of Mainz (see note 3), and the Elector Louis V of the
Palatinate (see *ADB* 19, 575 ff.).
15 This is a reference to the trip to Brussels which Count Palatine Frederick, the
brother of Count Palatine Louis (see *ADB* 7, 603 ff.), had made at the turn of
the year in order to present the articles to the Emperor, and to receive the Emperor's approval of further negotiations with the evangelicals; see Winckelmann,
pp. 110 ff.

might stand in the way of such a treaty and peace except perhaps the article concerning the king, etc.,[16] it is my humble petition that Your Electoral Grace donate this article to Christ, and give it up. If the king was illegally elected, then by now he has suffered enough for it. Your Electoral Grace has sufficiently opposed such injustice, and has certainly demonstrated Your Grace's opposition. One also has to permit the functioning of the Christian precept which is called forgiveness of sins. Otherwise, if one blows one's nose too hard (says Solomon)[17] blood comes, and if one wrathfully pursues an issue, strife will result from it. Certainly many unjust events will continue to be a part of this world; but once they have occurred they should remain unaltered, as the laws teach us, in order to prevent even greater trouble.

One also has to consider seriously that God is offering us such opportunities for peace because he perhaps intends to spread his gospel by means of this peace. We certainly are obligated even to deny ourselves and abandon our plans, if [thereby] we can glorify and promote God's honor, name, and Word. All of these will be obstructed if there is no peace; perhaps even the opposite [of peace] might arise, so that we might be hindered in [the promotion of] the gospel by war or lack of peace, or even might be robbed of it.

Christ our Lord, to whose glory this article [concerning the king] will be donated, will in turn glorify Your Electoral Grace, as he promises. Thus in Romans 12 [:18] St. Paul speaks out, and teaches that we Christians ought to live in peace with every man, as much as it depends upon us. This means that we ought to abandon our right for the sake of peace, so that we do not suffer. For peace is more important than that which is legal; in fact, the laws are established for the sake of peace.

If—God forbid—the treaty should not come about because of this article [concerning the king] then the final outcome would be that a war would develop from this situation, whether the Emperor remains in the country or not, etc.[18] Without doubt, Your Electoral

---

[16] See notes 7, 12.
[17] Prov. 30:33.
[18] Here one can see how thoroughly Luther was informed of the situation. The Landgrave had used the phrase, "whether the Emperor . . . " in his February 12 letter to Duke John Frederick; see Introduction.

Grace would also be one of the causes of such a war. It would be an unbearable burden for [Your Grace's] conscience if afterwards Mr. Remorse appeared and bit, saying: "Oh, why didn't I abandon my right and accept the peace, so that such great misfortune and grief would not have arisen?" Certainly it might happen that because of such a war the Empire would be torn apart and exposed to the Turk, and thus both the gospel and everything else would perish.

We also see that foreign kings are not faithful, and we have often experienced how effectively the cities control their citizens in time of a crisis; at present the people of Zürich are a good example of this.[19] I know that God is strongly opposed to such alliances, and he also sees to it that they do not stand firm; the prophets are full of examples of this.[20] For alliances are nothing but thoughts and plans of man, undertaken in human cleverness, without God's Word or order. Therefore it is not possible that these alliances stand firm when the need arises, and do not falter. Here is Scripture, [where we read]: "All men are liars."[21] That is, they do not come [to one's] aid, but falter. Therefore Isaiah calls Egypt a "broken reed of a staff," which will pierce the hand of him who leans on it.[22] We have a divine cause, which God alone will and ought to protect, as he has faithfully done till now; the thoughts of men certainly will not do it.

May Your Electoral Grace accept this, my humble judgment, with a benevolent attitude toward me; for I, too, mean well, God

---

[19] According to Luther's letter to the Electoral prince (see note 1), Luther means that in a time of crisis the upper German and Swiss cities would not stand up for the evangelical sovereigns of the Empire, and that there is a great difference between words and actions. See WA, Br 6, 263. Luther here makes a reference to the Second Peace Treaty of Cappel, which the city of Zürich (after its defeat on October 11, 1531, at Cappel, at the hands of the propapal Cantons) had to sign on November 20, 1531. In this treaty the people of Zürich had to make far-reaching concessions to their enemies, among them the renunciation of the *Burgrecht* (i.e., an alliance for mutual aid) which Zürich had signed with Strassburg and the Landgrave of Hesse on November 16, 1530 (see Winckelmann, pp. 24 ff.); see Kidd, No. 227; Ranke 2III, 225 ff. For Luther's reaction to these events, see his December 28 letter to Nicholas von Amsdorf (see LW 48, 218); WA, Br 6, 236.
[20] See, e.g., Isa. 31:3.
[21] Ps. 116:11 (Luther Bible); see also Rom. 3:4.
[22] Isa. 36:6.

knows it, and I hope not to have spoken with smooth lips but an evil heart.[23]

For doing his own good will, may the gracious Father enlighten and strengthen Your Electoral Grace. Amen. Amen.

Your Electoral Grace's humbly dedicated

MARTIN LUTHER

247

To Mrs. Martin Luther
[Torgau,] February 27, 1532

On February 19 Luther and Jonas[1] visited Elector John[2] in Torgau[3] for the purpose of consoling the Elector, who was suffering from something similar to gangrene in one of his feet.[4] For reasons which cannot be established with certainty, Luther's return was delayed.[5] In the following letter Luther informs his wife that he hopes to return "tomorrow or the next day." He also assures his wife that he is sleeping well. Then he briefly tells of the Elector's health, which seems to be improving. The major portion of the letter deals

---

[23] Luther wrote: *Dass ich nicht aus Menschenscherben rede*, i.e., literally: "That I do not speak out of [as?] human debris." According to WA, Br 6, 262, n. 13, Luther was apparently thinking here of Prov. 26:23, which is rendered in the Luther Bible as "Eager lips and an evil heart are like a potsherd covered with silvery foam."

[1] See LW 48, 275, n. 3.

[2] See LW 48, 269, n. 8.

[3] The city in which the Electoral Saxon residency was located. For this trip to Torgau, see also Buchwald, *LK*, p. 85; WA 36, viii.

[4] Apparently one of the Elector's big toes had to be amputated; see WA, Br 6, 269.

[5] On February 25, 1532, Melanchthon wrote to Jonas that he was expecting them to return "shortly"; *C.R.* 2, 569. Fabian, *ESBV* (1st ed.), p. 94, n. 378, suggests that Luther stayed in Torgau because of the negotiations with the special envoy of Landgrave Philip of Hesse, mentioned on p. 42, n. 10, and that Luther influenced these negotiations so that Electoral Saxony did not comply with the Landgrave's request to delay the peace negotiations between the propapal Estates and the evangelicals. This is, of course, a possibility. On the other hand it is also quite possible that Luther's stay in Torgau had nothing to do with these negotiations. Luther himself did not feel well (see WA, Br 6, 269; WA, 36, viii); in addition he spent quite some time in pastoral conversations with the Elector; see WA, Br 6, 268, 282.

with Luther's famulus,[6] John Rischmann, who was about to leave him. Luther urges his wife to find the means necessary for an appropriate farewell gift, even though he also expresses the opinion that the Common Chest should give such a present to Rischmann in his behalf. As an afterthought Luther asks his wife to tell Nicholas Hausmann to be content with the quarters provided to him. Luther also promises to report in person on a dinner he attended. In closing he asks his wife to give a kiss to their son John for him, to continue to urge the family to pray, and to have some presents ready for him to give to the children upon his return.

Text in German: WA, Br 6, 270–271.[7]

To my dearly beloved[8] mistress of the house, Catherine Luther:[9]
Personal

God in Christ be with you![10] My dearly beloved Katie! As soon as Doctor Brück[11] is granted permission to leave the court—he puts me off with this prospect—I hope to come along with him tomorrow or the next day. Pray God to bring us home chipper and healthy! I am sleeping very well,[12] about six or seven hours without interruption, and then thereafter again for two or three hours. It's the beer's fault, I think. But just as in Wittenberg I am sober.[13]

Doctor Caspar[14] says that the gangrene in our Gracious Lord's[15] foot will spread no further.[16] But neither Dobitzsch[17] nor

---

[6] See *LW* 48, 164, n. 4.

[7] The letter is extant in a manuscript copy, in a separate eighteenth century edition which is based on this copy, and in the common editions of Luther's works. See *WA*, Br 6, No. 1908, Introduction, and 13, 205 *ad loc. cit.*

[8] See *LW* 49, 312, n. 1.

[9] The text reads: *Katharin Lutherin,* i.e., literally: "Catharine the female Luther."

[10] The text reads: *Gott zum Gruss in Christo!* I.e., literally: "God as a greeting in Christ!" Or: "God in Christ as greeting!" This is a rather solemn greeting; it is still today occasionally used among Christian people in Germany, but only in a solemn context, while *Grüss Gott* has become so popular that it has lost its religious depth.

[11] See *LW* 49, 51 f.

[12] Did Luther's wife know that her husband was not feeling well? (See note 5.)

[13] On Luther's "drinking" habits, see Bainton, p. 298; H. Grisar, *Luther 2* (Freiburg, 1911), 244 ff.

[14] I.e., Dr. Caspar Lindemann, the Elector's personal physician; see *LW* 49, 291, n. 30.

[15] I.e., Elector John; see note 2.

[16] Literally: "that our Gracious Lord's foot will not eat [*fressen*] further."

[17] This is a reference to an infamous outlaw knight who had been executed on

any prisoner on the stretching-rack in jail suffers such agony from John the jailer as His Electoral Grace suffers from the surgeons. His Sovereign Grace is, in his whole body, as healthy as a little fish, but the devil has bitten and pierced His Grace's foot. Pray, and continue to pray! I trust God will listen to us, as he has begun. For Doctor Caspar, too, thinks that in this case God has to help.

Since John[18] is moving away, it is both necessary and honorable that I let him go honorably from me. For you know that he has served me faithfully and diligently, and conducted himself with humility, and done and endured all [he was required to do], according to the gospel. Remember how often we have given something to bad boys and ungrateful students, in which cases all that we did was lost. Now therefore reach into your wallet[19] and let nothing be lacking for this fine fellow, since you know that it is well used and God-pleasing. I certainly know that little is available; yet if I had them I wouldn't mind giving him ten gulden.[20] But you shouldn't give him less than five gulden, since we didn't give him a new suit of clothes [upon his departure]. Whatever you might be able to do beyond this, do it, I beg you for it. The Common Chest[21] might, of course, make a present to my servant in my honor, in view of the fact that I am forced to maintain my servants at my expense for the service and benefit of the local congregation.[22] But they may do as they please. Yet under no circumstances should you let anything be lacking as long as there is still a fine goblet [in the house]. Figure out from where you will take the money. God certainly will provide more; this I know. With this I commend you to God. Amen.

November 30, 1531; for bibliographical references, see Enders, *Briefwechsel* 9, 156, n. 4. See also *WA*, Br 13, 205, addition to *WA*, Br 6, 271, n. 4.

[18] I.e., John Rischmann of Brunswick. He had studied in Wittenberg since 1527, had been Luther's *famulus*, and had lived with the Luther family. With Luther's fine letter of recommendation, dated February 27, 1532 (*WA*, Br 6, 272), Rischmann became assistant principal of a school in Husum (Schleswig-Holstein) in 1533; soon thereafter he was appointed deacon and archdeacon there. In 1544 he visited Luther again in order to get advice on a marital problem of one of his parishioners. See Enders, *Briefwechsel* 9, 157, n. 1; *WA*, Br 6, 272.

[19] Literally: "So, now touch yourself here [i.e., in this case]."

[20] On the gulden, see *LW* 48, 11, n. 2.

[21] See *LW* 49, 28 ff.

[22] Literally: "benefit of their [i.e., the citizens of Wittenberg] church." See also *LW* 49, 61, n. 9.

Tell the pastor of Zwickau[23] he really ought to be pleased and content with the quarters. Upon my return I shall tell you how Mühlpfort and I have been guests of Rietesel,[24] and how Mühlpfort has demonstrated much wisdom to me.[25] But I wasn't eager for his wisdom.[26]

Kiss young Hans for me;[27] keep after Hänschen, Lenchen,[28] and Aunt Lena[29] to pray for the dear Sovereign[30] and for me. I am unable to find anything to buy for the children in this town even though there is now a fair here. If I am unable to bring anything special along, please have something ready for me!

February 27, 1532   DOCTOR MARTIN LUTHER

248

To Thomas Zink
[Wittenberg,] April 22, 1532

John Zink was a very young undergraduate student at Wittenberg and a frequent guest in the Luthers' house. On March 24, 1532, he became seriously ill, and on April 20 he died. In the following letter of consolation, written to John's father, Luther points out how well-liked John Zink was, and what a great personal loss John's death is

---

[23] I.e., Nicholas Hausmann; see *LW* 48, 399 f. He had run into extreme difficulties with the mayor of Zwickau, Hermann Mühlpfort, so that he had to leave Zwickau and stay for a while with Luther. See *WA*, Br 6, 50 ff.; see also *LW* 49, 161 ff.

[24] I.e., John Rietesel, the Electoral chamberlain; see also *LW* 49, 425. Apparently this dinner meeting was designed to bring about a compromise between the Zwickau mayor, Herman Mühlpfort, and Luther, who wholeheartedly supported Hausmann against the city council; Luther's position was perhaps not completely justified, as Rückert (*LB*, p. 405, n. 13) suggests.

[25] I.e., Herman Mühlpfort told his, i.e., the city's, side of the conflict with Hausmann in an attempt to convince Luther that Hausmann was to be blamed for the conflict. See also *WA*, Br 6, 50 ff.

[26] Literally: "But I wasn't eager to drink such drink." I.e., Luther was not eager to listen to Mühlpfort's arguments.

[27] John Luther; see *LW* 49, 152, n. 7, 323, n. 7.

[28] Magdalen Luther; see *LW* 49, 218, n. 4.

[29] Magdalene von Bora; see *LW* 49, 271, n. 28.

[30] I.e., Elector John.

for him. Luther encourages the parents to be grateful to God for the opportunity they had had to raise such a fine boy, and for the fact that their son had had such a blessed and peaceful death. He assures the parents that their son died affirming his faith and in full possession of his rational faculties, facts which in turn are sure signs that the boy is now with God in eternal blessedness. In closing Luther mentions that Veit Dietrich, the boy's tutor, would write down some of the statements which the boy made during his final days, and that these statements should bring some consolation to the parents.

Text in German: WA, Br 6, 301–302.[1]

To Thomas Zink at Hofheim[2]

Before all else—grace and peace in Christ, our Lord! My dear Friend! I think that by this time you will have learned that your dear son, John Zink, whom you sent here to study with us, was overtaken by a severe illness and, although nothing was spared in the way of care, attention, and medicine, the disease became too powerful and took your son away, carrying him off to heaven, to our Lord Jesus Christ. We were all very fond of the boy; he was especially dear to me—so that I made use of him many an evening for singing in my house[3]—because he was quiet, well-behaved, and especially diligent in his studies. Accordingly we all are deeply grieved by his death. We would have been very happy to have him saved, and to keep him with us, had this been at all possible. But he was even dearer to God, who desired to have him.

As is natural,[4] your son's death, and the report of it, will distress and grieve your heart and that of your wife, since you are his parents. I do not blame you for this, for all of us—I in particular—are stricken with sorrow. Yet I exhort you now rather to thank God

---

[1] The letter is extant in many manuscript copies, in the common editions of Luther's works, and in sixteenth-century collections of Luther's writings of pastoral counseling. See WA, Br 6, No. 1930, Introduction; WA, Br 13, 207, addition to WA, Br 6, 301. For the following translation, the translation provided by Theodore G. Tappert in LCC 18, 64 f. has been consulted.
[2] Hofheim is a small town in lower Franconia, in the area of the Hassberge.
[3] According to material presented in WA, Br 6, No. 1930, Introduction, John Zink had been a boy soprano.
[4] Or: "As is right."

for having given you such a good, devout son, and for having considered you worthy of investing your money and efforts so well. Let this be your best comfort (as it is ours), that he fell asleep (rather than departed) so peacefully[5] and softly, and with such a fine testimony of faith on his lips and in full possession of his rational faculties[6] that we all marveled. There can be as little doubt that he is with God, his true Father, in eternal blessedness, as there can be doubt that the Christian faith is true. For such a beautiful Christian end cannot fail to lead heavenward.[7]

In addition, you should also consider how grateful you ought to be, and how much comfort you ought to derive from this, that he (unlike many others) did not perish in a dangerous and pitiful way. Even if he had lived a long time, you could not, with your efforts, have helped him to anything higher than some sort of office or service. Now, however, he is in a place which he would not wish to exchange for all the world, not even for a moment. Grieve in such a way, therefore, as to console yourselves even more. For you have not lost him, but have sent him on ahead of you to be kept in everlasting blessedness. St. Paul says:[8] "You should not mourn over the departed, or those who have fallen asleep, as the heathen do," etc.

I am confident that Master[9] Veit,[10] your son's tutor, will write down for you some of the beautiful words which your son uttered before his death, and they will please and comfort you.[11] I, however, have not wished to omit writing these lines to you, out of love for the devout boy, so that you may have a reliable witness of what happened to him.

---

[5] Literally: "cleanly."
[6] Literally: "such fine faith, intellect, confession."
[7] Literally: "end, which cannot miss the kingdom of heaven."
[8] See I Thess. 4:13.
[9] I.e., Master of Arts.
[10] I.e., Veit Dietrich; see LW 49, 282, n. 13. John Zink's brother Albert, or Albrecht, was also one of Dietrich's students. While Dietrich was with Luther at the Coburg in the summer of 1530, he copied Luther's notes on the Decalog (WA 30II, 357 ff.) for the Zink brothers.
[11] According to Klaus, p. 112, it cannot be documented that Dietrich wrote down or sent these statements to the parents. In Dietrich's collection of Luther's Table Talks there is, however, a record dealing with the last days and words of John Zink, and this material confirms the picture sketched by Luther in his letter to Zink's parents. See WA, TR 1, No. 249.

Christ, our Lord and Comforter, allow me to commend you to his grace. Amen.

In the evening of April 22, 1532

DOCTOR MARTIN LUTHER,
written with my own hand
although now I, too, am weak

249

To Nicholas von Amsdorf[1]
[Wittenberg,] June 13, 1532

Excusing his silence on the basis of his own recent poor health, Luther first expresses his hope that Christ may restore von Amsdorf's health. Then he communicates news and rumors: a new attack against the Empire by the Turks is imminent; the Pope and the King of France refuse to aid the Emperor in the fight against the Turks; the mobilization against the Turks might make necessary an early closing of the Diet of Regensburg and the termination of the peace negotiations between the Emperor and "our" party; Karlstadt has gone to Friesland in search of a refuge and of suitable work. In closing Luther expresses his hope that Christ's will may be done, and commends von Amsdorf to Christ's grace.

On Nicholas von Amsdorf, see LW 48, 218.

Text in Latin: WA, Br 6, 318–319.

Grace and Peace in Christ

This has been the reason for the fact that I have not written to you,[2] my Amsdorf: the condition of my head—which gradually

---

[1] The letter is extant in manuscript copies, and in the common editions of Luther's works. Even though the address is missing in all witnesses, the content of the letter confirms von Amsdorf as addressee.

[2] Luther's last extant letter to von Amsdorf was written on April 2 (*WA*, Br 6, No. 1916), and in that letter, too, Luther excused his silence by stating that he had been suffering from illness connected with his head. What it was that bothered

improves because of your prayers, for I have definitely despaired of [my] natural strength. I hear that you, too, are ill, and I do not like to hear this. May Christ restore you also and preserve you a long time for us.

I do not know what to expect concerning the peace which is to be established at Nürnberg between the Emperor[3] and us.[4] While still traveling,[5] our friends wrote that the Turk, who has been totally immobile[6] thus far, is now moving against Germany with a horrifying army of countless soldiers in order to attack[7] Ferdinand and Charles simultaneously, and to devour both brothers. The Pope

---

Luther at this time (for more references, see WA, Br 13, 208, addition to WA, Br 6, 318, line 2) cannot be exactly defined; it seems, however, that he was suffering from severe headaches and tinnitus, apparently due to high blood pressure.

[3] I.e., here and throughout the letter, Emperor Charles V; see LW 48, 175 f.

[4] On the peace negotiations between the Electors of Mainz and of the Palatinate on the one side, and the evangelicals on the other side, see letters No. 242, 246. The meeting in Schweinfurt in the spring of 1532 brought no results beyond a clarification of matters. It was decided that the next meeting should be in Nürnberg on June 3. Nürnberg was selected because it was close to Regensburg, where (see LW 48, 70, n. 1) had been in session since April 17, at which the Emperor himself was present; See Ranke 2III, 253 ff.; Winckelmann, pp. 234 ff.

[5] This is a reference to the trip of the Electoral prince, Duke John Frederick (see LW 48, 181 f.), to Nürnberg, where in June and July a meeting took place (see note 4) between the Archbishop of Mainz and the Count Palatine (who were in constant consultation with the Emperor at the Diet of Regensburg) on the one side, and the evangelicals on the other side. This meeting brought about the Nürnberg Truce, which was signed on July 23, 1532, and ratified by the Emperor in two separate documents on August 2 and 3. For the text of the Nürnberg Truce, see Kidd, No. 125; for other important documents in connection with these events, see St. L. 16, 1821 ff., 1835 ff.; ZKG 12 (1891), 383 ff. For details, see Ranke 2III, 255 ff.; Winckelmann, pp. 234 ff.

[6] Literally: "dead."

[7] Literally: "against Germany with a horrible and infinite army in order to attack." The source of this news could not be exactly determined. For possibilities, see WA, Br 6, 319, n. 3; WA, TR 1, No. 245. Notwithstanding great efforts on the part of King Ferdinand to gain peace from the Sultan, the Turkish army had begun its advance against the southeastern border of the Empire on April 26, 1532. For a description of the pomp and might of the Sultan's army on the basis of a contemporary Venetian account, see Ranke 2III, 252; the strength of the army was estimated to be 350,000 men. This Turkish danger in turn substantially influenced the policies of King Ferdinand and of Emperor Charles toward the evangelicals, and contributed to the conclusion of the Nürnberg Truce; see Ranke 2III, 250 ff.; Brandi 1, 270. In view of the Turkish danger even Pope Clement VII (see LW 49, 161, n. 12) was willing to deal lightly with the evangelicals in order to enable the Emperor to come to terms with them, so that they might join in the defense of the Empire; see Ranke 2III, 257. For the general development, see ARG 47 (1956), 160 ff.

is in France,[8] and he and the King of the French[9] have broken off with the Emperor, and refuse him any help against the Turks.[10] Look at these monstrosities of our age! This is [how they use] the money which the popes have been collecting for so many centuries by means of the indulgences for fighting the Turks.[11]

It is said that the Emperor presses the sovereigns for their promised aid against the Turks.[12] Perhaps for this reason the diet and the peace negotiations may shortly come to an end. Karlstadt[13] is said finally to have gone to Friesland in search of a refuge, since in Switzerland[14] he was unable to find any work other than farmwork; earlier, when he was still with us, he quickly had enough of farmwork.[15] This is the news we have.

---

[8] This rumor was unfounded. On April 3 Spengler (see *LW* 48, 184) reported to Dietrich (see *LW* 49, 282, n. 13) in Wittenberg that the Curia in Rome was panicking in the face of the imminent Turkish attack, that Pope Clement VII was hiring soldiers, and that the Pope intended to move to Avignon in order to better protect himself against the Turks; see *WA*, Br 6, 319, n. 4. There was worry in Rome about possible naval operations by the Turks against Italy; see *NB* I.Abt.,E.1, 450 f., 463.

[9] I.e., Francis I.

[10] In connection with the Peace Treaty of Cambrai (see *LW* 49, 222) the French King had obligated himself to assist the Emperor in the fight against the Turks (see Brandi 1, 233 f.; 2, 201 f.), and in April, 1532, the Emperor requested this aid (see Brandi 2, 224). But France had no intention of fulfilling this pledge; to the contrary, it was busy initiating contacts with the enemies of the Hapsburgs, the Smalcaldic League and Zapolyai in Hungary (see *LW* 49, 185, n. 32). See Brandi 2, 225. And rumors concerning an alliance directed against the Emperor, in which also the Pope would participate, were circulating in Germany as early as October, 1531; see *NB* I.Abt.,E.1, 347 f. On the other hand, the Pope did support Ferdinand's mobilization, if not with money then certainly with letters; see *NB* I.Abt.,E.1, 355.

[11] Literally: "This is the money which the popes have collected against the Turk through so many centuries by means of indulgences." See also *LW* 48, 82, and below, pp. 270, 272.

[12] On the Emperor's demands for the troops and money promised by the 1530 Diet of Augsburg for war against the Turk, and on the general mobilization, see Ranke 2[III], 253 f., 264 f.

[13] Andrew Karlstadt; see *LW* 48, 79, n. 12.

[14] This rumor was unfounded. On January 3, 1532, Luther wrote to Martin Görlitz in Brunswick (*WA*, Br 6, 243) that Karlstadt had become the successor of Zwingli, who had been killed in the battle at Cappel. This was not true, because on December 9, 1531, Henry Bullinger (see *O.D.C.C.*, p. 206) was made Zwingli's successor in Zürich; see also *Zwingliana* 12 (1964–1968), 668 ff. Karlstadt remained in Zürich till 1534, where he received some kind of pension from the city council; see *WA*, Br 6, 243, n. 6.

[15] According to *WA*, Br 6, 319, n. 6, this statement has to be seen against the background of Karlstadt's letter to Luther, dated November 17, 1526; *WA*, Br 4, 131; *S-J* 2, 381 f.

May the Lord do whatever is good in his eyes; I commend you to his grace. Amen.

June 13, 1532   MARTIN LUTHER

250

To Elector John[1]
Wittenberg, June 29, 1532

The Nürnberg peace conference was scheduled to begin on June 3.[2] Since the Electors of Mainz and the Palatinate[3] had not yet received their final instructions from the Emperor,[4] the beginning had to be delayed. Finally on June 10 the two Electors presented to the evangelicals articles which were to function as the basis for a truce between the evangelicals and the Emperor. These articles were rejected by the evangelicals on June 13. Now the Electoral negotiators had to seek new instructions from the Emperor. In the meantime they tried their best to influence the evangelicals to accept the articles. Both sides, however, stubbornly clung to their positions, and refused to give in. On June 24 Duke John Frederick[5] sent to his father, Elector John, a detailed report of the negotiations which had taken place, together with the necessary documentation. On June 28 the Elector forwarded this material to Wittenberg, requesting a judgment on the situation by return mail. This request was addressed to Luther, Jonas, Bugenhagen, and Melanchthon.[6] On June 29 Luther and Jonas jointly issued a brief and forwarded it to the Elector.[7] Letter No. 250, also dated June 29, is Luther's covering letter for this brief. On that same day Luther also wrote a

---

[1] The letter is extant in one manuscript copy, and in the common editions of Luther's works. Even though the address is missing in the earliest witness, content and form of the letter establish he identity of the addressee.
[2] The following presentation is based on Winckelmann, pp. 234 ff.
[3] See p. 44.
[4] Here and throughout this letter "Emperor" or "His Imperial Majesty" refers to Emperor Charles V; see *LW* 48, 175 f., and above, p. 54, n. 5.
[5] See *LW* 48, 181 f., and above, p. 54, n. 5.
[6] See *WA*, Br 6, 324.
[7] *WA*, Br 6, No. 1944. For a possible brief by Melanchthon, see *WA*, Br 6, 331.

short personal letter to Duke John Frederick in Nürnberg,[8] *and dispatched it via the Electoral court at Torgau. Even though on June 30 the Elector had just (about one hour before) sent off a letter to his son in Nürnberg, upon receipt of the material from Wittenberg he immediately dispatched another messenger to forward this material to Nürnberg.*[9] *While in the covering letter the Elector did not bind his representatives in Nürnberg, he nevertheless strongly endorsed Luther's position.*[10] *By July 4 this material was well known among the evangelicals in Nürnberg,*[11] *and it contributed substantially to getting the negotiations off dead center, since the Emperor, too, was ready to bend.*

In his covering letter Luther points out that the time has come to demonstrate whether there is an honest interest in peace on the part of the evangelicals. If there is, then the conditions for peace should be accepted with trust that God will take care of the problems which might arise. If there is no genuine interest in peace, then Luther does not wish to have any further part in the matter. Whatever evil might come from a refusal of the peace offered by the Emperor would be someone else's responsibility, says Luther. He sees in the stubbornness with which some members of the evangelical party insist on having their own way in (what Luther considers to be) unimportant matters an attempt at perfection, a lack of faith, and a type of cleverness which does not want to yield to divine governance. Therefore Luther admonishes the Elector to do everything possible so that the offered peace is not rejected by the evangelicals. He concludes his letter with a short prayer for God's guidance, and a blessing for the Elector.

On Elector John, see LW 48, 269, n. 8.

Text in German: WA, Br 6, 325–327.

Grace and Peace in Christ!

Most Serene, Noble Elector, Most Gracious Lord! I am herewith returning to Your Electoral Grace the documents, together with our humble judgment.[12]

---

[8] *WA*, Br 6, No. 1945.

[9] See *WA*, Br 6, 324 f.

[10] *Ibid.*

[11] See *WA*, Br 6, No. 1944, Introduction.

[12] I.e., Luther's and Jonas' brief; see Introduction, and note 7.

Since I notice in all the proceedings that some of our party wish to be too clever and too much on the safe side, and wish to have what they call a peace beyond debate, etc.,[13] I certainly cannot but assume that these people have no desire for peace, or (and this would be the same thing) are aiming for the impossible. For when has there ever been signed, made, or promulgated a treaty, law, contract, sealed document, or letter[14] against which one could not debate, or through which one could not poke a hole? If we want cleverly to arrange matters exactly as we wish them to be, and not to entrust everything to God in these matters, and let him also have a word, then certainly nothing good will come out of it; it will be for us as Solomon says: "He who blows his nose too hard forces blood from it,"[15] and he who despises little things will never own bigger ones.

Certainly if His Imperial Majesty approves these articles, as we have received them now, changed through this one amendment (concerning the [privilege to grant] protection to persons who flee to us),[16] then His Imperial Majesty has done enough, and it would be both our responsibility and our fault [if peace did not come about]. God meets us graciously; if we are ungrateful to him, we shall sin against him heavily, and in addition shall have no success.

I[17] most humbly beg Your Electoral Grace, therefore, to write

---

[13] This is a reference especially to the policies of Landgrave Philip of Hesse (see LW 49, 124, n. 18), who with political farsightedness wanted to use the tight situation in which the Emperor found himself to force the Emperor to make as many concessions as possible. (See also LW 49, 251 f.) On June 20, e.g., the Landgrave had instructed his representatives in Nürnberg not to yield an inch, even if the Saxons would yield; see Neudecker, op. cit. (see p. 4, n. 15), pp. 216 f. Serious tensions did indeed come to the fore between Hesse and Electoral Saxony in the weeks before and after the meeting at Nürnberg, and for a while it looked as if Hesse would not join in the Nürnberg Truce. See Urkunden und Akten der Reformationsprozesse, ed. E. Fabian (Tübingen, 1961), pp. 48 ff., 68 ff.; Ranke 2III, 262 f.

[14] Literally: "contract, seal, or letters."

[15] Prov. 30:33; see also p. 45.

[16] As early as the meeting in Schweinfurt (see p. 54, n. 4), this point was controversial; see Enders, Briefwechsel 9, 202, nn. 3–5. The issue was whether the evangelical Estates had the right to grant asylum to subjects of propapal Estates, if these subjects, fleeing their state for the sake of the gospel, were seeking refuge in an evangelical territory. The propapal Estates denied this right, though in highly ambiguous language, while the evangelical Estates insisted on this right, and Luther and Jonas supported them; see WA, Br 6, 328.

[17] In the text, the following, down to "marginal issues," is one sentence.

a serious, precise, and sharp letter to our friends,[18] honestly admonishing them to consider the many and gracious concessions His Imperial Majesty is making to us, which we may accept with a good conscience, and that in addition His Imperial Majesty himself does not wish to mix the issue of the king[19] into this matter. [Therefore] they should by no means reject such a gracious [offer of] peace for the sake of some highly detailed and forced marginal issues. God certainly will heal and take care of these unimportant, quibbled-over deficiencies (if the central points are continued in peace).[20] Our friends will not, after all, make a bull's eye,[21] and it is not necessary to make one; it is enough to hit the target. All our lives and dealings with God and man (being full of shortcomings) have to be based on toleration and forgivenesss of sins. If we wished to be absolutely perfect[22] in relationship to God and our neighbors, and absolutely pure and spotless, we would never be saved, and would never be at peace with our neighbor. If our friends seriously desire peace, then (as [I] said) they ought definitely to accept these articles. If they do not desire peace, however, then they need neither our counsel[23] nor judgment. They are easily clever and capable[24] enough all by themselves to cause a disaster, but they have to do it without our approval. If they cook too much soup they must eat it.[25] I for my part shall thank His Imperial

---

18 The Elector fulfilled Luther's urgent request; see Introduction.

19 I.e., Ferdinand's election as Roman king. See pp. 41, n. 7, 43, n. 12.

20 The text placed in parentheses by Luther has been translated as literally as possible. While the general intention of Luther's statement is clear, the text itself is somewhat unclear; the reason for this is the ambiguity of *Hauptstück*, i.e., "central point(s)." Does Luther mean that peace itself is the central point of the negotiations? If so, then one would have to paraphrase: "If peace as such is continued (or guaranteed) through the peace which is to be established now, and is not replaced by war, then God will take care of all the possible deficiencies in these articles." Or does Luther mean that the central points are the Christian faith, or its proclamation, or its confession? Then one would have to paraphrase: "If the proclamation or confession of the Christian faith can be continued (or guaranteed) through this peace which is to be established, then God will take care of the possible deficiencies in these articles."

21 Literally: "will not split [i.e., as with an arrow] the wooden peg." A peg going through the center of a target fastens it to the pole.

22 The text reads *fromm*, i.e., pious, devout, godly, good.

23 See note 12.

24 Literally: "and satisfied," i.e., as one is satisfied after a good meal.

25 The text reads: *Sie* [i.e., the evangelical "hotheads" in Nürnberg] *mögen's ausessen, brocken sie zu viel ein.* There is a (German) custom of breaking pieces

Majesty from my heart if His Imperial Majesty approves these articles.

Should there be something fraudulent in the articles, which words never reveal anyhow, then I commend it to him who knows, judges, and governs all hearts; he will protect me well in such a danger and keep me unharmed. It is not up to me to be suspicious of His Imperial Majesty, much less to perhaps ascribe evil to His Imperial Majesty's intention—which is unknown to me—and [therefore] judge it as being evil. For I certainly know that he who deceives a heart which trusts in God and someone who loves his neighbor deceives himself, while faith and love remain unharmed. Should this peace accomplish nothing else, this [alone] would be a great gain, that by this peace the threats, obstinacy, insistence, and bragging of the papists, our enemies, would be cut down. This would truly be a great grief[26] and pain for them.

Most Gracious Lord, God knows that in this matter I know nothing further to do or suggest. If [in spite of everything] no peace comes, or if a war should develop over this gracious offer of His Imperial Majesty, then truly we are not guilty of all the evil which might arise.

God has graciously listened to our humble prayer and offers us peace. May that same dear Father further give us also a grateful heart which recognizes such grace, and accepts and uses it well to his praise and honor. Amen. To this same faithful, kind God I faithfully and diligently commend Your Electoral Grace with my humble prayer.

Wittenberg, June 29, 1532   Your Electoral Grace's
                                 humbly dedicated
                                 MARTIN LUTHER

---

of bread into a thin soup of water, flour, and browned onions (*Brotsuppe*). The more pieces of bread one adds, the thicker the soup gets. Luther is saying that whether or not one likes the soup, which has become too thick because one has put too much bread into it, one has to eat it.
[26] Literally: "grief of [or: in] the heart."

251

To the Regents and Councilors of the Margraviate of Brandenburg-Ansbach and to the Council of the City of Nürnberg
Wittenberg, August 1, 1532

Since the first half of 1528 the Margraviate of Brandenburg-Ansbach and the city of Nürnberg had cooperated, with some interruptions, in organizing the evangelical church, first by jointly drafting a church ordinance and conducting a visitation of the parishes, and then by working toward a new church ordinance.[1] After many delays, the Nürnberg theologians, in November of 1531, produced a draft of a church ordinance for which the councilors and theologians of the Margraviate sent suggested changes from Ansbach. The officials in Ansbach also suggested that the ordinance be submitted to Luther for an opinion. After new delays, a version of the church ordinance was finally sent to Wittenberg on July 17, 1532, and the judgment of the Wittenberg theologians was requested.[2] Letter No. 251 is the response to this request.

The reply of the Wittenberg theologians is divided into a summary judgment and a brief of details. In the summary judgment Luther and his colleagues wholeheartedly approve of the church ordinance itself, and also of the attempt to organize the church in the two territories on the basis of such an ordinance. The brief of details is divided into two sections, the first one dealing with the ban, the second one with the "dry mass" (missa sicca).[3] (Actually it ought to be divided into three sections, since in the second section, in addition to the dry mass, a number of miscellaneous items are discussed.) Concerning the ban, it is pointed out that at the present in the Wittenberg parish only that ban is being used by which someone who is living publicly in sin is excluded from the Lord's Supper. Concerning the dry mass the Wittenberg theologians point out that this "spectacle" ought to be abolished, just as the custom of

---

[1] The following presentation is based on H. Westermayer, *Die Brandenburgisch-Nürnbergische Kirchenvisitation und Kirchenordnung, 1528–1533* (Erlangen, 1894), pp. 90 ff.; Sehling 11, 116 ff.

[2] *WA, Br* 6, No. 1947.

[3] See note 23.

reserving the elements of the Lord's Supper ought to be abolished. Luther and his colleagues also urge the elimination of the paragraphs in the ordinance which deal with a government that acts unjustly and with the exegesis of Acts 13:38 f., since the interpretation of this passage does not do justice to the Pauline teaching concerning the law. Finally Luther and his colleagues point out that the whole ordinance needs to be polished in order to avoid repetitions; they suggest Osiander for this task.

Text in German (with some words, especially technical terms, in Latin): WA, Br 6, 339–342.[4]

To the Noble, Honorable and Brave, Respectable,
Distinguished, and Prudent[5] Margravial Viceroys and Councilors,
and to the Mayors and the Council of the City of Nürnberg,
our Dear Sirs and Friends[6]

God's grace and peace in Christ! Noble, Honorable, Brave, Respectable, Distinguished, Wise, and especially Gracious Sirs and Friends! We have carefully read through the church ordinance[7] and the institution of a visitation[8] which was sent to us and which is to be unanimously and uniformly introduced and instituted throughout the territory[9] of the serene, noble sovereign and lord, Sir George, margrave in Brandenburg,[10] and also in the territory which is subject to Your Honors, the lords of Nürnberg,[11] in order to avoid diversity both in teachings and also in certain external ceremonies. We have studied this document carefully, and as much as was possible at this time have scrutinized it. We have come to

---

[4] The letter is extant in the original, which is written in the handwriting of a secretary unknown to us; the signatures are in the personal handwriting of the four authors.

[5] For this rather flowery address, see *LW* 48, xiv.

[6] Literally: "Our Sirs and Friends who favor us."

[7] For an edition of the version which was finally issued, see Sehling 11, 140 ff. The version which was forwarded to Wittenberg is no longer extant.

[8] Luther and his colleagues assumed that the church ordinance was to serve as basis for a visitation of the parishes (just as was the case in 1528; see Westermayer, *op. cit.*, pp. 1 ff.), because in their letter the Nürnberg-Ansbach officials justified the ordinance by pointing to the poor conditions which were uncovered in the 1528 visitation, and which were to be eliminated by this ordinance. See *WA*, Br 6, 336.

[9] Literally: "in the countries and the principality of."

[10] On Margrave George of Brandenburg-Ansbach, see *LW* 49, xvi, n. 16.

[11] Literally: "in Your, the lords of Nürnberg, *Oberkeit* [i.e., governmental authority] and districts [or: areas]."

the conclusion that in its core it does not conflict with God's Word, and that it agrees with our visitation ordinance.[12] Therefore we are highly pleased with it. Attached, however, you will find our opinion on certain articles which in part you too, have specially marked, as, for instance, concerning the ban,[13] how it is to be used and practiced, and certain other points. As understanding people, you certainly will know how to consider and judge this material with a Christian mind, according to opportunity and necessity, so that especially pure teaching and preaching are preserved, and that nevertheless, for the sake of unity and good order, Christian ceremonies might also be conducted without abuse. For even though events occur everywhere so rapidly in our days that church ordinances cannot be drawn up and instituted everywhere as quickly as necessary, nevertheless in order to maintain pure teaching, and also external Christian discipline and behavior, and to prevent much wrong from occurring, one must daily improve on the situation[14] until the Almighty grants more peace and unity both in ecclesiastical and secular governments. If there is any way in which we are able to be of service to you in such or similar Christian undertakings, we shall be ready to do it, according to the best of our abilities.

Written at Wittenberg, August 1, 1532

DOCTOR MARTIN LUTHER

JUSTUS JONAS, DOCTOR[15]

JOHN BUGENHAGEN POMER[16]

PHILIP MELANCHTHON[17]

---

[12] The articles concerning Christian freedom and free will (Sehling 11, 169 ff.) have been taken over from Melanchthon's *Instructions for the Visitors* (see *LW* 49, 168, n. 7); see Westermayer, *op. cit.*, p. 90; Sehling 11, 169, n. 1; *Melanchthon:* Studienausgabe 1, 252 ff.

[13] See *WA*, Br 6, 337. A document was sent along with the version of the church ordinance which had been drawn up by the Ansbach theologians and officials with the help of John Brenz (see *LW* 49, 177 f.). In this document, among other issues (see note 23), the Ansbach position on the ban was set forth (a subject on which there was a great deal of disagreement between the officials of Nürnberg and Ansbach; see Westermayer, *op. cit.*, pp. 86, 97). For the text of the Ansbach document, see G. Strobel, *Miscellaneen Literarischen Innhalts* 2 (Nürnberg, 1779), 151 ff.

[14] I.e., the general situation is to be improved by maintaining pure teaching and preaching, as well as by good Christian behavior; this could be best done through a church ordinance.

[15] See *LW* 48, 275, n. 3.

[16] See *LW* 48, 303, n. 44.

[17] See *LW* 48, 77, n. 3.

Concerning the Ban

1. At present we have instituted no other ban than that those who live in public sins[18] and do not desist are not admitted to the sacrament of Christ's body and blood. This can be accomplished because no one among us receives the holy sacrament unless he has first been examined by the pastor or deacon. Further, we do not see how at this time another ban could be introduced, for many matters occur for which a preliminary investigation[19] would be necessary. We are unable to see how at this time such a procedure of investigation could be instituted and organized, since secular government does not wish to be bothered with such an investigation. Therefore we are content to withhold the holy sacrament from those who live and remain in public sins, even though the world is now so crude and beastly as to be in no hurry at all for the sacrament and church, so that this exclusion from the Lord's Supper might not be considered to be a punishment. If someone excommunicates himself in this way, be content; when even secular authority is ready to permit the existence of public vices [what are we to do?] Nevertheless, in their sermons the preachers ought to censure such pagan ways and behavior by reciting the divine threats[20] in all seriousness; at the same time they ought to admonish the authorities[21] to check such pagan ways.

If discipline would again be restored by instituting examination prior to communion, as certainly would be very useful and good, then one could more easily come to the point where one could institute a system of ecclesiastical discipline[22] which would hold parents responsible for urging their children and members of their household to go to the sacrament and to church, [and] for preventing the young people from falling into such pagan contempt of the sacraments and of all divine matters.

If the public ban is also instituted, then, of course, the secular

---

18 I.e., people of whom it is publicly known that they live in vice. See also p. 24.
19 The text reads *cognitio*.
20 I.e., against sin and vice.
21 The text reads *potestates*; see also LW 49, 379, n. 12.
22 The text reads: *Ein Zucht und Straf anzurichten*: i.e., literally: "to organize a discipline and punishment."

authority has to enforce an order for ostracizing the person who has been banned, if the public ban is to do any good at all; at the present this might cause many wrongs, especially in the large cities and territories. But our type of ban, by which someone is excluded in private from the sacrament, has no impact on citizenship and business dealing. In spite of this action, a Christian may work and have other civic dealings with the person who is banned, as one would have dealings with a pagan, but in such a way that he makes clear to the one who is banned and to others that he does not approve of, nor is pleased with, the ungodly and censurable teachings and actions [which caused the ban].

On the Dry Mass[23]

2. Concerning the mass which is to be celebrated without [giving] the sacrament, we are very much pleased with Brenz's judgment;[24] we, too, are of the opinion that one is not to conduct this spectacle of the dry mass. For what else would this be than a public and

---

[23] On the "dry mass" (*missa sicca*) see NCE 9, 414; J. A. Jungmann, *The Mass of the Roman Rite: Its Origins and Development* (New York), 1 (1951), 385 f., and *ibid.*, n. 46; 2 (1955), 449 f. The dry mass was originally a mass with an abridged liturgy which generally was celebrated in the sick room and in which only bread was used. Later it developed into a devotional act which was practiced apart from the Eucharist. On the basis of the above statement and its background, it is safe to suggest that the Wittenberg theologians used the term "dry mass" for the private mass, for in connection with the visitation of 1528 the celebration of masses without communicants (i.e., private masses) was abolished in the Margraviate, but not in Nürnberg. In 1531 the Ansbach theologians insisted that in the proposed ordinance this type of mass had to be excluded, while the Nürnberg theologians hesitated to go along with this demand. See Westermayer, *op. cit.*, pp. 82, 93. At this point the Ansbach theologians requested an opinion of John Brenz and of Luther. For Luther's reply, dated September 14, 1531, see *WA*, Br 6, No. 1865; for Brenz's reply, dated August 30, 1531, see *Anecdota Brentiana*, ed. T. Pressel (Tübingen, 1868), pp. 106 ff. The Nürnberg clergy and city council insisted on maintaining the celebration of masses without communicants, even though on June 21, 1532, Spalatin strongly urged the Nürnberg clergy to abandon this scandalous practice; see *WA*, Br 6, 453 f. Spalatin thus repeated what Luther had demanded from the Nürnberg clergy and city council as early as August, 1528; see *LW* 49, 204 ff. The version of the church ordinance which was forwarded to Wittenberg did contain a section on the celebration of masses without communicants, notwithstanding the demands of the Ansbach theologians, made in the document mentioned in note 13, that this type of mass be abolished; see Westermayer, *op. cit.*, p. 93; Sehling, 11, 118 ff.

[24] I.e., the document mentioned in note 13, of which the Wittenberg theologians thought Brenz to be the sole author.

powerful confirmation of the papal private masses,[25] a confirmation by which people would be incited to think more highly of the papal private masses and to run to them more than previously? If people became accustomed to thinking anything at all of this dry mass, then they would consider the papal private mass to be even more important and sacred, while one obviously knows that the papal private mass is an abomination, and a wrong service of God.[26]

[Miscellaneous Items]

3. Concerning the reserving of the sacrament in the ciborium, we think that even though it might still be the custom to reserve the sacrament and lock it up, this custom ought to be abolished; for sacrament and Word ought to be together. We know, of course, that this sacrament has been instituted for the purpose of being used and not for the purpose of making a special worship of God with [one] piece of the sacrament apart from the usage of the sacrament and the Word.

[4.] On the fifty-seventh folio[27] the following is written concerning secular governmental authority which abuses its office: Whoever conducts himself in the exercise of secular authority and its power in such a way that one has to be afraid of him, even if one is doing what is right, is in God's eyes no governmental authority, etc. It is our opinion that it would be better to omit this paragraph in order to avoid offense and a difficult disputation. Even though Holy Scripture and secular law teach how to deal with an unjust ruler, nevertheless an evil governmental authority still remains governmental authority, as every understanding person knows. For if in God's eyes an evil governmental authority should be no governmental authority, then the subjects would be free of all obligations, etc. Even if one intends to bring said words into a tolerably clear meaning by means of a commentary and explanation, it is nevertheless

---

25 See LW 48, 281, n. 26, 317.

26 The Nürnberg city council finally gave in on this point, and the celebration of masses without communicants was abolished; see Sehling 11, 121; Westermayer, op. cit., pp. 98 f.

27 I.e., of the copy of the ordinance which had been forwarded to Wittenberg; see note 7.

better to avoid such a disputation by omitting said paragraph, which after all is unnecessary here.[28]

[5.] On the sixtieth folio[29] the verse of Acts 13 [:38 f.] is interpreted [as follows]: Christ has abolished the law in those portions which do not justify. These words sound as if there is a portion of the law which [if observed] would justify, just as our opponents, too, teach that we are justified because of morally good deeds. But we are now teaching—and this is the truth—that we are definitely acceptable to God only by mercy, when we trust in such mercy as promised in Christ, and not because of our works or virtues, whatever their name may be. Therefore we are of the opinion that that paragraph, too, ought to be omitted. [For] Paul speaks in a Hebrew sense and in a universal context that all things in the law could not have justified us; this includes also those portions of the law which deal with morals. Why should one then change this into a context of particulars?

[6.] It also seems as if this visitation ordinance has not been put together by one person and at one time; in addition, there are many corrections in it, and certain paragraphs have been repeated often, as, for instance, is the case with the material on confession. If one were to entrust this document to one man, for instance to Mr. Osiander,[30] he might put it into another [and better] form, etc.[31]

DOCTOR MARTIN LUTHER
JUSTUS JONAS, DOCTOR[32]
JOHN BUGENHAGEN POMER
PHILIP MELANCTHON

---

[28] The section which deals with this issue is omitted in the final text of the ordinance.
[29] See note 27.
[30] Andrew Osiander; see LW 49, 238, n. 26.
[31] The aides of the Margrave and the officials of Nürnberg entrusted the final revision of the ordinance to Brenz and Osiander. On October 5, 1532, the church ordinance was ready for the printers. Due to internal circumstances the whole project, however, was once more delayed. Finally on January 1, 1533, the city council promulgated the ordinance, as did the Margrave on March 1. See Westermayer, op. cit., pp. 99 ff.; Sehling 11, 121 ff.
[32] For the signatures, see notes 15–17.

252

To Duke Joachim of Brandenburg
[Wittenberg,] August 3, 1532

The Diet of Regensburg granted, though hesitantly, troops and money to Emperor Charles for the defense of the southeastern border of the Empire against the advancing Turks. The Imperial army was to be mobilized according to the Imperial Circuits,[1] and circuit-captains were to lead the individual contingents. The Lower Saxon Circuit offered the position of captain to Duke Joachim, the Electoral prince of Brandenburg, who accepted the offer. The Duke wrote about this decision to Luther and Melanchthon, requesting their prayers for his undertaking, and a letter of spiritual instruction. Letter No. 252 is Luther's reply.

Luther assures the Duke of his prayers and expresses his hope that God may be with this defense of the Empire and Christian people against the Turks. Then Luther comments on the frame of mind in which Christians ought to go into this war. He makes three points, and underscores some of his arguments with observations made in connection with the David and Goliath story. First of all, Luther emphasizes, Christians ought not depend on their military might in this war, but on God's help. Secondly, Christians ought not to presuppose that God is on their side and will give them victory because of their own goodness or because of the wickedness of the Turks. And finally, under no circumstances should Christians see in this war an opportunity to gain glory or booty. For Christians the only purpose of this war should be a glorification of God's name and the defense of Christian people. If the Imperial army should go to war in another frame of mind, then, Luther assures the Duke, this war will result in more damage for God's people than for the enemy.

---

[1] In Luther's time the Empire was divided into ten *Reichskreise* (Imperial Circuits). This division was to facilitate the maintenance of peace, the collection of taxes, the representation of the Estates in the Imperial Supreme Court (see *LW* 48, 70, n. 1), and the mobilization of an Imperial army. For details, see *DRTA.JR* 2, No. 21; *The New Cambridge Modern History* 1, *The Renaissance*, ed. G. R. Potter (Cambridge, 1964), 199 ff., 208 ff., 211 f.; Elton, pp. 477 f.; F. Hartung, *Deutsche Verfassungsgeschichte vom 15. Jahrhundert bis zur Gegenwart* (8th ed.; Stuttgart, 1950), pp. 14, 25 f., 42 ff.

TO DUKE JOACHIM OF BRANDENBURG, AUGUST 3, 1532

Text in German: WA, Br 6, 344–345.[2] The following translation, with minor changes, is by Theodore G. Tappert, and is used by permission from LCC 18, 330–332. Published 1955, The Westminster Press.

Grace and peace in Christ,
our Lord and Savior. Amen

Serene, Noble Sovereign, Gracious Lord! We have received Your Sovereign Grace's letter[3] and learned of Your Sovereign Grace's intention to move personally, as a captain of the Saxon Circuit, against that miserable tyrant, the Turk. For this reason, then, Your Sovereign Grace requests our prayers and a letter of Christian instruction.

We are heartily glad to hear that Your Sovereign Grace has such a Christian heart and disposition in these matters and undertakings. We are reluctant, therefore, not to accompany Your Sovereign Grace with our Pater noster,[4] to the best of our ability. For apart from [Your Grace's] request, since we ought not nor are able to go along bodily, we know that we are obliged to move out to war spiritually with our earnest prayers, to join with the dear Emperor

---

[2] The letter is extant in several manuscript copies, and in the common editions of Luther's works. Together with Melanchthon's letter to the Duke (C.R. 4, No. 2496, where a wrong date is given), Luther's letter was printed as a pamphlet of pastoral counsel as early as the middle of the sixteenth century. The WA, Br text is based on this printed version of the text. Luther's thoughts as set forth in this letter should be compared with his Whether Soldiers, Too, Can be Saved (1526; WA 19, 623 ff.; LW 46, 93 ff.) and his On War Against the Turk (1529; WA 30ᴵᴵ, 107 ff.; LW 46, 161 ff.). Duke Joachim of Brandenburg (1505–1571), the son of Elector Joachim I, and one of Luther's early foes, succeeded in the Electoral office as Joachim II in 1535, and ruled till 1571. Even though Joachim I officially had opposed the Reformation, he could not prevent Luther's teachings from penetrating Electoral Brandenburg. After much hesitation Joachim II affirmed the Lutheran teachings in 1539, and from that date the Reformation rapidly transformed Brandenburg into an evangelical territory. For some time Elector Joachim II tried to mediate between the Reformation and the political supporters of the papal church within the Empire, and he was quite successful in this attempt. The church ordinance which was promulgated by Joachim II in 1540 was approved by both Emperor Charles V and by Luther. In secular affairs Joachim was best known for his lavish spending for cultural and military programs, spending which plunged his territory into great debt. On Joachim II, see ADB 14, 78 ff.
[3] This letter is not extant.
[4] I.e., the Lord's Prayer; the term may also be applied to prayer in general.

69

Charles[5] and his soldiers, and to help fight under his banner against Satan and his adherents. God grant that this may be the time when Michael, the sovereign of God's people, will arise and deliver his people, as Daniel 12 [:1][6] prophesies.

Thus, above all else, I wish and I pray God through Jesus Christ, our Lord, to give the devout Emperor, all the sovereigns, and all those who are now to fight against the Turks, first of all, a courageous heart that relies cheerfully on God's help. May God graciously keep them from depending, under any circumstances, on their own power and strength, as the Turks do, for such reliance would be disastrous. May he rather make them sing with David, "I shall not trust in my sword";[7] and again, "Lord, thou art the one that gives victory unto kings";[8] and again, "Some trust in chariots and some in horses, but we will remember the name of the Lord our God"[9]—and whatever more verses there are in the Psalter.

This is what David did when he killed Goliath and said, "You come to me trusting in your sword and spear, but I come to you in the name of the Lord," etc.; I Samuel 17 [:45]. It is said that the Turkish emperor, when moving out [to war], swore by his sword, which is his god.[10] May God help now that this idol [of the Turkish emperor] may become for him a filthy object of ridicule because of his folly, pride, and presumption. Amen.

Second, I beg our people not to place their reliance on the Turk's being altogether wrong and God's enemy while we are innocent and righteous in comparison with the Turk—for such presumption is also vain—but rather to fight in the fear of God, and in reliance on his grace alone. For we, too, are unrighteous in God's sight. Some [on our side] have shed much innocent blood, have persecuted, despised, and disobeyed God's Word, so that under no circumstances are we to take our stand on either our own righteousness or the unrighteousness of the Turks. For the miserable devil is God's enemy, too, and does us great injustice and wrong; in comparison with the devil we are innocent; nevertheless we must not boast of our innocence and the superiority of our claims, but must

---

[5] Emperor Charles V; see LW 48, 175 f.
[6] Luther by mistake wrote Dan. 7.
[7] See Ps. 44:6.
[8] See Ps. 144:10.
[9] See Ps. 20:7.
[10] Or perhaps: "his sword, that it is his god."

70

fight against him in all fear and humility and depend solely on God's help. This is what David, too, did in his fight against Goliath; he did not boast of his claims, but with God's help he fought and said, "You have blasphemed that God in whom I put my trust."[11] In like manner we must pray to God, not to avenge our innocence on the Turk, but [rather] to avenge and glorify his name through the Turk,[12] that great blasphemer, and meanwhile graciously to forget our sins.

Third, I hope and pray that in such a war our people by no means seek honor, glory, land, booty, etc., but only the glory of God and of his name, together with the defense of poor Christians and subjects. For the glory should and will be God's alone. As sinners and unworthy people we deserve nothing but shame, dishonor, and even death, as Your Sovereign Grace knows better than I can write. But since Your Sovereign Grace has so earnestly requested spiritual instruction, I have wished to set down this brief opinion to be of service to Your Sovereign Grace. I have no doubt that if Your Sovereign Grace inculcates such sentiments in others, so that the war is conducted on a high plane, the devil and all his angels will be too weak for our soldiers, and the Turks will encounter men who are different from those whom they have fought before, when both sides were insolent and fought without God, which has always harmed God's people more than their enemies.

May Your Sovereign Grace now go forth in God's name, and may the same God send his angel Michael to accompany Your Sovereign Grace and help all of you to gain a glorious victory and return home to the praise and honor of God. Amen. Our *Pater noster* shall follow after you and go along with you, and, if it pleases God, [our prayers] will await Your Sovereign Grace in the battlefield, that they may be found there.

May it please Your Sovereign Grace graciously to accept these lines, [which] I have written in haste. Herewith I commend [Your Grace] to God. Amen.

August 3, 1532

Your Sovereign Grace's willing [servant],

DOCTOR MARTIN LUTHER

---

[11] See I Sam. 17:45.
[12] I.e., through the defeat of the Turk.

71

253

To Nicholas von Amsdorf[1]
[Wittenberg,] November 2, 1532

Luther tells of the worries of Mrs. von Pack on behalf of her husband, Otto von Pack. Luther also voices skepticism about a naval victory over the Turks. Then he tells of his translation of Ecclesiasticus, and of the condition of his wife, who is suffering from fever and insomnia while awaiting the delivery of their fifth child.
On Nicholas von Amsdorf, see LW 48, 218.
Text in Latin: WA, Br 6, 381–382.

Grace and Peace in Christ

My Amsdorf: Mrs. [von] Pack is worried about her husband, Doctor Otto [von] Pack,[2] because there is a rumor at Leipzig that he has been seen in the duchy[3] of Sir George, and she is afraid that her husband might perhaps have been imprisoned. I have comforted that excellent woman as much as I could, [suggesting that] I think something else may be the case, etc. Therefore, she asked that I beg you, should you perhaps run into him in Magdeburg,[4] to admonish him seriously to stop moving around, especially in the duchy of Sir George, because dangerous traps are prepared for him there. According to your kindness you will do this.

There is no news [around here]. What is said about the capture of Turkish ships would be happy news, if it were true.[5] I am totally occupied with the translation of Ecclesiasticus. I hope to be freed from this drudgery within three weeks.[6]

My Katie is ill with fever and insomnia, [and] close to her

---

[1] This letter is extant in one manuscript copy, and in the common editions of Luther's works. Even though the witnesses do not give an address, the content of the letter establishes von Amsdorf as the addressee.
[2] Otto von Pack; see *LW* 49, 189 f., 197 f.
[3] I.e., Ducal Saxony; see *LW* 48, 110, n. 20.
[4] Von Amsdorf was a pastor in Magdeburg.
[5] This is a reference to a number of smaller naval victories which Andrea Doria, the admiral of the fleet of Genoa and an ally of Emperor Charles V, had won in the fall of 1532 over the fleet of the Turks in the Aegean and Ionian Seas. While, on the one hand, the news communicated by Luther was indeed based on events, Luther was, on the other hand, correct in being skeptical, since none of these "victories" was decisive. For details, see *WA*, Br 6, 382, n. 2; 427; Elton, p. 518.
[6] Luther used *pistrinum* (a term used in a similar context by Cicero *De oratore*

delivery.[7] I commend her to your prayers, and also myself, and all that belong to me. Our [Lord] Christ be with you. Amen.

November 2, 1532   MARTIN LUTHER

254

To John Löser
[Wittenberg,] January 29, 1533

In the evening of January 28, 1533, Luther's fifth child,[1] a boy, was born. Later that night Luther wrote to John Löser asking him to be godfather, and to come to the baptism.

John Löser was an Electoral Saxon marshal by inheritance.[2] He had a distinguished career of service to the Saxon dukes, and also to other ruling families of the Empire. His military service to Emperor Maximilian, and his service to the Saxon duke Henry the Pious, in connection with his pilgrimages to the Holy Land and to Compostella, were highlights in Löser's career. Luther had close relations with Löser, in whose house he was several times a guest, and to whom he dedicated some of his works.[3] Luther performed Löser's marriage, apparently baptized one of Löser's sons, and supposedly preached Löser's funeral sermon in 1541.

On John Löser, see WA, Br 3, No. 640, Introduction.

Text in German: WA, Br 6, 426.[4]

To the Brave and Honorable John Löser, marshal[5] in Saxony, my Most Gracious Lord and Dear Friend[6]

---

ii. 33. 144), i.e., pounding-mill. For the hard work Luther had put into translating this book and the difficulties he experienced, see WA, TR 2, No. 2761a. See also WA, DB 12, xxx ff., xlix.
[7] See letter No. 254.
[1] John (see LW 49, 152, n. 7), Elizabeth (*ibid.*, 181, 203), Magdalen (*ibid.*, 218), Martin (November 7, 1531–March 2[?], 1565).
[2] On this office and its development, see *Hilfswörterbuch, s.v.* Marschall.
[3] See WA 12, 92 f.; WA 31[I], 430 ff.; LW 14, 110 ff.
[4] The letter is extant in several manuscript copies, of which one supposedly was made from the autograph, while another one was handed down by Luther's descendants. For more details, see WA, Br 6, No. 1997, Introduction.
[5] Luther used *Erbmarschall*, i.e., marshal by inheritance; see also note 2.
[6] Literally: "Lord and kind, dear Friend." For "friend" Luther used *Gevatter*;

Grace and peace in Christ! Brave, Honorable Dear Sir and Friend![7] As I asked recently,[8] so for the sake of our Lord Christ I ask Your Honor again to humble yourself in God's honor, and to appear in assistance of my young son, whom God has given to me this night by my dear Katie, so that he may come out of the old Adam's nature to the rebirth in Christ through the holy sacrament of baptism, and may become a member of sacred Christendom. Perhaps God the Lord may wish to raise [with this boy] a new enemy of the pope or the Turk.[9] I would like very much to have him baptized around the Vesper hour so that he remain a heathen no longer, and I might become the more assured [of his salvation]. Your Honor is asked to come here unencumbered[10] and to aid in fulfilling this service[11] in God's praise. I am willing and ready to do whatever I can to make it up to you.

Herewith I commend you and yours to God. Amen.

At 1 A.M. *in the night of January 29, 1533*

Your Honor's willing servant,

MARTIN LUTHER

---

see *LW* 48, 201, n. 2. It is possible that in Löser's case *Gevatter* has to be translated as "(fellow [?]) godfather," since apparently Luther was the godfather of one of Löser's boys; see *WA* 36, xix.

[7] See note 6.

[8] On July 15, 1532, Luther apparently had baptized one of Löser's sons; at least he was apparently the godfather and preached that day; see *WA* 36, xix.

[9] The boy's name was to be Paul; according to Luther's own statements he chose this name because of the Apostle Paul, who had given him many good arguments. See *WA*, TR 3, No. 2946; *LW* 54, 184. Paul Luther (January 28, 1533–March 8, 1593) was perhaps the most gifted of Luther's children. He studied medicine and was graduated in 1557 as Doctor of Medicine. Soon thereafter he was called as professor to the University of Jena. In 1560 he became personal physician of the dukes of Saxony, and in 1571 he became personal physician of the elector of Saxony. On Paul Luther, see *ADB* 19, 692 ff.

[10] The meaning of this sentence is not clear. It seems as if Luther was suggesting that Löser should not be concerned about the customary present (usually in the form of a valuable coin).

[11] Literally: "sacrifice."

255

To the Council of the City of Nürnberg
Wittenberg, April 18, 1533

In addition to many other problems, the evangelical church had to come to terms with the question of ecclesiastical discipline.[1] In this connection confession and absolution were of special importance. While in the papal church private confession and absolution administered in the confessional box were the universal and mandatory practice, there was also the custom of administering a general, public confession and absolution immediately after the sermon.[2] Luther had summarized his position on these matters in his Babylonian Captivity of the Church *(1520) and* On Confession *(1521). In the spring of 1533 he became involved in a controversy on confession and absolution which was boiling in Nürnberg.[3] The issue was private confession and absolution (advocated and demanded by Osiander[4] to the exclusion of general, public confession and absolution) versus general, public confession and absolution (advocated by the majority of the Nürnberg clergy, among them Link,[5] though not to the exclusion of private confession and absolution). While the city council tried to do justice to both sides, it leaned definitely toward Link and his followers.[6] On April 8, 1533, the city council asked Luther and Melanchthon for an opinion on this controversy.[7] In their joint answer, letter No. 255,[8] Luther and Melanchthon set forth what seems to be a compromise, but which nevertheless was based on solid theological considerations. Since the preaching of the*

---

[1] See, e.g., pp. 64 f.
[2] See Klaus, p. 148.
[3] See Klaus, pp. 147 ff.; G. Seebass, *Das reformatorische Werk des Andreas Osiander* (Nürnberg, 1967), pp. 254 ff.; *Concordia Theological Monthly* 39 (1968), 106 ff.; *Una Sancta* 22 (1965), 18 ff., esp. 30 f.
[4] See *LW* 49, 238, n. 26; see also Seebass, *op. cit.*, pp. 255 ff.
[5] See *LW* 48, 169 f.
[6] See Klaus, pp. 150 ff. The controversy broke out because the city council insisted that the clergy use public confession and absolution. While the majority of the clergy complied with the city council's demand, Osiander balked, and began to preach against public confession and absolution.
[7] *WA*, Br 6, No. 2008.
[8] The extant original was written by a secretary unknown to us; the signatures are in Luther's and Melanchthon's own handwriting.

gospel is identical with the proclamation that forgiveness of sin is at hand, Luther and Melanchthon say, and since this preaching can and ought to be done both in public and in private, both forms of confession and absolution ought to be retained. Both forms of absolution demand and aid faith. Private absolution, as the personal application of forgiveness, has a great advantage, however, because it speaks to the individual personally, and thus directly helps the faith of the individual and aids in the proper understanding of the public absolution. On the other hand, general public confession and absolution need not be rejected only because there might be people in the congregation who do not believe the word of forgiveness.

Text in German (with some words in Latin): WA, Br 6, 454–455.[9]

To the Honorable and Wise Mayors, and to the
Council of the City of Nürnberg,
Our Dear Sirs

God's grace through our Lord Jesus Christ! Honorable, Wise, Dear Sirs! Regarding Your Honors' inquiry, we have discussed this matter among ourselves and do not see that public, general absolution is to be censured or rejected, for the [following] reason[s]:

The preaching of the holy gospel itself is principally and actually an absolution in which forgiveness of sins is proclaimed in general and in public to many persons, or publicly or privately to one person alone. Therefore absolution may be used in public and in general, and in special cases also in private, just as the sermon may take place publicly or privately, and as one might comfort many people in public or someone individually in private. Even if not all believe [the word of absolution],[10] that is no reason to

---

[9] For the whole letter, see also WA 21, 250 ff., esp. 262 f.

[10] Luther here tried to nullify Osiander's main argument against general, public absolution. Osiander was afraid that through a public absolution people ("thieves and crooks") might be absolved of sins which should be retained; see Klaus, pp. 150 f. Because of pastoral concern, Osiander insisted on private confession and absolution, esp. in view of the Lord's Supper and the necessity of practicing ecclesiastical discipline. Luther agreed with this concern; see p. 24. But Osiander *demanded* private confession and absolution, and the center of his argumentation was legalistic and rested upon disciplinary matters. Luther (and Melanchthon) demanded private confession and absolution, too, but the center of his argu-

76

reject [public] absolution, for each absolution, whether administered publicly or privately, has to be understood as demanding faith and as being an aid to those who believe in it, just as the gospel itself also proclaims forgiveness to all men in the whole world and exempts no one from this universal context. Nevertheless the gospel certainly demands our faith and does not aid those who do not believe it; and yet the universal context of the gospel has to remain [valid].

Regarding the idea that no one might desire private absolution if one has public absolution and keeps it in use, we say that this is definitely a weighty issue, [but] that consciences nevertheless are in need of this special comfort. For one has to instruct consciences that the comfort of the gospel is directed to each individual particularly; therefore, as you people who understand these matters know, the gospel has to be applied through Word and sacrament to each individual particularly, so that each individual in his conscience is tossed about by the question whether this great grace, which Christ offers to all men, belongs to him too. Under these circumstances it can easily be understood that one is not to abolish private absolution in favor of public absolution; also, this application[11] makes more clear the meaning of the gospel and the power of the keys. For very few people know how to use public absolution or apply it to themselves, unless in addition this application reminds them that they also ought to apply the general absolution to themselves as if it belonged to each individually; for this is the true office and task of the gospel: definitely to forgive sins by grace.

For these reasons we do not consider that general absolution is either to be rejected or to be abolished, but[12] that nevertheless the personal application and [private] absolution should be maintained.

May God always graciously protect Your Honors. We are always ready and willing to serve Your Honors.[13]

---

mentation was pastoral and rested upon the personal application of the Word of forgiveness; consequently Luther saw nothing wrong with general, public confession and absolution, although private confession and absolution were also necessary for him.
[11] I.e., of the gospel to the individual through private absolution.
[12] Literally: "and."
[13] Since this opinion satisfied neither of the parties, and since Osiander continued

Written at Wittenberg, April 18, 1533

DOCTOR MARTIN LUTHER

PHILIP MELANCHTHON[14]

256

To John Schlaginhaufen
[Wittenberg,] March 10, 1534

Having heard that Schlaginhaufen was ill, Luther sends his greetings and good wishes for total recovery. He complains about the speed with which time passes and about his own lack of productivity, and asks for his friend's prayer in this matter. He closes with general greetings, asking for Schlaginhaufen's love, and assuring his friend of his own willingness to be of service in any brotherly task.

John Schlaginhaufen of Neunburg/Upper Palatinate, had studied in Wittenberg and was a frequent guest in Luther's home. In 1532 he became a pastor in Zahna (near Wittenberg), and in 1533 in Köthen (southwest of Dessau), where he rose later to the position of superintendent. He was a studious recorder of Luther's Table Talks and a collector of Luther's letters. He died in approximately 1560.

On John Schlaginhaufen, see ADB 31, 329 ff.

Text in Latin (with some sentences in German): WA, Br 7, 24.[1]

---

to preach against general, public confession and absolution, the controversy continued. The city council demanded that both parties present position papers, which in turn were forwarded to the Wittenberg Theological Faculty for a judgment; see *WA*, Br 6, No. 2048, dated September 27, 1533. On October 8, 1533, the Faculty issued its verdict (*ibid.*, No. 2052), and on the same day Luther wrote a personal letter to Osiander (*ibid.*, No. 2053). As a result of this verdict by the Wittenberg theologians the controversy gradually calmed down. The issues were not settled, however, as the second phase (1536), and the third phase (1539) of this controversy demonstrate. For details, see Klaus, pp. 155 ff.; Seebass, *op. cit.*, pp. 259 ff.

[14] See *LW* 48, 77, n. 3.

[1] The letter is extant in one manuscript copy, apparently originating with Schlaginhaufen himself, and in the common editions of Luther's works.

To my dearest brother in the Lord, John Schlaginhaufen, a faithful minister of Christ at Köthen

Grace and peace in Christ. I hear, excellent Sir, that you are ill. I am really sorry about this, and I pray Christ to be merciful with you, restore your health, and enable you faithfully to fulfill your ministry.[2] I am quite well, thank God, but I do not know how the days pass without me accomplishing what I should and would like to. I live such a useless life that I cannot stand myself. I do not know where the time goes and why I accomplish so little. This is the sum of it. Pray for me that my work will bear more fruit.

The Lord be with you. Greet your wife and children in my behalf. Trust in the Lord and continue loving me who, in Christ, will never neglect serving you in any brotherly task.

March 10, 1534   MARTIN LUTHER, DOCTOR

257

To Mrs. Martin Luther[1]
[Dessau,] July 29, 1534

During the summer of 1534 Luther and some of his friends twice visited the court at Dessau[2] in order to give spiritual counsel to the sovereign Joachim of Anhalt, who at that time was seriously ill and was experiencing great spiritual struggles.[3] During his second visit to Dessau Luther wrote this personal note to his wife. He tells first of the pending return of Melanchthon, and of the necessity for his

---

[2] This sentence is freely translated.

[1] Until 1945 the autograph of this letter was extant in Königsberg/East Prussia (the Kaliningrad of today); now nothing is known of its whereabouts. It came to Königsberg, together with the autographs of letters No. 290, 292, 293, 320, by way of Luther's youngest daughter, Margaret (born December 17, 1534), who married George von Kunheim (a nobleman and high-ranking civil servant of East Prussia) in 1555 and moved to East Prussia, where she died in 1570. See *WA, Br* 14, xxvi, addition to *WA, Br* 5, 633; *WA, Br* 14, 86 f.

[2] See Buchwald, *LK*, p. 97 f.

[3] On Joachim of Anhalt and his relationship to Luther, see Luther's letters to Joachim in *WA, Br* 6 and 7; see also *LCC* 18, Index, *s.v.*, Anhalt.

*own continued stay in Dessau. Then he informs his wife that "yes-
terday" he drank something which did not agree with him, and asks
his wife to send him his whole wine-cellar and some of her home-
brewed beer, because otherwise the beer at Dessau, to which he is
not accustomed, would make him totally unable to return home. He
concludes by commending his household to God.*

Text in German: WA, Br 7, 91.

To my kind, dear lord, Lady Catherine von Bora,
Mrs. Doctor Luther,[4] at Wittenberg

Grace and peace in Christ! Dear Sir Katie! I know of nothing to
write to you since Master[5] Philip,[6] together with the others, is
coming home. I have to remain here longer for the devout Sovereign's sake.[7] You might wonder how long I shall remain here, or
how you might set me free.[8] I think that Master[9] Francis[10] will set
me free, just as I freed him—but not so soon.

---

[4] For "Luther," see p. 48, n. 9.

[5] I.e., Master of Arts.

[6] Philip Melanchthon (see LW 48, 77, n. 3) was among those of Luther's friends
who had traveled to Dessau. He and some of the others apparently left for
Wittenberg on July 28 (see WA, Br 7, 92, n. 1), while Jonas (see LW 48, 275,
n. 3) stayed with Luther in Dessau; see Kawerau, *Jonas Briefwechsel,* 1, No.
254. The date of Melanchthon's departure from Dessau is open to question.
Luther's statement above seems to suggest that Melanchthon is about to leave
Dessau, and therefore will take along this letter in which Luther informs his wife
that he, Luther, would continue to stay in Dessau. As long as Melanchthon's
return to Wittenberg cannot be more precisely established, however, one cannot
establish the carrier of the present letter.

[7] See Introduction.

[8] By August 6, Luther and Jonas were again in Wittenberg; see Buchwald, *LK,*
p. 98; Kawerau, *Jonas Briefwechsel* 1, No. 256; WA 37, 504.

[9] See note 5.

[10] I.e., Francis Burchart (1504[?]–1560), who had been one of Melanchthon's
favorite students and who was one of the professors of Greek at Wittenberg
University; he was president of the University in 1532, and from this time on
became increasingly involved in the affairs of the territorial government. After
the death of Christian Beyer (see LW 49, 349, n. 8) in 1535, he was called into
the service of the Electoral Saxon chancellery, and in 1536 he was appointed
vice-chancellor. He remained in the service of the Ernestine branch of the ruling
family of Saxony even after the Smalcaldic War (when the Electoral office was
transferred to the Albertine branch; see LW 48, 110, n. 20) and followed Duke
John Frederick (the former Elector) to Weimar. There he died in 1560. On
Francis Burchart, see NDB 3, 33. Burchart had visited Joachim of Anhalt several
times in June and July. He was in Dessau on July 15, the day on which Luther
arrived there for his first visit. On the basis of Luther's statement above, one has

Yesterday I drank something which did not agree with me, so that I had to sing: If I don't drink well I have to suffer, and [yet] I do like to do it.[11] I said to myself what good wine and beer I have at home, and also [what] a pretty lady or (should I say) lord. You would do well to ship the whole cellar full of my wine and a bottle of your beer[12] to me here, as soon as you are able; otherwise I will not be able to return home because of the new beer.[13]

With this I commend you to God, together with our young ones and all the members of our household. Amen.

July 29, 1534   Your loving[14]

                          MARTIN LUTHER, DOCTOR

258

To Elector John Frederick[1]
[Wittenberg,] August 20, 1535

In the resolution of the 1530 Diet of Augsburg,[2] Emperor Charles promised to enter into negotiations with Pope Clement VII to bring about a general council of the church; this council was to meet at a

---

to assume that Burchart left Dessau on July 15/16, i.e., after Luther had arrived there. On August 2 Burchart was still in Wittenberg (see Kawerau, *Jonas Briefwechsel* 1, No. 255), and it cannot be established when he again came to Dessau and "freed" Luther. On August 13 Jonas thought that Burchart might be in Dessau (*ibid.*, 214), and Clemen suggests (*WA*, Br 7, 92, n. 3) that Burchart went to Dessau on August 9, bringing letters from Melanchthon to the sovereigns of Anhalt; *C.R.* 2, Nos. 1210, 1211. In this case, Luther would have left Dessau prior to the arrival of Burchart, his "replacement."

11 It has been suggested that here Luther might have been thinking of a drinking song. The last portion of the sentence has been translated as literally as possible. The meaning of this clause is not clear, because the antecedent for "it" is unclear. Apparently Luther wanted to say that he enjoys a good drink but that he suffers when he has drunk poor wine or beer. See also p. 48, n. 13.

12 Luther's wife brewed the beer for the family. Köstlin-Kawerau, 2, 491; Schwiebert, pp. 266, 594.

13 I.e., the beer of Dessau, to which Luther is not accustomed, might make Luther ill, so that he would not be able to return home.

14 Or: "[The man] whom you love."

1 Even though the address is missing in all witnesses, the form of the letter and the circumstances set forth in it make clear to whom Luther was writing. The letter is extant only in printed form.

2 See *LW* 49, 423. For the following see Jedin, pp. 245 ff.

place convenient to all parties involved, and was to enact a Christian reformation.³ As a first, half-hearted, politically motivated step⁴
in this direction a special papal envoy came to Germany in the
spring of 1533 to negotiate with the German bishops and sovereigns, among them Elector John Frederick of Saxony, who functioned as spokesman for the Smalcaldic League. Even though the
league protested some of the notions of the papacy concerning the
council, it did not reject outright the plan of the council.⁵ By year's
end Pope Clement VII, however, buried the whole council matter
again.⁶ The council plan was revived by Pope Paul III,⁷ and in

---

³ See Urkundenbuch zu der Geschichte des Reichstages zu Augsburg im Jahre
1530, ed. K. E. Förstemann, 2, (Halle, 1835; reprint: Hildesheim, 1966), 478,
716.
⁴ Jedin, p. 280, called it "no more than a facade." In reaction to fifteenth century conciliarism, the papacy was extremely hostile to the idea of a council
having power of decision over matters of the church. Even though Luther himself had called for a council as early as 1518, and even though some of the diets
of the 1520's demanded a council, and even though many devout Roman
Catholics supported this demand, Pope Clement VII (see LW 49, 161, n. 12)
successfully circumvented this threat to his power and style of life, and the
council became a pawn in the political game between Emperor and Pope. Consequently when, in the aftermath of the Diet of Augsburg, Emperor Charles V
approached Rome with the request for a council, the Curia was most reluctant
to comply. Rome finally approved the idea, but added specific conditions which
jeopardized the plan from the beginning. See Ranke 2ᴵᴵᴵ, 183 ff. The negotiations
between the Emperor and the evangelicals which led to the Nürnberg Truce of
1532 were an opportunity for the papacy to forget about the plan to call a
council. When the 1532 Diet of Regensburg renewed the request for a council,
however, and even stated that further delay could mean that a German national
council would be called, the Pope finally acted. See Ranke 2ᴵᴵᴵ, 260 ff.; St. L.
16, 1839 ff. The papal envoy, Udo Rangoni, dispatched to Germany (on his
mission, see Jedin, pp. 281 ff.; see also below, note 13), specified the conditions
under which the Pope was willing to call a council (text: WA, Br 6, 480 f.); he
was to reach an agreement on these conditions with the German bishops and
sovereigns. These conditions clearly show that the Pope wanted to have full
control over the council, and that he did not at all see the council as a forum in
which the issues could be discussed on the basis of what the Reformers called
the "free Word of God." The Pope wanted the council to meet in an Italian
city, and this certainly must have left the Germans unimpressed. Further, the
council was to be held in freedom "according to the established custom of the
church"—whatever this phrase meant—and the participants were to agree in
advance to submit to the council decisions.
⁵ For the briefs of the Wittenberg theologians on the papal conditions, and for
the answer given to the papal envoy, see WA, Br 6, 483 ff.; C.R. 2, No. 1117;
St. L. 16, 1879 ff.
⁶ See Jedin, p. 284.
⁷ Paul III (1468–1549), the former Alessandro Farnese, had been educated at
the humanistically oriented court of Lorenzo the Magnificent in Florence. After
a remarkable ecclesiastical career, he became dean of the Sacred College of

1535 the papal representative at the Hapsburg court in Vienna, Pietro Paolo Vergerio the Younger,[8] traveled through Germany in an attempt to gain support for the council, especially for an Italian city as the place where the council would meet.[9] On August 3 and 4 he visited Margrave George of Brandenburg-Ansbach-Kulmbach, who on August 5 informed Elector John Frederick of Vergerio's visit and of Vergerio's travel plans, which included a visit to the Elector. On August 19 the Elector acknowledged receipt of this letter and pointed out that he would stand by the answer given to the papal envoy two years ago. On the same day the Elector forwarded copies of this correspondence to Brück and requested his counsel. Luther was also informed[10] of this situation and was requested to give his judgment. Letter No. 258 is Luther's reply.

Cardinals in 1524, and was elected pope in 1534. He was the last of the worldly Renaissance popes who, nevertheless, on the basis of his humanistic training, clearly saw the necessity for internal reforms if the Roman church was to survive the threat of Protestantism. He worked efficiently for the reform and revitalization of the church; on June 2, 1536, he called a general council to meet in Mantua, which was finally opened on December 13, 1545, in Trent. Probably his most important actions, however, were his confirmation of the Jesuits in 1540 and his reorganization of the Inquisition in 1542. On Paul III, see *O.D.C.C.*, p. 1032; *NCE* 11, 13 f.

[8] Vergerio (1497/98–1565), a poet laureate from Padua and a humanistically trained lawyer, entered the service of the Curia in approximately 1532 as secretary of cryptography. Immediately he was involved in diplomatic missions for the Curia (Sept. 1532 to Venice; 1533 nuncio to the court of Ferdinand I in Vienna). In 1535 he was charged with the negotiations with the German bishops and sovereigns regarding the city of Mantua as possible locale for the council. (On Vergerio's mission, see *NB* I. Abt. 1, 25 ff.; Jedin, pp. 292 ff.) Vergerio's mission accomplished little (see Jedin, p. 299). At the end of 1535 he was recalled to Rome, and was appointed to the commission which drafted the bull by which the council was called (see Jedin, p. 311). Apparently he proved himself incompetent for further top-level work in ecclesiastical diplomacy, for he abruptly disappeared from the papal diplomatic service, and in 1536 Pope Paul III appointed him bishop of an inconsequential Italian diocese. The remainder of Vergerio's life was tumultuous, to understate the matter. In 1544 he was charged with heresy and in 1549 he was excommunicated, but was able to escape to Graubünden, Switzerland, where he functioned as a pastor for a short time. From 1553 he lived as a councilor of Duke Christopher of Württemberg in Tübingen, and in this capacity he traveled extensively. Vergerio was a somewhat tragic figure. Apparently extremely ambitious, his theological abilities were limited, though his stylistic work as theological polemical satirist was quite remarkable. He definitely was not a Protestant in the strict sense of the word, though he must be considered an evangelical and a reformer. On Vergerio, see *NB* I. Abt., 1, 12 ff.; A. Jacobson Schutte, "Pier Paolo Vergerio: The Making of an Italian Reformer" (Stanford, Cal.: Unpublished Ph.D. Diss., 1969).

[9] For the following, see *C.R.* 2, No. 1294; *WA. Br* 7, No. 2225, Introduction.

[10] The Elector's letter to Luther is no longer extant.

Luther points out that the answer given to the papal envoy two years ago says all that has to be said. He leaves to the Elector's discretion the matter of the city proposed by the papacy for the meeting of the council. He voices skepticism, however, as to the seriousness and honest desire of the papists to bring about a free and Christian council, and then places the whole issue into God's hands.

On Elector John Frederick, see LW 48, 181 f.

Text in German: WA, Br 7, 238.

Grace and peace, and my poor *Pater noster!*[11] Most Serene, Noble Sovereign, Most Gracious Lord! I have received and carefully read Your Electoral Grace's letter, and also the copies [of the material] pertaining to the council.[12] Since Your Electoral Grace graciously requests my judgment as to whether Your Electoral Grace should make another statement which goes beyond the earlier answer given two years ago to the legate of His Imperial Majesty and of Pope Clement,[13] it is my humble opinion that in that answer[14] everything pertaining to this matter has been dealt with sufficiently, and certainly in a Christian way. As far as I am concerned I do not care about the place,[15] wherever it were located in the whole world, since I am not yet able to consider this to be serious business.[16] If they were serious, I would long ago have deserved to be taken and burned by these wrathful saints.[17] Your Electoral Grace will certainly know what to reply, if they continue to insist on [their choice of] locale. I hope and pray that God will let the papists at least once come to their senses so that they will be forced to undertake in all seriousness a council which would have to be

---

11 See p. 69, n. 4.

12 These were copies of the exchange of letters mentioned in the Introduction.

13 See notes 4, 5. Rangoni, who was not a *legatus* (papal legate, or ambassador) but only an extraordinary nuncio (envoy), was accompanied by an Imperial official who functioned as a kind of diplomatic travel companion and watchdog.

14 See notes 4, 5.

15 I.e., the locale where the council is to meet; see note 8.

16 Literally: "since I am not yet able to consider it [i.e., the council] as serious, and whether it would be to them [i.e., the papists] a matter of seriousness." The tactics of the papacy are sufficient basis for justifying Luther's skepticism, and Luther was not alone in this skepticism; see Jedin, p. 281.

17 I.e., if Luther attended a council outside of Germany and thus exposed himself to the danger of being arrested and executed.

called free and Christian.[18] But in this matter I am like unbelieving Thomas; I have to put my hands and fingers into the side and scars, otherwise I do not believe it.[19] Yet God, in whose hands are the hearts of all men,[20] is able to accomplish even more than that.

Herewith I commend Your Electoral Grace to the dear Father's, our God's, grace and peace. Amen.

In the evening of August 20, 1535

Your Electoral Grace's
dedicated
MARTIN LUTHER, DOCTOR

259

To Philip Melanchthon[1]
[Wittenberg,] August 29, 1535

In the summer of 1535 most of the faculty and students of Wittenberg University, including Melanchthon, moved to Jena because of the plague which was again harassing the people of Wittenberg.[2] The University in Wittenberg was not closed, however, but continued to function. In the following letter Luther, who was dean of the Theological Faculty at that time, asks Melanchthon to distribute the enclosed theses for two doctoral disputations among the theological students who are in Jena. He also invites Melanchthon and others to the graduation festivities. Then Luther reports some details: he has heard nothing from the Electoral court regarding the "synod";

---

[18] In the 1533 dealings with the papal envoy the major issue was the "freedom" of the council; for the documents, see note 5. Luther and his friends were afraid, and justly so (see note 4), that the council would simply rubber-stamp the condemnation of the Protestants rather than discuss the issues freely and arrive at a decision based on the Word of God.

[19] See John 20:25.

[20] This is perhaps an allusion to passages such as Exod. 13:3; I Kings 8:39; Prov. 21:1.

[1] Even though the address is missing in all witnesses, the opening sentence and the content of the letter establish Melanchthon as the addressee. The letter is extant in one manuscript copy of secondary value, in a collection of Melanchthon's letters published in 1565, and in the common editions of Luther's works.

[2] See, e.g., *LW* 49, 173 ff.

Brück has arrived in Wittenberg; he, Luther, is ill with diarrhea, but hopes to be better by "tomorrow." In conclusion Luther mentions the French envoys who are trying to get Melanchthon to come to France, a certain letter of the Elector to Melanchthon, and his latest confrontation with the Archbishop of Mainz.
    On Philip Melanchthon, see LW 48, 77, n. 3.
    Text in Latin: WA, Br 7, 244–245.

Grace and Peace

Here we are sending the theses of the disputations,[3] excellent Philip, which we would kindly ask you to distribute to the theological candidates; we also ask you, in our behalf, to invite everyone to the disputation at the time and place mentioned. Unless it seems wise to you to do otherwise I do not believe it is necessary to post the theses on the doors there,[4] since you are strangers there and do not live in the town where the University is located. When you people come, however, you will find them posted on the doors here according to custom and in the usual form. Then we shall also officially invite you to the banquet, even though we would like to know [now] (as you can guess) how many of you will come. The festivity will be on the day of the Holy Cross,[5] [and] we look forward with joy to your coming. For now another constellation of the stars has passed without doing any damage,[6] and in three days not even one case of death has occurred. Today one occurred, but it had nothing to do with the plague.

    From the court I hear nothing about that synod which you

---

[3] These were the theses, written by Luther himself, for the doctoral disputations of Jerome Weller (see *LW* 49, 321, n. 2) and Nicholas Medler (see Drews, p. 9). Text: *WA* 39^I, 44 ff.

[4] I.e., in Jena.

[5] I.e., September 14; the disputations took place on September 11. For details concerning this graduation, which Luther himself very carefully prepared, see Drews, pp. 7 ff.; *WA* 39^I, 40 ff. For the disputation and graduation in general, see Schwiebert, pp. 195 f.; R. H. Fife, *The Revolt of Martin Luther* (New York, 1957), pp. 180 ff.

[6] According to *WA*, Br 7, 245, n. 3, this is a slight mockery of Melanchthon's superstition regarding astrological guidance. Luther apparently wanted to assure Melanchthon that neither stars nor the plague were doing any damage which should be feared to the degree that Melanchthon would not come. On Melanchthon's interest in astrology, see Manschreck, pp. 102 ff.

mention.[7] Perhaps they are diligently hiding such great mysteries from us, and I am willingly ignorant of such mysteries. Today Doctor Brück[8] arrived. I shall visit him tomorrow if I am in a position to do so, for yesterday and today I have been suffering from diarrhea, and my body has been weakened so that I cannot sleep and have no appetite, and we have nothing to drink.[9] I hope to feel better tomorrow. In the last two days I have had fifteen bowel movements.

Write to me whether you have swallowed that letter of the Sovereign[10] by which I was quite disturbed because of you (as I wrote),[11] and also how your health is.[12] I have become suspicious (as you have read [by now])[13] of those envoys of yours.[14] You know that faithless and rotten disciple of mine,[15] and he has many people who go along with him and who are like him.

May the Lord guide and preserve you. Amen.

August 29, 1535[16]

---

[7] Since Melanchthon's letter to which Luther refers here is not extant, what "synod" is supposed to mean cannot be determined. It could refer to any gathering or conference (see e.g., LW 49, 239), or it could refer to the Vergerio mission in connection with the pending general council of the church. In a September 1 letter to Jonas, Luther also mentioned that the court was silent, this time in connection with the matter discussed in the Excursus; see WA, Br 7, 246.

[8] On Gregory Brück, see LW, 49, 51 f.

[9] On August 19 Luther assures Jonas that by God's grace life in the city is quite comfortable, except that no beer is available, so that people are forced to do their own brewing; WA, Br 7, 232.

[10] Elector John Frederick; see LW 48, 181 f. For the letter, see Excursus.

[11] This letter is not extant. See also Excursus.

[12] On July 29, 1535, Melanchthon wrote from Jena to Luther complaining about the poor conditions at the University; see WA, Br 7, 214 f. Perhaps Luther's inquiry above was motivated by his concern for Melanchthon, a concern which in turn was heightened by the news he had received from Jena.

[13] This letter is not extant; it is safe to assume that it is identical with the one mentioned in note 11.

[14] A September 1 letter of Luther to Jonas (WA, Br 7, 246) throws some light on this statement: "I have become suspicious." In this letter Luther reported the rumor that the real French envoys (see Excursus) had been killed, and that the people who had visited Melanchthon were in reality papistic agents who were trying to entice Melanchthon to leave the security of Electoral Saxony.

[15] This is a sarcastic reference to Albrecht, archbishop of Mainz (see LW, 48, 44 f.). At that time Luther was engaged in a controversy with Albrecht concerning the execution of one of Albrecht's creditors, an affair in which bribes, courtly intrigues, and actual and fictitious embezzlements were interwoven. For details, see WA 50, 386 ff.; WA, Br 7, No. 2215; Enders, *Briefwechsel* 10, 180 f.

[16] The signature is missing because in the witnesses Luther is identified in the title as the writer.

LETTERS

EXCURSUS

In February of 1535, in an attempt to gain the good will of the Smalcaldic League, the French king, Francis I, wrote a letter to the league in which he explained his general policies. He especially tried to justify the persecution of the evangelicals in France as police action against criminals. See *C.R.* 2, No. 1247; *WA*, Br 7, 227. Pursuing the same goal of establishing closer ties with the German Protestants, in the spring of 1535 Francis dispatched the French nobleman Barnabé Voré with an invitation to Melanchthon to come to France. Melanchthon declined this invitation (see *C.R.* 2, No. 1275), but this discouraged neither Voré nor the King. On June 23 Francis wrote to Melanchthon and again invited him to come to France for consultations with "our" learned men for the purpose of bringing about "harmony" in Christendom; *C.R.* 2, No. 1279. Voré, apparently with a small legation, brought this letter to Melanchthon, whom he met in Jena sometime between August 4 and August 8. Now Melanchthon was persuaded to accept the invitation (see *C.R.* 2, No. 1295 and *WA*, Br 13, 232, addition to *WA*, Br 7, 215, n. 8; *C.R.* 2, No. 1297), and on August 15/16 he was at the Electoral court in Torgau (not Weimar, as Manschreck, p. 224, states), seeking a leave of absence; *C.R.* 2, Nos. 1300, 1302, 1304, 1305.

Melanchthon's request was turned down. Through his councilors the Elector informed Melanchthon of his displeasure over the fact that Melanchthon had entered into negotiations with the French without the prior knowledge of and approval by the court. Melanchthon was told to abandon his plan to go to France; if he should desire it, however, the Elector would write to King Francis and excuse Melanchthon for not coming; *C.R.* 2, 907 f. Melanchthon accepted this offer from the Elector, and on August 17 the Elector promised to send to Melanchthon in Jena a copy of his letter to the French King; *C.R.* 2, No. 1300. The Elector's letter to Francis is dated August 18; *C.R.* 2, No. 1303. Thus the Elector and his councilors had every reason to believe that the case was closed; see *C.R.* 2, 908, 910. Whether they really thought so or only later said they had thought so is an open question; in view of Melanchthon's request for the letter to Francis I, however, they could have felt justified in assuming that Melanchthon was, if not content, then at least agreeable.

In connection with his visit to Torgau, Melanchthon had presented a written petition to the Elector (*C.R.* 2, No. 1302), asking for his leave of absence. The date of this petition is uncertain. The *C.R.* editors assign August 18 to the document, yet in a note they also give August 17. Clemen, *WA*, Br 7, No. 2221, Introduction, dates the document August 15; he does so on the basis of the Elector's August 19 statement (*C.R.* 2, 907) to the effect that Melanchthon had been at court on August 15, and had "then" presented a document to which an oral reply had been given. Clemen's date seems to have the most solid foundation, even though Clemen bypasses certain facts and fails to make certain observations. (*a*)

One may ask whether Clemen has the right to deduce from the Elector's statement everything which he does. The statement was made in a summary report in which a document by Melanchthon, marked (A), was forwarded to Brück; no details about the negotiations with Melanchthon were mentioned, except that the answer which had been orally given to Melanchthon was summarized, and Melanchthon's seeming acceptance of this answer was underscored. Clemen in no way documents that the "writing" which the Elector forwarded as exhibit (A) to Brück on August 19, and which according to the Elector's statement Melanchthon had presented on August 15 (*C.R.* 2, 907), is identical with the extant, undated Melanchthon petition, *C.R.* 2, No. 1302. Only further research in the archives could establish this. (*b*) Melanchthon received the Elector's answer, at least the portion assuring him that a letter would be written to the King of France, on August 16; see *C.R.* 2, No. 1300. Consequently Melanchthon was in contact with the Electoral officials at least twice, once on August 15 (see *loc. cit.*), and again on August 16 (see *C.R.* 2, 907). (*c*) The Electoral officials considered the case closed, and they and the Elector thought that Melanchthon had accepted the negative answer given him. In his report to Brück the Elector presented the situation in such a way that it is clear beyond any doubt that after an answer had been given to Melanchthon which he seemingly had accepted, the case was *reopened* by Melanchthon and Luther. See *C.R.* 2, 908, 910. (*d*) And finally, on August 19 the Elector mentioned *two* letters from Melanchthon which he forwarded to Brück: one marked (A) given to the Elector on August 15 and orally dealt with by the Electoral officials, and one characterized as an "additional" letter; *C.R.* 2, 907, 908. On August 24 the Elector replied to a *second* letter from Melanchthon; *C.R.* 2, 910. This second letter is not extant; at least it is not printed in *C.R.*

In light of these observations, events must have taken place as follows: On August 15 Melanchthon was at court in Torgau, apparently turning over to the Electoral officials a petition to the Elector in support of his request for a leave of absence; *C.R.* 2, 907. On that day or the next Melanchthon orally received a negative reply from the Elector, and on August 16 he received the promise that the Elector would write to King Francis, excusing Melanchthon for not coming to France; *C.R.* 2, Nos. 1300, 1304. The officials believed that Melanchthon was satisfied; they went ahead and drafted the letter to France, completing it on August 18 (*C.R.* 2, 908, and *ibid.*, No. 1303), and thought the case closed. They were wrong, for they received a second letter from Melanchthon, and even more, Luther got into the act. One of the two Melanchthon letters is missing. The one which is extant, *C.R.* 2, No. 1302, could be the one of August 15, as Clemen suggests, but it could also be the one written *after* Melanchthon's request had been rejected by the Elector. That the dateline of the extant letter is Torgau only establishes the fact that, provided this extant letter was the second letter, Melanchthon wrote it after his second meeting with the Electoral officials, the one of August 16, and before he left for Wittenberg, where he was on August 17. At least the Elector thought that Melanchthon was in Wittenberg on that day (*C.R.* 2, No. 1300). And on August 18 Melanchthon wrote from Wittenberg (not Jena, as Clemen, *WA*, Br 7, 229 states) to Jonas that he has been for "two days" in Wittenberg; he also told Jonas that "thus far" he had not yet received the Elector's permission to go to France—a statement which would make no sense at all, if Melanchthon had not still been expecting an answer from the Elector, i.e., an answer to his second letter with which he had tried to change the court's position which had been made clear to him on August 15/16—but that he did not really expect to receive this permission. See *C.R.* 2, No. 1301. By August 19 Melanchthon had left Wittenberg for Jena "quite angry" about the Elector's refusal to grant him the leave of absence, as Luther wrote to Jonas on that day; *WA*, Br 7, 232.

On August 19 the Elector informed Brück in Wittenberg that, in addition to Melanchthon, Luther also was at court in Torgau, that Luther had been informed of the reasons for the denial of Melanchthon's petition, and that the court had the impression that Luther was satisfied. In spite of all this, Luther wrote a letter, says the Elector, which was included for Brück. See *C.R.* 2, 908. It is difficult to establish any details about this journey of Luther to Torgau; Luther would have needed approximately a day and a half to two days in order to make this round-trip journey of about 90 kilometers and to take care of his affairs at court. On August 19 Luther was back in Wittenberg; *WA*, Br 7, No. 2223; *C.R.* 2, 909. On August 17 the Elector had thought Luther to be in Wittenberg; *C.R.* 2, 903. The Elector's report to Brück (*C.R.* 2, 908) would seem to justify the assumption that Luther was at court on August 18, the day on which the letter to Francis I was completed. And further, Melanchthon would hardly have gone to Wittenberg had he met Luther in Torgau on August 15/16. It is safe, then, to suggest that under the impact of the news which Luther received from Melanchthon personally about the frosty reception that had been accorded him at court, Luther, who favored Melanchthon's trip to France (*WA*, Br 7, 232), traveled to Torgau sometime on August 17 in an attempt to support Melanchthon's (second) petition for a leave of absence. After Luther had been informed of the reasons for the denial of this petition (and feeling that little else could be done) but prior to leaving again for Wittenberg, Luther left at court his own official letter to the Elector (*WA*, Br 7, No. 2221, dated August 17) in a last attempt to change the Elector's mind. If one wishes to wring every possible inference from the Elector's report to Brück, then one may deduce that all these events took place on August 18, probably in the morning, and that Luther used the afternoon for returning to Wittenberg. Then Luther would either have redated his letter to the Elector, or he would have actually written it on the 17 (perhaps while still in Wittenberg) and would have taken it along. It is reasonable to assume that Luther also took along the second letter of Melanchthon to the Elector mentioned above, and left it at court, along with his own. This would explain the fact that on August 18 (see above), while still in Wittenberg, Melanchthon had still been waiting, though with little hope, for a positive answer from the Elector. In any event, Luther returned to Wittenberg with mixed emotions; on the one hand he realized that his mission had been as unsuccessful as that of Melanchthon; on the other hand he did not know what would happen next (*WA*, Br 7, 232); i.e., Luther was uncertain how Melanchthon would react to the frigid reception, and how the court would react to the renewed pleas made by Melanchthon and himself.

The Elector found himself in a dilemma. By August 18, when the letter to King Francis had been completed, the Elector had thought that the case was closed; while he and his officials must have been aware of possible unhappiness on the part of Melanchthon and Luther, they must nevertheless have felt that things had been smoothed over. At that point the two petitions appeared, undoubtedly much to the surprise and annoyance of the Elector, who was now more than ever determined not to let Melanchthon go; see *C.R.* 2, 910. And so on August 19 (*C.R.* 2, No. 1304) the Elector sent to Brück in Wittenberg a brief report about the events, together with Melanchthon's two letters, the letter from Luther, and a draft of a reply to Melanchthon's second request for a leave of absence. He left it to Brück's discretion to pressure Luther and Melanchthon (whom the Elector thought still to be in Wittenberg) in an attempt to make them withdraw their petitions. In his own handwriting the Elector, in a postscript, spelled out his determination not to let Melanchthon go, as well as some of the reasons for this decision. Whether the envisioned meeting between Brück and Luther actually took place could not be established, though it is almost certain, for Luther tells of having seen the draft of the Elector's tart, brusque, final reply to Melanchthon. Luther referred to it above, p. 87 (at note 10). Since the date of the final version of this letter is August 24 (*C.R.* 2, No. 1305), and since Brück in his answer to the Elector's August 19 request for counsel on the draft of this final reply obviously informed the court that Melanchthon was no longer in Wittenberg, so that the Elector's August 24 letter was sent to Melanchthon in Jena, it was impossible for Luther to have seen the final version and to have already communicated with Melanchthon about it by August 29; see p. 87, at notes 11 and 13. Luther was disturbed about the content and tone of the draft of this letter (see also *WA*, Br 7, 243) which he could have seen on the evening of August 19 at the very earliest; consequently soon after this date he wrote to Melanchthon the no-longer extant letter mentioned above (p. 87), obviously in an attempt to prepare Melanchthon for this letter and comfort him with, among other thoughts, a certain rumor about the French envoys (which Luther had most probably heard while he was in Torgau); see p. 87, n. 14. While in his letters to Brück and Melanchthon the Elector gave a long list of reasons why he refused to grant Melanchthon the requested leave of absence, in the final analysis it is quite clear that the Elector was annoyed at Melanchthon, that he would have felt embarrassed if his famous professor had gone to France, the enemy of the Empire, and that he simply did not wish Melanchthon to go to France. Melanchthon had no choice but to accept the Elector's verdict, and on August 28 he wrote to King Francis declining the invitation to France; C.R. 2, No. 1306. And Luther tried to make the best out of these events, as his September 1 letter to Jonas demonstrates; see WA, Br 7, 246.

260

To Justus Jonas[1]
[Wittenberg,] September 4, 1535

Luther, anticipating Jonas' arrival in Wittenberg to participate in a graduation, jovially explains the suggestions he had made regarding the speech Jonas is to deliver at this graduation. He also asks Jonas to buy, or somehow help to acquire, some of the supplies necessary for the banquet[2] which the Luthers intend to give in connection with this graduation. Then Luther mentions the victories which Emperor Charles had gained over the Turks in Africa, and tells of the establishment of some religious regulations enjoined by Duke George of Saxony and Cardinal Albrecht of Mainz upon their people in an attempt to assure the successful outcome of the Emperor's campaign. He concludes by sending his wife's and his own good-humored greeting to the Jonas family.[3]

On Justus Jonas, see LW, 48, 275, n. 3.

Text in Latin: WA, Br 7, 249–250.[4]

Grace and peace!

---

[1] Even though the address is missing in all witnesses, the opening sentence of the letter and some of the circumstances mentioned in it establish Jonas as the addressee.

[2] This was the banquet to which Luther had invited Melanchthon and others in letter No. 259. On September 1 Luther had invited Jonas to these festivities; see WA, Br 7, 246. The Luthers gave the banquet in honor of Jerome Weller, who at one time had been the tutor of their son Hänschen; see LW 49, 321; WA, Br 7, 488.

[3] Jonas was absent from Wittenberg in July and August of 1535; he was not, however, with the University in Jena (see p. 85; WA, Br 7, 233, n. 1; Enders, Briefwechsel, 10, 190, n. 1). His absence from the city was connected with the plague (see also LW 49, 176, n. 35; Kawerau, Jonas Briefwechsel 1, 228), but Jonas apparently also had to fulfill some obligations for the Elector in connection with the visitation, for on August 24 Luther addressed him as visitor; WA, Br 7, 241; see also Kawerau, Jonas Briefwechsel 1, 228. On September 9 Jonas signed a letter in Schlieben, near Wittenberg, where relatives of his wife had an estate; see Kawerau, Jonas Briefwechsel 1, 231. Since in the present letter Luther extends greetings to Jonas' wife and family, it may be assumed that the letter was addressed to Jonas, who was in Schlieben with his family, i.e., in the country. After September 11, Jonas was again in Wittenberg (WA, Br 12, 441), and participated in the graduation festivities. See also note 7.

[4] The letter is extant in several manuscript copies, and in the common editions of Luther's works.

I hope that you have received the letter[5] and disputations,[6] my Jonas, and that at the same time you learned that we, the pig, wanted to teach you, Minerva,[7] what to say at the graduation. Now the chief cook, our lord Katie, asks you to accept this coin[8] and to buy for us poultry or fowl,[9] or whatever in that airy kingdom of our feathered friends is subject to the dominion of man (and may be eaten)[10]— but (for God's sake) no ravens, though we are quite eager to devour all the sparrows at once.[11] Should you spend more, it will be

---

[5] WA, Br 7, No. 2232, dated September 1, 1535.

[6] See p. 86, n. 3.

[7] The portion of the sentence beginning with "and that at the same time" has been freely translated. Luther uses here a slightly modified (i.e., more earthy) classical saying, recorded by Erasmus in the Adagia, I: 1, 40 (Clericus 2, 43). The saying deplores the fact that illiterate people try to teach those by whom they should be instructed. For other instances where Luther used this saying, see WA, Br 1, 288, n. 6. In his September 1 letter Luther, as dean of the Theological Faculty, had asked Jonas to function as the faculty's official graduator and to deliver the address; in this connection Luther had made some suggestions to Jonas regarding this address; WA, Br 7, 246. Jonas complied with Luther's wish; see the entry for September 14 in the Liber Decanorum Facultatis Theologicae Academiae Vitebergensis, ed. C. E. Förstemann (Leipzig, 1838), p. 31, cited in WA, Br 12, 441.

[8] Here a word is used which would have to be translated into German as Taler. The Taler was a coin of fluctuating silver content. According to pre-World War I currency standards the value of an "old" Taler, i.e., a Taler in circulation prior to 1857, was the equivalent of $0.71. Of course one has to consider that in Luther's day a fully grown hog was valued about $13.40 in terms of the 1913 dollar value. See Schwiebert, p. 257 ff. Whatever the actual value in grams of silver might have been, the one Taler enclosed by Luther would not have bought much for the pending banquet, at which seven to eight tables were actually served (see WA, Br 7, 488), and for which the Electoral court provided a substantial amount of wine (see ARG 25 [1928], 87). Luther must have felt that the money included would not be adequate for his request; hence his offer to repay any additional expenses and his request that Jonas try to do some hunting. Luther's "order" has to be seen against the background of the fact that Wittenberg was harassed by the plague and that food was probably not too easy to get, that Jonas was "in the country" (see note 3), and that Luther expected a large crowd for the banquet. As early as August 7, Luther had approached the Elector for some venison (see WA, Br 7, 223), and on August 19 Luther informed Jonas that the Elector had promised to send some venison and the best wine of the castle; see WA, Br 7, 232.

[9] The names of the ordered supplies are freely translated.

[10] This could be an allusion to Acts 10:12, 14, 15.

[11] The meaning of the last portion of the text is not clear and the translation is based on St. L. 21b, 1999. For "sparrow," the text reads passer; this is probably a reference to the German field sparrow which is slightly larger than the sparrow usually seen in America, esp. in the cities. (Passer also designates some kind of fish, probably a type of flounder; the context in which Luther used passer here and in other cases [see WA, Br 7, 250, nn. 6, 7], however, strongly suggests that Luther was thinking of sparrows.) The statement about the ravens could be an

repaid you. Further, if you can buy, or hunt at no expense to yourself, some rabbit or similar meaty delicacies send them along, for we intend to satisfy the bellies of all of you, if that drink called beer finally turns out all right. For my Katie has cooked 7 *Quartalia* (as they call them) into which she has mixed 32 *Scheffel* of malt, because she wants to satisfy my palate.[12] She hopes it will turn out to be good beer. Whatever it is, you and the others will taste it.

There is no news, except what you already know[13] about the Emperor's victory in Africa.[14] Duke George[15] and the Bishop of Halle,[16] however, held a meeting and decided to require their people, for the good of the Emperor, to fast three times per week, and to receive only one part of the sacrament[17] so that in the future everything will turn out successfully. If Charles should reach Constantinople[18] (which God may grant), then it will not be God who

---

allusion to Gen. 8:7, I Kings 17:6, Ps. 147:9, Luke 12:24. This would suggest that Luther considered ravens not to be "devoured" because they played an important role in Scripture. On the other hand, in a Table Talk (*WA*, TR 4, No. 4644) Luther voiced a negative opinion about ravens.

12 The malt of which Luther speaks is a mixture of grains (barley, wheat) and hops to which water was added for the purpose of fermentation. Luther means to say that his wife brewed beer by using 32 *Scheffel* (or *ca.* 384 liters) of this soupy substance, adding to it 7 *Quartalia* (or *ca.* 10 liters) of water, "cooking" (i.e., simmering) this mixture, and finally passing it through a sieve. The alcohol content of this beer would depend on the amount of water added to the grain in the preparation of the malt, and the time used for the fermentation and "cooking" processes.

13 It is not clear how Luther knew that Jonas had already heard the following news. See also note 18. On the basis of the extant Luther-Jonas correspondence from July/August 1535 it is, however, clear that some letters are missing.

14 This is a reference to the naval expedition which Charles V (see *LW* 48, 175 f.) undertook in the summer of 1535 against the ally of the Turks in Algeria and Tunisia, the pirate Chair-ed-Din Barbarossa. On July 14 the Emperor conquered La Goulette, the gateway to the city of Tunis, and also severely damaged the Turkish fleet in the process; shortly thereafter the Emperor conquered Tunis itself. Since the Emperor did not capture Barbarossa, however, the victory was not as decisive as it had appeared to be, and soon Barbarossa was as big a threat as ever to Spanish power in the western Mediterranean Sea. See Ranke 2[IV], 7 ff.; Brandi 1, 303 ff. The Imperial victory was celebrated and propagandized in pamphlets, one of which Luther sent to Elector John Frederick on August 7; see *WA*, Br 7, 222, and *ibid*, 223, n. 1. See also note 18.

15 I.e., Luther's old foe, the duke of Saxony; see *LW* 48, 110, n. 20.

16 I.e., Cardinal Albrecht of Mainz, who was also the bishop for Halle; see *LW* 48, 44 f. No details about this meeting could be established. Pope Paul III issued an indulgence bull ordering a three-day fast in order to assure the Emperor's final victory; see *WA*, Br 7, 250, n. 16.

17 See *LW* 48, 143 f.

18 According to Ranke 2[IV], 12 f., the Pope urged the Emperor to attack the

LETTERS

will have accomplished this, but [rather] those three fast days and the one part of the sacrament. The poet certainly is right when he says: "Those who are as smart as you are can easily transfer to themselves the glory created by the efforts of others."[19] Now I understand why Terence[20] calls that Thraso[21] a wicked person. [But] these words originate with Scipio and Laelius, and not with Terence.[22] Yet Christ lives and sees this wickedness of devils and men, wickedness too great to be put into words. We, however, live too, and rejoice in that raging of devils and men, and intend even to put on a banquet and a feast day while they miserably chafe— especially if you happily arrive here[23] with some captured feath-

---

Turks, now that Barbarossa had been defeated. While the Emperor intended only to continue the war in the western part of the Mediterranean Sea, an attack on Constantinople was also discussed at court. How Luther heard of this plan is not clear. Perhaps the pamphlets, mentioned in note 14, were Luther's source.—One manuscript copy of the present letter, deposited in Strassburg, is followed by a brief report on the Emperor's campaign in Africa. The report ends with the statement that, due to carelessness on the part of "our" army, Barbarossa slipped away, repaired his fleet, and escaped to Constantinople. Text: WA, Br 13, 234, addition to WA, Br 7, 249. If indeed this report originated with Luther, as is suggested *loc. cit.*, then it is clear how thoroughly Luther was informed of the situation. Further, if indeed this report was added by Luther to the present letter to Jonas, as is also suggested *loc. cit.*, then one would have to see in this report the source for Jonas' knowledge of the events. The opening sentence of the paragraph would then have to be paraphrased thus: There is no news around here, except what you already know about the Emperor's victory in Africa, because you have read my attached report.
[19] Terence *Eunuchus* iii. 1. 399 ff.
[20] On Publius Terentius (195[?]–159), a Roman comedian, see *O.C.D.*, pp. 884 f.
[21] Terence *Eunuchus* iv. 7. 780 ff. Thraso is a bragging soldier in the *Eunuchus*, who runs away when confronted with serious danger.
[22] According to WA, Br 7, 250, n. 19, this sentence was originally a marginal note which a copyist included in the text. If the sentence was indeed a marginal note then one can, of course, not determine whether it was a part of Luther's text, or an editorial comment by a copyist. The statement could originate with Luther, for in the Table Talks (WA, TR 4, No. 5023) there is recorded a statement, supposedly made by Luther, to the following effect: the style and subject matter of the comedies of Terence suggest that not Terence but Scipio Africanus Minor (see *O.C.D.*, p. 816) and Gaius Laelius Minor (*ibid.*, p. 477) were the authors of these comedies. Luther repeats a rumor here which was quite widespread in antiquity and mentioned in the biography of Terence by Suetonius (see *The Comedies of Terence*, ed. S. G. Ashmore [Oxford, 1910], p. 2). The rumor originated because Terence was a member of the Scipionic Circle of writers (see *O.C.D.*, p. 877) to whom he probably read aloud his plays before they were produced, and "availed himself, independently and according to his choice, of their [i.e., Scipio, Laelius, and others] criticisms and suggestions." So Ashmore, *op. cit.*, p. 29.
[23] Literally: "arrive with us."

96

ered animals and force them, after they have been taken from the freedom of the kingdom of the air, to walk into the jail of the cooking pots upon[24] a city stove.

My Katie cordially and reverently greets you and all your family. But hold a minute, if my wife greets you, I, in turn, greet your wife. What is sauce for the goose is sauce for the gander.[25] Farewell in the Lord!

September 4, 1535   Yours, MARTIN LUTHER

261

To George Spalatin
[Wittenberg,] September 6, 1535

Luther asks Spalatin's help for an elderly pastor who has been expelled from office. He also reports some news: Robert Barnes is in Wittenberg in order to get Melanchthon to come to England; Hartmuth von Cronberg is searching for his sister and has visited Luther; the cities of Greece supposedly call Emperor Charles the liberator from the Turkish tyranny; there is no plague in Wittenberg. Luther closes by sending greetings from his wife to the Spalatin family.

On George Spalatin, see LW 48, 8 f.

Text in Latin: WA, Br 7, 251.[1]

To the most distinguished Mr. George Spalatin,
Master [of Arts],[2] superintendent
in Meissen,[3] my dearest brother in the Lord

---

[24] Literally: "under."
[25] Literally: "A mate has to be referred to a mate." Or: "One has to return like for like." See also Terence *Eunuchus* iii. 1. 445.
[1] The letter is extant in manuscript copies, and in the common editions of Luther's works.
[2] Literally: "Distinguished man, Mr. Master George Spalatin."
[3] In 1528/29 Spalatin had been appointed to the visitation commission for the districts of the Electoral administration of Meissen and Vogtland. See, Höss, *Spalatin*, pp. 330 ff. On December 22, 1528, Spalatin was appointed superinten-

Grace and peace in the Lord! The pastor in Burkartshain by the name of Wolfgang Götzel[4] is being expelled by his lord, [even though] he is now old, has an abundance of children, and has so far faithfully discharged his official duties. Help this man, my George, as much as you are able to. For it is cruel that Christ's poor are so afflicted by our people, and such arbitrary cruelty of the nobility will cause great harm to our gospel. Therefore I heartily commend him to you.

There is no news, except that Doctor Antony, that unfortunate Englishman,[5] is here as envoy of his King[6] to our Sovereign,[7] and asks that Master[8] Philip[9] come to England for a colloquy with the King.[10] [Also,] Hartmuth von Cronberg[11] was here in search of

---

dent, with residency at Altenburg; *ibid.*, p. 337. In referring to Spalatin as superintendent in Meissen, Luther is not quite correct, since the area of competence of Spalatin's office did not encompass the whole area commonly known as Meissen, but only a part, i.e., the *Amt* (subdistrict; county), or as Luther sometimes called it, the diocese, of Altenburg. On February 24, 1535, Luther called Spalatin "archbishop and vistor of Meissen" (*WA,* Br 7, 160), and this suggests that Luther considered Spalatin to be superintendent of all of Meissen, because since September of 1533 the commission which was charged by the Elector with the visitation of all the parishes in the districts of Meissen and Vogtland was again operating (Höss, *Spalatin,* pp. 370 ff.).

[4] On this pastor, Wolfgang Götzel of Burkartshain (near Wurzen, east of Leipzig), see *WA,* Br 7, 251, n. 1.

[5] I.e., Robert Barnes. See also Rupp, *Tradition,* p. 95, n. 1. "Unfortunate" would have to be understood as an allusion to the dangers to which Barnes was exposed by the English papists and their agents on the Continent (*L.P.* 8, No. 652; Tjernagel, p. 145), of which dangers Barnes must have told Luther.

[6] Henry VIII of England; see note 10.

[7] Elector John Frederick; see *LW* 48, 181 f.

[8] I.e., Master of Arts.

[9] Philip Melanchthon; see *LW* 48, 77, n. 3.

[10] Through the Acts of Supremacy of 1534 (*EHD* 5, No. 100), Henry VIII completed his break with the papacy. Simultaneously the King sought the support of the Smalcaldic League, i.e., political support for his precarious position vis-à-vis France and Emperor Charles, and moral support in connection with his divorce, his remarriage, and the status of his offspring from this second marriage. He still hoped that the evangelical theologians in Germany would issue a verdict in favor of the divorce. "That he continued to press for this after Katherine had been put away, even after her death in January of 1536, is proof that for Henry the whole matter was closely bound to his concern for the succession." So Rupp, *Tradition,* p. 92. This interest in support by the league was, however, carefully balanced by the King's determination not to appear as the one who was seeking help, but to have the German evangelicals initiate the contacts. In order to get things off the ground, Robert Barnes, in a semiofficial capacity, came to Wittenberg in March of 1535 and established friendly contacts between Henry and Melanchthon, who wrote a "tactful letter" (*C.R.* 2, No. 1264, dated March 13, 1535) to the King "which walked delicately among

his sister. For this most honorable woman was indeed here for some months, though we did not know it. A certain Jew had abducted her, a widow, and made her his wife. But while traveling he was killed by her relatives, and his wife, called by her relatives to return to them in peace, left town.[12] From Silesia comes word that the cities of Greece are calling Emperor Charles[13] the liberator from the Turkish tyranny.[14] The fortune of that man is unheard of; may

the verities." So Rupp, *Tradition*, p. 93; see also Tjernagel, p. 142. Barnes also invited Melanchthon to come to England—whether officially or privately is not clear, and neither is Melanchthon's reaction. It is clear, however, that Melanchthon did not discourage Barnes (see *L.P.* 8, No. 1061; *C.R.* 2, 872; p. 101, n. 10), for Barnes, upon his return to England, saw to it that a safe-conduct for Melanchthon was issued by the King (see p. 101). In August Barnes again left for Wittenberg, this time as the King's envoy. His instructions (see *L.P.* 8, Nos. 1061, 1062, and *ibid.*, p. 423, note; Prüser, p. 23, n. 7) were to block Melanchthon's possible trip to France (see pp. 88 ff.), entice Melanchthon to come to England, and negotiate with Elector John Frederick accordingly. See further, p. 106, n. 29. The exact date of Barnes's arrival in Wittenberg could not be established. See also Tjernagel, pp. 143 ff.

[11] On Hartmuth von Cronberg, see *LW* 48, 216, n. 11.

[12] According to *WA*, Br 7, No. 2220, Introduction, the following circumstances are the background for Luther's statement: Von Cronberg's sister, Lorche, had been widowed since 1527/28. In the spring of 1535 she traveled to Erfurt, from where she informed her relatives that she had been secretely married, and was expecting a child about July 25. Pressed for an explanation, she stated that she was married to a Jew by the name of James who was living with her, his wife, and his four children in Hesse; that according to Jewish law a man was permitted to have several wives; and that she had been attached to James for the last three years. The relatives went into action, and requested the Elector's help in taking Lorche out of this situation. Apparently they also demanded that Lorche return to them. They met James, who admitted that he had abandoned Lorche six days earlier in Wittenberg, and they killed him. Meanwhile Lorche, having been abandoned by James, approached Luther for help without telling him who she was, though telling him some sad details which Luther believed, at least to the extent that he functioned as godfather at the child's baptism. However, Luther was not totally convinced. At any rate, on August 8 Luther commended "this woman" to Justus Menius, the superintendent in Eisenach, because she had asked him for such a recommendation to a pastor in this area in order to seek help from her relatives; *WA*, Br 7, 226. Lorche left Wittenberg, and went to Eisenach; *WA*, Br 7, No. 2227. After August 8 Hartmuth von Cronberg, searching for his sister and obviously angry with her for having brought shame on the family, came to Luther, who now finally found out who "this woman" really was, and that she had been called away from Wittenberg by her relatives, so that her departure from Wittenberg was in compliance with the demands of the relatives. Luther used all his influence with Hartmuth to calm him, and thus to prepare for an eventual reconciliation between Lorche and her family. Hartmuth traveled to Eisenach, and on August 24 Luther asked Menius to help in this reconciliation.

[13] On Emperor Charles V, see *LW* 48, 175 ff., and above, p. 95, n. 18. For a possible source of this news, see *WA*, Br 7, 252, n. 5.

[14] Or: "are calling on Emperor Charles to be the liberator."

Christ complete it. Amen. Of our plague[15] I know nothing; thus all is a lie. Of many it is said that they have been buried already for three days, but behold they are alive and most healthy. May God punish those miserable people who are masters in lying and seducing the people!

Farewell in the Lord, and pray for me!

September 6, 1535. My lord Katie reverently greets you together with your whole flesh.[16]

Yours,

MARTIN LUTHER

262

To Elector John Frederick
[Wittenberg,] September 12, 1535

Luther and some of his colleagues urge the Elector to grant a private audience to Robert Barnes, the English envoy. They also mention Barnes's efforts regarding a possible trip of Melanchthon to England, and point out that it would cause sadness to Melanchthon if he were not permitted to go. A brief blessing closes the letter.

On Elector John Frederick, see LW 48, 181 f.

Text in German: WA, Br 7, 266–267.[1]

To the Most Serene, Noble Sovereign and Lord,
Sir John Frederick, duke in Saxony and elector,
archmarshal of the Holy Empire, etc.,
landgrave in Thuringia and margrave in Meissen,
our Most Gracious Lord

Grace and peace in Christ, and also our poor *Pater noster!*[2] Most Serene, Noble Sovereign, Most Gracious Lord! Doctor Antony,[3]

---

[15] See p. 85.

[16] I.e., Spalatin's wife and children; see Gen. 2:23; Matt. 19:5.

[1] The letter is extant in Luther's handwriting; the signatures of Luther's colleagues are in their own handwriting. See WA, Br 7, No. 2240, Introduction, and WA, Br 13, 135, addition to *loc. cit.*

[2] See p. 69, n. 4.

[3] Robert Barnes.

envoy of His Royal Majesty of England,[4] has shown us letters[5] and asked us to intercede in his behalf with Your Electoral Grace for a secret or private audience, since he wishes to have his mission[6] withheld from public knowledge until a settlement has been reached. Since Your Electoral Grace is well acquainted with this man from the past,[7] and since in our opinion he brings good news as far as his orders are concerned, it is our humble request that Your Electoral Grace graciously grant such an audience to this man.

Further, with Master[8] Philip's[9] consent,[10] Barnes has diligently negotiated with the King; he has accomplished much, so that the King highly desires Master Philip [to come], advises against the trip to France (as Doctor Antony can report further), and in addition sends an official[11] safe-conduct and also offers bond, etc. [Therefore] it is our humble request that if Your Electoral Grace is unable to grant [an audience to Barnes] prior to the trip to Austria,[12] then [Your Grace] would not deny it after the return home (which, God may graciously grant). Who knows what God intends to accomplish? His wisdom is greater than ours, and his will better than ours. Should Master Philip not go, now that he has been officially invited as a result of his readiness [to go to England], then this might cause him many sad thoughts. Even without this problem he is and almost always has been overburdened with work, worry,[13] and spiritual struggles.[14] Your Electoral Grace certainly will know

---

[4] Henry VIII.
[5] It is not clear which "letters" are meant here. It is certain, however, that Luther saw the safe-conduct for Melanchthon (see the next paragraph of the letter); text in excerpt: WA, Br 7, 251, n. 3. Barnes also carried with him a letter of Henry VIII to the Elector (dated July 8, 1535) which constituted Barnes's credentials; text in excerpt: WA, Br 7, 251, n. 3; see also L.P. 8, 423, note.
[6] See pp. 98, n. 10, 106, n. 29.
[7] This is a reference to Barnes's former visits to Wittenberg. Whether a meeting between Barnes and John Frederick took place on these occasions—if Luther's statement were to be understood in this sense—could not be established.
[8] I.e., Master of Arts.
[9] Philip Melanchthon; see LW 48, 77, n. 3.
[10] An "official" expression on Melanchthon's part regarding his readiness to go to England could not be established; see also p. 98, n. 10. Whatever statements Melanchthon did make, he must have made them orally to Barnes in March.
[11] Luther used stattlich, i.e., literally, splendid, magnificent, commanding, noble.
[12] See p. 112, n. 21.
[13] Literally: "sadness."
[14] Luther used Anfechtung; see LW 48, 28, n. 10. Luther's statements must be seen against the background of the Elector's refusal to let Melanchthon go to France (see pp. 88 ff.).

how to consider graciously such matters, and kindly act accordingly. Christ our Lord be with Your Electoral Grace eternally. Amen.

September 12, 1535

Your Electoral Grace's dedicated

MARTIN LUTHER, DOCTOR

JUSTUS JONAS, DOCTOR[15]

CASPAR CRUCIGER, DOCTOR[16]

JOHN BUGENHAGEN POMER, DOCTOR[17]

263

To Gregory Brück[1]
[Wittenberg, about September 15, 1535][2]

Following up his letter of recommendation of Robert Barnes to the Elector (No. 262), Luther writes to Gregory Brück, the Electoral Saxon chancellor emeritus, and expresses his hope that Brück will help Barnes get the desired private audience with Elector John Frederick. In view of the willingness of Henry VIII to affirm the gospel and join the Smalcaldic League, Luther advocates the King's admission to the league. He sees in the King's desire God's hand at work, and sees a possibility of confounding the plans of the papists. Luther informs Brück that he, Luther, and his colleagues will deal with the next English envoy on the matter of the King's marriage. And he finally strongly recommends that Melanchthon be permitted to go to England, or even be sent there.

On Gregory Brück, see LW 49, 51 f.

---

[15] See *LW* 48, 275, n. 3.

[16] See *LW* 49, 104, n. 12.

[17] See *LW* 48, 303, n. 44.

[1] The only manuscript copy of this letter, and it is a poor one, is deposited in the Public Record Office in London. It is entirely possible that this copy got there by way of Barnes; see also note 5. The copy carries a Latin title which reads in translation: "Martin Luther's Letter to Doctor Brück, chancellor." See *WA*, Br 7, No. 2241, Introduction. Since addressee and sender are identified in this title, they are omitted in the text proper.

[2] The date can be established on the basis of a comparison of the content of this letter with that of letter No. 262. See also note 5.

Text in German (with some words, phrases, and sentences in Latin): WA, Br 7, 268.

Grace and peace in Christ!

Honorable, highly-learned, dear Sir and Friend![3] The Englishman, Doctor Antony, the envoy of his King,[4] comes[5] and, as you know,[6] requests of my Most Gracious Lord[7] an audience which should be gracious, yet secret or private, something about which I do not worry. If Your Honor promotes this matter, then my Most Gracious Lord will not feel imposed upon, especially since His Electoral Grace is well acquainted with this man from before,[8] and since Barnes comes under different circumstances than the French legation.[9]

Since the King now also offers to accept the gospel, join the

---

[3] For "Friend," see LW 48, 201, n. 2.
[4] I.e., Robert Barnes.
[5] Even before Elector John Frederick received letter No. 262, Brück (who was in Wittenberg at that time) informed (see WA, Br 7, 270; C.R. 2, No. 1326) the Elector of Barnes's arrival in Wittenberg and of a meeting between himself, Barnes, and Luther, during which he found out details about the purpose of Barnes's mission. Brück then went to Jena, and received there a September 13 letter from the Elector (C.R. 2, No. 1326; WA, Br 7, 270), informing him that the Elector would be willing to receive Barnes, who in the Elector's (correct) opinion would be traveling from Wittenberg to Jena. On September 17 Brück confirmed receipt of this letter (see WA, Br 7, 270), and informed the Elector that Barnes, together with Melanchthon, would arrive any minute. (Melanchthon was returning from Wittenberg where he had attended the graduation of Weller and Medler; p. 86.) On September 18 Brück informed the Elector (C.R. 2, No. 1328) that Barnes had arrived in Jena and was waiting for further instructions.—Since the graduation festivities were scheduled for September 14, and since one may not assume that Melanchthon and Barnes left immediately thereafter (i.e., on the same day), and since Luther says that Barnes "comes," it is safe to suggest that Barnes took the letter along. Thus it is more realistic to suggest September 15 as the probable date for the present letter rather than September 12, as the WA, Br editor does. It is, of course, possible that Luther, knowing that Barnes would join Melanchthon on the trip to Jena, wrote both the letter to the Elector, which was probably dispatched at once, and the letter to Brück, which was given to Barnes, on the same day.
[6] This is a reference to the conversations held in Wittenberg between Barnes, Brück, and Luther, of which Brück informed the Elector sometime prior to September 13; see note 5.
[7] Elector John Frederick; see LW 48, 181 f.
[8] See p. 101, n. 7.
[9] What Luther meant here is not clear. In WA, Br 7, 268, n. 4, it is suggested that this is a reference to the rumors surrounding the French legation, mentioned on p. 87, n. 14.

federation of our sovereigns,[10] and permit our *Apologia*[11] to circulate in his kingdom, it seems to me that, if His Royal Majesty would be honorably[12] received into the federation, it would confound the papists with regard to both the council[13] and all [their other] plans. For since all of this is taking place by itself in this way without our seeking it, God may, indeed, intend something which is bigger and better than we are capable of understanding. If God intends graciously to meet us in this way,[14] it is up to us not to let him pass by in ungratefulness. One has to seize an opportunity head on, because behind it is [only] emptiness.[15] Neglect an opportunity (says Bonaventure),[16] and the opportunity will neglect you.

Regarding the royal marriage[17] it has already been decided that the other envoy, once he has arrived,[18] is to deal with us

---

[10] I.e., the Smalcaldic League.

[11] I.e., the *Augsburg Confession*. As early as during the negotiations between Henry VIII and John Frederick which took place in 1532/33, the Elector insisted on the King's subscription to the *Augsburg Confession* as condition for the King to join the Smalcaldic League. See *L.P.* 6, No. 1079.

[12] The text reads *ehrlich*, i.e., literally, honestly, but also honorably. In Luther's usage the second meaning is the dominant one; see Dietz, *s.v.* Ehrlich. Barnes's mission was, among other things (see also note 29), to discuss the possible membership of Henry VIII in the Smalcaldic League, provided that a place could be found for the King which was worthy of his status; see *C.R.* 2, 942. It is quite possible that Luther, in discussing the "honorable" reception of Henry VIII into the league, was thinking of possible problems of protocol which might develop regarding the King's desire for a seat in the league.

[13] See pp. 81 ff.

[14] See also p. 58.

[15] Cato *Disticha de moribus* ii. 26. See also *O.C.D.*, p. 174.

[16] According to *WA*, Br 7, 268, n. 9, and Enders, *Briefwechsel* 10, 228, n. 5, the origin of this quotation from Bonaventure (see *O.D.C.C.*, p. 184) cannot be established.

[17] See pp. 27 ff. In the spring of 1533 Thomas Cranmer, in his capacity as archbishop of Canterbury, dissolved the marriage of Henry VIII to Catherine of Aragon, and legalized the King's marriage to Anne Boleyn. In 1534 Nicholas Heath (*DNB* 9, 345 f.) and others were sent to the Continent. Heath was to join Henry's roving ambassador on the Continent, Sir Christopher Mont (*DNB* 13, 651 f.) and travel to several courts in Germany, among them that of Saxony, and explain the King's position on the divorce and remarriage. Neither Mont nor Heath ever conferred with anyone in Electoral Saxony, and their missions failed to produce tangible results. See Tjernagel, p. 140 f.

[18] In the correspondence between Elector John Frederick and Brück (see note 5) it is noted that another English legation was on the way; see also note 29. Consequently Brück must have mentioned this legation to the Elector because Barnes had mentioned it to him and to Luther. On September 13 the

theologians about this matter; one may not deny him this. This issue is of no concern to the sovereigns. I myself would like to hear the reasons of the English since they appear to be so certain on this issue.

I would very much like to see Master[19] Philip[20] travel to England on his own, or be sent there,[21] for he has previously agreed [to go],[22] and as a result negotiations with the King have brought matters to this point.[23] Should he again[24] be prevented [from going], then he might feel that his reputation is being too much harmed; in the final analysis such stubbornness[25] might produce anger, or perhaps an eel's tail.[26] If it cannot be accomplished now [that Melanchthon may go], then it should certainly be arranged after my Most Gracious Lord's return.[27] Melanchthon has done much and worked hard, as we all know. But if one were not to have any consideration for him, or put up with him a little bit,[28] that would be dealing too harshly with him, and poorly rewarding his merits. After all, all the jurists and physicians are free to go to foreign lords if they wish to do so. I am writing this so that this good man is not forced to overburden himself with sad thoughts.

Elector instructed his captain at Wittenberg, Hans von Metzsch, to receive this English legation with all honor, and Metzsch confirmed receipt of these instructions on September 19; WA, Br 7, 281 f. In an undated letter written about the time of his departure for Vienna (see p. 112, n. 21), the Elector informed the Wittenberg theologians that Barnes had announced an official legation which was to discuss theological articles; see also note 29. The Elector also gave detailed instructions as to how to deal with this legation; WA, Br 7, 283 f. These are all references to the mission of Fox and Heath; see pp. 114 f. The reference made by Luther above regarding the "other envoy" also pertains to the Fox-Heath mission, and not to another mission of Christopher Mont, as Clemen argues in WA, Br 7, 269 f. See also Rupp, *Tradition*, p. 96, n. 2.

[19] I.e., Master of Arts.
[20] Philip Melanchthon; see *LW* 48, 77, n. 3.
[21] I.e., go as a private person to England, or be officially sent there by the Elector or by the Smalcaldic League.
[22] See p. 101, n. 10.
[23] I.e., that the safe-conduct for Melanchthon had been issued; see p. 101, n. 5.
[24] As Melanchthon was prevented from going to France. See pp. 88 ff.
[25] Or: "such holding on to [Melanchthon]."
[26] I.e., something which slips easily through one's hand.
[27] See p. 112, n. 21.
[28] I.e., one should not "punish" Melanchthon by refusing him permission to go to England just because he has again, as in the case of the invitation to France, agreed to accept an invitation without having first cleared the matter with the Electoral court.

Your Honor certainly will do what is best in this matter. With
this be commended to God. Amen.[29]

---

[29] The Elector received Barnes with all honors in or near Jena sometime after
September 18 (see note 5) and prior to September 28 (see *WA*, Br 7, 283, n. 2),
for on that day the Elector wrote a short, courteous letter to Henry VIII (*C.R.* 2,
No. 1330; *L.P.* 9, No. 468), saying very little, however, beyond praising
Barnes's diligence, and the King's efforts in behalf of the gospel. More important
than this letter is the Elector's letter addressed to Barnes (*C.R.* 2, No. 1329;
L.P. 9, No. 543), and obviously given to Barnes as instructions concerning what
to tell the King and his officials. In this letter the Elector informed Barnes (*a*) of
the Elector's willingness to receive the next legation (announced by Barnes),
which was to arrive with "certain orders" and was to discuss "certain articles"
with the Wittenberg theologians; (*b*) of the postponement of a decision regarding Melanchthon's trip to England; and (*c*) of the fact that the plenary assembly
of the Smalcaldic League would have to deal with the problem of the King's
possible membership in the league, as well as with the problem of possible joint
action of all evangelicals, including the King, regarding the pending council.
What one may read between the lines of this letter only substantiates what is at
one point set forth in the words of the letter: all further negotiations would have
to depend upon the King's acceptance of the *Augsburg Confession*. On September 27 Barnes left Jena again and returned to Wittenberg; see *WA*. Br 7, 282.
For the letter which he dispatched to England after his audience with Elector
John Frederick, see *English Historical Review* 36 (1921), 430 ff. On the basis
of the information which can be drawn from Luther's letter to Brück, from
notes which were taken during Barnes's audience with the Elector (text: *WA*,
Br 7, 269), and from the Elector's letter to Barnes, it becomes clear that the
purpose of Barnes's mission was more far-reaching than had been thus far
established (see p. 98, n. 10), and as, e.g., Tjernagel, p. 144, describes it;
Prüser, p. 19, gives a more complete picture of the situation, though one has to
wonder about the basis of his statements. In addition to inducing Melanchthon
to visit England instead of France, Barnes was to pave the way for Henry's
membership in the Smalcaldic League, and for possible joint action of all
evangelicals, i.e., the German evangelicals and the King, regarding the pending
council. Barnes was to open the door for an official (see note 18) legation
which was to do the theological and diplomatic groundwork through which
these two goals of English policy could become a reality. Barnes also was to re-
open the door for discussions of the King's divorce, which, so the English
hoped, would lead to a change of the position that had earlier been taken by
the Wittenberg theologians (see letter No. 245).

264

To Justus Jonas[1]
[Wittenberg,] October 28, 1535

Forwarding a letter from Melanchthon, Luther informs Jonas of the death of Christian Beyer, and of the fact that Gregory Brück is not in Prague at the moment. Then he tells of some events in Wittenberg: As yet no news has been received from the Electoral party which is on its way to Austria; Schadewalt has died from the plague; at the moment there are no other deaths from the plague; students are returning; and he himself is suffering from a catarrhal chest cold. He also wonders about the silence surrounding the papal envoy, Pietro Paolo Vergerio, and the council. As an afterthought Luther mentions his intention of writing theses against the private mass, and also on I Corinthians 13 and other passages dealing with justification. He also extends the greetings of his wife, and briefly describes her daily activities, which range from farm chores to Bible reading.

On Justus Jonas, see LW 48, 275, n. 3.

Text in Latin: WA, Br 7, 316–317.

Grace and peace in Christ!

Eight days ago, Doctor Christian Beyer[2] departed from this life; so Philip[3] writes. He suffered from a fever; during the trip[4] he also got a cough and a catarrhal cold[5] which moved from the head to the

---

[1] The address of this letter, which is extant in one manuscript copy and in the common editions of Luther's works, is missing in all witnesses. Although there is no material available to substantiate the traditional assumption that Jonas was the addressee of this letter, it is safe to suggest that this is the case, and that at the time that Luther wrote the present letter Jonas was again in Schlieben (see p. 93, n. 3).

[2] See *LW* 49, 349, n. 8.

[3] Philip Melanchthon's (see *LW* 48, 77, n. 3) letter from Jena (see p. 85) is not extant.

[4] Or: "because of the trip." Beyer was a member of the Electoral party that was traveling to Vienna (see p. 112, n. 21). He went along, though he had a "fever" (see also *WA*, Br 13, 237, addition to *WA*, Br 7, 317, n. 3), but returned to Weimar sufficiently ill that several "foreign" physicians were called to help. He died on October 21 (*ibid.*).

[5] The text reads *stillicidium*.

chest. I am sending the letter.[6] As you will read in Philip's letter, Brück is not in Prague.[7] Up to now we have received nothing from those who are traveling to Austria.[8] Last Sunday[9] the plague carried away Schadewalt,[10] our best citizen. Since then, however, we are again at peace with the plague.[11] I am suffering from a salty catarrhal cold,[12] and sometimes from a slight cough. Many students are returning.[13] Besides this I have nothing [to write about]. I am wondering where the papal legate is,[14] or where he might have gone; concerning him, and concerning the whole council[15] there is such great silence.

Greet your whole family, and pray for us!

October 28

I am thinking about putting together theses against the private mass, and also on I Corinthians 13 and certain other passages that pertain to the topic of justification.[16] My lord Katie sends greetings; she drives the wagon, takes care of the fields,[17] buys and puts cattle

---

[6] I.e., most probably Melanchthon's no-longer extant letter mentioned above.

[7] Apparently Jonas and the Wittenbergers were of the opinion that Gregory Brück (see *LW* 49, 51 f.) also had accompanied the Elector to Vienna.

[8] See also p. 112, n. 21.

[9] I.e., October 24.

[10] For some information on Bartholomew Schadewalt, see *WA*, Br 5, 201, n. 1. While Schadewalt was ill, Luther visited him at least once; see *WA*, TR 5, No. 5503, p. 195.

[11] It was not until the beginning of December, however, that Wittenberg was sufficiently free of the plague that the city fathers were in a position officially to request the return of the University; see *WA*, Br 7, 332, n. 15. And it was not until February 13, 1536, that Melanchthon returned; *C.R.* 3, 42.

[12] See note 5.

[13] I.e., either from Jena (see p. 85), or from other places to which they had moved in order to escape the plague.

[14] I.e., Pietro Paolo Vergerio, the papal nuncio, not legate, as Luther states.

[15] See pp. 81 ff.

[16] During Weller's and Medler's disputation (see p. 86, n. 5), Dan. 4:24 and I Cor. 13:2, 13 were used in an attempt to contradict Luther's position on justification by faith. On October 16 Luther conducted a disputation on Dan. 4:24 (*WA* 39I, 63 ff.). Luther was now collecting material on I Cor. 13 (*ibid.*, 77). He also was preparing a disputation on justification (conducted on January 14[?], 1536). See *ibid.*, 78 ff., 134 ff.; see also *WA*, Br 13, 237, addition to *WA*, Br 7, 317, n. 12; Drews, pp. 33 ff. Both disputations have to be viewed in connection with the English legation (announced by Barnes; see p. 106, n. 29), since esp. the retention of the private mass by the English Reformers was a major obstacle in the negotiations between the English and the Smalcaldic League.

[17] More accurately, "gardens." At the time that Luther wrote this letter he had

out to pasture, brews,[18] etc. In between she has started to read the Bible, and I have promised her fifty gulden[19] if she finishes before Easter. She is very serious[20] and is now starting the Book of Deuteronomy.

October 28, 1535 Yours,

MARTIN LUTHER

265

To Justus Jonas[1]
[Wittenberg,] November 10, 1535

Luther thanks Jonas for a hare and some birds, and reports on some of his daily activities and correspondence matters: he has written to Jonas about an as yet undecided affair of a procuress; he and Bugenhagen have had breakfast with the papal envoy, Pietro Paolo Vergerio, who had suddenly come to Wittenberg; the people of Frankfurt have written to him about the pressure which Albrecht of Mainz is putting on them to restore the celebration of the mass. In this connection Luther points out that he needs the help of his friends for all the problems he faces, and that it is a shame that the plague (which barely does any harm in the city) should keep his friends away. Luther also includes a letter from the pastor at Colditz and an "eloquent" writing by Hans von Dolzig. Then Luther mentions that the Elector has thus far had a good trip, and that there must be a mix-up regarding the persons who supposedly are accompanying the Elector on this trip. In conclusion Luther extends

---

to be considered a *Stadtbäuerlein*, i.e., a "farmer" who lived in the city and owned a little land in the immediate surroundings of the city. Luther owned several large gardens and meadows from which the Luthers derived some of their necessary supplies. For details, see *WA*, Br 12, 415 ff.; Köstlin-Kawerau 2, 490 ff.; Schwiebert, pp. 266 ff.

[18] See p. 81, n. 12.

[19] For the gulden, see *LW* 48, 11, n. 2.

[20] This sentence is written in German.

[1] The letter is extant in several manuscript copies, and in the common editions of Luther's works. Even though the address is missing in all witnesses, it is clear to whom Luther is writing this letter since he greets Jonas by name in the opening sentence.

*his wife's and his own greetings to the Jonas family, and mentions
the sale of linen which Jonas had offered.*
*On Justus Jonas, see LW 48, 275, n. 3, and above, pp. 93,
n. 3, 107, n. 1.*
Text in Latin: WA, Br 7, 321–322.

Grace and peace!

I thank you for the hare and the birds,[2] excellent Jonas. I have
much too much that I could write [about], but I am sluggish, and
affairs are too complicated for me to be able to write about them in
view of all the work I have to do. I have written about that procuress.[3] As yet I do not know what will happen to her, but I hope
that she will be evicted from town.

Suddenly, out of the blue,[4] the legate of the Roman pope
showed up also in this town.[5] Now he is with the Margrave.[6] This
man seems to fly rather than ride. How I wished that you had been
here! The legate invited me and Pomer[7] for breakfast, since I had

---

[2] It seems highly dubious that this sentence refers to the circumstances mentioned
in letter No. 260, as is suggested in WA, Br 7, 322, n. 1. Luther had had opportunities to thank Jonas if Jonas did bring the supplies for which Luther had
asked in that September 4 letter: Jonas had been in Wittenberg (see p. 93,
n. 3), and Luther had in the meantime written to Jonas at least twice (see also
note 3): WA, Br 7, Nos. 2262 (October 17) and 2267 (letter No. 264). It
seems far fetched to assume that Luther had previously forgotten to express his
appreciation for Jonas' help. It is more logical to assume that Jonas had sent
these supplies recently, perhaps as a (belated?) gift in honor of the 23rd anni-
versary of Luther's graduation as Doctor of Theology; Luther had informed
Jonas in a letter of October 17 that Katie was planning a banquet to celebrate the
occasion on October 18; see WA, Br 7, 301; LW 48, 5 ff.
[3] The text reads *lena*. Some witnesses (see Enders, *Briefwechsel* 10, 268, n. a.)
use an upper case "l" for this word, which would then designate a woman by the
name Lena or Magdalen. Was she a procuress? In any case, the background of
Luther's statement cannot be established beyond the fact that in a no-longer
extant letter Jonas had inquired about this matter, and that Luther had already
written to Jonas about the matter.
[4] The text reads *satis subito*.
[5] I.e., Pietro Paolo Vergerio, the papal nuncio (not legate, as Luther states). He
arrived in Wittenberg on November 6, and as guest of the Elector stayed in the
castle (see *ARG* 25 [1928], 59 f.). Luther and Bugenhagen had breakfast with
Vergerio on November 7. On this meeting, see WA, TR 5, Nos. 6384, 6388;
Jedin, p. 298 (where, incorrectly, November 13 is given as date of the Vergerio-
Luther meeting); *St. L.* 16, 1890 ff.; *NB* I.Abt. 1, 539 ff.; Köstlin-Kawerau 2,
371 ff.
[6] I.e., Joachim II of Brandenburg.
[7] John Bugenhagen; see *LW* 48, 303, n. 44.

refused an evening meal because of the bath.[8] I came and ate with him in the castle. But I am not permitted to write to anyone about what I said. During the whole meal I played the role of Luther himself;[9] I also acted as the representative of the Englishman Antony,[10] whom the papal legate had also invited,[11] [and I did so] in an extremely vexing way (as Anthony has written to you).[12] [More] about this in person.

The people of Frankfurt have written to me[13] and complained that they are pressured by the [Arch]bishop of Mainz[14] to restore masses and ceremonies. In all these matters I need you people[15] here. But I am forced to carry these burdens alone and answer by myself because of that plague (that is, the devil), which rejoices that it is able to keep us apart for such a long time through one or two funerals.[16] May God set free and protect his Word.

I am sending you the letter of Augustin,[17] the pastor at Col-

---

8 Or: "after the bath." The exact meaning of this phrase is not clear.

9 This is apparently a reference to the fact that on the one hand Luther stated to Vergerio that the evangelicals did not need a council since they have the true evangelical teaching, but that the papists needed a council in order to amend their ways. On the other hand Luther assured the nuncio that he would attend a council, regardless of where it met, and would defend his teachings. See Köstlin-Kawerau 2, 374.

10 Robert Barnes.

11 Vergerio was interested in meeting Barnes and in finding out any possible information about the moves made by the English to join the Smalcaldic League. For obvious reasons, Barnes refused to attend the breakfast, and made Luther his "legate," who was to convey his regrets.

12 The adjective connected with "way" is a Latin superlative of the German adjective *verdriesslich*, i.e., vexing, annoying, disgusting. But "vexing" for whom? Were Barnes's letter to Jonas extant, the sentence would be clear. At the present one may assume two possible answers: (a) The way in which Luther played the role of Barnes's representative annoyed Vergerio, because Luther was tight-lipped about Barnes's mission; Barnes knew of this, from Luther or Bugenhagen, and reported this to Jonas. (b) The way in which Luther played the role of Barnes's representative displeased or annoyed Barnes, who reported this to Jonas, and Luther found out about this in a way unknown to us.

13 See WA, Br 7, Nos. 2264 (the evangelical preachers of Frankfurt to Luther), 2266 (the Frankfurt city council to Luther and Melanchthon).

14 Albrecht of Mainz; see LW 48, 44 f.

15 I.e., Jonas, whose whereabouts at this moment cannot be established, and Melanchthon and other faculty members who had gone to Jena because of the plague (see p. 85).

16 See pp. 100, 108, n. 10; WA, Br 7, 283, n. 3.

17 On this pastor, Augustin Himmel, or Hymmel, who since 1516 had belonged to the circle of Luther's friends, and who since 1529 had been the pastor and superintendent at Colditz, near Leipzig, see WA, Br 1, 69, n. 25, and WA, Br

ditz, in which you can read about that turbulent sect of the Epicureans among those braggarts.[18] Nevertheless God is able to revenge himself, when he is despised. I am also sending the eloquent writing of [von] Dolzig.[19]

Concerning our Sovereign's[20] good trip up to Prague[21] you need not have any doubts. Philip[22] writes for the third time[23] already that Brück[24] is in Jena. Perhaps it is Bleycardus,[25] for he is with the Sovereign, and affairs and names have been mixed up: that is, previously Brück was ill, and Bleycardus went with the Sovereign, as if he were Brück.

My Katie greets you and your whole family. She continues

13, 7, addition to *loc. cit.* Nothing could be established about the background of the following statement.

[18] The text reads *thrasones*. Thraso is the name of a bragging soldier in Terence's comedy *The Eunuch*.

[19] On Hans von Dolzig, whose eloquence Luther recognized also in a letter written about the end of 1523, see *LW* 49, 69, n. 7. Nothing could be established about the background of this statement; perhaps one may assume that von Dolzig's writing had something to do with the information communicated in the following paragraph.

[20] Elector John Frederick; see *LW* 48, 181 f. According to one manuscript copy (see Enders, *Briefwechsel* 10, 268, n. i; *WA*, Br 13, 237, addition to *WA*, Br 7, 321) one has to translate: "I am also sending the eloquent writing of Dolzig concerning our Sovereign's good trip up to Prague. You need not have any doubts that Brück is in Jena. Philip writes this already for the third time; perhaps it is Bleycardus."

[21] On October 10 the Elector and a contingent of councilors and courtiers left Weimar for the court of King Ferdinand I in Vienna to settle dynastic matters. At the beginning of December the Elector returned to Weimar. See *WA*, Br 13, 238, additions to *WA*, Br 7, 328, n. 2, 343, n. 3; Ranke 2[IV], 45. According to *WA*, Br 7, 323, n. 11, the Elector arrived in Prague on October 30.

[22] On Philip Melanchthon, see *LW* 48, 77, n. 3, and above, p. 85.

[23] None of these letters is extant.

[24] On Gregory Brück, see *LW* 49, 51 f.

[25] Nothing can be established about the background of this statement beyond the fact that in a no-longer extant letter Jonas had made a statement to the effect that Brück was accompanying the Elector. Luther replies now that Brück is in Jena, and that Jonas' statement applies perhaps to "Bleycardus," who is indeed accompanying the Elector. "Bleycardus" could refer to a Swabian nobleman Bleikard von Sindringen, a member of Wittenberg's Law Faculty and one of the Elector's councilors. On Bleikard, see *WA*, Br 5, 139, n. 6; Friedensburg, *GUW*, pp. 206 f. De Wette (*Dr. Martin Luthers Briefe* 4 [Berlin, 1827], 649, n. 1) suggests that "Bleycardus" refers perhaps to Francis Burchart who, according to Melanchthon's November 5 letter (see *C.R.* 2, 964) to Veit Dietrich (see *LW* 49, 282, n. 13), had followed the Elector to Austria. This suggestion would fit Luther's next sentence: After Beyer, the chancellor, had become fatally ill and returned to Weimar, Burchart followed the Elector to take Beyer's place. Among Luther's friends it was assumed, however, that it was Brück, the

reading,[26] only the tragedy concerning that procuress[27] has robbed her of eight days. Concerning the sale of linen (which you offer), she answers that you can easily imagine what she would do in such a dangerous[28] situation, especially in view of such great, promising freedom to make up the reading, [or] fear to lose this opportunity.[29]

Kind greetings in Christ to your whole family!

November 10, 1535   Yours,

                                                    MARTIN LUTHER

266

To Philip Melanchthon
[Wittenberg, beginning of December, 1535][1]

Announcing the coming of Robert Barnes to Jena, Luther asks Melanchthon to prepare himself to receive an English legation, and to do so in a manner worthy of the ambassadors' dignity and Elector John Frederick's honor. Then Luther briefly mentions the threats made in Wittenberg by the papal envoy, Pietro Paolo Vergerio,

---

chancellor emeritus, who had become ill, but had recovered, and had then followed the Elector; in reality Brück was healthy and in Jena (see also *C.R.* 2, 961), and "Bleycardus," i.e., Burchart, had folowed the Elector.

[26] See p. 109.

[27] See note 3.

[28] I.e., tempting.

[29] I.e., of making up the lost reading time (and thus of getting the fifty gulden; see p. 109) instead of spending the time necessary to get the linen on her own.

[1] This letter is extant in one manuscript copy, and in the common editions of Luther's work. The date can be established on the basis of the following observations: On December 6 Melanchthon informed Luther that Barnes had arrived in Jena, but that he had not greeted Barnes since he had just this minute (i.e., late afternoon) returned from an investigatory hearing regarding some Anabaptists; WA, Br 7, 334. If one assumes that Melanchthon would probably have been eager to see Barnes at the earliest possible moment in order to find out how things were in Wittenberg, but was busy on December 6, one may suggest that Barnes arrived in Jena on December 5 in the evening, as is suggested in WA, Br 7, No. 2276, Introduction. If Barnes had left Wittenberg on December 4, or thereabouts, the present letter was then written shortly before Barnes's departure from Wittenberg, i.e., the beginning of December; the WA, Br editor suggests "about December 3" as the date for this letter.

against Henry VIII. In the remaining portions of the letter Luther deals with two topics: (a) Archbishop Albrecht of Mainz has taken away, and supposedly sold for a large sum of money, the crosier of the abbot of the monastery at Zinna and some of the sacred vessels of a church in Jüterbog. In this connection Luther muses on the greed of the cardinals, especially Albrecht. (b) The friends in Jena should not be deterred from returning to Wittenberg by rumors concerning the plague. In closing Luther extends greetings from his wife. In a humorous way he mentions that his wife is thinking of Melanchthon; he warns his friend not to make him jealous since then he would take revenge by thinking of Melanchthon's wife.

On Philip Melanchthon, see LW 48, 77, n. 3, and above, p. 85.

Text in Latin (with some words, sentences, or phrases in German): WA, Br 7, 330–331.

Mr. Philip Melanchthon, Master [of Arts],[2] a faithful
disciple of Christ, my dearest brother, who is
in Jena

Grace and peace in the Lord! Since Doctor Antony[3] himself comes, there was nothing for me to write about; from his report you will find out everything that goes on here. You see to it now that you be a companion and debator worthy of the two ambassadors,[4] and of the honor of their King[5] and our Sovereign.[6] I rejoice that Doctor

---

[2] Literally: "Mr. Master Philip Melanchthon."

[3] Robert Barnes. Barnes obviously went to Jena in order to meet the English legation which was expected to be in Jena or Weimar by December 6; see WA, Br 7, No. 2277, Introduction.

[4] I.e., Edward Fox, bishop of Hereford (see DNB 7, 553 ff.), and Nicholas Heath, archdeacon at Canterbury (see DNB 9, 345 f.), whose coming had been officially announced to Elector John Frederick by Barnes in September; see p. 106, n. 29. See further, note 5, and letter No. 267.

[5] Henry VIII. According to their highly detailed instructions (L.P. 9, No. 213), dated approximately September 30 (see Witt.Art., p. 3, n. 2), the ambassadors were to discuss doctrinal matters in order to enable all the evangelicals to act in unison at the upcoming council; further, they were to discuss the King's divorce, using this issue to illustrate the pope's craftiness; and finally, if the German Protestants would agree to the King's joining the Smalcaldic League, the ambassadors were to request the league's constitution for further study by the English government, and make further negotiations dependent upon a discussion in England between English scholars and a legation of the league.

[6] Elector John Frederick; see LW 48, 181 f. Prior to his departure for Vienna

Antony has been freed from his worries.[7] For I, too, started to have very grave thoughts, since the other ambassador[8] delayed so long. It is quite easy for someone who knows what kind of traitors, thiefs, robbers, and even devils the most reverend lord cardinals, popes, and their ambassadors are, to have second thoughts. I wish there would be more kings of England who would slay them.[9] For with these words the legate, Paolo Vergerio,[10] answered me here: "Yea! (I know) the King of England kills cardinals and bishops. But," etc. Then, gesturing with his hand and gnashing his teeth, he threatened that King with sufferings greater than the emperors ever had experienced before;[11] [he did this,] to be sure, not with open words but with lips pressed together. In the flesh, even in the heart, they are malicious people! May the Lord grant that you, too, can see this.

Priest Albrecht[12] at Halle has taken away the crosier of the abbot at Zinna, and the monstrance in Jüterbog, together with many other chalices; [he did this] out of such great devotion that he even replaced them with letters sealed by him.[13] They say that

---

(see p. 112, n. 21), the Elector had given detailed instructions concerning the reception of this legation; see *WA*, Br 7, No. 2249. While returning from Vienna, the Elector repeated some of these instructions. He also ordered Luther and Barnes to go to Jena for theological discussions with the English legation, and sent Francis Burchart ahead to meet the ambassadors. See *WA*, Br 7, No. 2277. To the best of our knowledge Luther did not go to Jena; we do not know why.

[7] According to *WA*, Br 7, 331, n. 2, Barnes, and also Luther (see the following sentences), were afraid that the sending of Fox and Heath would be sabotaged by enemies of the Reformation in England, since Fox's departure from England was delayed; see note 8.

[8] I.e., Fox, who because of illness did not leave England until approximately October 12; see *WA*, Br 7, 331, n. 2; see also Prüser, p. 20.

[9] I.e., "cardinals, popes, and their ambassadors." Does this statement have to be seen against the background of the execution of John Fisher, bishop of Rochester, who had been created a cardinal on May 20, 1535, and who had been executed for high treason June 22, 1535 (see *DNB* 7, 61 f.)?

[10] See pp. 110 f.

[11] This is perhaps a reference to the way in which some of the popes dealt with some of the emperors during the high Middle Ages.

[12] I.e., Cardinal Albrecht of Mainz (see *LW* 48, 44 f.), to whose ecclesiastical jurisdiction Halle and Jüterbog belonged, and who had a collegiate chapter in Halle; see also *LW* 48, 339 ff.; *LJB* 33 (1966), 9 ff. For details regarding the events, see the material cited in *WA*, Br 7, 331, n. 11, and in *WA*, Br 13, 238, addition to *loc. cit.*

[13] I.e., Albrecht issued a receipt for the items, thus making the transaction legal. "Out of such great devotion" could be either sarcastic, referring to Albrecht's zeal for acquiring precious things, or, serious, because Albrecht argued that he wished to protect these items from being taken over by the evangelicals.

that crosier of the abbot and the monstrance brought a large sum.[14] It is truly right that Albrecht became a cardinal since he, in his ingenuity, so successfully competes with all the cardinals, and soon will have outdone them if he is permitted to continue. For in this way they[15] have robbed all the churches in Rome and in Italy of altars, masses,[16] incomes, and treasury; yet nevertheless they strictly insist on the masses and the worship in the churches. If you believe Cicero, then you think that Verres or Dionysius really are something;[17] but now one most reverend cardinal of the holy catholic church not only has a hundred Verres and a thousand Dionysiuses in his heart, but also publicly and without any shame practices their ways in works for everyone to see. How do the sovereigns and lords tolerate this! And thus they vex us through crimes and the rape of churches.[18]

We expect your return,[19] and should a rumor reach you, then endure and overcome it. We hope that, even if there should be any future cases of contagious disease [around here], we will nevertheless have clean air (instead of this Scythian sky).[20] Were it the

---

[14] This rumor was false; according to the material presented in WA, Br 7, 331, n. 11, the items were not sold.

[15] I.e., the cardinals, or the papists in general. This sentence has to be viewed against the background of the absentee practice, in which clergy, esp. "higher" clergy, held a benefice and controlled its income, but did not reside in or take care of the benefice, but appointed a curate (who was only too often poorly paid) to fulfill the pastoral and liturgical tasks.

[16] I.e., the income derived from endowments given to a church by the faithful for the purpose of maintaining altars, or maintaining priests who would celebrate "ordered" masses. See LW 49, 28 ff.

[17] On Gaius Verres, "a notorious governor of Sicily," see O.C.D. p. 942. "In his governorship of Sicily (73–70) he showed, according to Cicero, a complete disregard of the rights both of the provincials and of Roman citizens." Ibid. Cicero prosecuted Verres for the restitution of a huge sum of money that he had supposedly extorted from the Sicilian people. In connection with this trial, Cicero composed his Verrine Orations, of which he delivered portions in court. When Luther says, "if you believe Cicero," then this suggests that Luther knew that just about all that is known about Verres has been transmitted through Cicero. In the Verrine Orations (ii. 5. 55. 143–144) Cicero also mentioned the jails built by the cruel tyrant Dionysius the Elder (see O.C.D., p. 287), and in the Tusculan Disputations (v. 20. 57–60) he described some of the actions of this tyrant. In WA, Br 11, 329, addition to WA, Br 7, 331, the references to Verres and Dionysius are interpreted as allusions to popular sayings.

[18] Literally: "through the crime of the violated churches."

[19] See p. 85.

[20] The time at which Luther wrote the present letter (the beginning of December) suggests that "Scythian sky" is to mean a dark, gloomy, rainy sky, which is

plague, it would need other symptoms. Everywhere on earth people are mortal; they are born and they die. We cannot all remain alive here on earth, otherwise we will not get yonder.

My lord [Katie] greets you reverently; she thinks more frequently of you. Take care not to provoke me to jealousy, since you, too, have a wife for my revenge. Farewell in the Lord; greet Doctor Caspar Cruciger[21] and all our friends, and pray for me!

Yours,

MARTIN LUTHER

267

To Elector John Frederick
[Wittenberg,] January 11, 1536

The English ambassadors,[1] who had arrived in Electoral Saxony at the end of November, 1535, attended the meeting of the Smalcaldic League which was in session in Smalcald in December of 1535, and which was addressed by Edward Fox. During this meeting the ambassadors had a conference with the Electoral Saxon chancellor emeritus, Gregory Brück, and presented to him a document of six articles; and the evangelicals, in turn, presented to the English 13 articles. Both documents[2] were to be the basis for further negotiations. In his address to one of the league's plenary sessions,[3] Fox underscored the necessity of common action on the part of all the evangelicals regarding the pending council, and of unity

---

not conducive to good health, but could contribute to the continuation of the plague. Luther means to say: In Wittenberg the air is clean, the sky is clear; at least we hope for this in view of the colder temperatures of winter which will replace the "Scythian" sky of the fall. Therefore whatever cases of contagious disease might occur in Wittenberg, they can have nothing to do with the plague, for a gray, rainy sky and the plague go together.

[21] See *LW* 49, 104, n. 12; he also was with the University in Jena. (See p. 85.)

[1] See p. 114, n. 3. For their instructions, see p. 114, n. 5. For their activities between November 25 and the end of December, see *Witt.Art.*, pp. 4 ff.; Prüser, pp. 20, 35 ff.; Tjernagel, pp. 153 ff.; Doernberg, *op. cit.* (see p. 27, n. 3), pp. 105 ff.

[2] *C.R.* 2, Nos. 1375, 1383; *L.P.* 9, No. 979.

[3] *C.R.* 2, No. 1382; *L.P.* 9, No. 1014.

among all who opposed the pope. The result of this meeting was that theological discussions (in which the matter of the King's marriage was to be of great importance) were to be conducted in Wittenberg. On January 1 the ambassadors arrived in Wittenberg, where they stayed until April as the Elector's guests.[4] *In Smalcald the English voiced their desire that Melanchthon be present at these discussions; Melanchthon excused himself, however, by citing the judgment regarding the matter of the King's marriage which he had given in 1531,*[5] *and his obligations to the University which, because of the plague, had been moved to Jena.*[6] *After the ambassadors had settled down in Wittenberg they approached Elector John Frederick and urged him to order Melanchthon to come to Wittenberg and attend the discussions. The Elector wrote to Luther for advice,*[7] *and letter No. 267 is Luther's reply.*

Luther underscores that he himself would be willing to bear the burden of these discussions without Melanchthon. Yet he encourages the Elector to send for Melanchthon, provided that Melanchthon wishes to attend the discussions. He gives three reasons for his stand: (a) to keep Melanchthon away from the discussions might be misinterpreted by the English as disrespect for them, and this could cause a bad reputation for the Elector; (b) according to a prior arrangement, Melanchthon was to attend the discussions; (c) to keep Melanchthon away from the discussions might do damage to Melanchthon's reputation. Then Luther informs the Elector that regarding the King's divorce he is curious to hear the ambassadors' arguments, but that he will not simply be talked into abandoning his opinion given in 1531.[8] *In conclusion Luther commends the Elector to God and thanks the Elector for a gift of venison.*

As a result of Luther's letter Melanchthon was called to Wittenberg,[9] *where he arrived sometime after January 17.*[10] *At the*

---

[4] See WA, Br 7, No. 2277, Introduction.
[5] See letter No. 245.
[6] See p. 85, and WA, Br 7, 340.
[7] WA, Br 7, No. 2282, dated January 9, 1536.
[8] Letter No. 245.
[9] The Elector's order could not be verified. Melanchthon felt that he was called to Wittenberg by Luther's letter (see C.R. 3, 26, 38), i.e., either the present letter to the Elector, or a no-longer extant letter directly addressed to Melanchthon (so argues Enders, *Briefwechsel* 10, 285, n. 1).
[10] Melanchthon left Jena on January 15 (see C.R. 3, 12), and on January 17

beginning of February he went back to Jena,[11] *and on February 13 he returned permanently to Wittenberg.*[12] *In February Heath made a short trip to Nürnberg.*[13] *Because of these travels, it was not until early March that serious theological discussions finally began,*[14] *the first two months of the year having been spent in occasionally heated discussions about the King's divorce and in academic disputations on certain theological subjects.*[15] *The ambassadors attended these disputations, though they did not participate in them actively or in great detail. Thus the discussions, which Luther had hoped could be finished quickly,*[16] *dragged on, and as early as January 25 Luther voiced his unhappiness about the whole matter.*[17]

On Elector John Frederick, see LW 48, 181 f.

Text in German: WA, Br 7, 342-343.[18]

To the Most Serene, Noble Sovereign and Lord,
Sir John Frederick, duke in Saxony, archmarshal
and elector of the Holy Roman Empire, landgrave
of Thuringia and margrave at Meissen, my Most
Gracious Lord

Grace and peace in Christ Jesus, and my poor *Pater noster!*[19] Most Serene, Noble Sovereign, Most Gracious Lord! I have obediently read[20] Your Electoral Grace's letter. First, regarding Master[21]

---

he was not yet in Wittenberg (see p. 124). Melanchthon's first extant letter from Wittenberg is dated January 19 (see *C.R.* 3, 17).

11 See *C.R.* 3, 35 ff.

12 See *C.R.* 3, 42.

13 See WA, Br 7, 360.

14 See *C.R.* 3, 45.

15 See *C.R.* 3, Nos. 1394, 1396, 1397. Especially at issue was the private mass; see *C.R.* 3, 12.

16 See WA, Br 7, 353 f.; 12, 197 f. This January 25 letter to the Elector is the only one extant in Luther's correspondence in which the negotiations between England and the Smalcaldic League are mentioned which has not been included in the present volume. The reasons for this elimination were considerations of space and the fact that in this letter Luther deals at length with other matters.

17 See letter No. 270, and the letter mentioned in note 16.

18 This letter is extant as autograph.

19 See p. 69, n. 4.

20 Luther wrote *verstanden*, i.e., literally, "understood" or "comprehended."

21 I.e., here and throughout the letter, Master of Arts.

Philip,[22] whether he is to be ordered by Your Electoral Grace to come [to Wittenberg] in order to assist us in the discussions of the King's matter[23] with the English legation: it is my humble judgment in this matter that Master Philip should also be present (provided that he himself does not wish to avoid getting entangled in this matter); for prior to the trip to Austria[24] Your Electoral Grace had written to Doctor Antony[25] that he should call us theologians together as soon as the other legation[26] arrived, either here or (should the other ambassador[27] be afraid of the plague)[28] at Torgau.[29]

Your Electoral Grace informs me that at Smalcald the ambassadors received favorably Master Philip's opinion;[30] yet I do not know how this happened, and whether the ambassadors are content [with this opinion. Therefore] I refer this issue back to Your Electoral Grace for consideration. For I would not like to see them cause us a bad reputation, as if they had been despised, since even without this, the constellation of the stars is so negative[31] for them that even I am compelled to wonder,[32] and in reality there is no limit to the praise and commendation of the honorable way in which Your Electoral Grace has treated the ambassadors until now,[33] etc.

---

[22] Philip Melanchthon; see *LW* 48, 77, n. 3.

[23] I.e., in a narrow sense the divorce and second marriage of Henry VIII, in a wider sense the King's eagerness to enter an alliance with the German Protestants.

[24] See p. 112, n. 21.

[25] Robert Barnes. This is a reference to a no-longer extant letter of the Elector written to Barnes at the time of Barnes's audience with the Elector at the end of September; see p. 106, n. 29. Brück mentioned this letter on September 27; see *C.R.* 2, 968, where according to *WA*, Br 7, 282 an incorrect date is given.

[26] I.e., Fox and Heath.

[27] Fox.

[28] See p. 85.

[29] Grammatically, the last portion of the sentence could refer either to "call us theologians together," or to "other legation would arrive." In a letter written by the Elector to the Wittenberg theologians at the same time that the letter to Barnes, mentioned in note 25, was written, statements are made that suggest that the theologians should come together when the "other legation" had arrived at Wittenberg. See *WA*, Br 7, 284.

[30] See Introduction.

[31] Literally: "childish [or: foolish, stupid]."

[32] What Luther wanted to say in this portion of the sentence is not clear. Perhaps Luther's statements have to be seen in the light of the phrase "Scythian sky" used on p. 116.

[33] Luther was correct in this statement. On the care the Elector showed for the

Of course, so far as I am concerned, I certainly do not begrudge Master Philip the opportunity to be spared this matter, since it looks as if I have to empty[34] this bathtub by myself. Regardless of whether I am alone [in doing this], or whether everyone else is with me, yet (I think) a large portion [of the work] certainly will rest on me. But I would not like to have Master Philip's reputation left unconsidered in this matter.

Second, I thank Your Electoral Grace with my whole heart that Your Electoral Grace so faithfully exhorts me to deal carefully with the matter,[35] etc. But since the ambassadors base themselves on Your Electoral Grace's letter regarding our own previously made offer,[36] I have to see and hear what they produce. For (to speak confidentially and in secret) Your Electoral Grace will certainly find out that I shall not let myself be talked into[37] publicly condemning the Queen and the young Queen,[38] together with the whole kingdom, as being incestuous, as they brag that the Pope and eleven universities have already done.[39] I will not get mixed up with their incest business,[40] even if I could do nothing more in this matter than say "gawk" like a goose. But I maintain that my former judgment is to stand; besides this I shall not be unfriendly toward the

---

English ambassadors, see, e.g., WA, Br 7, 333, 355. Apparently the ambassadors felt somewhat embarrassed for, as Luther reported to the Elector on January 25, 1536 (see note 16), they wanted to pay their own way; WA, Br 7, 354.

[34] Literally: "since nevertheless [or: of course] I am in the suspicion [that] I have to empty."

[35] See the postscript to the Elector's January 9 letter to Luther; WA, Br 7, 341. On the basis of this postscript, and Luther's following sentences, it is clear that "matter" refers to the King's divorce and second marriage.

[36] This correspondence between Luther and the Elector, and the Elector and the English (Barnes?) could not be verified.

[37] Literally: "Find out that I shall not myself be put in such conscience [or: frame of mind] that the Queen . . . should be publicly condemned as."

[38] Catherine of Aragon and Mary Tudor.

[39] Pope Julius II, by granting a dispensation for Catherine to marry Henry (see p. 32, n. 35), confirmed that without such dispensation the marriage would have been illegal. And by approving the annulment of Henry's marriage to Catherine, the universities (see p. 27) confirmed the argument that in this marriage the King had committed incest.

[40] Luther wrote *mich . . . vertiefen*, i.e. literally, "to sink myself deeply into." Luther seems to say that he does not intend to discuss the argument that the King's marriage had to be annulled because the marriage was an incestuous one. Regarding the incest argument, he, Luther, intends to hold on to the position set forth in letter No. 245.

ambassadors regarding one or the other issue,[41] so that they do not think that we Germans are made of stone and wood, etc. I will not discuss my opinions casually,[42] just as the English, too, are not committing themselves,[43] etc. Otherwise all the stable hands[44] would first have to justify this matter all over town.

May Your Electoral Grace graciously receive this letter as my humble answer. With this be commended to God—and also my humble thanks to Your Electoral Grace for the presented venison, etc.

January 11, 1536   Your Electoral Grace's dedicated
MARTIN LUTHER, DOCTOR

268

To Nicholas Hausmann
[Wittenberg,] January 17, 1536

Luther asks Hausmann not to pay any attention to the protests made by Master Peter regarding the marriage of the Master's widowed daughter. Then Luther informs Hausmann that at the moment he knows of no vacant parish for the pastor at Wörlitz, that in Wittenberg there is nothing new except what Hausmann has heard from Francis Burchart, and that the English legation in Wittenberg is awaiting the arrival of Melanchthon. Luther closes by extending his wife's greetings, and by assuring Hausmann that he would write

---

[41] I.e., a detail in the argument in favor of the divorce.
[42] Literally: "Such things [or: words] I do not talk over the table."
[43] Literally: "just as they too are stopping [i.e., are holding on to their argument] up to the final decisive moment."
[44] Literally: "stable boys." According to WA, Br 7, 343, n. 27, Luther used this term here and at other places in a contemptuous way, meaning something like "street punks." In these last sentences Luther meant to say: Regarding the King's divorce I am ready to listen to the ambassadors, but I shall not let my arm be twisted to agree with their argument that the divorce was necessary to stop incest on the King's part. On this point I shall maintain my position set forth in 1531, even though I shall be flexible regarding other arguments. Right now the English are not ready to give up their position either. So, the matter has to be discussed further among us scholars. Were it otherwise, the decision on the divorce issue would have to be made by the rabble.

shortly about Spiegel and the personal matter about which Hausmann had asked him.
On Nicholas Hausmann, see LW 48, 399 f.
Text in Latin: WA, Br 7, 347.[1]

To the excellent and venerable Mr. Nicholas Hausmann,
Master [of Arts],[2] a minister of the gospel in Dessau,
my elder[3] in the Lord

Grace and peace in Christ! I ask you, my Hausmann, to let the marriage of the daughter of Master Peter take its course.[4] For Master Peter has no authority over her, since she, as a widow, has been taken out of her father's jurisdiction and been independent for a long time. Master Peter has even been deprived of his house and all possessions by means of a public judgment. She marries at her own risk. It is enough that Master Peter has had such a sad experience with the former son-in-law; now he should not concern himself with this [new son-in-law], but take care of his own affairs.

At this point I know of no vacancy for the pastor at Wörlitz ([I say this] not to make empty promises).[5] Should I be in a position to help him, however, I shall be delighted to do so if there is a vacancy somewhere.

I have no news except what you no doubt have heard there

---

[1] The letter is extant as autograph.
[2] Literally: "Venerable man, Mr. Master Nicholas Hausmann, a minister."
[3] Or: "superior."
[4] According to WA, Br 7, 347, n. 2, the background of this first paragraph is as follows: Luther's barber and friend of many years (see WA, Br 1, 106, n. 8; 1517), Master Craftsman Peter Beskendorf, had a married daughter, Anne. On March 27, 1535, perhaps while drunk, Peter killed his son-in-law, for which he was banned from Electoral Saxony. His sentence was not more severe because Luther and Melanchthon pleaded for Peter, with Luther arguing that Peter was possessed by the devil when he committed the crime. Peter, stripped of home, property, and fatherland, moved to Dessau in the territory of Anhalt. His daughter apparently also moved to Dessau where she intended to remarry. Peter protested this second marriage on grounds unknown to us, and either Anne or Peter appealed to Hausmann for help, and he, in turn, consulted with Luther. Anne remarried in the fall of 1536, and Peter apparently died sometime in the second half of 1538. See also WA, Br 13, 239, addition to WA, Br 7, 347, n. 2.
[5] Literally: "That I do not nurse him in vain". On this pastor of Wörlitz, near Dessau, who was searching for another parish because he was quarreling with the lord of his parish, see WA, Br 7, 348, n. 3, 373 f.

from Master[6] Francis.[7] The English legation here is still awaiting Master[8] Philip[9], so that they may unfold[10] the matter of the King of England.[11] Yet I, who am afflicted with many things, continuously grow less able to handle one single thing. My Katie greets you reverently. Farewell in Christ! Regarding Spiegel and your own matter,[12] I shall write shortly in detail. Again, farewell!

January 17, 1536　　　　　Yours,

MARTIN LUTHER, DOCTOR

269

To Caspar Müller
[Wittenberg,] January 19, 1536

Throughout the letter[1] Luther complains, in a serious yet humorous way, about a severe cough and cold, and about his advancing age. In addition the letter is filled with details about Luther's day-by-day life. At the moment Luther cannot accept a student as boarder; there is nothing new to write about the English legation which is in Wittenberg; the issue of the divorce of Henry VIII has been settled by the death of Catherine of Aragon; it was only right that the pope was disavowed in England in connection with this marriage issue, since he played games in this serious matter; the papal envoy, Pietro Paolo Vergerio, has been at Wittenberg and at the Smalcald meeting of the Smalcaldic League. Luther also voices his skepticism

---

[6] I.e., Master of Arts.
[7] Francis Burchart, who for reasons unknown had been in Dessau. Luther assumes that Hausmann has met Burchart. In view of the following sentence it seems safe to suggest that the "news" Hausmann was to have heard from Burchart had to do with events pertaining to the English ambassadors.
[8] See note 6.
[9] See p. 118.
[10] Or: "promote."
[11] After Melanchthon's arrival in Wittenberg, the issues pertaining to the divorce and remarriage of Henry VIII were discussed; see *C.R.* 3, 37, dated February 6, 1536.
[12] The background of this statement is unclear. For a possible identification of Spiegel, see *WA*, Br 7, 348, n. 8; 9, 14 f.
[1] See note 8.

about some development in the Mansfeld smelting business and his disappointment that none of the people of Mansfeld, including his brother James, has informed him of this development. He tells Müller that he has to go to Torgau, and adds that his wife and his son, John, send greetings. In closing he expresses the hope that Müller will accept the letter in good humor, as Luther intends it.

On Caspar Müller, see LW 49, 341, n. 26.[2]

Text in German (with a few words in Latin): WA, Br 7, 348–350.[3]

To the honorable and wise Caspar Müller, chancellor at Mansfeld, my kind lord[4] and dear friend[5]

Grace and peace! My dear Mr. Chancellor and Friend![6] I certainly would like to write Your Honor[7] many things and thus comply with Your Honor's request. But I, too,[8] am sick with a cough and catarrh. Yet the most serious illness begins with me; that is, the sun has shone on me for such a long time,[9] a vexation which, as you well know, is common, and certainly many people die of it.[10] For people

---

[2] See also Enders, *Briefwechsel* 17, 178, n. 2. It must be pointed out that notwithstanding Müller's position, Luther and he were close friends (see note 45; Luther dedicated his *Open Letter on the Harsh Book Against the Peasants* to Müller [WA 18, 384 ff.; LW 46, 63 ff.]) and wrote to him as an equal, someone from home; see the present letter, and WA, Br 7, No. 2185, dated March 18, 1535.

[3] The letter is extant in one manuscript copy, and in the common editions of Luther's works.

[4] Literally: "My lord, who favors [me]."

[5] The text reads *Gevattern*; see note 45, and LW 48, 201, n. 2.

[6] See note 5.

[7] Throughout the letter, when addressing Müller, Luther used only the personal pronoun with an uppercase first letter. This practice could simply be in conformity with custom, but it could also designate an attempt to convey an honor to the addressee, so that one could translate "Your Honor."

[8] Luther's letter is an answer to a no-longer extant letter from Müller in which Müller informed Luther of his illness (see note 13), apparently complained about Luther's silence, and asked for a letter.

[9] I.e., I have seen the sun shining for a long time, or I have grown old and weary.

[10] This editor is unable to accept the interpretation given to this sentence by the WA, Br editor (7, 350, n. 1), namely, that Luther is stating ironically that winter lasts too long. Whether Luther is speaking ironically may be debated; the text does not make this clear. Further, this interpretation could be accepted only if in the text the portion translated as "the sun has shone on me for such a long time" were negated, which it is not. In view of the context it is farfetched to contend

finally become blind from such prolonged sunshine,[11] some turn grey, black, and wrinkled from it.[12] Who knows whether Your Honor[13] didn't step on a stone which, heated by the rays of the sun,[14] caused Your Honor such days of pain? Of course, it is not the dear sun's fault that by its shining mud becomes hard and wax becomes soft.[15] Everything has a unique nature which develops and reveals itself; in the final analysis, a thing develops in accord with its basic nature.

For several reasons I would have liked to have Kegel[16] as a boarder;[17] but since the students are returning from Jena[18] my table is filled, and I cannot simply oust the old companions.[19] If a place becomes vacant, however, as might happen after Easter, I would be happy to inform Your Honor accordingly, provided that lord Katie will then be gracious to me.

Concerning the English legation[20] (how nosy you gentlemen of Mansfeld are!) I know of nothing special to write. For the Queen

---

that it is exactly this lack of a negation which gives the sentence an ironic quality. Finally, the last clause of the sentence ("and certainly many people . . . ") is not clear beyond doubt; and this observation, overlooked by the WA, Br editor, is significant. In this last clause Luther says that *fast viel* die of this common vexation. Luther uses *fast* (which has been translated quite freely as "certainly") in an affirmative, enlarging sense, and only very seldom in a limiting sense ("almost"); see Dietz, *s.v.* Fast. Luther would speak ironically only if *fast* would have to be understood in this limiting way, so that one would have to paraphrase: This vexation (i.e., according to the WA, Br editor, the fact that winter lasts so long) is common, and yet few people die of it. Still, the sentence would be most awkward, esp. in view of Luther's statement in the following sentence, and the sentence is too unclear to justify the departure from Luther's common usage of *fast*. Finally, in view of note 44 it seems natural to adopt the interpretation mentioned in note 9.
11 Or: "From such a long lasting light." I.e., with old age blindness can develop.
12 I.e., too much exposure to the sun makes the skin look old; or, with advancing years the skin wrinkles.
13 Literally: "Your thigh." Apparently Müller had informed Luther (see note 8) of some pain in his thigh (sciatica?).
14 Literally: "brightness of the sun."
15 According to Enders, *Briefwechsel* 10, 290, n. 1, Luther took this observation, used several times by him (see WA, Br 13, 239, addition to WA, Br 7, 350, n. 3), from the writings of Theodoret (*ca.* 393–458) who was a bishop at Cyrrhus in Syria (see *O.D.C.C.*, p. 1341); see Migne, *Patrologiae cursus completus. Series Graeca* 80, 237B.
16 For a possible identification of this otherwise unknown student from Mansfeld, see Enders, *Briefwechsel* 10, 290, n. 2.
17 See also Köstlin-Kawerau 2, 486 f.
18 See p. 108, n. 11.
19 Literally: "companions in such a way." One has to add a phrase to the effect: "companions [in order to make room for Kegel]."
20 See letter No. 267, Introduction.

is dead;[21] it is also said that the child, her daughter is deathly ill.[22] In the eyes of the whole world she[23] has lost her case;[24] we poor beggars, the theologians at Wittenberg, are the only exceptions who would like to maintain her in royal honor, where she should have stayed. This has been the end and solution [of this matter].[25]

In this case the Pope has acted like a real pope, and has issued contradictory bulls.[26] He has played such a game that it served him right to be ousted from England—and not even for the sake of the gospel. He has played his game[27] well against the King, so that I am forced to stand up for the King, and yet I am unable to approve of the matter.[28] For goodness sake,[29] pray[30] the *Pater noster*[31] at least once against the papacy, that St. Valentine may grab it by the neck![32]

The Pope's orator has been here,[33] as Your Honor knows. But in my present haste I am unable to send [a copy of] the answer

---

21 Queen Catherine of Aragon had died on January 7, 1536; see *DNB* 3, 1211. Luther's source for this statement, as well as for the next, could not be established.
22 It could not be established whether this rumor concerning Mary Tudor was based on fact. Since the annulment of Catherine's marriage, she and her daughter had been "banned" from court, and this disappearance could easily have caused the assumption that Mary also was deathly ill. In the summer of 1534 Mary had indeed been seriously ill (see *DNB* 12, 1221).
23 I.e., Catherine of Aragon.
24 I.e., the claim to have been legitimately married to Henry VIII.
25 See also letter No. 245. Luther's statement could suggest that the matter has been ended by Catherine's death, or that at the time he wrote the present letter, i.e., January 19, the discussions between himself and the English on this matter were deadlocked in view of his conviction that Catherine's marriage should never have been annulled in the first place.
26 On the unclear position of Pope Clement VII regarding Henry's petition for annulment of his marriage to Catherine of Aragon, see the materials cited on p. 27, n. 3, and *WA*, Br 7, 350, n. 13.
27 Literally: "He has thrown the King well." For "thrown" the text uses technical term for throwing dice.
28 I.e., the divorce.
29 The text reads *Lieber* in the sense of "lieber Mensch." See also *LW* 48, 249, n. 4; *American Historical Review*, 69 (1963/64), 1137.
30 Literally: "curse."
31 See p. 69, n. 4.
32 Literally: "That St. Valentine get it [i.e., the papacy]." Or: "That it [i.e., the papacy] get [i.e., get sick with] St. Valentine." St. Valentine was supposed to protect one against epilepsy. Calling on certain saints by way of a curse (see note 30) turns their protective activity into a harassing activity; see Enders, *Briefwechsel* 10, 291, n. 9. Luther intends to say that one should pray against the papacy so that the papacy might fall down as an epileptic does. See also *WA*, TR 3, No. 3028; *WA*, Br 7, 246.
33 See pp. 110 f. "Orator" is one of the technical terms for envoy.

given him at Smalcald,[34] for I am having a coughing spell, and because of this cough I am unable to search for the copy; as soon as the cough stops I will look for it. I think that the cough certainly would stop if Your Honor would pray for me.

Since Your Honor received a part of the smelting houses, I wish you well.[35] But I have no hope at all, for my theology tells me that man's planning and God's blessings are against one another.[36] If this is to happen to my dear fatherland, I will not stand in the way. But you people are really fine fellows, since neither Your Honor nor James Luther nor the Kaufmanns[37] wrote how they fared in this matter. With your silence you are causing us poor children (who live here) to think that all of you together have become beggars. Yet God will nevertheless still feed us. Amen.

Tell my brother[38] that my cough and his silence kept me from answering him! Give my greetings to his black hen, together with the chicks.[39] I have to cough [now], and yet I have to think of

---

[34] While in Wittenberg, Vergerio wrote to Elector John Frederick that he intended to meet with the Elector while the latter was returning from Vienna (see p. 112, n. 21), and that at the court of Duke George in Dresden he would be waiting to receive news about the Elector's return route. See *St. L.* 16, 1892. Then Vergerio went to the court of the Margrave of Brandenburg in Berlin, and to Dresden, and from here he hurried to Prague in order to meet the Elector. The Elector returned to Prague and met with Vergerio on November 30 (*St. L.* 16, 1893 ff.), but refused to commit himself regarding the pending council without consulting with his allies in the Smalcaldic League. Vergerio then returned with the Electoral party to Weimar, and then attended the December meeting of the league in Smalcald. On December 21 the league turned over to Vergerio a document drafted by Melanchthon (*C.R.* 2, No. 1379)—the "answer" mentioned by Luther in the text above—in which the league flatly rejected any council which would be convened outside of Germany, and could thus easily be dominated by the pope, even though the league affirmed its readiness to attend a "free" council. *St. L.* 16, 1904 ff.
[35] For the mining business in the county of Mansfeld, see Schwiebert, pp. 106 f.; for the background of this paragraph, see *WA*, Br 12, 364.
[36] I.e., Luther has little hope that the division of the Mansfeld mining business, until now jointly owned by the counts of Mansfeld and leased to citizens for operating, would bring an end to the tension existing between the counts (see also pp. 281 f.).
[37] I.e., Luther's nephews in Mansfeld, or relatives of these nephews; see *LW* 49, 269. On James Luther, see *LW* 49, 268, n. 4.
[38] I.e., James Luther; see note 37.
[39] I.e., James Luther's family. On this family (by which the Luther name was preserved down to the early 1900's), see O. Sartorius, *Die Nachkommenschaft D. Martin Luthers in vier Jahrhunderten* (Göttingen, 1926), A 4 ff. No material could be found to clarify "black hen" as an allusion to James Luther's (apparently unknown) wife.

Shrove Tuesday[40] at Torgau; I don't know what I am to cough there.[41] Maybe I will have to keep company with John of Jena.[42]

My lord Katie sends cordial greetings to Your Honor and asks that, if it is in Your Honor's power, Your Honor not let the sun shine upon Your Honor more[43] than upon me, even if the sun intends to shine on me too much.[44]

Your godchild, Master John,[45] greets you. He is set on really growing up (not growing to be a bad boy); may God grant it! With this be commended to God!

Accept my ways (as Your Honor knows them); for I am quite rough and coarse, big, grey, green, overburdened with, excessively mixed up in, and overtaken by [all kinds of] affairs, so that some-

---

[40] I.e., February 29, 1536.

[41] I.e., speak or do in Torgau. On February 27, 1536, Luther was in Torgau in order to preform the marriage ceremony for a member of the Electoral family. See Buchwald, *LK*, p. 105; *WA*, 41, xxxi.

[42] The expression "Hans von Jena," used quite often by Luther (see *WA*, Br 5, 522, n. 2), designates anyone who is extremely curious or bored, or always yawning, or has lots of time to look around, and stand around gaping. The saying is derived from a fool's head, carved in wood and fixed above the clock of the city hall in Jena. Each time that the clock strikes the fool opens his mouth and tries unsuccessfully to catch a golden ball (apple?) which is brought before him at the tip of a staff held in the hand of a pilgrim. Luther seems to be saying that he will be only a spectator at the festivities scheduled in Torgau for Shrove Tuesday, or some days prior, and a bored one at that.

[43] Literally: "not let the sun shine too much upon Your Honor and earlier than upon me."

[44] The *WA*, Br editor (7, 350, n. 26) interprets the second portion of the sentence ("and asks that . . . ") to mean that Luther's wife asks Müller not to be jealous, or greedy, and snap away from Luther the warmth of the sun. This interpretation is extremely awkward; one has to ask what the sentence is supposed to mean, esp. since the idea of greed is forced on the sentence, which in literal translation is quite clear. Further, this interpretation does not do justice to the sentence for it overlooks the clause translated as: "even if the sun intends to shine on me too much." And finally, this interpretation is the direct result of the *WA*, Br editor's interpretation of the second portion of the third sentence of the letter; see note 10. The present translation is as literal as possible. Paraphrased, Luther says: Katie asks Müller, if Müller can manage it, not to get too much sun or to do so earlier than Luther gets the sun, even though the sun intends to shine too much on Luther. Adopting the suggestions made in notes 9 and 10 that the statement about the long shining of the sun is a different way of saying "to grow old," then it is clear that Luther meant to say that his wife requests Müller not to grow old and weary before Luther does, even though old age is doing a "good" job on Luther anyhow. In the last paragraph Luther takes up this idea again when he bemoans his present condition and contends that, just in order to survive, he now and then has to force a joke, such as the present letter.

[45] Müller was one of the godfathers of John Luther; see *LW* 49, 152, n. 7; *WA*, Br 4, No. 1013.

times, in order to preserve myself,[46] I have to force myself to make a joke.[47] Of course, a man is not more than a man, even if God can make out of a man what he wishes—yet we have to do our part too.[48] Greet all good gentlemen and friends!

January 19, 1536   Doctor Martin Luther

270

To Francis Burchart

[Wittenberg,] January 25, 1536

Luther informs Burchart of the receipt of a present of wine, and congratulates him on his appointment as vice-chancellor. Then Luther mentions that he is debating, or rather wrangling, with the Englishmen, that he is bothered by the expenses which the visit of the Englishmen causes for the Elector, and that he is tired of these useless talks. Finally, Luther announces the date of an upcoming disputation on private mass, and encourages Burchart to come to Wittenberg for this disputation.

On Francis Burchart, see p. 80, n. 10.

Text in Latin: WA, Br 7, 352.[1]

Grace and peace from the Lord!

The wine about which you write has been sent and given to me as a present,[2] about six buckets,[3] my Francis. I congratulate you on

---

[46] Literally: "in order to rescue the poor corpse."

[47] Literally: "have to break a little pleasure off a fence," i.e., as one breaks a piece of wood from a fence. Luther uses a popular saying here (see also WA, 51, 646, No. 32, 668, No. 32) which speaks of dragging someone in by the head and shoulders or forcing an issue. He meant to say that he has to joke about his condition (as he has done in the letter by using the sun-image) in order to maintain his well-being.

[48] Literally: "wishes, yet not without our salve," i.e., the salve of making light of one's condition.

[1] The letter is extant in one manuscript copy, and in the common editions of Luther's works.

[2] According to Luther's January 25 letter to Elector John Frederick, the wine (a

your success, and the new honor or occupation,[4] and I am asking the Lord[5] Christ to multiply and preserve this, your success, with all blessings. Amen.

Here we are debating with the Englishmen,[6] if debating is wrangling. I am bothered by the fact that our Sovereign[7] is burdened with such great expenses. I certainly am sick and tired;[8] already in the cases of Karlstadt and Zwingli I started to hate such useless talks by which, as Paul says,[9] the hearts are hidden[10] so that you lose all that you have learned and become a fool. "They have become fools"[11] (he says)[12] "while they want to be wise." But more about this[13] in person.

The disputation on private mass will take place this coming Saturday,[14] God willing, and the sum of it is contained in this syllogism:[15] Every human cultic action[16] in divine matters is an abomination; every private mass is of this kind; therefore every private mass is an abomination.

Farewell in the Lord, and come if you are able.[17]

January 25, 1536   Yours,

                                                  MARTIN LUTHER

---

barrel containing six buckets) was a present from the Elector. In the same letter Luther thanked the Elector also for a boar. See WA, Br 7, 353; 12, 197.
[3] The text reads 6 *Eimer*, i.e., buckets; an *Eimer* holds approximately 70 to 75 liters.
[4] Burchart was appointed vice-chancellor in early 1536.
[5] Literally: "God."
[6] "Debating" refers to the discussions which Luther had with the English ambassadors on the King's divorce, since the ambassadors did not actively participate in the January 14 disputation on justification (see p. 108, n. 16), or in another disputation which was conducted about January 21 (see Drews, pp. 34 f.); at least nothing is mentioned in the records.
[7] Elector John Frederick; Luther made a similar statement in the letter cited in note 2. For the Elector's expenses, see ARG 25 (1928), 60 f.
[8] I.e., either of the discussions, or of the Englishmen. Literally: "I certainly am satiated to [the point of] nausea."
[9] See Rom. 1:21.
[10] Or: "the minds are darkened."
[11] The text uses a Greek word.
[12] Rom. 1:22.
[13] Literally: "these [i.e., discussions or ambassadors]."
[14] January 29. See also note 6.
[15] See Thesis 3 of this disputation; WA 39^I, 138.
[16] The text reads *cultus humanus*.
[17] Burchart did come from Weimar to Wittenberg and participated actively in the disputation; see WA 39^I, 137.

271

To Elector John Frederick
[Wittenberg,] March 28, 1536

Luther informs the Elector that Francis Burchart will present to him a German translation of the articles which are the result of the discussions held between the English legation and the Wittenberg theologians.[1] Luther endorses the articles and approves of proceeding with the negotiations to establish an alliance between the Smalcaldic League and the King of England, provided that the King accepts the articles and makes no efforts to change them. Luther also tells his Sovereign that, compared with the articles, the King's divorce is of minor importance. Then Luther chastises his old foe, Duke George, for his latest effort to harass the evangelicals in the Duchy of Saxony. In an enclosed note Luther, in behalf of his colleague, Caspar Cruciger, asks the Elector to make available the castle at Eilenburg for Cruciger's wedding, since this wedding could not take place in Leipzig or Wittenberg.

On Elector John Frederick, see LW 48, 181 f.

Text in German: WA, Br 7, 383–384.[2]

To the Most Serene, Noble Sovereign and Lord,
Sir John Frederick, duke in Saxony and elector,
etc., landgrave in Thuringia and margrave in
Meissen, my Most Gracious Lord

Grace and peace in Christ Jesus, our Lord, together with my humble prayer![3] Most Serene, Noble Sovereign, Most Gracious Lord! From Master[4] Francis, the vice-chancellor,[5] we have humbly received Your Electoral Grace's order concerning the English, etc.[6] Said Master Francis will turn over [to Your Electoral Grace] the

---

[1] See pp. 117 ff.
[2] The letter is extant as autograph.
[3] See also p. 69, n. 4.
[4] I.e., Master of Arts.
[5] Francis Burchart.
[6] The background of this statement could not be established.

articles, all of them translated into German,[7] from which Your Electoral Grace will see how far we have progressed with the English by this time.[8] Since they do not know, however, how their Lord King[9] will react to these articles, especially to the last four,[10] they have taken a recess in order to inform His Royal Majesty accordingly. If His Royal Majesty should accept these articles,[11] then one may proceed to form the alliance.[12] For these articles are certainly

---

[7] Or: "Grace] all articles translated into German." The document which Melanchthon, in consultation with his Wittenberg colleagues, and Fox, Heath, and Barnes, had drafted, are the *Wittenberg Articles* of 1536. Text: *Witt.Art.*, pp. 18 ff.; for an English translation, see Tjernagel, pp. 255 ff. The textual history of these articles is not clear. On the basis of Luther's statement, as it has been translated above, one may assume that this document was written in Latin, that in order to keep the Elector and his staff informed a (preliminary) German version was produced at a time when the discussions and all the articles had not yet been completed, and that now, on March 28, a (final) German version of *all* articles was being sent to the Elector. On the basis of the alternate translation suggested at the beginning of this note one may assume that only one final German version of all articles had ever reached the Elector (because it was now, on March 28, being sent to him), and that those sections in the articles which are now different in the Latin text were drafted after this German version had been dispatched to the Elector on March 28. See also note 10; *C.R.* 3, No. 1409, and *WA*, Br 13, 240, addition to *WA*, Br 7, 382, Introduction.
[8] Or: "have progressed with the English here [i.e., in Wittenberg]."
[9] I.e., here and throughout the letter, Henry VIII. It could not be established whether at the time that Luther wrote this letter the articles had already been dispatched to England, or whether the English ambassadors took the articles along to England when they left Wittenberg after the discussions were recessed.
[10] This is a reference to the last four articles of the *Wittenberg Articles* (see note 7) as they are extant in the Latin version of the articles. They deal with the Lord's Supper as mass (Art. XII), with the giving of bread and wine to the communicants (Art. XIII), priestly celibacy (Art. XIV), and monastic vows (Art. XV). As late as March 20 Elector John Frederick wrote to Landgrave Philip of Hesse (see *Witt.Art.*, p. 8) that the Wittenberg theologians had little hope that agreement on these articles could be reached. By March 28, the date of the present letter, agreement, though tentative, was reached even on these issues. On March 28 the discussions were not yet completed however; see the *C.R.* reference cited in note 7, and the facts that in the extant German version material can be found which is missing in the Latin version, and that the ambassadors continued to stay in Wittenberg for almost two more weeks. One has to assume, then, that the final Latin text of the *Wittenberg Articles*, which has to be considered the "official text," and which shows significant differences from the German text inasmuch as it is less precisely formulated, was established after the German translation made from an earlier Latin draft had been sent to the Elector on March 28. Had it been otherwise, one would have to assume that on March 28 Luther mentioned to the Elector what was in reality not a translation but an interpretation of the articles. See also Rupp, *Tradition.* pp. 104 f.
[11] Literally: "accept these articles accordingly [or: likewise; i.e., just as the English theologians in Wittenberg had done]."
[12] Literally: "then the alliance may have its continuation." For "alliance," see p. 98, n. 10.

in agreement with our teaching.[13] And[14] then in due time one may, of course, dispatch a legation to England—since the English desire it[15]—to inform the King in greater detail. If His Royal Majesty should not accept these articles, however, or if he searches in them for much to be discussed or changed,[16] then, indeed we are not in a position again to confuse or upset our congregations—which have hardly been brought to peace and quiet—just because of the English.

Your Electoral Grace may exclude from these theological issues the matter of the King's marriage; or, should it be considered wise, [Your Electoral Grace] may offer to defend it to the degree to which we have approved of it.[17]

Regarding Duke George's matter[18] our people have acted quite carelessly, and this has deeply troubled me. But Your Electoral Grace [may have] a good conscience [regarding this issue] since Your Grace has honestly and with a Christian attitude offered to let all bad will fall by the wayside. Thus God's will has been fulfilled, and in his time he certainly will not forget it. But that man,

---

[13] For a theological evaluation of the articles, see Tjernagel, pp. 160 ff.; Rupp, *Tradition*, pp. 104 ff.; *Witt.Art.*, pp. 11 f.

[14] Literally: "Upon this [or: therefore; i.e., as a result of the fact that the articles agree with "our" teaching]."

[15] Or: "provided that the Englishmen [now one would have to add: still] demand it." For "legation," see p. 106, n. 29.

[16] It has to remain open whether Luther simply anticipates further delaying actions on the part of Henry VIII, or whether Luther's statements were the result of Henry's answer (*L.P.* 9, No. 1016; *C.R.* 3, No. 1407) to an official communication of the Smalcaldic League; this answer had been communicated to the Elector in Wittenberg on March 12, 1536; see Prüser, p. 51. In this answer Henry underscored that he could subscribe to the *Augsburg Confession* only if certain issues would be clarified first by means of theological discussions.

[17] On March 29 Melanchthon wrote to Camerarius (*C.R.* 3, No. 1407) that no agreement could be reached regarding the issue of the King's divorce. While the Wittenberg theologians continued to uphold in principle their rejection of the divorce, they nevertheless agreed with the English ambassadors on certain details. Consequently something similar to a compromise was worked out. See *C.R.* 2, No. 1001. See Tjernagel, pp. 159 f.; Rupp, *Tradition*, pp. 104 f.; Prüser, pp. 46 ff.

[18] The following statements reflect a quarrel between the Elector and Duke George of Saxony (see *LW* 48, 110, n. 2), who, since 1532, had been harassing some members of the nobility of his territory because of their open affirmation of the Reformation. Since these noblemen also had properties under the jurisdiction of Electoral Saxony, they appealed to the Elector for help, and the Elector promptly ordered retaliations. Long drawn-out and apparently half-hearted negotiations—the source for Luther's "troubles"—resulted in nothing. It was not until June of 1536 that the matter was settled. For details, see *WA*, Br 7, 384, n. 4.

eager for revenge and without any peace, remains as he has always been, ravenous for blood and murder; one day he is going to discover, as Psalm 8 states: You execute the enemy and him who is eager for revenge.[19] The best thing[20] is that he, together with all his hangers-on, is unable to pray because of such unrepenting wickedness; of course he is not in need of prayer, so haughty is he. Yet we who are seeking and offering peace and pardon are able to pray—praise be to God. Therefore God will listen to us, provided that we humbly confess our sins and seek his honor.

May Jesus Christ, our dear Lord, strengthen and comfort Your Electoral Grace's heart against the devil's threats and gloomy thoughts. The devil had worse things in mind [on other occasions]. Amen.

March 28, 1536   Your Electoral Grace's dedicated
MARTIN LUTHER, DOCTOR
and the others, etc.[21]

Further, Doctor Caspar Cruciger[22] has asked me to write to Your Electoral Grace and ask that Your Electoral Grace would graciously grant him [the use of] the castle at Eilenburg for his wedding. For otherwise he does not know where to go, since his wedding cannot take place at Leipzig[23] or Wittenberg.[24] Your Electoral Grace certainly will know how to act graciously in this matter. For in such matters one has to help [others to] overcome obstacles.[25] Herewith [Your Electoral Grace] be commended to God. Amen.

---

[19] Ps. 8:3 (Luther Bible).

[20] On the basis of the following statement it is clear that Luther is being sarcastic here.

[21] I.e., the other Wittenberg scholars who participated in the discussions with the English ambassadors, esp. Melanchthon.

[22] See *LW* 49, 104, n. 12. He had been a widower since May of 1535, and was about to marry Appollonia Günterrode of Leipzig; see *WA*, Br 7, 384, n. 5.

[23] Leipzig was located in the Duchy of Saxony, the territory of Luther's old foe, Duke George.

[24] As Luther later advised Jerome Weller not to celebrate his wedding festivities in Wittenberg because of the expenses involved (see *WA*, Br 7, No. 3056), so he apparently now considered that Wittenberg was not the right place for the wedding festivities.

[25] The Elector approved of this request, and on April 24 Luther preached Cruciger's wedding sermon at the Eilenburg castle; see *WA*, 41, xxxii; Buchwald, *LK* p. 106.

272

To Thomas Cromwell
Wittenberg, April 9, 1536

Luther explains the fact that he had not yet answered a letter from Cromwell by telling of the sudden departure of Robert Barnes from Wittenberg. Luther, thanking Cromwell for his kind letter, sidesteps the praise with which Cromwell had showered him. He emphasizes that by God's grace he has much good will, but that he lacks the power to put his will into operation. Turning to Cromwell and the affairs in England, Luther voices his pleasure with Cromwell's efforts on behalf of the gospel, and assures Cromwell of his prayers. In conclusion Luther refers Cromwell to Barnes for information pertaining to the situation in Wittenberg.

Luther wrote this letter at a time when Cromwell's fortunes were about to reach their apex. Born in approximately 1485, Cromwell had studied law and had entered the service of Cardinal Thomas Wolsey. A member of the House of Commons since 1523, Cromwell successfully weathered Wolsey's downfall in 1529; he moved on into the service of King Henry VIII, and in 1531 he was appointed privy councilor. Thereafter his career advanced rapidly, and in January of 1535 he was appointed the King's vicar general in ecclesiastical affairs, a position in which he executed the secularization of the monasteries. In July of 1536 Cromwell was made lord privy seal, and for the next three and a half years he was perhaps the most influential man around the King. In his interior policies he advocated royal supremacy in church and state, and his religious policies, in which traditionalism and Erasmian reform were blended, served that principle. His foreign policy was aimed at bringing about an alliance between England and the Smalcaldic League. "The King's disgust at the marriage [that is, with Anne of Cleve, arranged by Cromwell] and the fact that he now had no further use for Cromwell were the causes of his [that is, Cromwell's] undoing; for though Cromwell had only recently been created Earl of Essex . . . he was arrested, sentenced for treason and beheaded on 28 July 1540." O.D.C.C., p. 357.

On Thomas Cromwell, see DNB 5, 192 ff.; G. R. Elton, Policy

and Police. The Enforcement of the Reformation in the Age of Thomas Cromwell *(Cambridge, 1972).*
Text in Latin: WA, Br 7, 396.[1]

To the highly esteemed and most excellent man, Sir Thomas Cromwell, chancellor[2] and councilor of the most serene lord, the King of England,[3] my Lord to be esteemed in Christ[4]

Grace and peace in Christ! Your Lordship—that I have not replied to Your Lordship's letter,[5] which Doctor Barnes has turned over to me, is the fault of that same Doctor Barnes, who suddenly left and did not consider me worthy of a greeting or a farewell, in such a great hurry was he.[6] But the place and time will come for me to revenge myself on him for this neglect of me. Nevertheless I most heartily thank you for your most friendly and kind letter, and I only wish that by Christ's blessing I would be and act as they[7] have pictured me to Your Lordship. For comparing myself with those virtues in which Your Lordship believes I excell, I consider myself far inferior. This one thing I confess to the Lord, namely, that by his grace I do not lack in eagerness and good will; or as Paul says,[8] the power to will has been given to me, but the power of execution I do

---

[1] The letter is extant as autograph which is deposited in the British Museum in London.
[2] Luther used *secretarius.*
[3] Henry VIII.
[4] The translation here is based on a variant reading taken from the autograph and printed in *WA,* Br 13, 241, addition to *WA,* Br 7, 396, line 2.
[5] This letter is no longer extant.
[6] The circumstances to which Luther refers here cannot be established since Barnes's activities at that time are unknown. The present letter raises questions regarding the date and the reason why Barnes suddenly left Wittenberg, and how Luther expedited his letter to Cromwell. The first two questions have to remain open, for Tjernagel's (pp. 158, 159) argumentation (to the effect that Barnes was to bring the verdict reached by the Wittenberg theologians on the King's divorce; see p. 134, n. 17) contributes no reason for Barnes's sudden return to England, since it is based on no evidence whatsoever. Regarding the last question one might perhaps suggest that, after Barnes had left Wittenberg, Luther wrote his letter to Cromwell and expedited it with the last "official embassy mail" from Wittenberg, by which mail Fox and Heath informed Cromwell of the outcome of the discussions, of the end of their stay in Wittenberg, and of their future travel plans, while at the same time seeking further instructions.
[7] I.e., Luther's friends in England, esp. Barnes.
[8] See Rom. 7:18.

137

not find in myself. Yet he who sees my imperfection is perfect, and in his time will finally make me perfect according to his good will; to him be glory for ever and ever. Amen.

Doctor Barnes has, however, made me extraordinarily happy in telling me of Your Lordship's earnest and determined will regarding the cause of Christ,[9] especially since because of your prestige,[10] by which you are capable of accomplishing very many things throughout the whole kingdom and with the Most Serene Lord King, you can do much good. I do pray and I shall pray to the Lord to strengthen abundantly his work, begun in Your Lordship, to his glory and the salvation of many. Amen.

Through Doctor Barnes Your Lordship, whom I commend to the Father's mercy, will become thoroughly acquainted with the situation here.[11]

Wittenberg, April 9, 1536   Your Lordship's dedicated

MARTIN LUTHER, DOCTOR

273

To Francis Burchart
Wittenberg, April 20, 1536

By April 10, 1536, the stay of the English ambassadors, Fox and Heath, in Electoral Saxony came to an end in a cool, though diplomatically correct, atmosphere.[1] The ambassadors returned to Lon-

---

[9] In order to help bring about the alliance between the continental Lutherans and the English, Barnes was engaging in wishful thinking in both directions; i.e., in the way in which he presented the situation in England to Luther (see above), and in the way in which he presented the situation in Wittenberg, esp. Luther's and Melanchthon's reaction to the English overtures, to Cromwell (see Barnes's letter cited on p. 106, n. 29).

[10] Or: "position of authority".

[11] Literally: "with all that which is among us, and is being handled [or: acted upon]." This is a reference to the discussions between the English ambassadors and the Wittenberg theologians, and the *Wittenberg Articles.*

[1] Fox and Heath stayed in Wittenberg until April 11; at least until that day the Elector provided food for the ambassadors; see *ARG* 25 (1928), 60 f. On April 8, in Torgau, Elector John Frederick signed a letter addressed to Henry VIII (text: *WA*, Br 7, 401 f.; *C.R.* 3, No. 1416) in which the ambassadors were being

don on June 30, having traveled via Frankfurt, where they had stayed from approximately April 25 to June 11, and had attended a meeting of the Smalcaldic League.[2] *Clemen argues that after the discussions in Wittenberg had been ended, and for reasons that are not absolutely clear, Elector John Frederick approached Luther through Francis Burchart with the question whether further concessions to Henry VIII could be made.*[3] *Letter No. 273 is Luther's reply to the Elector's inquiry. Luther emphatically points out that the theological position set forth in the* Wittenberg *Articles must be maintained even though theological formulations might be changed,*

---

discharged. The letter is filled with praise for Fox and Heath, is polite, and says very little beyond giving the impression that the Elector was determined that Henry would have to accept the Lutheran theological position before further negotiations could take place. This letter was intended to be given to the ambassadors to take along to England. The Elector politely but determinedly refused to grant Fox a farewell audience, even though Fox asked twice for it; see *WA, Br* 7, 401 ff. Instead of the desired audience, the ambassors were given detailed instructions by Francis Burchart pertaining to what to tell the King, esp. in reply to the King's "answer," mentioned on p. 134, n. 16. These instructions (*C.R.* 3, No. 1415; *L.P.* 10, No. 771) make it quite clear that the Elector was not interested in entering an alliance with the King on the King's terms. Certainly one reason (commonly overlooked) for the cool and rather unbending way in which the Elector acted at the time that the ambassadors were being discharged was Henry's "answer," in which the King had in no way committed himself but had suggested that he expected the Lutherans to make certain doctrinal concessions. Insofar as the Saxons were concerned, all possible concessions had been made and set forth in the *Wittenberg Articles*, and it was now up to the King to act. Therefore no further discussions would be necessary, helpful, or even desirable. It was only upon the urging of Landgrave Philip of Hesse that the Elector reluctantly consented to allow the ambassadors to come to the meeting of the Smalcaldic League in Frankfurt; see *Prüser*, pp. 60 f., 71.

[2] On this Frankfurt meeting, and on the activities of Fox and Heath, including their return to England, see *Prüser*, pp. 60 f., 88 ff.; *WA, Br* 8, 220 f.

[3] Clemen (*WA, Br* 7, 403) suggests that the Elector had a slight change of heart which, according to Clemen, might have been due to pressures by Landgrave Philip of Hesse—brought to bear upon the Elector at the end of March/beginning of April, but certainly prior to the time that the English ambassadors were being discharged by the Elector—because the Landgrave did not wish to see the possibility of an alliance with England radically jeopardized through stubbornness in doctrinal matters on the part of the Saxons. This seems to be farfetched, for if the Elector had been willing to give way to these pressures then he certainly could have acted differently at the time that the ambassadors left Wittenberg. It is more natural to suggest that the Elector's inquiry has to be viewed in connection with the upcoming meeting of the Smalcaldic League in Frankfurt. Here the plenary meeting of the league had to be informed of the King's "answer," mentioned in note 1, and an *official* reply of the league had to be drafted. The Elector's inquiry was, then, simply a last check with Luther in preparation for the discussions within the plenary meeting of the league, discussions which were to result in an answer to the king on behalf of the league. See also note 8.

that patience regarding the practical application of doctrine has to be exercised, and that issues pertaining to ceremonies might in due time be properly handled by reasonable rulers. At this point, Luther argues, one should not worry about ceremonies as long as the proper foundation of the faith is being laid. The political problem, that is, whether the Smalcaldic League ought to enter into an alliance with Henry VIII if the King does not accept all the articles, is up to the politicians to decide, says Luther, though he points out that it seems to him to be dangerous to enter into an alliance if the hearts of those entering are not united.

On Francis Burchart, see p. 80, n. 10.

Text in German: WA, Br 7, 403–404.[4]

Since my Most Gracious Lord[5] has requested an answer to the question of how far one could go in making concessions to the King of England regarding the articles, it is my judgment, dear Mr. Vice-Chancellor, that in this matter we are unable to concede anything beyond what has been already conceded.[6] If one wishes to talk about the issues or to formulate the results in different words it suits me fine (so that we do not appear to be contemptuous of the ability[7] of other people).[8] Yet it is impossible that the articles[9] and the central points be believed or taught differently. Were it otherwise, it certainly would have been easier for us at Augsburg[10]—and might still be today—to become one with the pope and with the Emperor; further, it would be a disgrace for us not to be willing to

---

[4] The letter is extant only in the common editions of Luther's works. The earliest witness is based on a now no-longer extant manuscript copy in the Weimar archive.

[5] Elector John Frederick; see *LW* 48, 181 f.

[6] I.e., Luther considers the *Wittenberg Articles* a document in which were set forth all the theological concessions to the King that could be made in good conscience, i.e., without abandoning one's own fundamental doctrines.

[7] Literally: "intellect."

[8] The text in parentheses supports the argument (see note 3) that the Elector's inquiry and Luther's letter have to be viewed in connection with the King's "answer," mentioned in note 1. For this answer underscored the facts that the King himself was learned in theological matters, and that England had its *own* learned men with whom certain modifications in the *Augsburg Confession* (i.e., the document pertaining to the faith and learning of foreigners) must be discussed.

[9] Literally: "other articles."

[10] This is a reference to the discussions at the 1530 Diet of Augsburg; see *LW* 49, 403 ff.

concede to the Emperor and to the pope what we would now concede to the King. Of course it is true that one must patiently realize that in England not everything can be abruptly put into practice according to the teaching (just as among us it also did not go swiftly). Nevertheless the central points[11] must not be changed or abandoned. Ceremonies are temporal matters, and in time they can be handled correctly by reasonable rulers; therefore there is no need to quarrel or worry a lot at this time about ceremonies, as long as the correct foundation is being laid.[12] But whether the alliance with the King should be initiated[13] in the event that the King does not agree with us on all articles—that is a matter I leave to the dear lords,[14] together with my Most Gracious Lord, to consider because it is a secular matter; yet it seems to me to be dangerous externally to make an alliance if the hearts are not united. But I shall not insist on my judgment; God, if he intends to be gracious, certainly knows how to use the thoughts of godly people, of the enemies, and of all people for the best results.

Written at Wittenberg, April 20, 1535[15]   MARTIN LUTHER

274

To George Spalatin
[Wittenberg,] June 10, 1536

Recommending Kilian Zimmermann, who is searching for a place to work, Luther informs Spalatin that there are no jobs left open in Wittenberg since so many poor people from other places have come to Wittenberg in search of a way to make a living. Then Luther

---

[11] Literally: "articles."
[12] See also *LW* 49, 262 f.
[13] Literally: "accepted." I.e., Luther knew that Henry VIII was highly interested in the alliance and, so to speak, offered it to the Smalcaldic League. See also p. 98, n. 10.
[14] I.e., the Estates of the Smalcaldic League.
[15] This is the date given to the letter in the earliest witnesses. The facts that in spring of 1535 no doctrinal discussions between Luther and the English had yet taken place, and that no articles had yet been drawn up, make clear that the letter belongs in the year 1536.

briefly mentions the execution of Anne Boleyn. Ending his letter, Luther promises to write as soon as possible about Spalatin's "Asmodeus," extends greetings to Spalatin's wife, and encourages the Spalatins to endure patiently the insults of Spalatin's mother-in-law.

On George Spalatin, see LW 48, 8 f.

Text in Latin: WA, Br 7, 430.[1]

To the excellent man of true godliness, George Spalatin,
Master [of Arts],[2] a most faithful servant of Christ,
my dearest brother in the Lord

Grace and peace in Christ! Excellent Spalatin! Here comes Kilian Zimmermann,[3] who either has been expelled or is fleeing from Glauchau,[4] and has asked for help in finding some kind of job. But since so many poor are streaming together here from all over, it is absolutely impossible to find any jobs. Therefore he has finally asked me to recommend him to you. I ask you to understand that this is being diligently done by me with this letter. For he also belongs to your diocese[5] since he had lived close to Altenburg.

I am sure that any news I have is already old stuff to you, such as that absolutely monstrous tragedy in England.[6] As soon as I am

---

[1] The letter is extant as autograph.

[2] Literally: "To the man, excellent and of true godliness, Mr. Master George Spalatin."

[3] For some information about the possible identity of this man, see the material collected by the WA, Br editor in WA, Br 7, 430, n. 1.

[4] "Expelled" or "fleeing," either because of some crime or trouble with the authorities, or (and this is probably closer to the truth) because of his evangelical convictions. Glauchau is located about thirty kilometers west of Chemnitz (Karl Marx Stadt) in what in Luther's days was the *Grafschaft* Schönburg. The Count of Schönburg, who was a staunch opponent of the Reformation, had died, and among the guardians of his minor children was Luther's old foe, Duke George of Saxony.

[5] See p. 97, n. 3.

[6] I.e., the execution of Anne Boleyn which had taken place on May 19, 1536. See also *EHD* 5, 723 ff. The source of the news could not be established. In view of the references to this event which can be found in the Melanchthon correspondence (*C.R.* 3, 82, 89, 90, 91) it is safe for the WA, Br editor (7, 431, n. 2) to suggest that a letter of Barnes to Melanchthon was the source of this news. Without documentation, Tjernagel, p. 160, states: ". . . it is plain enough that her [i.e., Boleyn's] execution was a shock to continental Protestantism and probably an important factor in preventing Melanchthon's visit to England." And Prüser (p. 98) states that Anne Boleyn's execution nullified the plans of the

able I shall write concerning your Asmodeus;[7] in the meantime may Christ grant you to be victorious through enduring. Greet your most pleasant wife and tell her that I have the highest opinion of her, and that she should endure those motherly (not to say stepmotherly) insults. All things will finally turn out in the best and happiest way; but those who have harmed her will be confounded. Farewell in Christ to you and your whole household. Amen.

June 10, 1536   Yours,

MARTIN LUTHER

Smalcaldic League to send a legation to England. Anne Boleyn's execution had nothing to do, however, with Melanchthon's not going to England. For as early as the beginning of April, Elector John Frederick had made clear to the English ambassadors that neither Melanchthon nor anyone else would go to England unless Henry VIII had first committed himself to the *Augsburg Confession* and the *Wittenberg Articles*; see *C.R.* 3, No. 1415, and above, p. 138, n. 1. This position dominated the Frankfurt meeting of the Smalcaldic League. The league put off Fox and Heath with halfhearted promises so that upon leaving Frankfurt the two ambassadors felt that they were leaving without any definite commitment on the part of the league as a whole regarding the legation; see *WA*, Br 8, 221. Whatever preparations the league made for such a legation, and there were indeed many (see Prüser, pp. 91, 93 ff.), they clearly demonstrate that all further negotiations would depend on the King's reaction to the *Wittenberg Articles*. For the Elector, and also for the league, the course of action to be pursued regarding the legation to England was clearly determined prior to the Queen's execution, or prior to the time that any news about this event was available to the German Protestants. While this event may have had something to do with the fact that the legation was finally not dispatched (see also *C.R.* 3, 89), it was not an *important* factor in this development, certainly not insofar as Melanchthon's possible trip to England was concerned. The Queen's fate was simply a postlude to a prior decision; it only confirmed the Elector in the position he had so clearly enunciated long before the Queen's execution, and made him only more determined not to let Melanchthon go to England. Consequently with the arrival of the news pertaining to Anne Boleyn's execution the final event in the 1535/36 English-Wittenberg contacts and negotiations has been reached, and the topic "England" disappears from Luther's correspondence for the time being. See pp. 150 f.
[7] "Asmodeus" is a demon, mentioned in Tob. 3:8, 17, who destroys marriages by killing husbands. In the 1534 preface to Luther's translation of the apocryphal book Tobit (*WA*, DB 12, 110), Asmodeus is described as an evil domestic demon. "Asmodeus" has to be seen in connection with the "insults" to which Spalatin's mother-in-law exposed the family, esp. her daughter, Spalatin's wife. According to Höss, *Spalatin*, p. 395 f., the Spalatins had lived in the house of Spalatin's parents-in-law since 1527, when Spalatin's wife had inherited it. The mother of Spalatin's wife lived with them, and apparently life was sometimes not easy. Luther's promised writing concerning "Asmodeus" could not be identified.

275

To Justus Jonas[1]
[Wittenberg,] August 17, 1536

Luther mentions that he has seen only a German translation of the papal bull by which a general council of the church is summoned, and gives a negative evaluation of the bull for "we are already condemned" in it. Then he refers to three "spooky" incidents, and briefly reports on the war over the succession to the Danish throne. In closing Luther sends greetings from his wife, and encourages Jonas to return soon to Wittenberg.

On Justus Jonas, see LW 48, 275, n. 3.

Text in Latin (with some words in German): WA, Br 7, 503–504.[2]

Grace and peace in Christ!

The reason that the bull of Sir Paul, that is, of the cardinals,[3] has not been turned over to me is perhaps due to the fact that Master[4] Philip,[5] in his eagerness, was the first to receive it personally from

---

[1] In April of 1536 the Naumburg city council asked Elector John Frederick and the Wittenberg theologians for an evangelical pastor, and Jonas was at once sent to Naumburg to serve as interim pastor during Holy Week and Easter Week. Thereafter Jonas returned to Wittenberg while the city council tried to get the Elector's permission for Jonas to serve in Naumburg until such time as a new pastor could be found. Shortly after May 24 Jonas moved to Naumburg, where he officiated until September 8, when the new pastor arrived. See *WA*, Br 7, Nos. 3007, Introduction, 3079.

[2] The letter is extant in one manuscript copy, and in the common editions of Luther's works.

[3] This was the bull *Ad Dominici gregis* of June 2, 1536, by which a council was summoned for May 23, 1537, to Mantua. The original text, signed by Pope Paul III and some cardinals, is no longer extant. St. Ehses edited the text of a later copy in *C.T.* 4, 2 ff.; see also *UASA*, pp. 15 ff.; see also Jedin, p. 312, n. 1. "As for the purpose of the Council, the Bull specified the traditional tasks, namely the extirpation of errors and heresies, the reform of morals, the restoration of peace in Christendom and preparation for a great expedition against the infidels. The Council was convoked. The great, long-expected step was taken. Yet the goal was further off than anyone would have imagined. . . . There . . . followed a whole chain of difficulties both old and new, with the result that after three whole years of discussion this way and that, the hope of a Council faded out once more." So Jedin, p. 312.

[4] I.e., Master of Arts.

[5] Philip Melanchthon; see *LW* 48, 77, n. 3. See also below, note 13.

Bernard,[6] and that since then he has not yet shown it to me (as there is between us both mutual reliance and negligence). For I usually handle his letters in this way too. But yesterday I saw the German bull,[7] which has been published here; I also saw and became aware of,[8] not those basic virtues[9] about which Seneca[10] and the other philosophers teach, but the cardinals—I should rather say, the central poles,[11] the chiefs,[12] indeed the heads of Satan themselves. In every respect they are cardinals, and are justly called so. For in that bull we are already condemned.[13] But of other things

---

[6] A Jewish man by the name of Bernard is frequently mentioned in Luther's correspondence, and in that of other persons contemporary with Luther, as a letter carrier. For references, see WA, Br 13, 244, addition to WA, Br 7, 464, n. 7.

[7] The official text of the bull (to be distributed to sovereigns and the higher ranking clergy and to be posted on the doors of important churches) was printed as a poster and sealed with the papal seal. In addition, some manuscript copies were circulating, and translations into German were produced. For bibliographical information, see WA Br 7, 469, n. 23, 504, n. 4; 13, 245, addition to WA, Br 7, 469, n. 23. Except for an occasional reference, nothing is known about the German Wittenberg edition of the bull which Luther saw on August 16. See also note 13.

[8] The following is a play on the word "cardinal."

[9] The text reads *cardinales virtutes*.

[10] This is most probably a reference to some of the *Dialogi* and the *Epistolae morales* of the stoic philosopher Lucius Annaeus Seneca (5 B.C.[?]–A.D. 65); see *O.C.D.*, pp. 827 f. The publishing house Froben in Basel had published Seneca's works in 1529.

[11] The text reads *cardines*.

[12] The text reads *capitales*.

[13] While in the bull the evangelicals were not condemned openly and by name, the references to heresies which had recently emerged within Christendom and which were to be eliminated by the council were a sufficiently clear indication of the directions in which the council would go for Luther's rather negative evaluation of the bull to be justified. When Luther in the opening sentence of this letter says that he has not yet seen the bull, then he was referring to the official poster version of the bull. Indeed, it was not until February of 1537 that an extraordinary papal nuncio to Germany, Peter van der Vorst, officially presented the bull to Elector John Frederick; see *UASA*, p. 17, n. 4. In the meantime, however, the Electoral policy-making machinery was working at high speed. For on July 6 Margrave George of Brandenburg forwarded to the Elector a copy of the official text of the bull (*ibid.*, pp. 17 f.), and perhaps also a printed copy of a German version. At least in the Weimar archive both documents are put together; see WA, Br. 7, 605. On July 24 the Elector ordered his Wittenberg theologians and jurists to draft a brief on the matter (see WA, Br 7, 478), and Melanchthon did so, drafting the brief which was issued on August 6; *C.R.* 3, No. 1456; see also WA, Br 7, 479. While Luther also signed this brief, Melanchthon was nevertheless the chief author. It is reasonable to conclude, therefore, that at this point Luther had turned the matter over to Melanchthon. And further, since discussion on the matter had taken place among the Wittenberg theologians one has to conclude that they were familiar with the bull. Yet Luther

[let us talk] in person. It is the most just wrath of God over the world. You have correctly interpreted the spook Eric.[14] But I believe that I have written to you also about our spook in Frankfurt in the Margraviate[15]—or perhaps you have heard about it from somewhere else—that is, about the virgin who plucks margravial coins from the beard of someone who stands around, or from his suit or

---

clearly stated above that as late as August 15 he had not yet seen any version of the bull, and he assumed that one reason was Melanchthon's eagerness to read the bull as soon as "Bernard" had brought it to Wittenberg. Yet at the end of July or beginning of August, Melanchthon was already working on a brief in connection with the bull. And finally, after the Elector had received the August 6 brief, he criticized it as being insufficient and poorly composed. He ordered Brück to meet with Luther and the other theologians and to demand a second brief. On September 3 Brück had fulfilled this order; see *C.R.* 3, No. 1464. Due to Melanchthon's absence from Wittenberg in the fall of 1536 (see *WA*, Br 7, 526, n. 4), the Wittenberg theologians did not issue this second brief until December 6; see *WA*, Br 7, 604 f., and *C.R.* 3, No. 1458. Brück had an additional order: he was to discuss the whole council issue with Luther in private and request from Luther a separate brief. This order Brück had also fulfilled by September 3; for on that day he informed the Elector that he was of the opinion that Luther was already hard at work "to open his [i.e., Luther's] heart to Your Electoral Grace regarding the matter of the faith, as if it would be his testament." *C.R.* 3, 147. (Here is the root of Luther's *Smalcald Articles.*) The situation becomes clear—i.e., Luther's August 17 statement that he has *not yet seen* the bull is confirmed, his assumption concerning Melanchthon's eagerness to see the bull becomes understandable, as does his minimal input regarding the August 6 brief, just as the Elector's reaction to the August 6 brief becomes understandable—if one considers the fact that for their work at the end of July and beginning of August the Wittenberg theologians did not have available the *text* of the bull; they had only received oral instructions and a set of articles drafted by Brück on the basis of the bull forwarded by Margrave George to the Elector; see *WA*, Br 7, 478 f. No wonder that Luther did not show too much interest in the work, but obviously wanted to wait until he could finally study the text of the bull itself! No wonder that he assumed that Melanchthon grabbed hold of the bull when Bernard brought it to Wittenberg! Was Melanchthon responsible for the German translation (a possible reason for the assumed "negligence" in showing the bull to Luther) which was published in Wittenberg and which Luther saw on August 16? (Apparently it was published approximately August 15, for it seems that it is mentioned for the first time on that day; see Enders, *Briefwechsel*, 11, 34, n. 4; *Archiv für Geschichte des deutschen Buchhandels* 16 [1893], 160, No. 491.)

[14] Nothing could be established about the background of this statement concerning this "spook Eric" about whom Luther had written to Jonas in a no-longer extant letter in which Luther also informed his friend about the following incident. Clemen (*WA*, Br 7, 504, n. 6) asks whether this "spook Eric" should be connected with a "spooky dog" mentioned by Luther several times in the Table Talks; *WA*, TR 3, No. 3745; 6, No. 6830.

[15] I.e., Frankfurt/Oder in the territory of the Elector and margrave of Brandenburg.

from anywhere, and then devours them.[16] Finally one hears from Halle a new and monstrous story, which you should investigate, namely, that during a shooting match, which had been organized by the [Arch]bishop,[17] a young groom disappeared from amidst the tents, carried away by a storm, and leaving behind his bow, arrows, coat, even his shoes.

In addition to this, the following is news: The Duke of Holstein has finally defeated Denmark, Copenhagen has been captured and subdued, and Duke Albrecht of Mecklenburg has been pushed out. Now there is hope for peace in that area since the Duke of Holstein finally has become king through the cold fact that he[18] is the victor. [There is hope for peace, that is,] unless the Emperor intends to harass that area through a new war, which I wouldn't want [to see happen].[19]

My Lord Katie reverently greets you, together with your whole family. See to it that you return, that you bring news, [and then] that you repair, put in order, open up, redecorate, and put back into good condition everything which needs it.[20] Christ be with you. Amen.

August 17, 1536   Yours,

                                     MARTIN LUTHER

---

[16] On this incident, see *LCC* 18, 44 f.

[17] I.e., Cardinal Albrecht, the archbishop of Mainz; see *LW* 48, 44 f. Nothing could be established about the background of this statement.

[18] Literally: "in that area since he [i.e., the Duke of Holstein] finally has become king through the cold fact that the Duke of Holstein is the victor."

[19] When Frederick I, duke of Schleswig-Holstein and king of Denmark, died in 1533, a struggle developed concerning his successor. Frederick's oldest son, Christian, succeeded his father as duke of Schleswig-Holstein, but was prevented from succeeding his father on the throne of Denmark because a propapal faction of the Danish nobility had swung its support behind Albrecht, the Duke of Mecklenburg, who was able to entrench himself in Copenhagen. Christian laid siege to Copenhagen, and on July 29, 1536, Albrecht had to surrender and renounce all claims to the Danish throne. Another of the claimants was a brother of the elector of the Palatinate for whom Emperor Charles, on the basis of dynastic relations, had made claims to the Danish throne. Even though the Emperor had made preparations for a military intervention, he cancelled all plans when he heard of the fall of Copenhagen. See Ranke 2[III], 363 ff.; [IV], 52. On Christian, who ruled Denmark as Christian III from 1536 to 1559, see *NDB* 3, 233 f.; on Albrecht VII of Mecklenburg, see *NDB* 1, 167 f.

[20] These are apparently references to Jonas' house in Wittenberg. Whether the house was literally in as poor condition as these exhortations seem to indicate could not be established.

276

To Nicholas Hausmann
[Torgau,][1] September 20, 1536

Even though Luther thinks that Hausmann is probably well in-
formed about all that is news, he communicates everything he
thinks might be news and comments on the various items: The
Margraves of Brandenburg have abandoned the gospel; Jerome
Weller has moved into his own house close by Luther's own; the
French campaign of Emperor Charles V has taken a large toll in
lives; Duke George of Saxony apparently is writing a thick book
against the bishops; it looks to Luther as if no one really works
seriously for the council; Jane Seymour, an enemy of the gospel, is
to be crowned on St. Michael's Day, and conditions in England
have changed so much that Barnes has to go into hiding; the En-
glish are boycotting the council. Luther also tells Hausmann that he
intends to call him to Wittenberg. In closing he asks for Haus-
mann's prayer in his behalf, and extends greetings to the sovereign
of Anhalt-Dessau.

On Nicholas Hausmann, see LW 48, 399 f.

Text in Latin: WA, Br 7, 546–547.[2]

To the very gifted[3] man, Mr. Nicholas Hausmann,
Master [of Arts],[4] a servant of Christ in the
congregation at Dessau,
my dearest brother in the Lord

Grace and peace. I seldom write to you,[5] excellent Nicholas, for I
think there is no need for writing since you are always best informed about everything that is news among us, and since your

---

[1] In September of 1536 Luther was at the Electoral court in Torgau several
times. See Buchwald, *LK*, p. 109; *WA* 41, xxxvii f.
[2] The letter is extant as autograph.
[3] Literally: "splendidly decorated."
[4] Literally: "Mr. Master Nicholas Hausmann."
[5] Luther's last extant letter to Hausmann is dated March 11, 1536; see *WA*, Br 7,
No. 2298.

court[6] finds out news faster than ours. Both Margraves have become alienated from our gospel;[7] should you not [yet] know this, then know it now; further, I don't know what evil is starting to burn among us here.[8] May Christ crush Satan under our feet.[9]

I hereby inform you of my new plan concerning you: I am thinking about calling you away from there and making you a member of my household, so that finally you can enjoy peace and quietness. Already I have the promise of your brother that he will maintain you here at my place. For I can see that position is not meant for you.[10]

Doctor Jerome Weller is happy and has moved away from me into his own house, close to me; I am pleased with this.[11]

The affairs of the Emperor are not as prosperous as people brag.[12] They say that approximately five thousand of his soldiers[13]

---

[6] I.e., the court of Anhalt in Dessau, to which Hausmann was attached as chaplain.

[7] I.e., from the way in which "we" understand and preach the gospel. This reference to Joachim II, elector of the margraviate of Brandenburg, and his brother, Margrave John of Brandenburg-Küstrin-Neumark (see ADB 14, 156 ff.) is unclear. For some material that might perhaps contribute to clarifying this statement, see Enders, Briefwechsel, 11, 85, n. 1; WA, Br 7, 547, n. 1.

[8] Nothing could be established about the background of this statement. For a good conjecture, see WA 39[I], 198 f.

[9] See Rom. 16:20.

[10] As early as February 24, 1535, Luther had intended to get Hausmann out of Dessau for health reasons; see WA, Br 7, 161. The statement above ("enjoy peace and quietness") could suggest that other reasons, perhaps "professional" difficulties, may also have been involved. The brother, who promised to "feed" (literally) Nicholas, was John Hausmann, a city judge and mayor in Freiberg/Saxony; see WA, Br 13, 66, addition to WA, Br 3, 304, n. 1.

[11] See LW 49, 321, n. 2. On August 18 Luther informed Jonas that Weller had married; WA, Br 7, 506. A part of the wedding festivities took place in Luther's home (see WA, Br 7, No. 3056), and the young couple stayed with the Luthers for some time.

[12] On September 5 Luther wrote to Jonas that there were rumors in Wittenberg of a victory of the Emperor; WA, Br 7, 526. In the meantime other rumors, or news, must have arrived in Wittenberg. Luther refers here to the third war between Charles V and Francis I; see Ranke 2[IV], 13 ff. On July 25 an Imperial army invaded the Provence (see WA, Br 7, 469, n. 24). The French, rather than meeting the Imperial army head-on, engaged in some skirmishes. One of these skirmishes was near Brignole, and as Enders, Briefwechsel 11, 68, n. 4, suggests, it could very well have been that the Emperor made a "victory" out of this engagement in order to frighten the Francophiles in the Empire. Thereafter the French pursued a scorched earth tactic which was so catastrophic for the Imperial army that it had to abandon the campaign by September 13. See also WA, Br 7, 547, n. 7.

[13] In the available sources the number of those who are said to have perished

have perished from starvation, among them some outstanding military men, such as Margrave Frederick, the provost of Würzburg,[14] [and] Caspar von Frundsberg,[15] and I don't know who else.

It looks to me as if in reality people only pretend to be concerned about the council[16] rather than actually working for it, although it is said that Duke George is writing a thick book[17] against the bishops, whom he thinks to bring into line with the Canon Law; that is, [he hopes] to bring about unity between the devil and God.

Our Alesius[18] writes to us from England that the new Queen Joanna,[19] an enemy of the gospel (as he says), is to be crowned on [St.] Michael's Day;[20] the conditions in the kingdom are now so different that Antony[21] has to go into hiding and be silent, and is

---

ranges from 1,500 to 10,000; see Enders, *Briefwechsel* 11, 86, n. 5; *WA*, Br 7, 547, n. 7. Luther's source for this and the following information could not be established.

[14] I.e., Frederick, margrave of Brandenburg-Ansbach-Kulmbach, who at one time had been provost of the collegiate cathedral chapter in Würzburg, but who had resigned from his clerical duties and became an Imperial military captain.

[15] I.e., Caspar von Frundsberg, the oldest son of George von Frundsberg (see *NDB* 5, 670) whose troops had been involved in the 1527 sack of Rome; see *LW* 49, 169.

[16] See pp. 81 ff.

[17] This book by Luther's old enemy, Duke George of Saxony (see *LW*, 48, 110, n. 20), cannot be identified with certainty. For a possibility see *WA*, Br 7, 548, n. 9; Enders, *Briefwechsel* 18, 49, n. 2. Apparently the book was to deal with the need to strip the bishops of some of their worldly rights and to restrict them to those spiritual duties outlined in the Canon Law.

[18] Alexander Alesius (1500–1565), who at one time was a canon at St. Andrew's Church in Edinburgh, was converted to the Reformation by Patrick Hamilton in 1528, and shortly thereafter was imprisoned for his convictions. He was able to escape to the Continent, and in 1533 he visited Wittenberg. Apparently upon Melanchthon's recommendation, Alesius became a theological professor at Cambridge University in 1535. As early as 1536, however, he moved to London and pursued studies in medicine there, while trying to make a living as well as he was able. While in London he stayed in touch with Melanchthon, via John Aepinus in Hamburg (see, e.g., *CR*. 3, No. 1450, to Aepinus, dated July 31, 1536), and informed his friends of the developments in England. In order to avoid the consequences of the religious policies of Henry VIII, Alesius returned to Germany in 1540, and became a theological professor first at the University of Frankfurt/Oder, and then in 1543 at the University of Leipzig. On Alexander Alesius, see *DNB* 1, 254 ff.; *NDB* 1, 191.—Alesius' letter, to which Luther refers, is not extant.

[19] I.e., Jane Seymour (see *DNB* 10, 678 ff.) whom Henry VIII had married on May 30, 1536, eleven days after the execution of Anne Boleyn.

[20] I.e., September 29.

[21] I.e., Robert Barnes. Alesius did not have the proper perspective on the situation in England. For with the *Ten Articles* of June 9, 1536 (see *EHD* 5, 795 ff.),

not without danger. Nevertheless the King persists in rejecting the pope; with the consent of the whole kingdom it was decided that no one is to attend the council, unless the King has first approved of the council,[22] which will never be the case. Thus the monarchs disagree,[23] and the council will turn out to be a fairy tale, or at least will not convene at the set date. Once this date has been missed who will set another one? The whole world is full of foul play.[24]

Farewell in Christ, and pray for me, my brother, for I am very much in need of it. In my behalf greet your excellent sovereigns[25] reverently.

September 20, 1536   Yours,

                                        MARTIN LUTHER

277

To John Luther
[Wittenberg,] January 27, 1537[1]

Luther tells of his pleasure with his son's studies and letters, and encourages his son to continue studying diligently. Pointing to the

England moved closer to continental Protestantism than ever before (see Tjernagel, pp. 165 f.), and whether Jane Seymour was hostile to the Reformation has to remain an open question. On the other hand, Barnes had indeed lost favor with the court, probably because he was no longer needed for the purpose of establishing contacts with Wittenberg, or because he had been bearer of the rather unfavorable opinion issued by the Wittenberg theologians on the King's divorce, as Tjernagel (p. 168) suggests. At any rate, Barnes was back in Wittenberg by the end of October; see *WA* 39I, 181, 191.

[22] From the very beginning, but at least since April of 1536, Henry VIII had been opposed to the idea of the council unless he could make it serve his own purposes; see Jedin, pp. 307, 343, n. 1. While the bull convening the council was not even publicized in England (so Jedin, p. 324), the King nevertheless, with the consent of parliament, denounced the bull. See *L.P.* 11, No. 80; 12I, Nos. 1310, 1311.

[23] This is a reference to the bickering that went on among the secular and ecclesiastical greats of Europe, esp. between the Pope, the Emperor, the King of France, and the King of England, concerning the council, which Jedin (pp. 301 ff.) describes in great detail. It cannot be established whether, and to what degree, Luther knew details of these events.

[24] This sentence is written in German.

[25] I.e., the sovereigns of Anhalt.

[1] Date, background, and contents of this letter, which is extant in several manu-

151

fourth commandment and to God's blessing for obedient children and God's curse for disobedient children, Luther admonishes John to fear God, to obey his parents, and to avoid all improper conversations. Then Luther sends greetings from the whole family, and informs John that it would be possible for him and his teacher to visit with the Luthers during Shrovetide.

On John Luther, see LW 49, 152, n. 7.

Text in Latin (with some words in German): WA, Br 8, 19–20.

Grace and peace in the Lord!

Thus far, my dearest son, your studies and the letters you have written to me have been a pleasure for me. If you continue this way then not only will you please me, your father who loves you, but you also will very much benefit yourself, so that you will not seem to have stained yourself with dishonor. Therefore take care to pursue diligently what you started. For God, who has commanded children to be obedient to their parents, has also promised his blessing to obedient children. See to it that you have only this blessing before your eyes, and that you do not let yourself be diverted from it by any evil example. For that same God has also threatened disobedient children with a curse. Therefore fear God who blesses

---

script copies, and in the common edition of Luther's works, are highly problematic. All witnesses give 1537 as the year in which the letter was written. De Wette (*Dr. Martin Luthers Briefe* 5 [Berlin, 1828], 46) places the letter in the year 1543, when John Luther was in Torgau, studying with Marcus Crodel. If one maintains the traditional date, 1537, then the circumstances mentioned in the letter (John Luther's absence from Wittenberg; the identity of the teacher; the wish of Aunt Lena) cannot be identified. Enders (*Briefwechsel* 11, 190, n. 1) and Clemen (*WA*, Br 8, No. 3129) maintain the traditional date, though Clemen leans heavily toward the de Wette correction. A final answer on the date cannot be given unless it can be clearly established that the Aunt Lena mentioned by Luther was indeed Magdalene von Bora (see *LW* 49, 271, n. 28), as is generally assumed, and that she died sometime in 1537, as Enders, *loc.cit.*, argues. Prior to preparing the Introduction to the present letter, Clemen affirmed this date (see *WA*, Br 5, 241, n. 11); in the Introduction to the present letter, however, Clemen produced some material from the Table Talks which could suggest that Magdalene von Bora was alive at least in the early summer of 1539. A reexamination of the other material on which Enders bases his argument also raises doubt regarding the traditional date of the letter, but Magdalene von Bora's death seems to be the key to the problem. Until this question is cleared up, the traditional date has to be retained, though the letter would definitely fit better in the year 1543, following letter No. 301.

and curses, who even though he delays with his promises and threats, a fact which leads to the ruin of the evil, nevertheless quite quickly implements them for the well-being of the good. Fear God, therefore, and listen to your parents—who certainly want nothing but the best for you—and run from disgraceful and disreputable conversations.

Your mother cordially greets you; so do Aunt Lena and your sisters and brothers, all of whom are looking forward to a successful progress and conclusion of your studies. Mother requests that you greet your teacher and his wife. Further, should they wish to be with you here during this Shrovetide, or these happy days, while I am gone from here, then this is fine with us. Aunt Lena very much asks for this.

Farewell, my son; listen to and learn from the exhortations given to you by good men. The Lord be with you.

January 27, 1537   Martin Luther,
                                your Father according
                                to the flesh and spirit

278

To Justus Jonas
Altenburg, February 1, [1537]

Notwithstanding a severe cardiac illness in the second half of December, 1536, Luther drafted the Smalcald Articles; *they were discussed, revised, and approved at a conference of theologians who had been especially called to* Wittenberg.[1] *On January 3, 1537, Luther forwarded the articles to Elector John Frederick.*[2] *In the*

---

[1] See WA, TR 5, No. 6079; WA, Br 8, 3. The illness was so severe that for the work on the later portions of the articles Luther had to use two secretaries to whom he dictated the text; see UASA, p. 35, n. 1. Text of this December version of the *Smalcald Articles: UASA*, p. 35 ff.; text of the revised version, published by Luther in June of 1538: *The Book of Concord*, ed. T. G. Tappert (Philadelphia, 1959), pp. 288 ff. For the Wittenberg conference, see *UASA*, pp. 30 ff., 69 ff.
[2] *WA*, Br 8, No. 3124.

meantime the Smalcaldic League had been called to meet in Smalcald on February 7, 1537, in order to work out a program of joint action in response to the papal summons of a general council to Mantua.[3] *Summoned by the Elector to attend this meeting, Luther, along with Melanchthon, Bugenhagen, and Jonas, left Wittenberg for Smalcald on January 30.*[4] *Their first stopover was Torgau, where Jonas suffered such a severe attack of (gall?) stones that he had to stay behind; on January 31 the others continued the journey. Luther's party spent the night of January 31 at the Electoral castle in Grimma, and arrived at the castle in Altenburg in the late afternoon of February 1; while there Luther wrote the following letter to the ailing Jonas in Torgau.*[5] *Luther expresses his hope that Jonas' health has in the meantime improved. Then he reports that the papal envoy, Peter van der Vorst, might come to Smalcald, and that the Imperial vice-chancellor, Matthias Held, will be present at the Smalcald meeting of the league, so that this meeting will turn out to be of greater importance than "both sides" had assumed. Luther mentions that a certain canon from Zeitz swears that the pending meeting at Smalcald will be attended by men more learned than will attend the council of Mantua, should it ever come about. Luther asks Jonas to visit his family, and that of Bugenhagen; he tells of the magnificent hospitality he is experiencing in the Elector's castles, and sends some verses which he has addressed to Spalatin.*

On Justus Jonas, see LW 48, 275, n. 3.

Text in Latin: WA, Br 8, 22–23.[6]

Grace and peace in Christ!

Even though I think that these lines might come to you too late,[7] excellent Jonas, yet I wished to inform you that we hope that at this

---

[3] See *UASA*, pp. 79 ff.

[4] *UASA*, pp. 82 f., 97, n. 2; for the itinerary, see *ibid.*, p. 96, n. 1.

[5] Jonas was so ill that he had to stay in Torgau till February 8; see *UASA*, p. 97, n. 2.

[6] The letter is extant in several manuscript copies, and in the common editions of Luther's works.

[7] I.e., either because in the meantime Jonas' condition had taken a turn for the worse (so *WA, Br* 8, 23, n. 1), or, and this seems to be closer to the truth, because Jonas' condition had so improved that in the meantime he had been able to return to Wittenberg.

hour you have finally recuperated from the stone, and that our prayers have been heard. Here we hear the rumor that the most sacred legate, that is, the man from Acqui,[8] comes straight from Nürnberg to our Sovereign.[9] This is being written from Coburg to the Sovereign, who has replied to the people in Coburg that, should the legate come, they should instruct him to go to Smalcald.[10] There he will be awaited, if he really comes. If, I say, he really comes, then no doubt he does not come because of reverence,[11] but because of the Turks,[12] to seek help, etc. For what else are the Lutherans than sheep for the slaughter,[13] except when per chance those furious murderers might be in need of the help of the Lutherans. But we shall see. The chancellor of the Emperor, Doctor Matthias Held, also will be present;[14] perhaps this meeting will be of greater importance than both sides have assumed. May God grant it to be a legitimate council.

A canon from Zeitz is here, but he is an apostate from his order since he has married;[15] he is a distinguished man, who swears and states[16] that in this meeting there will be men more learned than

---

[8] I.e., Peter van der Vorst, bishop of Acqui (in northwestern Italy, in the province of Piedmont); see *LThK* 10, 894. Vorst was not a *legatus* (ambassador), as Luther states, but a nuncio extraordinary; i.e., an envoy especially sent for one task, namely, the delivery of the bull in which the council was summoned. On Vorst's mission, see Jedin, pp. 316 ff.

[9] Elector John Frederick; see *LW* 48, 181 f.

[10] Except for the statement that Vorst would come *straight* from Nürnberg to Electoral Saxony, Luther's information was correct, as can be seen from Vorst's itinerary; see *WA*, Br 8, 23, n. 3; Jedin, p. 317. Vorst stayed in Smalcald from February 24 to March 3; see Enders, *Briefwechsel* 11, 193, n. 2.

[11] The text reads *timore*.

[12] Literally: "but through the persuasion and intercession of the Turk." Luther meant to say that Vorst would come to Smalcald, if he came at all, not because of reverence (for the evangelicals)—or according to another possible translation of *timor*, because of anxiety (for bringing about the council)—but because of the threat of an attack by the Turks (see Ranke 2[IV], 17 f., 22 f.; *C.R.* 3, No. 1522), or a possible crusade against the Turks, mentioned in the bull in which the Pope summoned the council; see *UASA*, p. 17.

[13] Ps. 44:22.

[14] On Matthias Held, who was Imperial vice-chancellor from 1531 to 1541, see *NDB* 8, 465 f. He arrived in Smalcald on February 13; see *UASA* p. 99, n. 4. The purpose of his mission was to press the members of the Smalcaldic League in the name of the Emperor for a positive response to the bull in which the council was summoned, and to deal with political and legal matters (aid for the fight against the Turks, interpretation of the Nürnberg Truce). On Held's mission, see Ranke 2[IV], 60 ff.; Jedin, pp. 318 ff.; Brandi 1, 335 ff.

[15] For the possible identity of this canon, see *UASA*, p. 99, n. 5.

[16] In the text a phrase is added to the effect that the canon states whatever he ought to say anyway.

even at the council of Mantua (should this ever come about). I write this in order to console you, for your desire is marvelous.[17]

Farewell, and visit my family, and also the Pomeranian Rome[18] and his little Quirites.[19] We are healthy and happy; indeed, we are treated magnificently as guests of the Sovereign, and are excellently cared for in his castles at Grimma and Altenburg.[20] We had expected to be guests of the old Pylades and Theseus.[21] Therefore, as is our custom (known to you), we have played a game with him in verses. I am including mine; Master[22] Philip,[23] that is Homer, sends his too; but here are those verses of mine, that is, of Choerilus:[24]

As to Christ your deeds, George, are most pleasing.
So let this crew of strangers be pleasing to you.
To famous Chalcis[25] we are traveling for our meeting.
God's great cause forces us to travel there.

---

[17] I.e., the fact that the Smalcald meeting will be attended by many learned men, in fact by men who are more learned than those who will eventually attend the council, should comfort Jonas who had eagerly wanted to attend this meeting but was prevented from doing so by his illness.

[18] I.e., the home of John Bugenhagen Pomer (see *LW* 48, 303, n. 44).

[19] I.e., little Romans (see P. Harvey, ed., *The Oxford Companion to Classical Literature* [Oxford, 1962], p. 357), or Bugenhagen's children.

[20] This sentence has been freely translated. For the expenses incurred by the Luther party in Altenburg, see *UASA*, p. 100, n. 7.

[21] I.e., George Spalatin, Luther's old friend and helper, who was superintendent in Altenburg; see *LW* 48, 8 f. Luther thought that he and his friends would stay with the Spalatins. The Elector had made arrangements, however, for the Luther party to stay at the Altenburg castle. Pylades was the friend of Orestes, and Theseus helped Heracles in the battles against brigands, monsters, and Amazons. See *O.C.D.*, pp. 898 ff.; Harvey, *op.cit.*, pp. 203, 427 f.; Erasmus, *Adagia* I: 5, 27 (Clericus 2, 191 f.).

[22] I.e., Master of Arts.

[23] Philip Melanchthon; see *LW* 48, 77, n. 3. According to *WA Br* 8, 23, n. 14, Melanchthon's verses are not extant. Extant is, however, a short note, dated Grimma, February 1, 1537, but actually written by Melanchthon on January 31, after the Luther party had left Torgau; *C.R.* 3, No. 1522. Since Melanchthon does not mention his verses in this note, it seems safe to suggest that Luther and Melanchthon wrote their verses on February 1, while traveling from Grimma to Altenburg.

[24] Choerilus of Iasus was a poet traveling with and paid by Alexander the Great to celebrate Alexander's victories. According to Horace, Choerilus was a poor poet; see *O.C.D.*, p. 187. In the text the following verses are in the form of an elegiac distich.

[25] Because of the mines in the area of Smalcald, Luther called this town Chalcis after *chalkos*, the Greek word for copper, or ore. According to *UASA*, p. 100,

You too, excellent man, have an important part in such great affairs.
You, leader and companion on the way, come with us.[26]

February 1, at Altenburg, at 8:00 P.M.
Yours,
MARTIN LUTHER, DOCTOR

279

To Elector John Frederick[1]
[Smalcald, about February 9, 1537]

On February 7 the Luther party arrived in Smalcald.[2] On February 9 Luther preached in the City Church,[3] and on February 10 the meeting of the Smalcaldic League, to which Luther had been summoned, was officially opened with an address by the Electoral Saxon chancellor emeritus Gregory Brück.[4] Many items were on the agenda of this meeting; the most pressing one dealt with a joint policy regarding acknowledgment of, and attendance at, the council summoned by Pope Paul III to Mantua.[5] On this topic Luther issued the following opinion. No details about background, possible addressee, or date of this document could be established, though it is clear that it is part of the negotiations about the council. It is commonly assumed that, while in Smalcald, Luther issued this opinion for Elector John Frederick and that he wrote this document in the days immediately preceding the official beginning of the meeting.[6] The tone of the document is critical. Luther chastises the

---

n. 9, a copyist misunderstood Luther and replaced "Chalcis" with *Chalcida*, and then added on the margin of his copy a sentence to the effect that the meeting in Chalcida would be another Council of Chalcedon (see *O.D.C.C.*, p. 259).
[26] Spalatin joined the Luther party and stayed in Smalcald until February 26; see *UASA*, p. 128, n. 2.
[1] For the addressee and the date, see notes 6, 8, 43.
[2] *UASA*, p. 96, n. 1.
[3] *WA*, Br 8, 40; see *WA* 45, xvi.
[4] *UASA*, pp. 147 f.
[5] See p. 144, n. 3.
[6] Without any basis, Clemen (*WA*, Br 8, No. 3134, Introduction) suggests that

"Roman scoundrels" for their intention of manipulating the council to their own advantage, so that the issues (Luther's own case, the Gravamina) *would not be freely debated. He sees in the council a forum designed to condemn the evangelicals and to justify the spilling of innocent blood; consequently, Luther argues, in the eyes of all impartial people the council will turn out to be a farce. Above all, Luther is not convinced that the papists are at all serious about the council, but feels that they would rather cancel it for any possible reason. Since the refusal of the evangelicals to attend the council would provide such a reason and thus would do great damage to the cause of the evangelicals, Luther affirms his readiness to attend the council. Yet he also underscores that he would in no way feel bound by this readiness.*[7]

On Elector John Frederick, see LW 48, 181 f.

Text in German: WA, Br 8, 35–38.[8]

These are my thoughts:

[1]

I definitely see and fear that it will finally come to a fight. One must not be terrified, etc., by this, for God is and is called almighty,[9] and until now has arranged many things differently than we thought.

2

I have no doubt that the pope[10] or his followers are afraid [of this council] and would rather see this council thwarted.[11] Yet they

---

the document was written on February 8 or 9, i.e., during the first days of Luther's stay at Smalcald which were free from official business. See also note 43.

[7] See note 44.

[8] The document is extant as autograph. The many corrections (see, e.g., note 18) in Luther's own writing suggest that the extant text is a first draft only. This fact raises the question whether the document, which simply presented Luther's "thoughts" (see below), had any official function or was an official communication to the Elector or anyone else. The fact that in section 8 Luther speaks only for himself seems to suggest that this document was highly personal; perhaps it was never intended to be sent to anyone, but was simply a collection of materials. For the whole document see also WA 50, 175.

[9] See, e.g., Gen. 17:1.

[10] It is academic to speculate whether here and throughout this document Luther was thinking of the papacy in general or of Pope Paul III in particular.

[11] Luther's statement has to refer to the procrastination on the part of the papacy

would like this to come about in such a way that they could boast—and do so with seeming justice—that [this failure] was in no way their fault, since they had summoned the council, sent out messengers, and called the Estates, as they certainly would underscore.

3

In an abominable way they have therefore presented us with a devil's head, so that we should be frightened and retreat; that is, they have summoned a council for which they announce [as agenda] nothing pertaining to matters of the church, nothing pertaining to a hearing, nothing pertaining to other matters, etc., but only that which pertains to the extirpation and eradication of the poisonous Lutheran heresy[12] as they interpret it for themselves in the bull *De reformatione curiae*.[13]

4

Thus we have not only already received the judgment on our case which is to be pronounced against us in the council, but in addition the appeal with a hearing, answer, and discussion of all matters has been moved to the background;[14] further, the papists have scared away all godly, honorable people who might perhaps have been

in calling a council; even such a strong supporter of the papal church as Duke William of Bavaria had doubts whether the council ever would take place; see Jedin, p. 316. See also below, note 49. If one considers the efforts of the Curia to summon the higher-ranking clergy to the council and to seek the cooperation of secular powers, as Jedin has set them forth (pp. 313 ff.), or if one considers the work of the reform party at the Curia which at that time was working on the *Consilium de emendanda ecclesia* (see J. C. Olin, ed., *The Catholic Reformation: Savonarola to Ignatius of Loyola* [New York, 1969], pp. 182 ff.), then it becomes clear that at this point Luther was more skeptical than he need have been.

12 While this evaluation of the bull *Ad Dominici gregis* may be too negative so far as specific details are concerned, for the over-all nature of the bull it is correct.

13 This is a reference to the papal bull *Sublimis Deus*, dated August 23, 1535, which the evangelicals wrongly connected with the pending council of Mantua; see Bugenhagen's February 13, 1537, letter to Jonas in *UASA*, p. 108. In this bull the extirpation of the poisonous Lutheran heresy is indeed given as reason for calling a council. Text: *C.T.* 4, 451 ff., esp. 452. See also *WA* 50, 93, n. 2.

14 I.e., since the evangelicals had been declared heretics already prior to the council (i.e., in the bull cited in note 13) there was nothing to be fairly considered, tried, or heard.

selected as mediators. These accursed scoundrels of the devil wish to act as they please, not only to condemn us (for they are certain of this on the basis of previous bulls[15] issued against us) but also immediately to command and start the execution and eradication [of us all]. And this notwithstanding the fact that we have not yet been heard[16] (as all laws require), and that they, the cardinals, etc., have not yet studied our writings nor understood [the point of our] teaching since our books are everywhere prohibited. They have only read the false writers and listened to the lying mouths, while in contrast to this they have not listened to us. Yet both bishops and sovereigns in the German territories, even if they belong [to the pope's] party, know that the authors in whom the pope, Italy, and other nations, etc., believe are liars[17] and scoundrels.

For[18] at Wittenberg we heard from the pope's orator, Pietro Paolo Vergerio,[19] that he thought and had been informed quite differently about many things among us than he finds them actually to be. Doctor Gervasius, the envoy of the King of France,[20] also publicly admitted to us that his King had been talked into believing[21] that among us Lutherans there is no matrimony, governmental authority, church, or anything else. One may easily figure out from where the King, the pope, and the other nations got such an opinion. The wicked one at Halle[22] and those similar to him have permitted these [evil] books, and perhaps also [other] writings, to be distributed[23] while obstructing our books. But God is not

---

[15] See e.g., note 13, and LW 48, 179, n. 1.
[16] Or: "investigated."
[17] Literally: "lying books."
[18] The text from "For" to "not fettered, etc." has been added by Luther on a separate sheet of paper.
[19] See pp. 110 f. "Orator" is one of the technical terms for envoy.
[20] This is a reference to Dr. Gervasius Waim, who in July of 1531 came to Torgau as special envoy of the French king, Francis I, in order to inform Elector John that in case war broke out between the Protestants and the Emperor, France would declare neutrality. His real mission, however, was to strengthen the opposition of the German sovereigns, both evangelicals and papists, to the election of Ferdinand of Austria as Roman King; see Winckelmann, p. 131. Following this visit, Waim was in the Empire several times as French envoy. See also WA, Br 2, 31, n. 4; 11, 320, addition to WA, Br 8, 39, n. 8; WA 50, 195.
[21] Literally: "that his King had been convinced and considered to be certain."
[22] I.e., Cardinal Albrecht of Mainz.
[23] Literally: "being put into [i.e., among people]."

fettered,[24] etc. Since in some matters the pope and his followers have been too quick to believe such shameful and abominable lies, they owe it to us to listen[25] to us. I am silent about the matters which their own party will raise against them,[26] such as the facts that the pope and the Cardinal (!)[27] confiscate and lay waste (!) to monasteries and collegiate chapters, that the Bishop at Halle has three dioceses,[28] and that some similar to him [and some] canons have many benefices, etc., and many [other] innumerable matters which, even regardless of the Luther case, are certainly in need of concil[iar action].[29] But the bull[30] is conveniently silent about all these matters, [for the papists] are afraid that during a council these issues might be stirred up.

5

Therefore they would like to frighten us[31] into refusing [to attend the council]. Then they would feel safe and could say that we obstructed the council, etc. Thus not only would the legal disadvantage hang over us,[32] but also we would be forced to hear that by our refusal [to attend the council] we helped to strengthen all such abominations of the pope which otherwise would perhaps have been remedied.

---

[24] See II Tim. 2:9.
[25] Or: "to investigate us."
[26] I.e., the *Gravamina*; see *LW* 49, 414, n. 13.
[27] See note 22.
[28] Cardinal Albrecht was bishop of the dioceses of Mainz (in which Halle was located), Magdeburg and Halberstadt.
[29] Because all these matters, at least the ones specially mentioned by Luther, are gross violations of ecclesiastical law; at least Luther thinks so.
[30] Luther's reference is unclear. Luther could be thinking of the bull mentioned on p. 144, n. 3 (in this case Luther's judgment would be correct), or of the bull mentioned in note 13 (in this case Luther's judgment might be too negative).
[31] I.e., by means of the statement which had already branded the evangelicals as heretics; see notes 13, 14.
[32] I.e., because of their refusal to attend the council, the evangelicals would be "declared contumacious, in which case they would be debarred by their own act from future opportunities." So Jedin, p. 319.

See the devil at work in his wicked scoundrels: the papists do not want to condemn us but to wipe us out. This means: Until now the papists have studiously used the canon, *Si papa*,[33] and in our time the papists have spilled much innocent blood, have done all kinds of damage to many godly, honorable people, exiled them, robbed them [of their property], and treated them shamefully, only because these people received the sacrament [in both kinds],[34] etc., since they definitely knew that this was right. Now the papists want to justify such spilling of blood and such persecution by means of a conciliar decree.[35] And not only this, but they intend really to begin and pursue such devilish raging; in addition, they want to compel us to consider such actions to be right, and to be their yes-men, so that consequently all the spilling of blood, persecution, blasphemy, and destruction of Christendom which they have previously committed, are now still committing, and stubbornly intend eternally to commit, may be loaded on our consciences and that we, knowingly, may [thus] be pulled with them to hell. The devil may do this, as he certainly is doing through them.

7

All this certainly would have been sufficient reason long ago to attack and destroy the papists.[36] Yet we have the advantage that (as the situation stands now) it will turn out to be a miserable, despised council which few rulers will attend,[37] and that in addi-

---

[33] *Decreti*, Pars I: Distinctio 40, cap. 6; *Corpus Iuris Canonici*, Ae. L. Richter, ed. (Leipzig, 1879; reprint: Graz, 1959), 1, 146. In his *Against the Papacy of Rome* (1545) Luther translated this canon; *WA* 54, 225; *LW* 41, 285.

[34] See *LW* 48, 143 f.

[35] Literally: "justify . . . in a council."

[36] The following text, down to "big fool after the little ones" in section 8, is one long sentence in which clauses are simply connected by a comma, and separated from one another by spaces or upper case letters for the word with which a new "sentence" begins. The sentence in section 7 is so constructed that it provides the reasons for the opening phrase of section 8, in which Luther states that he is not afraid of the council and therefore does not refuse to attend it.

[37] Literally: "council in which few rulers will be." For "miserable" Luther used a word which sounds like the English "lousy," and which literally means full of lice. It cannot be established whether this was wishful thinking on Luther's part,

tion the [effectiveness of the] ban (should the papists intend to pursue the matter) has long since been nullified. Also, [any] council has now come into such a bad reputation, namely, that it is able to err and has often erred; thus the council has lost its power and prestige, so that in order for the council again to be respected the papists are forced to demonstrate a high degree of fairness for everyone to see. For if this bull[38] were to be made public and be commented upon, what a mockery and an absurdity this council would then be considered by all godly and honorable people! Also, this council would then be an absolute duplication of other councils, as, for instance, the Council of Constance,[39] etc., the stupidity of which has now also become clear through God's Word.

8

[For these reasons] I shall not be afraid of this scarecrow,[40] but shall let the papists continue, and let them completely pour out their foolishness.[41] I also would not give a negative answer to the legate (were His Haughtiness[42] to demand an answer);[43] yet I

---

or whether Luther was thinking of the negative attitude toward the council on the part of the Kings of England and France, or on the part of the members of the Smalcaldic League; see Jedin, pp. 306 ff., 320 ff., 324 ff.; UASA, pp. 22 ff.
[38] I.e., most probably, the bull by which the council had been summoned (see p. 144, n. 3); for another possibility, see note 13.
[39] See LW 48, 147, n. 24.
[40] I.e., the bull (see note 38), or the pending council.
[41] Literally: "completely pour out their fools and bells [i.e., as on a fool's cap]."
[42] This translator takes Luther's words (seine hoffart) to be a title, such as His Excellence. Another possible translation, perhaps, would be: "(were he, in his haughtiness, to demand an answer)."
[43] "Legate" can refer either to the "legate" of the Emperor, Matthias Held (so in Luther's February 14 letter to Jonas; WA, Br 8, 42), or to the "legate" of the pope, Peter van der Vorst. It seems that Luther was thinking of Vorst, however, not only because of the tone of the context in which Luther refers to this legate, but also because of the following circumstances which provide some background for this document. On February 1 Luther informed Jonas of the rumor that Vorst might visit the Elector (see p. 155), while on the same day Melanchthon stated positively that Vorst was on the way to the Elector (C.R. 3, 265). On February 5 Melanchthon informed Jonas that Vorst had been in Weimar but that the Elector requested him to go to Smalcald; C.R. 3, 266. Yet on February 9 Luther wrote Jonas that Vorst, perhaps angry because he could not get an audience with the Elector in Weimar, went from Weimar to Halle, and had not yet come to Smalcald. Luther continued by saying that it was of little importance that superbia [the Latin word for the German hoffart used by Luther above; see note 42] pontificia, i.e., "the papal haughtiness," or perhaps "His

shall also not bind myself,[44] for, if God grants it, the papists will also pour out the big fool after the little ones. It is not necessary to be in a hurry in this matter. One has to learn the ways of God, who does not hurry, but with great patience coaxes [the tongues of people out of their mouths] and then puts little sticks through their tongues so that people are unable to pull them back into their mouths.[45]

9

Were we unnecessarily in a great hurry, and were we to try to overtake God,[46] we might labor in vain. For we whose own logic is much too weak against the devil need God's help at our side.

10

In addition it would create a great scandal, perhaps even also the apostasy of many good people, if we, just at this time when the Turk is again around and the Emperor is in distress,[47] rejected the coun-

---

Papal Haughtiness", was growling. See WA, Br 8, 40. I.e., on the basis of Luther's February 9 statement about the papal haughtiness, i.e., about Vorst, it is safe to suggest that the legate of whom Luther speaks above is also Vorst. For on February 9 Vorst had not yet appeared in Smalcald; in fact it then looked as if for the time being Vorst, being angry, would not show up at all. And as late as February 13 Vorst was still expected to come to Smalcald (see UASA, p. 108); this situation is reflected in Luther's statement concerning Vorst above. Were it certain that Vorst would show up in Smalcald, then it would also be certain that he would demand an answer regarding the papal summoning of the council, for the only purpose of his coming to Smalcald would be to get such an answer. The situation does not fit Held, the Emperor's "legate," of whom it had been known, at least since February 1 that he would come to Smalcald (see p. 155). And on February 14 Luther informed Jonas that Held had "yesterday" arrived; WA, Br 8, 42. The observation concerning "His Haughtiness Vorst" can also substantiate Clemen's suggestion that the present document was written by Luther on approximately February 9, i.e., the date on which Luther made a similar statement about Vorst in the letter to Jonas.

[44] To what Luther does not bind himself is not clear; it could be either his affirmative answer to attend the council, or any decision which the council will make.

[45] See also WA, 51, 656, No. 313, 707, No. 313. Luther means to say that either God would prevent the papists from further speaking by immobilizing their tongues, or that God would prevent the papists from retracting their foolishness.

[46] Luther used the expression: Fur dem hamen fischen. See LW 49, 263, n. 16.

[47] Francis I was still at war with the Emperor (see p. 149, n. 12), and in this war the Turks were the allies of the French (see Ranke 2^IV, 22 f.), so that the

cil.[48] (To be honest, however, I think that since the papists knew what the situation would be this year insofar as the Turk and the Frenchman are concerned, the Roman scoundrels have arranged for the council precisely this year so that even if the Lutherans did not obstruct it, it would certainly be obstructed by the Turks and the French.[49] Of course the Roman scoundrels would really prefer to have it said that the council had been obstructed by the Lutherans. For this would then have to be called obstinacy; but [if the papists canceled the council] then this, of course, would have had to be done out of necessity, that is, because the Turks kept them from conducting the council, etc.) In summary, they are unable to endure a council, not even one of their own, unless they are able to manipulate it as they wish.

280

To Mrs. Martin Luther[1]
[Tambach,][2] February 27, 1537

While Luther was in Smalcald he suffered one attack after the other of what was probably kidney stones,[3] and he became so

---

possibility for a two-front war could develop. That the Emperor felt himself cornered can be seen from his secret instruction for the mission of Held, dated October 1536; text: E. McNall Burns, ed., *The Counter Reformation* (Princeton, 1964), pp. 153 ff.; commentary: Ranke 2[IV], 61 ff.

[48] The period is missing in the text. Literally: "council (even though I am of the opinion . . . " Thus starts one long sentence which ends with "conducting the council, etc." Then Luther left some space and started a new sentence with "In summary." While Luther forgot to put in the closing parenthesis, it is obvious that it should follow the "etc."

[49] Even Emperor Charles was afraid that Pope Paul, out of consideration for France, might cancel the council or lose interest in it; see Ranke 2[IV], 61. Indeed, Francis I did everything possible to prevent the council from taking place; see Jedin, pp. 324 f., 330 f.

[1] While the address is missing in all witnesses, the content of the letter makes clear to whom Luther was writing.

[2] See note 8.

[3] On February 8 Luther passed one or more stones with little pain; WA, Br 8, 40. On February 11 and 18 Luther did experience severe pain, however, and from February 19 on he could not pass any urine. It is not clear whether these stones were in the kidney or bladder, though it is clear that they had become

severely ill that there were serious doubts whether he would live.[4]
*His wife was informed accordingly, and she sent a "carriage" to
Smalcald in order to bring Luther home. In the meantime, however,
Luther lapsed into total weakness; stones blocked his urinary system and apparently some early signs of uremic poisoning developed.
Luther's health was up and down, but the general tendency was
poor. Feeling that his end was near, Luther wanted to die at home,
and so every effort was made to get him back to Wittenberg.*[5] *After
Elector John Frederick had visited Luther in the morning of February 26,*[6] *Luther, along with Bugenhagen, Spalatin, a physician, and
others, left Smalcald for Wittenberg in several carriages, among
them the Elector's private carriage. They traveled only about 15
kilometers to Tambach, where during the night of February 26
Luther's health suddenly improved.*[7] *In the following letter, written
from Tambach in the very early hours of February 27,*[8] *Luther
informs his wife of these developments. He tells of his past severe
illness, of the many unsuccessful efforts to help him, and of the
miracle which God has now accomplished in him. He asks his family to thank God for this rescue. He also tells Catherine that for the
time being the Elector would retain the horses sent from Wittenberg and that it would not be necessary for her to travel from
Wittenberg to meet him, for he is confident of coming home soon.*

Text in German: WA, Br 8, 50–51.[9]

Grace and peace in Christ!

---

wedged in the urinary system. For details, see *WA*, Br 8, 46 ff.; *UASA*, *passim*;
for a thorough discussion of medical details, see *Chicago Medicine* 69 (1966),
107 ff., esp. 111 f.

[4] See notes 5, 6.

[5] See *UASA*, pp. 117 f.; *C.R.* 3, 271, 296; *WA*, TR 3, No. 3543; 4, No. 5147;
5, No. 5368.

[6] See *UASA*, pp. 128 f.

[7] On February 27, at approximately 2:30 A.M., Luther wrote from Tambach to
Melanchthon (who had remained in Smalcald) and informed him, and through
him the people in Smalcald, of his improvement; *WA*, Br 8, No. 3139. It is
quite possible that the trip over the poor roads literally jolted loose some of the
stones.

[8] That this letter was written from Tambach can be seen from its relationship to
the letter cited in note 7, from the reference to the trip to Gotha (see note 22),
and from one witness not used by the *WA*, Br editor; see note 9.

[9] The letter is extant in several manuscript copies, and in the common editions of
Luther's works. For the witnesses see also *WA*, Br 13, 255, addition to *WA*, Br 8,
50.

In the meantime you might rent some extra horses, should you need them, dear Katie, for my gracious Lord[10] will retain your horses and send them home with Master[11] Philip.[12] I myself left Smalcald yesterday and traveled up to this place in my gracious Lord's private carriage.[13] This is the reason: I had not been healthy there for more than three days,[14] and from the first Sunday[15] to this night not one little drop of water passed from me; I had no rest nor did I sleep, and I was unable to retain any drink or food. In summary, I was dead; I commended you, together with the little ones, to God and to my gracious Lord, since I thought that I would never again see you in this mortal life. I felt great pity for you, yet had resigned myself to the grave. But many people prayed to God so hard on my behalf that their tears moved God to open my bladder this night, and in two hours about one *Stübig*[16] passed from me, and I feel as if I were born again.

Therefore thank God and have the dear little ones, together with Aunt Lena,[17] thank the real Father, for you certainly would have lost this father. The good Sovereign ordered people to run,

---

[10] I.e., here and throughout the letter, Elector John Frederick; see *LW* 48, 181 f.

[11] I.e., Master of Arts.

[12] Philip Melanchthon; see *LW* 48, 77, n. 3.

[13] Apparently in view of the elaborate preparations made and the precautions taken (see *WA*, Br 8, 47) the conveyance sent by Catherine was not suitable for transporting Luther; consequently the Elector made one of his own carriages available and retained the conveyance sent by Catherine for Melanchthon's return trip. Another possibility would be that Catherine's conveyance had not yet arrived in Smalcald by the time Luther left on February 26; see however note 19. Since Luther talks about "renting" horses, it seems reasonable to assume that Catherine sent their *own* horses. Apparently these were the horses used by Katie for "driving the wagon"; see p. 108. Whether these horses were from Zölsdorf, as Rückert (*LB*, p. 407, n. 20) suggests, seems to be open to question, since it is generally assumed that the Luthers did not acquire Zölsdorf until 1540.

[14] I.e., February 8–10; see note 3.

[15] According to one of Melanchthon's letters (*C.R.* 3, 296), the *retentio urinae* begun on February 19, i.e., the Monday after Invocavit Sunday, the *second* Sunday that Luther spent in Smalcald, and not on Estomihi Sunday (February 11), the *first* Sunday that Luther spent in Smalcald. The physicians attending the Smalcald meeting in the entourages of the sovereigns were helpless, and consequently on February 20 Melanchthon called for a Dr. George Sturtz to come from Erfurt; *UASA*, pp. 117 f.

[16] I.e., according to *WA*, Br 8, 51, n. 4 about 3–4 liters. According to a different decimal equivalent of the *Stübig* the amount would be about 1 liter, and this figure seems to be more probable.

[17] Magdalene von Bora; see *LW* 49, 271, n. 28.

ride, fetch, and with all his might tried his best to help me.[18] But it was not to be. Your manure cure didn't help me either.[19] [But] this night God has accomplished a miracle in me, and he continues to do it through the intercession of godly people.

I am writing this because I think that my most gracious Lord has ordered the bailiff[20] to send you to meet me, fearing I would die on the way, so that prior to this you could talk with me or see me.[21] Now this is not necessary, and you can certainly stay at home, since God has so abundantly helped me that I am confident I can come happily to you. Today we will spend the night at Gotha.[22] By the

---

[18] For expenses incurred, see *ARG* 25 (1928), 12 f.; for the care given to Luther, see also Köstlin-Kawerau 2, 387.

[19] Literally: "Your skill with the manure also does not help me." Except for the obvious, that Luther was probably referring here to some home remedy given to him by his wife at some other time, the background of this statement is unclear. Did Catherine send the medication along with the driver of the conveyance (so *WA*, Br 8, 51, n. 6)? This suggestion would presuppose that the conveyance had arrived in Smalcald at least a day or so prior to Luther's departure, so that the medication could have been tried. Or was it prepared upon Luther's instructions? The reference to "manure" suggests a liquid "medication" which the doctors in Smalcald gave to Luther, and which was prepared by boiling (?) cloves of garlic with horsedroppings. See *WA*, TR 5, No. 5368. Luther himself supposedly stated that he was given drinks as if he were an ox; see Köstlin-Kawerau 2, 387. Among other cures given consideration was the opening of the bladder either by incision or by some procedure (similar to a present day cystoscopy?) performed with a "golden" instrument: see *ibid.*

[20] I.e., Hans Metzsch.

[21] Catherine indeed left Wittenberg to meet her husband, and the Elector paid her traveling expenses; see *WA*, Br 8, 52, n. 7. It cannot be established, however, that Catherine left as a result of an Electoral summons issued from Smalcald—so Luther's assumption above—or prior to the date she received the present letter—so Clemen, *loc.cit.* See also below, note 22. Luther's niece, Magdalen Kaufmann (see *LW* 49, 269, n. 8), who was staying with the Luther family in Wittenberg at that time (see Köstlin-Kawerau 2, 485), had gone to meet Luther. So had Justus Jonas. The meeting between Jonas and the Luther party took place in Gotha on or prior to March 3; see *C.R.* 3, 308; see also *C.R.* 10, 549, No. 135; *ARG* 31 (1934), 262.

[22] On February 27 the Luther party arrived in Gotha in the late afternoon, and soon the good mood of everyone was shattered by an abrupt and sharp worsening of Luther's condition; see *C.R.* 3, 297. Luther said later that on February 27 he went to bed certain that the next day he would see his coffin; *WA*, TR 3, 394. For the following, see *WA*, Br 8, 54 f. On February 28 Luther made his confession to Bugenhagen and received absolution; he also told his last will to Bugenhagen (see *WA*, Br 8, 55 f.), and discussed funeral arrangements. Even though Luther was still extremely weak, on March 1 he had a lengthy conversation with Martin Bucer (see *LW* 48, 247, n. 13) who had been in Smalcald and had traveled to Gotha to see Luther. Yet Luther's condition was so poor that he could not continue the journey. He eventually passed six stones, among them one supposedly the size of a bean (see *WA*, Br 8, 54 f.). In connection

way, I have written four times,[23] and I wonder that nothing has reached you.

February 27, 1537   MARTIN LUTHER

The messenger has been paid but give him a tip.[24]

281

To George Spalatin
[Wittenberg,] March 21, 1537

Luther finally returned home from Smalcald on March 14.[1] He was still ailing, and only slowly recuperated.[2] In the following letter Luther informs Spalatin of his gradual improvement, and of his wife's gratitude for the hospitality extended to her in Spalatin's home. He also tells Spalatin his wife was sorry that she did not bring along some gifts for Spalatin's daughters, and that she intends to send them some booklets.

On George Spalatin, see LW 48, 8 f.

Text in Latin: WA, Br 8, 59.[3]

---

with these events Catherine Luther apparently was (again? see note 21) summoned to her husband's side (by whom cannot be established), for the Electoral Saxon financial records state that Catherine received money for a *trip to Gotha,* where her husband was ill. It must have taken even a mounted messenger at least a day and a half to get from Gotha to Wittenberg; if February 28 was the day of crisis, then March 2 would have been the earliest date for a possible departure of Catherine from Wittenberg. See also letter No. 281.

23 None of these letters is extant.

24 Literally: "rewarded but do him an honor." This postscript can be found only in one witness; see note 9.

1 See letter No. 280. Because of his illness Luther's return trip was slow; see *UASA,* p. 97, n. 3. Leaving Gotha on March 4, the Luther party spent some time in Weimar, where Spalatin left the party in order to go ahead to Altenburg and prepare Luther's lodging (*C.R.* 10, 549, No. 135; *ARG* 31 [1934], 262). Leaving Weimar on the 10th, Luther spent March 10–12 in Altenburg with the Spalatins (*WA* 35, 602, No. 3; *ARG* 31 [1934], 262), and then returned via Grimma and Torgau to Wittenberg on March 14 (*C.R.* 3, 327).

2 See *C.R.* 3, 327, 329.

3 The letter is extant in several manuscript copies, and in the common editions of Luther's works.

To the most illustrious and excellent man, Mr. George
Spalatin, archbishop of the congregations in Meissen,[4]
my dearest brother

Grace and peace in Christ! Finally I am writing to you, my Spalatin, after my pen has celebrated so many Sabbath days. By God's
grace I gradually recuperate, and learn to eat and drink again.[5] Yet
my thighs, knees, and bones are still shaky, and are thus far not
sufficiently strong to carry my body. I am more exhausted than I
thought, but I shall take care of myself with rest and other nourish-
ment until through God's help I have regained my strength.

My Katie greets you reverently; she is sorry that she brought
along nothing in the line of a present[6] for your daughters,[7] but she is
now having some little books[8] bound, which she has decided to
send as a memento. In the meantime she asks that you accept her
gratefulness and her good intentions. She raves about your thought-
ful treatment, and your great kindness [to her].[9]

Farewell in Christ, and pray for us!

March 21, 1537   Yours, MARTIN LUTHER

---

[4] See p. 97, n. 3.

[5] See WA, TR 3, No. 3558A.

[6] On the basis of the extant Electoral Saxon financial records (see WA, Br 8,
52, n. 7) it is clear that Catherine intended to travel to her ailing husband in
Gotha. On the basis of the statement above it is further clear that Catherine was
in the Altenburg parsonage. Since March 2 is about the earliest date Catherine
could have left Wittenberg for Gotha (see p. 168, n. 22), and since it probably
took her some time to get to Altenburg—on the return trip the Luther party
needed three days (see note 1)—one may assume that Catherine arrived in Altenburg on about March 4. At that point she apparently heard that Luther's health
had sufficiently improved for the Luther party to have left Gotha for Weimar.
The sources do not indicate whether she stayed in Altenburg to await her husband, or whether she returned to Wittenberg prior to Luther's arrival in Altenburg. See also note 9.

[7] Spalatin had two daughters: Anne (born on January 16, 1532) and Catherine
(born on August 28, 1533); see Höss, *Spalatin*, pp. 355 f., 394 f.

[8] It is not clear whether these were copy booklets (so Enders, *Briefwechsel* 11,
215, n. 2), or some of Luther's books; at one time Catherine gave away a copy
of a *Catechism* (WA, Br 7, 151).

[9] Or: "[To all of us]." The text does not make clear to whom the Spalatins
showed this kindness. In the former case one could assume that Catherine
stayed for some days in Altenburg, and then returned to Wittenberg, even
though Luther had not yet arrived in Altenburg.

282

To Wolfgang Capito
[Wittenberg,] July 9, 1537

*In May of 1536 the Wittenberg Concord was signed. This agree-
ment established unity in the interpretation of the Lord's Supper—
and thus ecclesiastical fellowship—between the evangelicals of
southwestern Germany, especially Bucer and Capito (the Reformers of Strassburg), and Luther.*[1] *Shortly thereafter the evangelicals
of Strassburg approached Luther with a plan to publish a collection
of his works in that city.*[2] *In the following letter Luther mentions
that he is not at all eager to have his works republished since,
except for his* On the Bound Will *and his* Catechism, *he would
rather see his books disappear. Then Luther talks about the Wittenberg Concord. He is confident that Bucer and Capito are working hard to make the concord work and that, not withstanding
Satan's work at Augsburg, Christ will complete the work he has
begun. Luther also sends his wife's thanks for a golden ring which
had been sent by Capito. Even though the ring has somehow disappeared, to Catherine Luther's bitter disappointment, Luther assures Capito that the hope for unity among the evangelicals has not
disappeared.*

On Wolfgang Capito, see LW 48, 305, n. 2.

Text in Latin: WA, Br 8, 99–100.[3]

To the most illustrious man, Mr. Wolfgang Capito, Dr. Theol.,
a most faithful servant in the congregation[4] at Strassburg,
my dearest brother in Christ

Grace and peace in Christ! Through those Frenchmen whom you
had recommended to me,[5] my Capito, I want[6] to write back to you.

---

[1] For details, see Köhler 2, 432 ff.; Sasse, pp. 295 ff.; Kidd, No. 127.
[2] For details, see *Archiv für Geschichte des Buchwesens* 7 (1966), 1131 ff.
[3] The letter is extant as autograph, in several manuscript copies, and in the common editions of Luther's works.
[4] Luther used *ecclesia*, i.e., church; see also *LW* 49, 61, n. 9.
[5] Nothing could be established about the background of this statement. Letter
No. 282 is the first extant letter written by Luther to Capito since the latter had

Perhaps they themselves will tell you what they have seen and heard. Regarding [the plan] to collect my writings in volumes,[7] I am quite cool and not at all eager[8] about it because, roused by a Saturnian hunger,[9] I would rather see them all devoured.[10] For I acknowledge none of them to be really a book of mine, except

been in Wittenberg in May of 1536 for the purpose of establishing the concord. Yet Bucer and Capito had in the meantime written to Luther several times. In fact, on September 4, 1536, Capito ever so carefully reproached Luther for his silence; WA, Br 7, 521. Since in the following lines Luther deals with Capito's letters of June 13 (see notes 7, 19), July 20 (see note 14), September 4, 1536 (see note 19), and January, 1537 (see note 13), one has to see in Luther's letter an answer to all the letters Capito had written—the delay in Luther's answer could be explained by the events occurring at the time Luther wrote his *Smalcald Articles* (see pp. 145, n. 13, 153 f.)—and one is tempted to assume that the "Frenchmen" had something to do with these letters. This would mean that the "Frenchmen" must have been in the area of Wittenberg for quite some time. "What they have seen and heard" could, then, be a reference to the events pertaining to the meeting of the Smalcaldic League. Yet Bucer was also in Smalcald (see *UASA*, p. 109, n. 7), so that he certainly could have given a detailed report about this meeting to Capito. In any event, Luther's reference to "those Frenchmen" and what they might report to Capito, is obscure.

[6] Literally: "wanted." I.e., Luther wrote here and throughout the letter from the standpoint of the reader for whom the activities mentioned by the writer were already in the past.

[7] On June 13, 1536, Capito asked Luther to give his permission to publish or republish some of his books in Strassburg. Capito hinted that by means of such a project he himself hoped to get out of a tight financial situation; WA, Br 7, 433. In the following letters Capito did not mention the project. On January 19, 1537, the Strassburg printer Wendelin Rihel wrote a letter to Joducus Neobulus, who was a kind of majordomo in the Luther house at that time (see Köstlin-Kawerau 2, 487; WA, Br 7, 436), and from this letter we find out the following: (a) Rihel had printed some of Luther's sermons, yet with little financial success. (b) In order to make Luther's *divina mens* known to all preachers, esp. in Switzerland and among the Waldensians, Capito and Bucer had for the last two years been planning an edition of Luther's *opera omnia* in Latin, which Rihel was supposed to publish. (c) Neobulus was to write what Luther thought of this plan, for without Luther's permission the people of Strassburg would not wish to undertake anything. Text: *Analecta Lutherana*, ed. T. Kolde (Gotha, 1883), p. 232, n. 1.

[8] E. Wolgast, *Die Wittenberger Luther-Ausgabe* (Nieuwkoop, 1971), pp. 14 ff., gives five reasons for Luther's negative attitude toward the attempts to have his collected works published: (a) his worry that reading his works might reduce the study of Scripture; (b) his realization that some of his writings originated in temporary, restricted circumstances; (c) his changed attitude toward the papacy; (d) his conviction that writings by other theologians were more significant than his own writings; (e) his realization that such an edition would be so expensive that the edition would collect dust in libraries, and that only the rich could afford to buy it, while the common man could by no means afford it.

[9] Kronos, the youngest son of Heaven and Earth, swallowed up all his sons except Zeus, born to him by his sister Rhea. When Kronos was forced to cough up his sons, they defeated him in a desperate struggle. "The ancients themselves supposed that he [Saturnus] was not a native [Roman] god, but imported from Greece, a story which blends with the flight of Kronos from Zeus, as in Verg.

perhaps the one *On the Bound Will*[11] and the *Catechism*. Nevertheless I have entrusted the matter to Doctor Caspar Cruciger[12] to see if anything ought to be done.

I have an idea that in this case[13] you people will put forth much effort; yet I do pray that our [Lord] Christ does not let you work in vain. Others, too, have given me a sufficiently clear picture of the satan at Augsburg;[14] but let us wait for Him who has begun His work.[15] When His time arrives He will come and will not delay;[16] therefore let us not despair. On the other hand, concerning you and Bucer[17] I am convinced that you act in a sincere and candid way; not only this, but I also rejoice that all who write to me or talk with me have the same opinion about you people when they mention you.[18]

Aen. 8. 319 ff." So *O.C.D.*, p. 797; see also *ibid.*, p. 476. Luther identifies Saturn with Kronos, and wants to say that he is as eager to see his books devoured, as Saturn, i.e., Kronos, was eager to devour his children.

[10] See also *WA*, TR 3, No. 3797; *LW* 54, 274; *WA* 38, 133 f.; 50, 657 f.; *LW* 34, 283 f.

[11] See *LW* 33, 15 ff.; 49, 140, n. 3.

[12] See *LW* 49, 104, n. 12. According to Wolgast, *op. cit.*, pp. 13 f., the project developed; there were even suggestions from Wittenberg pertaining to an organization of the edition which would please Luther. It is not known why the project did not finally materialize.

[13] "This case" refers to the efforts of Bucer and Capito to have the concord accepted by as many of the upper German cities and Swiss evangelicals as possible. In letters written between January 15 and 19 Luther was informed of these developments; see *WA*, Br 8, Nos. 3126, 3127, 3128. On these efforts, see also Köhler 2, 456 ff.

[14] In his July 20, 1536, letter Capito informed Luther of the attitude of the people of Augsburg toward the concord. Then Capito mentioned the quarrel between John Forster, the pro-Luther pastor at Augsburg's St. John's Church, and a certain Michael. *WA*, Br 7, 466 f. On September 24, 1536, Forster wrote to Neobulus (see note 7) that Michael is a son of perdition (Kolde, *op. cit.*, p. 238, n. 1). On August 7, 1536, Luther answered a no-longer extant letter from Forster in which Luther mentioned a *Meister Michel* who agitates against "us"; *WA*, Br 7, 492 f. These are references to the pro-Zwingli preacher Michael Keller in Augsburg; see *LW* 49, 146, n. 24. Among the "others" who, in addition to Capito, had informed Luther about Keller's activity in Augsburg was certainly Forster, who must have done this in the no-longer extant letter just mentioned. But who else had informed Luther, so that the plural would be justified? One possibility would be a woman mentioned by Luther in his August 7 letter who talked to von Amsdorf about Keller; von Amsdorf, in turn, informed Luther about this discussion. Another possibility would be Forster's letter to Neobulus mentioned above.

[15] See Phil. 1:6.

[16] See Hab. 2:3.

[17] See *LW* 48, 247, n. 13.

[18] Since very few of the letters addressed to Luther are extant it is impossible to substantiate this statement.

My Catherine thanks you for the golden ring.[19] Hardly ever have I seen her more indignant than when she realized that the ring either had been stolen by a thief, or had been lost because of her own negligence (this seems to me unlikely, though I always nag her about it), for I had convinced her that this present had been sent to her as a good omen and token of the fact that your church really is one with ours. And so the woman is crushed. I am writing this for you to know that [nevertheless] we have total and sincere hope regarding unity. May Christ complete the matter. Amen. But this I add: send nothing further to my wife, so that you do not double the sadness, for Christ is sufficient for both of us.

Do greet all your and our friends and tell them to think the best of us as we do of you people. The Lord Jesus be the seal of this [good] will; to him, with the Father and the Holy Ghost be glory for ever. Amen.

July 9, 1537   Yours,

MARTIN LUTHER

283

To Nicholas Hausmann
[Wittenberg,] February 23, 1538

Luther tells of being worn down by vexations of Satan which have kept him from writing long letters to Hausmann. He asks Hausmann to thank the sovereigns of Dessau for the gift of a fish, and to extend his congratulations to Sir John upon his reconciliation with his wife. In connection with this reconciliation, Luther speaks of the power of prayer, and asks for Hausmann's prayer in his behalf. Then Luther informs Hausmann that the Consilium de emendanda ecclesia *will be published in Latin and in German, and voices his*

---

[19] In his June 13 letter to Luther, Capito extended greetings to Catherine and announced the pending dispatch of a gift; WA, Br 7, 434. In his September 3 letter to Neobulus (see note 7), Capito included a golden ring for Catherine as a sign of his appreciation for the kindness with which she cared for Luther; see Kolde, *op. cit.*, p. 234, n. 1. It is peculiar that in his September 4 letter to Luther (WA, Br 7, No. 3075), Capito did not mention this ring.

negative opinion of this document. He extends greetings from his wife and his wishes that Master Peter may be strong in Christ. In a postscript Luther tells of enclosing a satirical woodcut of the papal coat of arms, and returns Hausmann's copy of the Consilium.
   On Nicholas Hausmann, see LW 48, 399 f.
   Text in Latin: WA, Br 8, 200.[1]

To the most distinguished man, Mr. John[2] Hausmann,
Master [of Arts], a faithful and sincere servant of
Christ in Dessau, my dearest brother in the Lord
and my elder[3] to be honored

Grace and peace in Christ! I have not the time to write to many people, my excellent and dearest Nicholas. Therefore I am also asking you first to thank the illustrious sovereigns[4] in my behalf for the fish given to me, and then also in my name to congratulate the sovereign, Sir John, upon his reconciliation with his wife.[5] May Christ strengthen his work which he has begun in them, [and] complete it.[6] Amen. To Him be also glory for having so graciously listened to our prayers in this matter. By this example we are taught to pray without ceasing,[7] for He who is coming will indeed come and save us.[8] But as I have said, I am now so worn down by certain vexations of Satan that I am unable to write more.[9] More at some other time, if [Christ][10] will grant the time. Pray diligently to the

---

[1] The letter is extant as autograph.
[2] Luther often used the name John (as did others at the time), either if he did not know a person's first name, or if he knew it, then simply as a somewhat humorous touch. For documentation, see *WA*, Br 8, 200, n. 2; 10, 182, n. 1.
[3] "Elder," or: "superior."
[4] I.e., the sovereigns of Anhalt-Dessau.
[5] In 1534 John of Anhalt had married Margaret, a daughter of Elector Joachim I of Brandenburg. As early as 1535 rumors spread that the marriage was shaky. Margaret's extravagance aroused resentment, and court intriguers were successful in having her income cut. When her husband did not take her side, she separated from him. It could not be established when the reconciliation was accomplished. For details, see *WA*, Br 8, 108 f.
[6] See Phil. 1:6.
[7] See I Thess. 5:17.
[8] See Hab. 2:3.
[9] Luther apparently thought that he had made this statement in the opening sentence of the letter, or at least that Hausmann would understand this sentence in this way.
[10] Or: "[Satan]."

Lord for me, therefore, that I might be able to do what is good in his eyes.

Those monstrosities of the Roman cardinals will be published both in Latin and in German.[11] But the malice of the matter and the wickedness of those people are beyond indignation and words. Christ will come and himself be the judge; punishment worthy of those mockers of God and men has to be reserved for him. As I have asked, do pray for me, for I am confident that your prayers accomplish much with God. My Katie greets you reverently, and I wish that Master Peter[12] may be strong in Christ.

Written on Saturday after Peter's Enthronement[13]—*that is, [the feast] which has been introduced by the pope in order to stabilize his tyranny—1538.*

Yours,

MARTIN LUTHER

I am sending the papal coat of arms, which I have drawn, or caused to be drawn, together with [that of] his cardinals.[14] I am returning the copy of the "Improved Church," for I had it already, also in a German translation.[15]

---

11 See p. 158, n. 11. The *Consilium* was presented to Pope Paul III early in March of 1537. Even though the Curia did not authorize its publication, a Latin version of the *Consilium* was soon published in Italy and in Germany. And in April of 1538 a German translation was published in Strassburg. Soon thereafter Luther himself published a German version with a preface and a commentary; *WA* 50, 288 ff.; *LW* 34, 235 ff. Luther apparently misunderstood this document when he declared that it was a mockery. "What was a most serious and vital declaration looking only toward the regeneration of the Church became unfortunately a weapon in the hands of the Protestants. . . . " So Olin, *op. cit.* (see p. 158, n. 11), p. 185. On the other hand, Luther's attitude becomes understandable if one considers that in April of 1537 the Council of Mantua had been postponed (see *UASA*, pp. 176 ff.), so that the honesty and good will of the papacy regarding the council and reforms in the church could indeed be doubted. For details see Jedin, pp. 328 ff., 432 ff.

12 This is apparently a reference to Luther's former barber, Master Craftsman Peter Beskendorf, who was then living in Dessau.

13 The day *Cathedratio Petri*, February 22, fell on a Friday in 1538.

14 See *WA* 54, 346 ff.; 38, 616; *WA, TR* 3, No. 3749.

15 Hausmann must have sent a (manuscript?) copy of a German version of the *Consilium* to Luther, which Luther now returned, for he had already received another German version prior to the time that he received the one from Hausmann. For bibliographical details, see *ARG* 33 (1936), 1 ff., and *WA* 50, 285 ff. For a different interpretation of this sentence, see Enders, *Briefwechsel*, 11, 336, n. 7.

284

To Edward Fox
[Wittenberg,] May 12, 1538

After the English legation returned home from the 1536 meeting of the Smalcaldic League at Frankfurt,[1] *the interest of Henry VIII in an alliance with the German evangelicals rapidly cooled.*[2] *The situation changed, however, when Pope Paul III summoned the Council of Mantua, and when papal envoys publicized this summons throughout Europe. In late February/early March, 1537, the Smalcaldic League rejected this summons,*[3] *and on March 26 the league informed Henry VIII of this action; at the same time the league renewed the idea of further theological discussions for the purpose of establishing unity, as well as a basis for common action regarding the council.*[4] *Henry, too, rejected the council, and did so in his famous* Protest, *a document which supposedly "shocked even Cromwell."*[5] *Henry sent a copy of this document to Elector John Frederick of Saxony in order to promote the renewal of alliance negotiations,*[6] *and in February of 1538 he sent Christopher Mont to the members of the Smalcaldic League. Mont's mission was to get a legation of councilors and theologians of first rank—Melanchthon was to be among them—to come to England for further negotiations.*[7] *Mont discharged his mission during and after the March/*

---

[1] See pp. 138 f.

[2] The religious-ecclesiastical policies of the King were set forth in the *Ten Articles*, which show an influence of continental Protestantism (see *O.D.C.C.*, p. 1330; *Witt.Art.*, p. 12 f.; Rupp, *Tradition*, pp. 109 f.; Tjernagel, pp. 163 ff.). Cromwell's *Injunctions* of 1536 (see *EHD* 5, 805 ff.) were designed to put these articles into operation (see Tjernagel, p. 167). "The deaths of Catherine of Aragon and Anne Boleyn had removed the principal source of friction between Charles V and Henry VIII. The English king had less reason to seek the aid of the emperor's Lutheran subjects than before." So Tjernagel, p. 168.

[3] See *C.R.* 3, Nos. 1540, 1543; see also Jedin, pp. 320 ff.

[4] *C.R.* 3, No. 1543; *L.P.* 12^I, No. 745; see also *ibid.*, No. 564.

[5] So Tjernagel, p. 171. See also Jedin, p. 307; Prüser, pp. 111 ff. Text of *Protest*: *L.P.* 12^I, Nos. 1310, 1311.

[6] See *L.P.* 12^{II}, No. 1089; *C.R.* 3, No. 1629; Tjernagel, pp. 171 f.; Prüser, pp. 119 ff.

[7] Mont's instructions, dated February 28, 1538: *L.P.* 13^I, No. 367; his credentials in the form of letters from Henry VIII to Elector John Frederick and Landgrave Philip of Hesse, dated February 25: *ibid.*, Nos. 352, 353. Mont's instructions (see also Prüser, pp. 121 f.) demonstrate that Henry's sole interest in the

April meeting of the Smalcaldic League in Brunswick.[8] *As was to
be expected, Elector John Frederick refused to let Melanchthon go.
As a result the Electoral Saxon Vice-Chancellor Francis Burchart,
the Hessian Councilor George von Boineburg, and the superintendent of Gotha, Frederick Myconius, were sent to England. The
purpose of this mission was to lay the doctrinal groundwork for a
legation to be dispatched later on.*[9] *Upon his return from the
league's meeting, Myconius visited Luther in Wittenberg,*[10] *and
when on May 13 Myconius and Burchart left Wittenberg for England,*[11] *Luther sent along with them the following letter, addressed to Edward Fox, one of the members of the English legation
which had been in Wittenberg in 1536.*

*Luther first reflects upon the kindness shown to him by Fox
during the latter's stay in Wittenberg. Then Luther mentions that
for a long time he has received no news from Fox, that this fact
worries him because it could be a sign that the cause of the gospel is
not faring well in England (a possibility supported by rumors), and
that he hopes to receive good news from the league's envoys upon
their return. The envoys, in turn, will give Fox all the news pertaining to the church and commonweal in Germany. Luther closes with
greetings from his wife.*

On Edward Fox, see p. 114, n. 4.

Text in Latin: WA, Br 8, 219–220.[12]

---

alliance with the league was political, and that theological matters were of
minor concern to the King. For the league members, however, these theological
concerns were primary.

[8] For the following, see Prüser, pp. 121 ff.

[9] See *L.P.* 13ᴵ, Nos. 648, 649, 650; see also Tjernagel, pp. 180 ff.; Prüser, pp.
124 ff.

[10] For Myconius' travels, see *ARG* 31 (1934), 205 f.

[11] On the stay of this legation in England (end of May 1538, to October 1,
1538) and the resulting *Thirteen Articles* (*L.P.* 13ᴵ, Nos. 1306, 1307; see also
O.D.C.C., pp. 1348 f.); see Prüser, pp. 125 ff.; Tjernagel, pp. 181 ff.; Rupp,
Tradition, pp. 115 ff.; *Witt.Art.*, pp. 13 ff.

[12] The letter is extant as autograph, which is deposited in the Wolfenbüttel
Library. The letter never reached its addressee since after the Germans had
arrived in England they found out that Fox had died on May 8 (see *DNB* 7,
555). The Germans apparently kept Luther's letter and brought it back to Germany; it eventually found its way into the library of the University of Helmstedt
(founded in 1576), and from there into the Wolfenbüttel Library. The Germans
also took along a personal letter from Melanchthon to Henry VIII; *L.P.* 13ᴵ, No.
985.

To the father who is to be revered in Christ,
Sir Edward, bishop of Hereford in England,
my superior[13] to be cherished in the Lord

Grace and peace in Christ, our Lord! Since these men, our friends
and the envoys[14] of the sovereigns, are getting[15] ready for the
journey to your most serene King,[16] I cannot, Reverend Sir, omit
writing a letter to you since [otherwise] I really fear being charged
with being an ungrateful and forgetful man. Since[17] in addition to
the most warm friendliness you showed in conversing with us
here, you have also shown me an overflowing measure of kindness
and helped me with your counsel [in the battle] against my enemy,
the stone, I am unable to forget you. We speak of you people often
and at great length, especially[18] since, in view of the changing conditions in your kingdom, either you are unable to write letters to
us with which we might satisfy our wish [for news concerning you],
or those letters which you did dispatch have perhaps been inter-
cepted. So[19] we are hanging in the air, and indeed are afraid that
this persistent silence[20] might perhaps be a sign of some harsh blow
struck against the progress of the gospel. In addition there are some

---

[13] Or: "elder."
[14] I.e. here and throughout the letter, Burchart, von Boineburg, and Myconius.
[15] Luther wrote the whole letter from the viewpoint of the reader of the letter
for whom the circumstances mentioned in the letter were in the past. Consequently in many cases Luther used the past tense for the verbs, while the
translator used the present tense in order to provide a smoother reading.
[16] I.e. here and throughout the letter, Henry VIII.
[17] The following is a reference to Fox's stay in Wittenberg; see pp. 117 ff. In
connection with that stay, nothing is known about an attack of stones (kidney,
bladder, gallstones?) on Luther's part; see, however, letter No. 269, and WA,
Br 7, Nos. 2292, 3018. Perhaps Luther's reference should be understood in the
sense that Luther and Fox had talked about the stone problem and that Fox
had told Luther of some remedy, or of some means (diet?) to prevent stone
attacks.
[18] For the following, see also pp. 150 f.
[19] Literally: "For we."
[20] One may assume, as Clemen (WA, Br 8, 220) does, that with "persistent
silence" Luther wanted to say that "we" had received no letters from Fox, or
other Englishmen, since the English legation had left Wittenberg in April of
1536, even though Luther did not state this explicitly. Luther is not quite exact
at this point for the last extant letter from England, written by Nicholas Heath
to Melanchthon, was dated August 29, 1536; text: WA, Br 8, 220 ff.; see also
WA, Br 13, 263, addition to WA, Br 8, 220 ff. In addition, the Wittenbergers
had also received other letters from England; see C.R. 3, 91, 104, 709 (incorrect
date).

who think that your King, finally ensnared by the Roman intrigues,[21] would like to get back into the pope's good grace. In this affair we pray and, [torn] between hope and fear, wish that Satan would be crushed under your feet.[22] At this point we are not certain how the cause of the gospel fares among you people. But we hope that through these envoys, when they return, we shall hear happy news and truly "good news" about your English church. On the other hand, what the situation is concerning both the church and the commonweal in our Germany, you will be able to find out in detail from our friends.

May the Lord Jesus Christ multiply in you people—and at the same time also in us—his grace and gifts[23] to the glory of God the Father. Amen.

My Katie reverently greets Your Lordship. In Christ farewell to Your Lordship, to whom I commend myself.[24]

May 12, 1538   Your Lordship's dedicated

MARTIN LUTHER

---

[21] Neither Enders (*Briefwechsel* 11, 362), nor Clemen (*WA*, Br 8, 220), nor the revisions of *WA*, Br (*WA*, Br 13, 263) comment on this sentence. One may, of course, ask whether the statement carries any weight, or should be understood as beating around the bush. If one does not wish to affirm this latter possibility, then one has to identify "some who think," and "ensnared by Roman intrigues." Where does one have to search for "some who think?" In Wittenberg? At the Electoral court? Among the members of the Smalcaldic League? Among Luther's friends in England? (see also pp. 150 f.) And finally, what were the "Roman intrigues"? Is the statement simply a cover-up for the opinions the Wittenberg theologians held of the *Ten Articles* of 1536 (see note 2), or of the *Bishops' Book* of 1537 (see *O.D.C.C.*, p. 175), if, indeed, they were familiar with these documents? This is possible, for on July 31, 1536, Alesius sent the *Ten Articles* via Aepinus in Hamburg to Wittenberg (*C.R.* 3, 104), and Melanchthon passed a negative judgment on them (*C.R.* 3, No. 1490). Whether at the time of the present letter the *Bishops' Book* was known in Wittenberg could not be established, though it seems to have been available in Germany; Fox apparently had sent a copy of it to Bucer in July of 1537 (*L.P.* 12[II], No. 410). Were the "Roman intrigues" perhaps a reference to the Northern Rebellion? (See J. D. Mackie, *The Earlier Tudors: 1485–1558* [Oxford, 1962], pp. 385 ff.) But how much of this situation was known in Wittenberg? In any event, Luther's statement needs further clarification.

[22] Rom. 16:20.

[23] This is perhaps an allusion to Eph. 4:7.

[24] Literally: "In Christ farewell to Your Lordship who should hold me as someone who has been commended."

285

To James Propst
[Wittenberg,] September 15, 1538

After a long silence (which was the result of Luther's work load, his aging, his spiritual struggles, and his conviction that Propst was not in need of his letters of counsel and guidance), Luther writes this letter to Propst. Luther first tells Propst that two well-educated but poor brethren have come from lower Germany to Wittenberg, and that one of them will be sent to Propst in Bremen. Then he communicates news: He, an old man, is becoming youthful again because of the many theological controversies in which he is constantly involved; in this connection he sends theses against the Antinomians. Further, Charles V, Francis I, and the Venetians are undertaking joint naval operations against the Turks, and thus a good beginning has been made in the war against this great enemy of Christendom; the council, transferred from Mantua to Vicentia, has breathed its last; the Pope promotes the interests of his sons by means of murder. Luther also extends greetings from his wife and his daughter Margaret (Propst's godchild), asks for Propst's prayers in his behalf, wishes God's blessing upon Propst, and asks Propst to extend his and his wife's greetings to Propst's wife.

On James Propst, see LW 48, 233, n. 34.

Text in Latin: WA, Br 8, 291–292.[1]

To the excellent man, Mr. James Propst, a theologian and
a faithful and sincere servant of Christ in the
area of Bremen, my dearest brother

Grace and peace in Christ! I write to you rather rarely, my James, and I do not answer your letters[2] as you would perhaps wish.[3] But

---

[1] The letter is extant in one manuscript copy, and in the common editions of Luther's works. It was printed, supposedly from the autograph, in a history of the evangelical clergy of Hannover, published in 1731; see WA, Br. 8, No. 3259, Introduction. The WA, Br text reproduces this printed version.

[2] Or: "letter."

[3] Luther's last prior extant letter to Propst is dated August 23, 1535; WA, Br 7, No. 2226. None of Propst's letters to Luther is extant.

I hope you make the best of this, since you know of my various burdens of business, work, age, and spiritual struggles.[4] Finally I think you do not need my letters, since in other ways you have been so richly endowed by God as to be able to guide and console both yourself and all others in this very evil age [in which people are] possessed by such great ungratefulness and contempt for the Word of salvation. But enough about these matters.

Let me go on.[5] Two excellent and learned brethren[6] [have come to us][7] from lower Germany. Of course, we, who are poor enough ourselves, are flooded with poor people who come from all over.[8] Yet we decided to feed them both, according to our ability. Since they are unable to be useful here on account of the language,[9] however, it seems wise to Mr. Philip[10] to send one of them to you people; Philip thinks there is a chance that a place of ministering might perhaps be free among you, so that they are not forced to be idle;[11] also, you people are wealthy, and the flood of your wealth can easily flow over into the lowliness of their poverty.[12] Should the ungratefulness of man have become so powerful among you people that you are unable to sustain him until he may be provided with [a place of] ministering, then send him back to us, and we shall share with him what we have.

News: I—an exhausted old man, tired out from so many labors[13]—constantly become younger from day to day; that is, new

---

[4] In the text this sentence is connected with the next in such a way that both sentences provide the basis for Luther's hope that Propst would make the best of his, Luther's silence. A literal translation would read: "Since you know of . . . struggles. And finally since I think you . . . "
[5] Literally: "By the way."
[6] The text reads *fratres*, which could also be translated as "friars." It is commonly assumed (Enders, *Briefwechsel* 12, 10, n. 1; WA, Br 8, 292, n. 1) that these "brethren" were Augustinian friars from the lower German-Dutch area, though nothing can be established about them.
[7] A note in the 1731 text points out that this phrase was missing in the source, and that Luther, perhaps in haste, had forgotten to add this phrase, and being very busy did not reread his letters and therefore did not catch this omission.
[8] See also p. 142.
[9] I.e., the low German dialect of the "brethren" could not be understood in Wittenberg or its surrounding area.
[10] I.e., Philip Melanchthon; see LW 48, 77, n. 3.
[11] Why Luther, after speaking of sending "one," suddenly speaks again of both brethren is not clear.
[12] This is an allusion to II Cor. 8:2 (Vulgate).
[13] In his last extant letter to Propst (see note 3) Luther made a similar statement.

sects always rise up against me,[14] and renewed youth is necessary to fight them. You will find out about the Antinomians from these theses.[15] Were there no other proof that we are the ones who have been called and elected to the Kingdom of God and have the true Word of God, this one fact would suffice: we are attacked by so many sects which constantly disagree with one another—sometimes they even originate within our own ranks—not to speak of the papists, and my personal wars with Satan, and the contempt for the Word in our midst. But we are not better than the apostles and prophets, or even our Lord himself.

We have certain news that the Emperor, the Frenchman, and the Venetians have joined their fleets against the Turks, and that at sea a good beginning has been made against such a great enemy.[16] May God bless and give success to the prayers of the Christian people.

---

[14] Or: "for me [i.e., for my benefit]."

[15] This is a reference to the Antinomian controversy (see *LW* 49, Index, *s.v.*), which in the early summer of 1537 had moved into its second phase, and in November of that year into its third phase. See also *LW* 47, 101 ff. Text of the theses mentioned by Luther: *WA* 39I, 489 ff.; Luther sent a poster print which is described *ibid.*, 338, No. 6a; see also *ibid.*, 336.

[16] The news reported by Luther is only partially correct. In May of 1538 Pope Paul III had been able to work out a ten year truce (signed at Nice) by which the third war between Emperor Charles V and Francis I was ended. The Turks, however, who were allies of the French, were not included in this truce. To the contrary, during the negotiations between the Emperor and the French which preceded and followed the signing of the truce, details of a joint action against the Turks were discussed. All through 1537 the Turks had successfully harassed the southeastern border of the Empire and the eastern half of the Mediterranean Sea. In fact, in July of 1537 they were able to gain a temporary foothold in southeastern Italy. Against this threat the Pope organized the Holy League (consisting of Venice, the Emperor, and the Pope himself). Above, Luther reported a minor skirmish which took place on August 10, 1538, between the papal fleet and the Turks (see *WA*, Br 8, 292, n. 8), and which was of no particular consequence for the war. On September 28, 1538, the Turkish fleet defeated the combined Venetian-papal fleet (to which a few Imperial ships had been added) in the gulf of Arta, a victory which gave the Turks mastery of the Mediterranean Sea until the Battle of Lepanto in 1571. France never participated in any of these naval actions, and the Emperor was more concerned with securing the southeastern border of the Empire than with naval actions against the Turks. How critical the situation actually was can be seen from the fact that in November of 1538 the Emperor expressed the hope of having 60,000 men mobilized against the Turks by spring of 1539, and from the additional fact that the only accomplishment of the allied fleet, the conquest of a castle on the Dalmatian coast, could not be maintained. For details, see Ranke 2IV, 69 ff.; Elton, pp. 518 ff.

The council which has been transferred to Vicentia has without much ado breathed its last.[17] And the Pope in Rome[18] leads the life of ease; by right and by wrong he strives to make his [sons] richer and more important, bravely killing or poisoning[19] those whose property his sons eagerly covet. Rome is so incomparably bad that God is in no position to consider it worthy of an opportunity for reform: "God's wrath has come upon it at last."[20]

My lord Katie greets you, and so does your little godchild, my daughter, little Margaret,[21] for whom you will please provide a decent suitor after my death. I write nothing about myself except to ask you to pray in my behalf that the Lord may free me from the blows and the thorns[22] of the angel of Satan, and that according to His will He may grant me a good hour when I am to be delivered from this misery.[23] The Lord be with you, and please greet your lord[24] for me and my Katie.

September 15, 1538   Yours,

MARTIN LUTHER

---

[17] On April 20, 1537, Pope Paul III postponed the opening of the council to November 1, 1537; on October 8, 1537, he postponed the date once more, this time to May 1, 1538, and designated Vicentia (in the territory of Venice) as the location of the council. On April 25, 1538, the Pope delayed the opening of the council indefinitely. Later the pope agreed to have the council opened on April 6, 1539. See *UASA*, pp. 176 f.; Jedin, pp. 332 f., 339 f.

[18] Paul III. For the nepotism of Paul III, see the references from Pastor's *History of the Popes* cited in *WA*, Br 8, 293, n. 10; see also Enders, *Briefwechsel* 12, 11, n. 6.

[19] Literally: "having bravely killed and wiped out by means of poison." Whether Luther speaks here on the basis of rumors or factual knowledge, or whether he is simply polemical, has to remain open.

[20] I Thess. 2:16.

[21] This was Luther's daughter Margaret, who had been born on December 17, 1534, and who died in 1570. In his last extant letter to Propst (see note 3), Luther also extended greetings from Margaret.

[22] See II Cor. 12:7.

[23] In his last extant letter to Propst (see note 3) Luther made a similar statement.

[24] I.e., Propst's wife (see *ADB* 26, 615), about whom nothing could be established. On the basis of Luther's letters to Propst it is clear that the Propsts and the Luthers were quite close.

286

To Elector John Frederick
[Wittenberg,] July 8, 1539

In April of 1539 Duke George of Saxony, Luther's bitter foe since the days of the Leipzig Disputation in 1519, died. He was succeeded by his brother, Duke Henry, during whose short reign (1539-1541) the Reformation was officially introduced in Ducal Saxony. This was a heavy blow for the papal party in the Empire, but especially for a printer named Nicholas Wolrab[1] whom John Cochlaeus[2] had set up in Leipzig in 1535 for the specific purpose of printing the works of papal theologians directed against the Reformers, and also any materials pertaining to the pending council. At the beginning of May, 1539, Duke Henry stopped Wolrab's work on the third volume of a Postil *by George Witzel.[3] On May 11 Wolrab approached the Duke and requested permission to complete the work, pointing out that in printing Witzel's* Postil *he was only following Duke George's order, and that he had invested large sums in the project which he would lose, were he to discontinue the half-completed project. Wolrab added a postscript in which he mentioned his intention of reprinting Luther's German Bible,[4] and asked for a ducal patent which would license him exclusively to print and market Luther's German Bible in the Duchy of Saxony. As one might expect, Luther found out about this plan. In the following letter Luther approaches his territorial lord, Elector John Frederick, with the request that he see to it that Wolrab not get away with this plan. Luther points out that it would be wrong to let Wolrab enrich himself at the expense of the hard work of the Wittenberg publishers and printers who took the financial risk for the German Bible in the first place. Were Wolrab successful, it would*

---

[1] On Nicholas Wolrab, and also for the following material, see *WA*, Br 8, No. 3356, Introduction; Enders, *Briefwechsel* 12, 200, n. 1; J. Benzing, *Die Buchdrucker des 16. und 17. Jahrhunderts im deutschen Sprachgebiet* (Wiesbaden, 1963), p. 263, No. 9. See also *WA*, Br 12, 284 ff.

[2] See *LW* 49, 273, n. 12.

[3] See *NCE* 14, 984 f.

[4] In the fall of 1534 Hans Lufft published in Wittenberg the first complete edition of the German Bible. Luther and his friends then thoroughly revised the whole work, and in the fall of 1541 a revised text was published.

certainly mean financial loss for the Elector's subjects, because the
people at Leipzig have better marketing opportunities.
On Elector John Frederick, see LW 48, 181 f.
Text in German: WA, Br 8, 491.[5]

To the Most Serene, Noble Sovereign and Lord,
Sir John Frederick, duke in Saxony, archmarshal and
elector of the Holy Roman Empire, landgrave in Thuringia,
margrave in Meissen, and count of the castle in Magdeburg,
my Most Gracious Lord

Grace and peace in Christ, and also my humble *Pater noster!*[6] Most
Serene, Noble Sovereign, Most Gracious Lord! Wolrab at Leipzig—
the scoundrel[7] who until now has printed and with great effort
distributed all the insulting books directed against us—has decided
to reprint our German Bible and take the bread out of the mouths
of our printers.[8] Your Electoral Grace knows how unfair it is that
this scoundrel should be able to use the labor and expense of our
printers for his own profit and their damage. This would mean that
he with his wickedness would manage to have even our work serve
him in the best possible way as the result of his unpunished foul
play, disgraceful action, and slander. Therefore it is my humble
request that Your Electoral Grace help see to it that Wolrab does
not reap such rich rewards from his wickedness, and that Your
Electoral Grace's subjects not have to pay so dearly for the expenses
and risk [they were willing to face]. I do not mention the fact,

---

[5] The letter is extant as autograph. For the background of this letter, and for the
development of Luther's case against Wolrab, see also the material cited in WA,
Br 13, 274, additions to WA, Br 8, 488 ff. In later years (1540–44) Wolrab did
print the whole Luther Bible as well as individual portions of it. But for the
time being Wolrab was unable to go ahead with his plan.
[6] See p. 69, n. 4.
[7] What a "scoundrel" Wolrab was—or what a good businessman he was—can be
seen from the fact that he intended to continue printing the Witzel *Postil,* and
also hoped to print a work by John Faber of Vienna (see LW 49, 41, n. 35),
while at the same time printing the Luther Bible; see Enders, *Briefwechsel* 12,
200, n. 1.
[8] Literally: "ours." Here and throughout the letter Luther was referring to Hans
Lufft, the printer of the Luther Bible, and to the *Buchführer* in Wittenberg, i.e.,
the "publishers" who had to take the financial risk of having the Bible (or any
book) printed before it was possible to make any money from its sale for which
they were also responsible. For details, see WA, Br 12, 284 ff.

which is annoying to me personally, that that slanderer and printer of insulting books should abuse my own hard work in this way, and in addition perhaps even scoff. For what he might deserve by his [past] printing [activity] insofar as God and we are concerned[9] I shall entrust to God. It would not be unfair, of course, if the printers at Leipzig, who until now have grown sufficiently rich with their insulting books, were forced to refrain for a time from becoming even richer with our books and by ruining our printers. For it can easily be figured out that the printers at Leipzig can more easily sell a thousand copies, because all the markets are in Leipzig,[10] than our printers can sell a hundred copies.

In this matter Your Electoral Grace certainly will know how to arrive at a solution worthy of Your Grace.[11] With this I commend you to the dear Lord. Amen.

July 8, 1539   Your Electoral Grace's dedicated
MARTIN LUTHER

287

To Martin Bucer
[Wittenberg,] October 14, 1539

Luther explains his long silence by referring to his work, his age, and his hope that true unity exists between the evangelical preachers of Strassburg and himself, so that it should be unnecessary for him to write a letter each time that Bucer writes one. Luther expresses his appreciation for the news Bucer had given him regarding the status of the evangelical cause in upper Germany, and sees in the activities of certain people a sure sign that II Peter 2:1 is about to come true for them. He emphasizes also, however, that "our sins . . . are signs of some great calamity for us." Then Luther

---

[9] Another possible translation would be: "by his [past] printing [activity] directed against God and us, I shall entrust to God."
[10] I.e., in Leipzig, a city bigger than Wittenberg, there were more marketing opportunities. Another possible translation would be: "all the fairs are in Leipzig."
[11] Literally: "In this matter . . . arrive at a sovereign counsel."

comments on some details: His Latin is not good enough to write the preface for the Postil *as requested by "our Crato," and therefore Bucer should write this preface; even though at the moment an envoy of Henry VIII is at the court of Elector John Frederick, there is no reason at all for hope that anything might be accomplished with the King; the Emperor has lost both luck and God's blessing by allying himself with the Pope. In closing Luther extends greetings to John Sturm and John Calvin, and makes a rather cutting remark about Jacopo Sadoleto and the Italians.*

On Martin Bucer, see LW *48, 247, n. 13.*

Text in Latin: WA, Br 8, 568–569.[1]

To the illustrious man, Mr. Martin Bucer, bishop[2]
of the church at Strassburg, a true servant of
the Lord, my dearest brother in Christ

Grace and peace in the Lord! I think, my Bucer, that you know it is not necessary for me to write more frequently to you.[3] You have more leisure and are younger, not to mention the work and the problems with which I am loaded down every hour. Therefore assume that you have been promptly answered each time you write to me. For I hope that there is real unity of heart between us. I assume the same regarding all your colleagues,[4] whom I ask you also to greet reverently in my name. We are grateful, of course, that you do not leave us in the dark about what is going on among you people, especially in matters pertaining to the Cross, that is, the Word of

---

[1] The letter is extant as autograph, which is edited in Pollet 1, 158 f., where following p. 144 a facsimile is reproduced.

[2] See LW 49, 87, n. 5.

[3] Luther's last extant letter to Bucer prior to this one is dated December 6, 1537; WA, Br 8, No. 3193.

[4] Capito (see LW 48, 305, n. 2) was the most prominent one among them. Even though for the period from January, 1537, to October, 1539, several of the letters written by Bucer and Capito to Luther are extant (see WA, Br 8, passim), specifics pertaining to the news communicated by Bucer and mentioned by Luther in the following sentence could not be established. In light of the following sentences it is safe to suggest, however, that either Luther's statement was a highly general one, or that Luther was referring to Bucer's April 19, 1539, letter (WA, Br 8, No. 3324) in which Bucer reported on some of the charges made by the papists against the evangelicals during the negotiations surrounding the Frankfurt Truce (see note 16).

the Crucified. St. Peter's word which says, "They[5] are bringing upon themselves a swift destruction,"[6] is coming true. They wish to perish.[7] Again they are spreading great threats, and (so they boast) efficacious ones. May God destroy their plans,[8] as he has done thus far, even though our sins, ungratefulness, and contempt[9] are signs of some great calamity for us. People among us [here] take as some kind of harsh punishment the fact that winds and waters have been raging so extraordinarily for six weeks already, so that[10] our old people can remember nothing similar.

Our Crato has requested of me a preface to my *Postils*. But I am not well versed in Latin; if I ever was, it must be that by not using any Latin for such a long time and by using German instead, I have forgotten it.[11] I have asked Crato to request the preface from you, and I am still requesting this.[12]

I[13] am afraid that your hopes regarding the King of England

---

[5] Is Luther thinking of the papists or the enthusiasts? It is most likely that he was thinking of the papists because only their threats could be "efficacious." This interpretation presupposes that one understands this phrase, "efficacious ones," in a political sense. See also note 16. Luther was apparently thinking of those propapal Estates of the Empire which, guided by the Imperial Vice-Chancellor Matthias Held, organized the Nürnberg League in June of 1538 (as a direct result of the March, 1537, rejection of the council by the Smalcaldic League). At the end of 1538 there was talk at several German courts of the possibility of a war between the Protestants and the papists. For details, see Ranke 2[IV], 65 ff.

[6] II Pet. 2:1.

[7] Luther wrote this sentence in German.

[8] This could be an allusion to II Sam. 15:34, as is suggested in *WA*, Br 8, 569, n. 4; at least Luther used one of the phrases found in the Vulgate text of this passage.

[9] I.e., contempt for the Word; see also p. 183.

[10] The translation is based on the autograph (see note 1), and not on the *WA*, Br text. Luther also mentioned these windstorms and floods in a letter of October 13, 1539; see *WA*, Br 8, 567.

[11] The last portion of this sentence (from "that by") has been freely translated. Luther is apparently thinking of his work on the German Bible.

[12] In the spring of 1539 the Strassburg printer Crato Mylius, or Kraft Mylius (see Benzing, *op. cit.* [see p. 185, n. 1], p. 418, No. 33), with Bucer and others, had attended a meeting of the Smalcaldic League in Frankfurt/Main; see *WA*, Br 8, 388, n. 9; Ranke 2[IV], 76 ff. He returned to Strassburg via Wittenberg (where he stayed for some time) and Nürnberg (see *C.R.* 3, 803). According to a Calvin letter of November 20, Mylius was the carrier of the present letter; see *C.R.* 38, 432. Mylius planned a new edition of Luther's *Postil* of which a Latin version had been published in Strassburg in 1535; see *WA* 10[I,2], xxxix f. While he was in Wittenberg he had asked Luther for a preface.

[13] For the following, see letter No. 288, Introduction, and p. 205.

are empty. We heard the English themselves, while they were here,[14] complaining about their King and admiring our freedom. Now the King has an envoy at our Sovereign's court; but that envoy neither brought nor reported anything that could give any hope. May the Lord direct the King's heart,[15] together with all the other kings, to his glory.

The prophecies about the Emperor have now become a reality: all luck and all of God's blessing left him after he had allied himself with the Pope whom God detests. But they blame all this on us.[16]

Farewell, and please greet reverently Mr. John Sturm[17] and

---

[14] See pp. 117 ff., 138 f.

[15] See I Kings 3:9; I Chron. 29:18; Prov. 21:1.

[16] This is a reference to the Holy League and the loss of Castelnuovo to the Turks on August 10, 1539; see also p. 183, n. 16. With the date of September 20, Francis Burchart (who was in London at that time [see p. 194, n. 14]) informed the Electoral court of this event; see WA, Br 8, 568, n. 4. To compound the Emperor's problems, in 1539 Venice initiated discussions with the Turks which were aimed at bringing about a truce, and a truce was indeed signed in October 1540; see Elton, p. 520. Thus Venice and her resources were neutralized so far as the Emperor's struggles against the Turks were concerned, and this at a time when military conflict in the Balkans seemed to be unavoidable; see *ibid.*, pp. 522 f. Luther also mentioned the loss of Castelnuovo in a letter to Albrecht of Brandenburg (see LW 49, 60), dated October 13, 1539 (WA Br 8, 566), and then continued: Charles V and his brother, Ferdinand of Austria, are angry at us and intend to attack us with great force, certainly by next summer, for they have let themselves be convinced that their disaster at the hands of the Turks is the result of the fact that they have let us live and have not yet offered us to God as a slaughtered sacrifice. Luther's view of the political situation in the Empire does not do full justice to the circumstances. Since it became increasingly clear that the council would not get off the ground, and as a result of the Turkish problem, the Imperial government and *some* of the propapal Estates of the Empire (see, however, also note 5) pursued a policy of peaceful co-existence with the Smalcaldic League. This policy led to the theological colloquy of Leipzig (January, 1539), the Frankfurt Truce (April 1539; see also note 12), and the colloquies of Hagenau-Worms (1540), and Regensburg (1541). See Kidd, Nos. 129, 136–140; Ranke 2IV, 75 ff., 117 ff., 3VI, 108 ff.; Jedin, pp. 355 ff. And yet, while Luther obviously knew nothing of the Emperor's motivation, Luther's view of the situation is based on a *feeling* which was correct. The Emperor did not ratify the Frankfurt Truce, but he did confirm the Nürnberg League (see note 5); further, he did affirm to the Curia his duty to use the sword, if necessary, against the Protestant heretics; see Ranke 2IV, 105. Did Luther feel that the Emperor was not interested in co-existence, but only in delay? Luther's attitude toward the colloquies would seem to suggest an affirmative answer (see Köstlin-Kawerau 2, 531 ff.).

[17] John Sturm (1507–1589) was one of the leading Protestant educators. He attended the famous St. Jerome School of the Brethren of the Common Life at Liège, and studied at the humanistic Collegium trilingue in Louvain. From 1529/30 to 1536 he taught humanistic studies in Paris, and under Bucer's influence he became an evangelical. In order to escape the harassment to which

John Calvin;[18] I have read their books with special pleasure.[19] I wish Sadoleto[20] would believe that God is the creator of men even outside of Italy. But this thought does not enter the hearts of the Italians since of course they alone, ahead of the rest of mankind, have totally lost their minds because of their arrogance. Again, farewell.

October 14, 1539   Yours,

                                    MARTIN LUTHER[21]

---

the evangelicals in France were periodically exposed at that time, in 1536/37 Sturm accepted an appointment to the *Gymnasium* in Strassburg, which was then being organized; he became the rector there. As a humanistic educator, Sturm became known as *Cicero et Nestor teutonicus*. His work as educator was crowned in 1566 when an *academia* was organized in Strassburg. As a theologian he attempted, in good Erasmian tradition, to bring about an agreement between the opponents. As a man of great diplomatic skill and international reputation he tried to bring about a rapprochement between the French crown and the evangelicals in France and Germany. Theologically seen, he had strong Calvinistic tendencies which led him into serious difficulties with the authorities when in approximately 1555 a strict Lutheran party began to dominate the ecclesiastical life of Strassburg. In 1581 Sturm was even dismissed from his position as rector of the institution he had helped organize and shape. He spent the last years of his life as a lonely man, impoverished and almost blind. On John Sturm, see *O.D.C.C.*, p. 1299. On March 3, 1539, Frederick Myconius informed Luther from Frankfurt (see note 12) that Sturm and Calvin were at Frankfurt with Bucer and others; *WA*, Br 8, 387.

[18] After Calvin had been forced to leave Geneva in April of 1538 he stayed for a short time in Basel. In September of 1538, called by Bucer and Capito, he went as pastor to Strassburg to minister to the French-speaking evangelical refugees in that city. He stayed there until September of 1541, when the Geneva city council called him back. Calvin had gone to Frankfurt with the Strassburg delegation (see note 12) in order to inform the evangelical Estates of the Empire about the situation pertaining to the evangelicals in France, and to discuss theology with Melanchthon; see *WA*, Br 8, 388, n. 9. Upon their return from Frankfurt, Luther's friends, but also Mylius (see note 12), obviously reported to Luther about Sturm and Calvin.

[19] The books mentioned by Luther included one by Sturm and one by Calvin; both were published in Strassburg in September of 1539, and both were directed against Jacopo Sadoleto (see note 20), who had tried, unsuccessfully, to have Geneva reaffirm obedience to the pope. For bibliographical details, see *WA*, Br 8, 569, n. 14. For Calvin's book, see J. C. Olin (ed.), *A Reformation Debate: Sadoleto's Letter to the Genevans and Calvin's Reply* (New York, 1966). For Calvin's reaction to Luther's greetings, see the Calvin letter cited in note 12.

[20] Jacopo Sadoleto (1477–1547), a humanistically oriented Italian clergyman of outstanding spiritual and intellectual qualities, was appointed secretary to Pope Leo X in 1513, bishop of Carpentras in 1516, and cardinal in 1536. Pope Paul III made him a member of the special commission which was charged with drafting proposals for the reform of the church (see p. 158, n. 11). On Sadoleto, see *NCE* 12, 846.

[21] In the autograph (see note 1) the "Doctor" of the *WA*, Br text is missing.

288

To Elector John Frederick
Wittenberg, October 23, 1539

When the legation of the Smalcaldic League left London for Germany on October 1, 1538,[1] they took along a letter to Elector John Frederick[2] in which Henry VIII praised the members of the legation for their piety and learnedness, and expressed his hope that Melanchthon and other learned men would soon come to England in order to conclude the matter, that is, an alliance between Henry and the league. The one condition of the league on which such an alliance depended was unity in doctrinal matters. And it was precisely on this point that the King intended to stay flexible. Whatever was accomplished in 1538 regarding doctrinal matters was of little importance, for the Thirteen Articles[3] (the result of the deliberations between the English and the envoys of the league) never gained official status in England; in addition the articles did not produce any solution to the crucial issues.[4] Yet for political reasons Henry VIII kept up his efforts to bring about an alliance with the German Protestants, and in January of 1539 he again dispatched Christopher Mont to Germany.[5] The King ordered him to find out as much as possible about the political plans of the Smalcaldic League, to press the league to send a legation of prestigious men to England, and to get from the league information about the political position and the religious views of the ruling family of Cleve. Cromwell ordered Mont to explore the possibilities of a marriage of Mary Tudor into the ruling family of Cleve, and a marriage between one of the daughters of the duke of Cleve and Henry VIII.

---

[1] For the following, see also Prüser, pp. 149 ff.

[2] *L.P.* 13[II], No. 497; see also Prüser, Appendix: document No. 13.

[3] See p. 178, n. 11.

[4] I.e., marriage of the clergy, communion "in both kinds," private mass, monastic vows. These had been at issue since the days of the Wittenberg discussions; see p. 133, n. 10, and below, note 29.

[5] For Mont's instructions, see *L.P.* 14[I], No. 103; Prüser, pp. 156 f. The plan regarding the marriage with a member of the ruling family of Cleve, discussed as early as the summer of 1538 (see *L.P.* 13[I], No. 1198), has to be seen as an effort on Cromwell's part to tie Henry even more closely to the antipapal, anti-Imperial forces in Germany.

In addition, Mont was to assure the league that Cromwell would do everything in his power to have Henry VIII participate in the affairs of the league.

Mont discharged his mission at the Frankfurt meeting of the Smalcaldic League in spring of 1539.[6] At this meeting the league dispatched Francis Burchart and the Hessian councilor, Louis von Baumbach, to England. In addition, the Germans informed the King that their position on controversial matters had been made sufficiently clear to the King, that they would not abandon their position regarding private mass, communion "in both kinds," and the marriage of priests, and that the King should finally shake off all the vestiges of papalism.[7]

Shortly after Burchart and von Baumbach had arrived in London a change in Henry's ecclesiastical policies occurred. On April 28 that Parliament was convened which on June 16 passed the Six Articles; on June 28 these articles became law, the transgression of which could be punished even by death. Thus the foundation of what is commonly called the "Catholic Reaction" in Henry's policies had been laid, and the King's interest in an alliance with the Smalcaldic League diminished. The German envoys were therefore forced to leave London empty-handed on May 31, 1539.[8]

In order to keep the contacts with the Smalcaldic League open, at the end of August, 1539, Cromwell again dispatched Christopher

---

[6] See Prüser pp. 155, 159 ff.

[7] For the league's answer to Henry VIII, see Elector John Frederick's letter to the King, *L.P.* 14[I], No. 698; *C.R.* 3, No. 1950 (with an incorrect date). The position of the German evangelicals also becomes clear from Melanchthon's personal letters written from Frankfurt to Henry VIII, Cranmer, Heath, and Cromwell; *C.R.* 3, Nos. 1788, 1790–1792; *L.P.* 14[I], No. 844. The purpose of this (second) mission of Burchart (see Prüser, pp. 169 ff.) is not clear. When on April 24 Cromwell announced Burchart's presence to the King, he added that the purpose of Burchart's mission was to arrive at doctrinal agreement and at arrangements for mutual aid in time of crisis; see *L.P.* 14[I], No. 844. The German envoys stayed in England from April 23 to May 31, 1539. For their reports about the situation in England, see Prüser, pp. 174 f.

[8] For the *Six Articles*, see *EHD* 5, 814 ff.; *O.D.C.C.*, p. 1262. One reason for the King's change of attitude was the truce, signed in Frankfurt between the Emperor and the Smalcaldic League, which prohibited the league from accepting new members. Thus the possibility for Henry to join the league was nullified, at least on paper. On the other hand, by establishing his catholicity in the *Six Articles*, the door was opened for a rapprochement with the Catholic powers on the Continent (Spain and France, and the Emperor).

Mont to Elector John Frederick and Landgrave Philip of Hesse.[9] *Mont was to tell the Elector that, even though there were some issues on which the King did not agree with the German evangelicals, the King nevertheless still repudiated the pope, and that a common foe made a common cause. Mont was further to try to win the Elector over to the idea that the Wittenberg theologians should not write against the* Six Articles, *and that another legation should be sent to England.*

Mont was with the Elector at the beginning of September,[10] *and on September 16 he received a polite yet firmly negative answer which was critical of the King: the Elector blames the King for the collapse of the negotiations; the* Six Articles *are an open affirmation of the papacy and condemnation of the evangelicals; the Elector is in no position to prevent his theologians from writing against the articles.*[11]

Thus at the end of September, 1539, the negotiations aimed at an alliance between England and the Smalcaldic League had collapsed. In view of the Six Articles *the German evangelicals felt betrayed by Henry.*[12] *Notwithstanding this development, the negotiations between the English and the court of Cleve aimed at bringing about the marriage between Henry VIII and Anne of Cleve were continued.*[13] *Since on the basis of dynastic relations Elector John Frederick was involved in this project, Francis Burchart was again sent to England, along with John von Dolzig and the representatives of Cleve.*[14] *The purpose of this mission was to negotiate the*

---

[9] For the following see the excerpts from the records in WA, Br 8, 563 f.; Prüser, Appendix: documents No. 16, 17.

[10] See also p. 190.

[11] The answer (*WA*, Br 8, 563 f.; *L.P.* 14[II], No. 211; *C.R.* 3, 783 f.) was given orally to Mont shortly prior to September 9; it was then sent to Melanchthon for translation, and on September 27 was dispatched to Mont, who in the meantime had traveled to Kassel to see Philip of Hesse; see Prüser, pp. 327 f. On September 23 the Landgrave gave Mont a similar answer, though somewhat softer in tone; see *ibid.* At the beginning of October Mont left again for England, taking the boat from Calais on October 12; *L.P.* 14[II], No. 525.

[12] See, e.g., WA, TR 4, No. 4699; *LW* 54, 361 f.; *C.R.* 3, No. 1828; *L.P.* 14[I], No. 1353.

[13] See note 5; Prüser, pp. 157 f., 159 ff., 195 f.

[14] Burchart and von Dolzig arrived in London on September 18 (see Prüser, p. 215), and returned to Germany in the second half of October. On October 20 Burchart was again in Düsseldorf (see *ibid.*, p. 213), and on November 21 he attended the meeting of the Smalcaldic League at Arnstadt, near Erfurt (see *ibid.*, p. 229). The primary purpose of Burchart's mission was to assist the repre-

*marriage contract. The mission was successful: the marriage con-
tract was completed.*[15] *And Burchart was able to gain a first-hand
view of the situation in England as it was developing under the
impact of the* Six Articles; *according to the impressions which he
took back to Germany, not all was lost for the cause of the gospel in
England.*[16] *Thus at the end of October, when Burchart for the third
time returned from England, prospects for a renewal of negotiations between England and the Smalcaldic League were not as dim
as at the end of September.*

*Meanwhile in another way the contacts between Henry VIII
and the German Protestants were kept alive, notwithstanding the*
Six Articles. *In attempts to counteract the papal party around the
King, to forestall the full consequences of the* Six Articles, *and to
save the cause of the gospel in England, Martin Bucer, on September 16, 1539, wrote to Landgrave Philip of Hesse. In his letter Bucer
blamed the developments which led to the* Six Articles *on the facts
that Melanchthon (who alone would have been capable of dealing
with the sophistry of the papal party in England) was never sent to
England, that in October of 1538 Myconius and Burchart had left
England prematurely, and that the Germans always lacked courage
and vision. In order to save whatever could be saved for the cause
of the gospel in England, Bucer argued, Melanchthon should be
sent to England at once.*[17]

*On September 30 the Landgrave informed the Elector of
Bucer's letter, and on October 7 the Elector informed his chancellor*

---

sentatives of Cleve in the negotiations for the marriage contract (see *ibid.*, p.
196); the secondary purpose was to find out as much as possible about the
religious situation in England.

[15] October 4, 1539; *L.P.* 14[II], No. 286.

[16] For Burchart's reports about the situation in England, see Prüser, pp. 213 ff.;
C.R. 3, No. 1744 (with an incorrect date); see also *C.R.* 3, 824.

[17] On Martin Bucer, see *LW* 48, 247, n. 13. Bucer's letter: Lenz, *BPB* 1, No. 29.
The Strassburg city government supported Bucer in a separate letter to the
Landgrave; see *WA*, Br 8, 563. It is quite possible that, when he was in Germany in September, Mont visited Bucer in Strassburg (whom he probably knew
from Frankfurt; see above), as Rupp (*Tradition*, p. 122) argues. In any case,
even prior to any possible visit by Mont, Bucer was remarkably well informed
about the situation in England; see Lenz, *BPB* 1, Nos. 27, 28. The Landgrave
received Bucer's letter on September 20, and answered it negatively on September 30 (Lenz, *BPB* 1, No. 30), just as he had answered Mont negatively (see
note 11). Bucer also wrote a no-longer extant letter to Luther asking for Luther's
cooperation which Luther answered with letter No. 287.

emeritus, Gregory Brück, of this correspondence. On October 11 the Elector replied to the Landgrave that there was no hope that Henry could be gained for the gospel, that Bucer was wrong in blaming the German evangelicals for the collapse of the negotiations, and that all further negotiations with the English would depend on the news which Burchart and von Dolzig would report from London. As he had done in the answer given to Mont, so in these letters the Elector put the blame for the collapse of the negotiations with England squarely where it belonged and thus clearly established his position; nevertheless on October 12 he requested his Wittenberg theologians to draw up a brief on the situation, especially on Bucer's argument that the German evangelicals were at fault for the developments in England, and were therefore obligated to take the initiative by sending Melanchthon to England.[18] Letter No. 288 is this brief. Luther and some of his colleagues point out that the German evangelicals have done everything possible in this matter, that the King's recent actions and statements make clear beyond doubt that he stubbornly acts contrary to his conscience, and that therefore he is to be abandoned as a stiff-necked person. Since the King was never serious about the gospel, but only used it whenever it suited him, says Luther, there is no further need or possibility of dealing with him. Even to send Melanchthon to England would accomplish nothing other than more useless discussion since the King refuses to commit himself to the gospel. Notwithstanding this position, the Wittenberg theologians leave it up to the Elector to decide whether to negotiate further with Henry VIII. They promise to compose swiftly an expostulatio of the King and to admonish him once more. In conclusion they also mention that arrangements have been made for the rapid printing of a book sent to them by the Elector.

On Elector John Frederick, see LW 48, 181 f.

Text in German: WA, Br 8, 572–575[19]

---

[18] See Lenz, *BPB*, 1. No. 30 (Landgrave to Elector); WA, Br 8, 564 (Elector to Brück); Prüser, Appendix: document No. 18 (Elector to Landgrave); WA, Br 8, 564 f. (Elector to Wittenberg theologians).

[19] The original is extant; it is written by a secretary unknown to us, and signed with the personal signatures of the authors. According to WA, Br 14, xxxiii, addition to WA, Br 8, 572, the brief was written by Melanchthon. The fact that Melanchthon speaks at one point in the first person seems to corroborate this argument. Yet this fact should not be overemphasized; the personal pronoun could simply have been used to underscore the fact that the following section

To the Most Serene, Noble Sovereign and Lord, Sir
John Frederick, duke in Saxony, archmarshal and
elector of the Holy Roman Empire, landgrave in
Thuringia, margrave in Meissen, and count of the castle
in Magdeburg, etc., etc., our Most Gracious Lord

First of all, God's grace through our Lord Jesus Christ! Most Serene, Noble, Most Gracious Elector and Lord! We have read
through Mr. Bucer's letter[20] and realize that it has been written in
great earnestness, 'no doubt with good intention, and as a direct
result of the information given by the refugees; we, too, heard
similar miserable lamentations from some of those who are at
Hamburg.[21] Even though these people hope to get help through us,
as all those afflicted [and] in need search everywhere for help, yet
we know of no way to help them. As far as we personally are
concerned, we do not shy away from any danger or labor; yet it is
also true that in the matter of instructing and admonishing the
King[22] enough has been done by our party, and this for the following reasons:

St. Paul says:[23] He who is weak is to be tolerated, but he who
is stiff-necked is to be let go, for according to Paul he is condemned
by his own judgment; that is, he openly acts contrary to his conscience. On the other hand, he is called weak who wants to learn

---

was added especially upon Melanchthon's request. Further, the source which
designates Melanchthon as author is late in comparison with the registry notation
on the original (*WA*, Br 8, No. 3396, Introduction), which designates this
document as a brief of the Wittenberg theologians. That Luther contributed
substantially to this brief can be seen from a comparison of this brief with letter
No. 289.

[20] I.e., Bucer's September 16 letter to the Landgrave; on September 30 the
Landgrave had forwarded a copy of this letter to the Elector, and on October 12
the Elector had a copy sent to the Wittenberg theologians, along with a copy of
his October 11 letter to the Landgrave; see note 18.

[21] Luther assumed (and apparently correctly; see Prüser, p. 198) that one source
for Bucer's information (see also note 17) about the situation pertaining to the
cause of the gospel in England was the news brought to Strassburg by English
evangelicals who had fled their country in order to avoid persecution because
of the *Six Articles*. Nothing could be established about the English refugees (?)
in Hamburg, or their contacts with Luther. Among the English refugees (?) was
Alesius; see *L.P.* 14I, No. 1353.

[22] I.e. here and throughout the letter, Henry VIII.

[23] Rom. 14:1; Titus 3:10 f.

and does not attack that which he understands, but accepts, affirms, and promotes it.

That the King of England acts contrary to his conscience may be seen from the following: He knows that our teaching and position on the usage of the whole sacrament,[24] on confession, and on the marriage of a priest are correct, or at least he knows that our teaching is not contrary to God's Word. [But] now he says in his articles and in his edict[25] that some of these points are contrary to God's law.

This the King certainly says contrary to his own conscience. For much written material has come to him, both publicly[26] and also addressed to him personally.[27] He has read this material, and he has received sufficient information from his[28] and from our envoys.[29] He himself has also had a little book by Sarcerius—in which these issues are dealt with briefly—translated into English,

---

[24] I.e., the celebration of the Lord's Supper in which both elements are given to the communicant.

[25] "Articles," i.e., the Six Articles, esp. Art II (communion "in both kinds"), III (against priestly marriage), VI (retention of auricular confession). "Edict," i.e., the edict issued by Henry VIII on November 16, 1538; Tudor Royal Proclamations, P. L. Hughes, J. Larkin, eds., 1 (New Haven, 1964), No. 186; L.P. 13II, Nos. 848, 890. This edict became known in Electoral Saxony in January of 1539 (see C.R. 3, No. 1771). While this edict was designed to curb the activities of the Anabaptists in England, it also established literary censorship and ordered the observation of priestly celibacy and of certain rites of the papal church. Therefore the edict could easily have been interpreted as being directed also against the "Lutherans" in England. In his letter to Henry VIII given to Mont in Frankfurt in spring of 1539 (see note 7), the Elector focused on this edict in particular in order to underscore the reasons for his unhappiness with Henry's policies.

[26] E.g., the Wittenberg Articles.

[27] This is a reference to the letters which Melanchthon had previously sent to the King; see, e.g., note 7.

[28] I.e., Fox and Heath; see pp. 117 ff.

[29] See pp. 117 ff. The authors of the brief were apparently thinking of the document which Burchart and his colleagues had turned over to Henry VIII on approximately August 5, 1538; see L.P. 13II, Nos. 37, 38; Prüser, pp. 135 ff.; Tjernagel, pp. 182 f. This material dealt with the celebration of the Lord's Supper "in both kinds," with priestly marriage, and with the private mass, issues on which no agreement had been reached between the Germans and the English prior to that time. Burchart and his colleagues set forth their position on these issues in this document, and considered this material a resumé of the work which still had to be done. They also used this document as a means of urging the King to abolish these reminders of the papacy. Then the Germans considered their mission at an end, and were ready to go home. As a result of this document, however, the King insisted that the Germans stay for more discussions which started on August 19; L.P. 13II, Nos. 165, 166. Even though promising news about these discussions reached Wittenberg, yet nothing was accomplished.

and ordered it to be printed, and has used it as his prayer book.[30] We also hear that [at one time] he talked quite differently about this teaching, and said about [the King of] France,[31] among other things, that that man does evil in attacking this teaching, for he understands it and knows that it is correct. In addition, the King has many godly, learned preachers, the deposed Bishop Latimer, Cranmer,[32] and others to whom he listened previously, and whom he tolerated for a while.

Notwithstanding all this, the King suddenly condemns this teaching more harshly than the pope who, of course, never stated that the marriage of a priest is contrary to God's law, etc., [or] that it is God's commandment to tell [all individual] sins in the confessional.[33] Like Nebuchadnezzar with his pillar,[34] the King

---

[30] Erasmus Sarcerius (1501–1559), evangelical educator and theologian (sometimes called the Reformer of Nassau), is one of the lesser known evangelicals of the first half of the sixteenth century, though on the basis of his literary productivity and his churchmanship he belongs in the frontline. For a biography and bibliography, see G. Eskuche, *Sarcerius als Erzieher and Schulmann* (Giessen, 1910); this work was not available to this editor, and the following references to this work are taken from *WA*, Br 8, 576, n. 8. While teaching at the Latin school in Lübeck, Sarcerius came in contact with the English, and wrote a brief for an English bishop (unknown to us) on the correct evangelical faith. In December 1538 he published this brief in Frankfurt under the title *Loci communes* (see Eskuche, *op. cit.*, p. 6, No. 8). Apparently while he was in Frankfurt in the spring of 1539 Mont made the acquaintance of Sarcerius, and perhaps even picked up a copy of the *Loci*; apparently Mont also told Sarcerius that the *Loci* had been translated into English as the result of a special command of Henry VIII. See *L.P.* 14[I], No. 496. (Was Mont trying to make out of the King a better evangelical than the King in reality was? Or did Mont have any special information?) In any case, it was rumored that Henry had ordered the translation of the *Loci* into English. As a result of this rumor, in 1540 Sarcerius dedicated his *Postil* (Eskuche, *op. cit.*, p. 7, No. 15) to Henry VIII. In this dedication he stated that English book dealers in Frankfurt spread the rumor that the King had ordered the translation of the *Loci* into English; see *WA*, Br 8, 576, n. 8. In the text above, the authors of the brief are on thin ice with their matter-of-fact statement regarding Sarcerius' book; inadvertently they communicate what, according to available bibliographical material, seems to have been only a rumor.
[31] I.e., Francis I.
[32] On Hugh Latimer, bishop of Worcester since 1535, see *DNB* 11, 612 ff. He had opposed the *Six Articles*, and therefore resigned (or was forced to resign) his office. Together with Nicholas Shaxton, the bishop of Salisbury (see *DNB* 17, 1390 ff.), and "eight" doctors, Latimer was imprisoned; so Bucer to Philip of Hesse (see note 17). Latimer was imprisoned only briefly, then pardoned and prohibited from preaching. On Thomas Cranmer, see *DNB* 5, 19 ff. Cranmer was not removed from office, though he, too, had opposed the *Six Articles*.
[33] One may wonder whether the authors of the brief are sarcastic at this point. While they are correct that the decisions on these issues can be found in Canon Law only, i.e., in man-made law, nevertheless the authors knew very well that

decrees punishments; [that is,] he intends to kill those who do not obey these articles.[35] He also started this persecution in a horrible way, for many are in jail and are awaiting the punishment.[36] That means, like Herod,[37] he has used this teaching for a while to his advantage, but now he attacks it, and [thus it can be seen that] the devil begins to use a new ruse: since the papal power has to fall, the devil now urges the great kings to use religion as it is opportune for them, for their profit and advantage.

A cruel blindness will follow from this, for there is [now] no reason that the kings of all territories, [of] Spain, France, England, Hungary, and Poland should protect the bishops and the estate of priests, on whom the mass and all the other errors depend,

---

the papacy attributed divine quality to the Canon Law. The phrase "contrary to God's law," or similar ones, can be found in the Six Articles.

[34] Dan. 3:15.

[35] I.e., the Six Articles; see note 8. In the articles capital punishment is stipulated for offenses against all articles, in some cases for the first offense, in some for the second.

[36] See, e.g., note 32. The reliability of the information which the Wittenberg theologians had at that time is open to question. It is certain, however, that the reports of Burchart and von Baumbach about the situation at the time that they left England (May 31, 1539; see note 7) did not comfort the German evangelicals. It is further certain that the Wittenbergers became familiar with conditions in England via refugees (how reliable were their reports?) and via Bucer; see note 17. (While Bucer's letter was intended to give the impression of being a "factual report," it cannot hide the author's tendentious position, i.e., an urgency to "rescue" the evangelicals in England from the persecutions and traps of the papists around the King by having Melanchthon sent to England to convert the King.) Last of all, it is certain that rumors about the situation in England did circulate in Germany (see, e.g., Prüser, p. 190). In the statement above one has to see an expression of an emotional overreaction and of tense anticipation rather than of exact knowledge. For the reaction of the German evangelicals to the developments in England, see also note 12. While the situation in England was tense (Tjernagel, p. 199, mentions that within two weeks after the Six Articles had become law a London grand jury had returned five hundred indictments for heresy), yet it was not as bad as one might assume on the basis of the statement above; see Prüser, pp. 191 f.; Mackie, op. cit., (see p. 180, n. 21), pp. 426 ff. By October 22, i.e., a day prior to the date on which the Wittenbergers made the rather pessimistic statement above, the Elector was in possession of a September 20 letter from his envoys in London (see note 1,, and on the basis of this letter the Elector felt justified in expressing the hope that maybe not all was lost insofar as the cause of the gospel in England was concerned; see Prüser, p. 213. At the end of October Burchart returned from London, and from his report it became clear that, notwithstanding the Six Articles, there was no mass persecution of evangelicals in England; see ibid.; see also C.R. 3, No. 1744 (with an incorrect date), and L.P. 14[II] No. 423, for Burchart's private report to Melanchthon; see also C.R. 3, 824.

[37] Mark 6:20.

except for this one reason—that the kings are eager to have people available for the chancellery, for legations, and for all kinds of evil actions, so that these same priests might maintain their status, even without the kings' expenses.[38]

Besides this, the kings see that the crude people are attached to the mass and the routine ceremonies, and do not like to have these idols taken away. Therefore the kings arrange it so that they and the priests are able to retain more authority. But the kings maintain what they want and make ordinances to their advantage. We worry, therefore, that this King is of such a mind, [and] that he does not seek God's glory, but wishes to do and decree what he himself desires. He said to the Vice-Chancellor that he alone intends to rule his kingdom;[39] by this he has shown that he does not think highly of this teaching, and intends to create a religion for himself, as Antiochus[40] and others did.

Second, since it is now out in the open that the King is acting contrary to his conscience, we think that we are not obligated[41] to admonish him once again, but that we are free to abide by St. Paul's rule[42] which states that one should twice admonish one's opponents, and if this does not help one should then avoid them as people who act contrary to their consciences. Such admonishing has now taken place,[43] yet the King flails against his conscience. With such people no instruction is of any use.

We also hear[44] that the King is a sophist and glossator who colors all articles with a little gloss, [yet] wants to pretend to affirm them. He who has no desire for clear, certain truth may easily get entangled and has to pay the price regardless of whether he

---

[38] I.e., expenses incurred in the protection of bishops and priests and the maintaining of their status.

[39] On what occasion this exchange between Francis Burchart and Henry VIII took place could not be established, though it is quite possible that it took place in connection with the circumstances mentioned in note 29, as Enders, *Briefwechsel* 12, 268, n. 11, suggests.

[40] I Macc. 1:43 ff.

[41] See note 55.

[42] Titus 3:10.

[43] This is apparently a reference to Elector John Frederick's letter to Henry VIII cited in notes 7, 25.

[44] The background of this statement could not be clarified. The material cited in *WA*, Br 8, 576, n. 21, contributes little if anything to the background of this statement.

must open his mouth wide like a pike[45] who tears himself off the hook.

In Ecclesiasticus 37[46] it is written that to him who uses sophistry God will not give grace; he will not receive wisdom, for there is no end to the mulling-over of things, and the twisting of them. Therefore nothing permanent can be accomplished with such people, and experience teaches us how harmful it is [to try to do so], especially for the lords.[47] Since the King is eager for such glossing, as we indeed hear, we have little hope that he will commit and submit himself wholeheartedly to the Word of God.

One also has to consider the people who are now in power and favor around the King. They too have no consciences. The man from Winchester,[48] while traveling around the country, is accompanied by two unchaste females dressed in men's clothing.[49] Yet he declares that the marriage of priests is contrary to God's law. He is so arrogant as to say in public that he intends to maintain against the whole world that the thesis,[50] "We are justified by faith," is wrong. Among tyrants he is the greatest; prior to this year he pushed for the burning of two people solely on the ground of transubstantiation.[51] And so the proverb is true: like master, like servant.[52]

From all this we conclude that thus far we have done everything possible.[53] We know that we did everything with the best

---

[45] Or: "bass." See Plutarch *Moralia* 977B.
[46] See Jesus Sirach 37:20–21; 38:24 ff.
[47] The text does not make clear whether the authors want to say that experience teaches how harmful it is for lords (i.e., rulers) if one tries to enact something which is supposed to be stable with someone who always mulls over things and twists them; or how harmful it is for the Lord (i.e., the cause of the gospel) that people never commit themselves.
[48] I.e., Stephen Gardiner, bishop of Winchester since 1531, whom Bucer (see note 17) considered the most cunning man (later Bucer called Gardiner even a "devilish bishop"; Lenz, *BPB* 1, 244) and whom he designated as the one who now "rules" at the King's side. On Stephen Gardiner, see *DNB* 7, 859 ff.
[49] Nothing could be established about this incident, or the following one.
[50] This word and the following phrases were written in Latin.
[51] This word was written in Latin. In November of 1538 John Nicholson (or Lambert) was burned because he denied transubstantiation; see Prüser, pp. 147 f. Who the other victim was, and the source for this statement, could not be established. Further, the authors are incorrect, for it was not Gardiner who was involved in the proceedings against Nicholson, but Barnes; see *ibid.*
[52] See Erasmus, *Adagia* IV: 5, 63; Clericus 2, 1068D.
[53] See note 55.

Christian intention, and maintain that we are not obligated to try further to deal with the King; there is little hope for such an undertaking. Perhaps God does not wish his gospel to be touted by this King who has such a bad reputation.

We leave it to Your Electoral Grace's further deliberations whether one should try once more. Nothing shall be omitted. We all shall put together an *expostulatio*[54] addressed to the King and exhort him once more in writing; more, however, we are not obligated to do. For when Mr. Bucer cites: "Go into all the world, preach," etc.,[55] then we have to reply that we are doing this with our writings; in addition to this, also to abandon our present work is not commanded us.

I, Philip, wrote to the King concerning the prior edict—of course in all humility and respect—and criticized it; the same criticism I wrote to Cromwell and to the man of Canterbury.[56] Yet letters have been sent to me from England to the effect that the King has received my letters most ungraciously.[57] From this one can easily see that even if I were in England the King would grant me only a short audience, or, as he did with the previous envoys,[58] refer me to his arrogant, poorly educated bishops and have me quarrel with them.

---

[54] I.e., a complaint combined with a challenge to abstain from or remedy the circumstances about which one is complaining. The most famous *expostulatio* of the first decades of the sixteenth century was the one written by Ulrich von Hutten and addressed to Erasmus of Rotterdam; see *LW* 49, 79, n. 13. In his letter to Elector John Frederick (see note 18) the Landgrave suggested as the only possible action under the given circumstances that Melanchthon write an *expostulatio*. In his letter to the Wittenberg theologians (see note 18), the Elector requested Melanchthon to draw up this document at the earliest possible moment, and forward a manuscript copy of it to the Elector for dispatch, but not have it published for the time being. Melanchthon finished the *expostulatio* by November 1; text: *St. L.* 17, 270 ff.; *C.R.* 3, 805 ff.; *L.P.* 14^{II}, No. 444.

[55] Matt. 28:19. In his letter to the Landgrave (see note 17) Bucer used this passage to prove his argument that the German Protestants were obligated to do something about the situation in England, or more precisely, to send Melanchthon to the King.

[56] Melanchthon refers here to the letters which he had sent to England from Frankfurt in the spring of 1539; see note 7. For "edict," see note 25.

[57] The background of this statement could not be clarified.

[58] This is a reference to the missions of Burchart (see notes 7, 29) and the long drawn-out discussions which took place between the Germans and some of the English bishops; see Prüser, pp. 132 ff., 174 ff.; Tjernagel, pp. 180 ff.; Rupp, *Tradition*, pp. 115 ff.

How ingeniously the King debates[59] about these matters can be seen from two of his arguments. Regarding good works he argues as follows: Since evil works earn eternal wrath, it must follow that good works earn eternal salvation. And as I hear, he does not intend to have this argument taken away from him. The other one, concerning the marriage of priests, is this: Since the King has power to decree that a man remain at court as long as the King desires, [and] not marry, the King has also the power to decree that priests do not marry. This is the ingenious mind by which the King has ridiculed and condemned us. Your Electoral Grace will carefully consider whether it is fruitful to enter into debate with persons who help themselves by such arguments.

Arrangements have been made that the book[60] which Your Electoral Grace has sent to us be speedily printed. The *expostulatio*,[61] too, will be swiftly produced.

May God protect Your Electoral Grace at all times.

Written at Wittenberg, October 23, 1539

> Your Electoral
> Grace's dedicated servants,
> MARTIN LUTHER, DOCTOR
> JUSTUS JONAS, DOCTOR[62]
> JOHN BUGENHAGEN POMER, DOCTOR[63]
> PHILIP MELANCHTHON[64]

289

To Elector John Frederick[1]
[Wittenberg,] October 23, 1539

To the official brief of the Wittenberg theologians regarding further negotiations with Henry VIII (letter No. 288), Luther adds this personal letter. After reviewing briefly the correspondence on this

---

[59] The background of the following statements could not be established.
[60] For the possible identity of this book, see WA, Br 8, 566, n. 3.
[61] See note 54.
[62] See LW 48, 275, n. 3.
[63] See *ibid.*, 303, n. 44.
[64] See *ibid.*, 77, n. 3.
[1] For the whole letter, see also letter No. 288, Introduction.

issue, Luther rejects any further dealings with the King, who was never serious about the gospel, but always bent it to his own advantage. The German evangelicals are better off without this unfaithful, wavering hypocrite, who in effect wants to be worshipped, and who thinks that God cannot get along without him. Therefore Luther requests his Sovereign to abide by the negative answer given to Christopher Mont.

On Elector John Frederick, see LW 48, 181 f.

Text in German (with some words, phrases, or sentences in Latin): WA, Br 8, 577–578.[2]

To the Most Serene, Noble Sovereign and Lord,
Sir John Frederick, duke in Saxony, archmarshal and
elector of the Roman Empire, landgrave in Thuringia,
margrave in Meissen, and count of the castle in Magdeburg,
my Most Gracious Lord

Grace and peace in Christ, and my poor *Pater noster*![3] Most Serene, Noble Sovereign, Most Gracious Lord! Martin Bucer has previously also written to me in the same way in which he wrote to my Gracious Lord, the Landgrave, requesting my assistance in urging that a legation, especially Master Philip, be sent to England.[4] For the time being I have answered him suggesting that he abandon such hope, for there is no hope so far as the King is concerned, etc. It is therefore my humble request of Your Electoral Grace that Your Grace allow nothing to move you into abandoning the position you have already taken.[5]

The King is a dilettante[6] and has no serious intentions. This we have certainly found out from the English who have been here,[7] although at the time out of Christian love we had to believe that he was serious. But finally, when we had debated *ad nauseam*[8]—at great expense to Your Electoral Grace[9]—everything was sealed

---

[2] The letter is extant as autograph.
[3] See p. 69, n. 4.
[4] Bucer's letter to Luther is no longer extant; its content can be partially reconstructed on the basis of Luther's statements above, and Luther's answer to Bucer, letter No. 287.
[5] This is a reference to the answer given by the Elector to Christopher Mont; see p. 194, n. 11.
[6] Literally: "tempter."
[7] See pp. 117 ff., 138 f.
[8] Literally: "we had debated until we were weary."
[9] See p. 131.

with a sausage[10] and left to the King's pleasure. The English themselves said: "Our King vacillates." And Doctor Antony[11] said several times: "Our King in no way respects religion and the gospel."

Since that time I have come to be glad that the King has shown by public action that he has fallen from the gospel and, even more, that he has revealed his hypocritical pretense. By no means would we have fared well with him, for we would have had to load his sins upon ourselves, and yet had a false friend in him. Above all, as the English let slip while they were here, we would have had to let the King continue to be and be called "Head and Defender of the Gospel," as he boasts that he is head of the English churches.[12] Away, away with this head and defender! Gold and money make him so cocky as to think that he should be worshipped, and that God could not get along without him. Let the King himself carry his sins, for which he is not ready to repent; we have enough of our own to carry. We have more than enough evidence [of his hypocrisy]: he [betrayed] Emperor Maximilian and soon thereafter King Louis of France as well.[13] He should be pope, as in fact he is in England.

May our dear Lord God protect Your Electoral Grace and all friends[14] from every evil, especially from such cunning, insidious[15] attacks of the devil. Amen.

October 23, 1539   Your Electoral Grace's dedicated

MARTIN LUTHER

[10] "To seal with a *Bratwurst*," a phrase frequently used by Luther (see *WA*, Br 5, 227, n. 8), means that a document or the action and circumstances to be documented are actually worthless.
[11] Robert Barnes.
[12] This is a reference to the *Act of Supremacy* of 1534 (see *EHD* 5, 745 f.) and to the attempts by Henry to be accepted into the Smalcaldic League with the title "Defender of the Gospel"; see Tjernagel, pp. 156, 159.
[13] In 1510 Henry VIII had entered into an alliance with Louis XII of France; yet he soon abandoned his ally and joined the Holy League, which was directed against France and sought to expel the French from northern Italy. In 1513 he entered into an alliance with Emperor Maximilian, defeated the French in the Battle of Guinegate (August 16, 1513), but then promptly, upon the payment of a large sum of money by France, abandoned Maximilian. Luther refers to these events to underscore his contention that the German evangelicals are far better off without such a questionable ally as Henry VIII.
[14] Luther used *mit verwandte*, i.e., relatives. This could designate the Elector's relatives. The phrase was also often used in a technical sense to designate members of a league (i.e., political "relatives") or subscribers to a particular document.
[15] Literally: "roguish."

290

To Mrs. Martin Luther
Weimar, July 2, 1540

On June 11, 1540, Melanchthon left Wittenberg for the Electoral court in Weimar, intending to go from there to Hagenau. He was to participate in a colloquy between evangelicals and Roman Catholic theologians which was to work out a theological basis for Emperor Charles's policy of reconciliation between the opposing religious-political parties of the Empire. Melanchthon arrived in Weimar on June 12 and became so seriously ill that he could not continue the journey.[1] *In order to make new arrangements, Elector John Frederick*[2] *summoned*[3] *Luther and Caspar Cruciger*[4] *to Weimar on June 16.*[5] *Luther arrived in Weimar on June 23*[6] *and stayed there until approximately July 4 when he and the others went on to Eisenach with (the now recuperated) Melanchthon. Luther and his friends stayed there from July 7 to 26, primarily for the purpose of finding a solution to the highly embarrassing problem of the bigamy of Landgrave Philip of Hesse.*[7] *On July 27 Luther and Melanchthon left Eisenach for Wittenberg, where they arrived on August 2.*[8]

---

[1] See *WA*, Br 9, No. 3492, Introduction; Kawerau, *Jonas Briefwechsel* 1, No. 501. Lenz, *BPB* 1, 338, gives June 13 as the date of Melanchthon's arrival in Weimar; for June 12 as the date of Melanchthon's arrival, see *WA*, Br 9, 140 f. For the Colloquy of Hagenau (June 12–July 16, 1540), see Jedin, p. 374; Ranke 2[IV], 117 ff.; Lau-Bizer, pp. 161 ff. Melanchthon's severe illness, marked by high fever and general weakness, was apparently a psychosomatic reaction to his worries about the bigamy case (see below)—at least Melanchthon himself interpreted it in this way, as did Luther (*WA*, Br 9, 137, 144 f.; Köstlin-Kawerau 2, 526); see Manschreck, pp. 267 f. A fever epidemic was circulating in the area at that time; see also note 8, and Enders, *Briefwechsel* 13, 153, n. 1.
[2] See *LW* 48, 181 f.
[3] See *WA*, Br 9, No. 3499.
[4] See *LW* 49, 104, n. 12. According to the Elector's summons, Cruciger was to go to Hagenau instead of Melanchthon.
[5] Jonas (see *LW* 48, 275, n. 3) joined Luther and Cruciger (see Enders, *Briefwechsel* 13, 89, n. 6) for unknown reasons; see also *C.R.* 3, No. 1979.
[6] See *ARG* 25 (1928), 21; Lenz *BPB* 1, 338, n. 3. For the following dates, see Buchwald, *LK*, p. 137.
[7] See *LW* 49, 124, n. 18; Rockwell, *op. cit.* (see p. 30, n. 22), pp. 170 ff.; Lau-Bizer, pp. 157 ff.; Köstlin-Kawerau 2, 528 ff.
[8] In Eisenach, Jonas became ill with a fever; and then, on approximately July 30/31, while returning with Luther and Melanchthon from Eisenach to Wittenberg, Jonas had to stay behind in Naumburg. He was back in Wittenberg on August 4 or 5; Kawerau, *Jonas Briefwechsel* 1, Nos. 506–508.

Luther's absence from Wittenberg of approximately six weeks is the background for the four following letters written by Luther to his wife. In letter No. 290 Luther informs his wife that he is well, that Melanchthon's health is improving, and that at Arnstadt a pastor has driven a devil out of a young girl. Luther also discusses business and family matters: Catherine should help Bugenhagen and others find a pastor for the parish in Greussen; he, Luther, has received the letters from his children, but as yet has received no letter from his wife; he encloses a "silver apple" which Catherine should divide among the children; he will stay until July 4 in Weimar and then go to Eisenach with Melanchthon; Wolfgang Seberger should not neglect the mulberries and should tap the wine. Luther adds greetings to all his boarders and friends and asks them to step in and help wherever the need arises.

Text in German: WA, Br 9, 168.[9]

To my dearly beloved[10] Katie, Mrs. Doctor Luther,[11] etc.,
to the lady at the new pig market:[12] *Personal*

Grace and Peace! Dear Maid Katie, Gracious Lady of Zölsdorf[13] (and whatever other names Your Grace has)! I wish humbly to inform Your Grace that I am doing well here. I eat like a Bohemian and drink like a German;[14] thanks be to God for this. Amen. The reason for this is that Master[15] Philip[16] truly had been dead, and

---

[9] The letter was extant as autograph; it was preserved by Luther's daughter Margaret; see p. 79, n. 1.

[10] See *LW* 49, 312, n. 1.

[11] See also p. 48, n. 9. A literal translation would be: "Katie, a she-doctor."

[12] Since June of 1531 Luther had owned a large garden outside the city wall, east of the Elster gate, with a little house, a barn, and a small fishpond on it, the so-called "garden at the pig market." For details, see *WA*, Br 12, 416.

[13] In the spring of 1540 Luther bought the little country estate Zölsdorf (or Zülsdorf), south of Leipzig, from his brother-in-law, John von Bora. This rather run-down estate was the last of the von Bora family property; it was not productive enough to provide a living for the family of John von Bora, who went into the service of the duke of Prussia. For details, see *WA*, Br 8, 214 ff.; Enders, *Briefwechsel* 13, 108, n. 2.

[14] Luther used rather strong words for "eat" and "drink." Luther himself later interpreted this passage (see p. 218) the way he wished it to be understood; in a Table Talk he stated: "One must make the best of the vices that are peculiar to each land. The Bohemians gorge themselves, the Wends steal, the Germans swill without stopping." *LW* 54, 207; *WA*, TR 3, No. 3476.

[15] I.e., here and throughout the letter, Master of Arts.

[16] Philip Melanchthon; see *LW* 48, 77, n. 3.

really, like Lazarus, has risen from death.[17] God, the dear father, listens to our prayers. This we [can] see and touch [with our hands], yet we still do not believe it. No one should say Amen to such disgraceful unbelief of ours.

I have written to Doctor Pomer, the pastor,[18] that the Count of Schwarzburg is asking that a pastor be sent to Greussen.[19] As a wise woman and doctor, you, with Master George Major[20] and Master Ambrose,[21] might also give counsel as to which of the three candidates[22] I suggested to Pomer might be convinced [to go]. It is not a bad parish. Yet you people are wise and will find a better solution [than I suggested].

There[23] at Arnstadt the pastor has driven a devil out of a young girl in a truly Christian way.[24] Regarding this event we say:

---

[17] John 11:5 ff. For Melanchthon's severe illness and for Luther's prayers in Melanchthon's behalf, see Manschreck, pp. 267 f.; Köstlin-Kawerau 2, 527; WA, TR 4, Nos. 5058, 5062, 5096; 5, No. 5407; LW 54, 387 ff.

[18] This letter to John Bugenhagen (see LW 48, 303, n. 44) is no longer extant.

[19] Count Gunther of Schwarzburg-Sondershausen who, though he was a faithful papist, nevertheless "tolerated" the evangelical movement in the district of Arnstadt-Greussen-Klingen (southwest of Weimar), which he inherited in 1538, and which stood under the overlordship of the elector of Saxony; on the basis of dynastic laws, he was even obligated to see to it that his subjects were provided with evangelical preachers and, as the statement above demonstrates, he took this obligation seriously. For details on the highly complicated dynastic and legal situation, and on the evangelical movement in the Schwarzburg territory, see WA, Br 11, No. 4075.

[20] George Major of Nürnberg (1502–1574) had studied in Wittenberg and was appointed headmaster of the Latin school in Magdeburg in 1529. In 1537 he was appointed chief preacher of Wittenberg's Castle Church, and in 1544 he became a theological professor at Wittenberg University. He is known for his Patristic interests, his concern to establish a consensus catholicus, his support of Melanchthon against the Gnesio-Lutherans, and for the way in which, in the Majoristic controversy, he affirmed the necessity of good works for the preservation of the faith which leads to salvation. See O.D.C.C., p. 844.

[21] Ambrose Berndt of Jüterbog had been graduated as Master of Arts from Wittenberg University in April of 1528. After a short stay away from Wittenberg he returned, became a member of the Arts Faculty and of the Wittenberg Consistory, but then suddenly died early in 1542. In 1538 he had married Luther's niece, Magdalen Kaufman. On Ambrose Berndt, see WA, Br 5, 696, n. 1; 6, 279 ff.; 8, 327, n. 3; 9, 578, n. 10; Friedensburg, GUW, p. 223.

[22] For possibilities, and for the pastor finally sent to Greussen, see WA, Br 11, 33 f.; see also WA, Br 9, 169, n. 8.

[23] Literally: "Here," i.e., there at Arnstadt, in the district in which Greussen was located, about which Luther just had written.

[24] The background of this statement, esp. the identity of the pastor, could not be established. On the basis of the material presented in WA, Br 11, 33, it seems as if there was still a "papistic preacher," at least in Greussen, but perhaps also in Arnstadt at that time. When Luther says that the pastor handled

may the will of God, who is still alive, be done, even though the devil should be sorry about this.[25]

I have received the letters from the children,[26] also the one from the *baccalaureus* (who is no child)[27]—(Marushe [is] also not [one])[28]—but from Your Grace I have received nothing. If it please God, then you might now, at least once, answer this, the fourth letter,[29] with your gracious hand.

I am sending along with Master Paul[30] the silver apple which

---

the matter "in a Christian way," this suggests that the pastor did not use the complicated, colorful, and dramatic papal rite of exorcism, but a more simple one. For Luther's practice of exorcism, see WA, TR 3, No. 3739.

[25] I.e., that God's will is being done. Another possible translation would be: "alive, even if it [i.e., the fact that God lives] should do harm to the devil."

[26] It seems to be most natural to assume that these no-longer extant letters were written by Luther's children, though Luther could, of course, also be talking about letters from the children of friends (Melanchthon, Jonas).

[27] This is a reference to Luther's fourteen year old son, John, who in 1539 had been graduated from Wittenberg University as Bachelor of Arts (see Enders, *Briefwechsel* 13, 108, n. 8); hence he is no longer a child.

[28] Literally: "Marrische also not." In the original the name of the person is difficult to decipher. According to Clemen (WA, Br 9, 169, n. 11), "Marrische" seems to be the most accurate reading. Rückert (LB, p. 414, n. 16) suggests one has to read "Marusche;" this could be an allusion to Luther's daughter Margaret, whom Luther on another occasion called "Marussala" (WA, Br 7, 492). This suggestion makes good sense, though by itself it contributes little to the understanding of the whole passage. Would Luther have said that six year old Margaret was not a child, while he calls his other offspring, who were *older* than Margaret, children? It is understandable that Luther says that the Bachelor of Arts, John Luther, is no longer a child, notwithstanding that he is only fourteen years old. If indeed the person named by Luther is Margaret, and there is little that prevents one from assuming this, then Luther's statement obviously would have to be understood as humorous. Another possibility of interpreting this passage should be mentioned. The last letter of the name, the "e," could be a corrupted transcription of the Latin female genitive ending "ae." This would mean that one would have to translate: "(also not of [or: from] Mariischa)." The text in the second parentheses would then not be an afterthought, but would have to be seen in the light of the following clause so that one would have to paraphrase: I have received the letters from the "children," and from John; but (as yet) I have received nothing from you, and also nothing from Margaret. This interpretation presupposes that either Luther anticipated a letter from Margaret, or that on the basis of the other letters he knew that Margaret had written a letter.

[29] The other three letters are not extant.

[30] Paul Eber (1511–1569), from Kitzingen/Franconia, was graduated from Wittenberg University as Master of Arts in 1536, joined the Arts Faculty in 1537, and became professor of Latin in 1541. In addition to Latin, he taught physics, natural history, world history, and anatomy. He was dean of the Arts Faculty in 1542 and 1550 and president of the University in 1551/52. In 1556 he became professor of Old Testament and chief preacher at the Castle Church. From his student days he had a close personal and professional friendship with

my Gracious Lord[31] presented to me. As I previously said,[32] you may divide it among the children and ask them how many cherries and apples they would wish in exchange for it; give them these at once, and you retain the stalk, etc.[33]

Give my hearty greetings and good will to our dear boarders,[34] especially to Doctor Severus or Schiefer,[35] and tell them to help in

---

Melanchthon. A deeply pious person, Eber was committed to the ideals of Christian Humanism; consequently he tried to reconcile the warring theological parties, a fact which in turn made him the target of the attacks of the Gnesio-Lutherans. On Paul Eber, see *NDB* 4, 225. Eber had traveled from Wittenberg to Weimar in order to visit the ailing Melanchthon. He returned to Wittenberg on July 3 (?), taking along the present letter and the gift mentioned by Luther; see *C.R.* 3, 1060; *WA*, Br 9, 169, n. 13.

[31] While Luther generally called the Elector "my Most Gracious Lord," it is safe to suggest that he had received the "silver apple" from Elector John Frederick (see note 2).

[32] This is a reference to one of the no-longer extant letters mentioned above.

[33] This passage is difficult to understand, and Rückert (*LB*, p. 414) and Enders (*Briefwechsel* 13, 107 ff.) do not explain the passage. It is clear that Katie was to divide the "silver apple" among the children in such a way that the part due to each child would at once be exchanged for cherries and apples. That would mean that Katie would be left either with all the parts of the "silver apple," or with the whole "silver apple" if she did not actually cut it up into parts, but simply showed it to the children and said each one would receive a part. But why does Luther say that Katie should retain (also? only?) the stalk, if she has the whole apple anyhow? Is the stalk to be taken as symbolic of the whole "silver apple?" What does the "etc." mean? Finally, and probably most important, what is a "silver apple"? Clemen suggests (*WA*, Br 9, 170, n. 15) that it was some silver piece in the form of an apple which could be opened or divided; or that it was a little silver perfume bottle in the form of an apple (the dividing would then have to mean that the children could take turns smelling the "apple," and thus getting their share). In any case, the children (probably? hopefully?) would not know what to do with their shares of the "silver apple," and therefore would willingly exchange them. Perhaps the apple was some fruit, or candy, wrapped in silver paper. But then one would immediately ask why the children would exchange their shares for some other fruit. While Clemen's suggestion is the only one that is available, it is highly unsatisfactory, as Clemen himself points out.

[34] See p. 126, n. 17.

[35] Wolfgang Schiefer, or Severus, from Austria, had been a student in Vienna and Wittenberg. After 1525 he served as tutor to the children of a high official at the court of Austria, and finally became tutor to the children of Ferdinand I. In 1539 his name appeared among those of the members of the Luther household, and in the following months he held an important place in the round table of the Luther house. Thirty-two times he supposedly appears as the main speaker or questioner in the Table Talks; see Enders, *Briefwechsel* 12, 277, n. 4. (Apparently he had to leave his position in Austria because of his positive attitude toward the Reformation, though the circumstances are far from clear.) Luther tried in vain to get him employment. It seems that Schiefer left Wittenberg after September 20, 1540, to return to Austria with a letter of recommendation written by Melanchthon to one of the councilors of King Ferdinand (*C.R.*

all affairs of the church, school, house—wherever the need arises. Also [tell] Master George Major and Master Ambrose[36] to help you around the house.[37] By God's will we shall be here until Sunday,[38] and then, with Philip, we shall travel from Weimar to Eisenach.[39]

With this I commend you to God. Tell our Lycaon[40] not to neglect the mulberries by oversleeping; of course, he won't oversleep unless he forgets about it. Also, he should tap the wine at the right time. All of you be happy and pray. Amen.

Weimar, July 2, 1540   MARTIN LUTHER,

who loves you from his heart[41]

291

To Mrs. Martin Luther
[Eisenach,][1] July 10, 1540

While Luther was in Weimar, he received a portion of his quarterly salary which normally would have been paid to him on St. Mi-

---

3, No. 2012, dated September 20, 1540). Much in the life of this fascinating man is unclear, and it would be highly interesting to investigate further. Some data pertaining to Schiefer's life can be found in Enders, *Briefwechsel* 12, 277, nn. 2, 4, and in WA, Br 8, 589, n. 2 (corrected in WA, Br 9, 6, n. 1).

36 See notes 20, 21.

37 Literally: "to be of comfort to you around the house."

38 I.e., July 4.

39 See Introduction. On July 3 Joachim Moller (one of Melanchthon's boarders who was to accompany Melanchthon to Hagenau) wrote from Weimar to a fellow student in Wittenberg that "we" shall continue the journey on July 5 or 6; see WA, Br 9, 169, nn. 5, 13. According to a Melanchthon letter of July 8 (see ZKG 4 [1881], 288), the Luther-Melanchthon party left Weimar on July 4. It is certain that the Wittenberg theologians arrived in Eisenach on July 7, after a stopover in Erfurt; see C.R. 3, 1060; WA, Br 9, 170.

40 Lycaon was a legendary king of Arcadia, who sacrificed a child on a Zeus altar and tried to trick Zeus into eating human flesh. Finally Zeus turned him into a wolf. See O.C.D., p. 520. Lycaon the Wolf is an allusion to Luther's servant, Wolfgang Seberger; see LW 49, 158, n. 7.

41 Or: "Whom you love from your heart."

1 See letter No. 290, Introduction. While at Eisenach, Luther stayed in the house of Justus Menius where he spent some good hours with Menius' son, Timothy, whom he taught to "steal" nuts; WA, Br 9, 212, 222.

chael's Day.[2] *He sends this and some other money to his wife with letter No. 291 and suggests how she could exchange this money for smaller denominations. Then he mentions certain events: Around Eisenach the devil is raging by means of arson and murder; Philip Melanchthon has recuperated, and for this one should thank God; the Colloquy of Hagenau will accomplish nothing except, perhaps, that the Pope will arouse the Turks to attack "us"; Nicholas von Amsdorf is visiting Luther in Eisenach. In a postscript Luther leaves the payment of the messenger to his wife. He also makes some suggestions for the remodeling of the house, though he is aware that his suggestions might come too late.*

Text in German: WA, Br 9, 171–173.[3]

To Mrs. Catherine Luther[4] at Wittenberg, etc.,
my dear mistress of the house, etc.

Grace and peace! Dear Maid Katie! Herewith I am sending you (via the driver of Doctor Bleikard,[5] etc.)[6] A [:][7] forty-two *Taler,*[8] the salary due this coming St. Michael's Day,[9] and also forty

---

[2] In Weimar, Luther stayed in the house of Sebastian Schade, the "chief clerk" of the Electoral revenue department. Luther had also stayed with him in March of 1537, when returning from Smalcald; see ARG 25 (1928), 15. For Luther's stay with Schade in June/July of 1540, see ARG 28 (1931), 271. On Schade, see the materials collected in WA, Br 12, 425, n. 3. On Luther's salary, the various sources from which it was made up, and the way in which it was paid, see WA, Br 12, 423 ff.; Schwiebert, pp. 257 ff., 266 ff.
[3] The letter is extant as autograph; see WA, Br 13, 287, addition to WA, Br 9, 171, No. 3511.
[4] For "Luther," see p. 48, n. 9.
[5] Bleikard von Sindringen of Schwäbisch-Hall studied (Canon and Roman) law at the Universities of Heidelberg and Wittenberg, and joined the Wittenberg Law Faculty in 1529. In the summer semester of 1537 he was president of the University, and shortly thereafter he was appointed to the Electoral council. After the Smalcaldic War he continued to serve the Ernestine family who, now deprived of Wittenberg University, founded the University of Jena. He died in Jena in 1551. For some material on von Sindringen, see p. 112, n. 25, and Enders, *Briefwechsel* 7, 152, n. 5. Apparently von Sindringen had gone to Eisenach in order to be available for the discussions on the case of the Landgrave's bigamy.
[6] "Etc." apparently refers to whatever other titles von Sindringen might have had.
[7] Apparently this was the inscription placed on the "envelope" or bag in which the money was being sent. Did Luther send additional enclosures, marked B, C, etc.? (see also p. 220.) Or did the enclosure, marked A, only contain the 42 *Taler,* while an additional bag (marked B?) contained the 40 gulden?
[8] For the *Taler,* see p. 94, n. 8. According to p. 220, this amount was equivalent to fifty gulden; on the gulden, see *LW* 48, 11, n. 2.
[9] I.e., September 29. See also note 2.

gulden on the account of George Schnell which you may use until we return.[10] We were unable to get one penny in change at court,[11] just as you cannot get any in Wittenberg.[12] George Schnell received his change from Weissensee in the territory of Duke[13] George.[14] However, I think that one thousand gulden in little *Groschen*[15] have now arrived or will arrive shortly from my Most Gracious Lord[16] for change, etc.[17] For this is what he has ordered.[18] But it would be good if the people themselves would begin to avoid [using] the *Merker*, as well as the Polish pennies,[19] for they certainly are doing too much damage to this principality,

---

[10] This was the income from a benefice awarded by Elector John Frederick to one of Luther's boarders, George Schnell (from Rothenburg/Franconia), who was also Luther's *famulus* (see *LW* 48, 164, n. 4) and the tutor of his children. The money was the interest derived from an endowment which was administered by the city council of Weissensee (see note 14). On behalf of Schnell, Luther accepted this "fellowship" while he was in Eisenach. Incidentally, Luther was shortchanged. See *WA*, Br 7, 43, and 13, 221, addition to *loc.cit.*; *WA*, Br 9, 107, n. 2, 212, 222; *WA*, DB 12, 534 ff.—Luther told his wife that she could use this money; upon his return the account would have to be settled, and Schnell's money would have to be divided between Schnell and the Luther family.

[11] I.e., in Weimar.

[12] In view of the circumstances mentioned in note 18, small coins were difficult to obtain.

[13] Or: "Sir."

[14] Even though Weissensee (northwest of Weimar) was located in Ducal Saxony (i.e., that portion of Saxony which was ruled by the Albertine family; see *LW* 48, 110, n. 2), the benefice administered by the Weissensee city council stood under the patronage and jurisdiction of Electoral Saxony.

[15] The *Groschen* (a small coin with a comparatively high silver content) was the coin between the penny and the *Taler*. In present-day coinage it would be equivalent to a silver dime.

[16] Elector John Frederick; see *LW* 48, 181 f.

[17] It is not clear whether Luther wants to say that the thousand gulden in *Groschen* would come to Wittenberg, or that this money would be available in the territory.

[18] The *Merker*, mentioned in the following sentence, was the *Groschen* minted in the Margraviate of Brandenburg, the neighboring territory of Saxony. Because of their low silver content "one of them is not worth five [Saxon] pennies." To protect the Electoral and Ducal Saxon currency and economy, the use of the *Merker*, together with all pennies and *Groschen* not minted in Saxony, was repeatedly prohibited; see Enders, *Briefwechsel*, 13, 112, n. 4; *WA*, Br 9, 173, n. 8; *WA*, TR 4, 331. This, in turn, caused some hardship (see above, and *WA*, Br 9, 173, n. 6), because the supply of small Saxon coinage often ran low and then people had to wait until Saxon *Groschen* were available for the proper exchange.

[19] This is a reference to the *Scotus*, or *skocice*, the Polish penny. See Du Cange, *s.v.* Scotus; *WA*, TR 2, 600, n. 6.

since one of them is not worth five pennies. In the long run they may not be tolerated without damage to my Most Gracious Lord, and also to his land and people, as we shall see,[20] if God wills it. You might see whether John von Taubenheim[21] at Torgau could or would change the *Taler* into smaller coins for you.

There is nothing new, except that around here, too, the devil is raging and gives horrible examples of his maliciousness,[22] and pushes the people [to commit] arson which often proves fatal, suicide, etc. The people[23] are quickly jailed for this and executed. In this way God admonishes us to believe, to fear, and to pray, for all this is God's punishment on account of the ungratefulness for and contempt of his dear Word.[24]

Master Philip is returning to life again from the grave;[25] he still looks sick, yet he is in good spirits,[26] jokes and laughs again with us, and eats and drinks with us as usual. Praise be to God! You people, too, should join us in thanking the dear Father in heaven who raises the dead and who alone gives all grace and blessings; praised be he in eternity. Amen. But pray zealously, as you people ought to do, for our Lord Christ, that is, for all of us who believe in him, [and pray] against the crowd of devils who now rage at Hagenau[27] and rebel against the Lord and his anointed;[28] they intend to burst their bonds, as is stated in Psalm 2,[29] so that God in heaven may deride them and finally shatter them like a potter's

---

[20] The translation here is based on the corrections of the WA, Br text made on the basis of the autograph in WA, Br 13, 287, addition to WA, Br 9, 171, No. 3511.

[21] See LW 48, 163, n. 3.

[22] Katie apparently had informed her husband of the June 29 execution of four men convicted of scattering poison in the countryside and also of poisoning wells; for details, see WA, Br 9, 173, n. 11, 289, n. 9; 13, 288, addition to WA, Br 9, 173, n. 11. For "arson which often proves fatal," see p. 222, n. 12.

[23] I.e., the arsonists, since one who had committed suicide could hardly be apprehended and executed.

[24] See also pp. 183, 189.

[25] See pp. 208 f.

[26] Luther wrote *leberlich*. This could mean "liverish," i.e., yellow, pale (so Clemen in WA, Br 9, 173, n. 14, on the basis of a sixteenth century collection of proverbial sayings), or it could mean something to the effect of "lively" (so Rückert, LB, p. 416, n. 14). In view of the context ("still . . . yet") the latter possibility has been adopted.

[27] I.e., at the colloquy at Hagenau; see letter No. 290, Introduction.

[28] See Ps. 2:2.

[29] See Ps. 2:3.

vessel.[30] Amen. What will happen there, however, we do not yet know, except that we expect they will command us: "Do this and that, etc., or we shall devour you." For they have evil intentions.

Also, tell Doctor Schiefer[31] that I do not have any further hopes regarding Ferdinand;[32] he goes to his own destruction. Yet I worry that the Pope,[33] as I often prophesied, will arouse the Turk against us, for Ferdinand would not really fight back, as he supposedly said in a veiled way, and that [we shall] see strange events. For the Pope already sings: "If I cannot bend the great, I shall move hell."[34] If he is unable to incite the Emperor against us,[35] he will try it with the Turk. He will not yield to Christ. May Christ intervene with force against the Turk as well as the Pope and the devil, and prove that he is the one and only lord, seated by the Father on his right hand.[36] Amen.

Amsdorf is also still with us here.[37] With this I commend you to God. Amen.

July 10, 1540   MARTIN LUTHER

You certainly will know how to pay and tip the driver Wolf. I[38] have an idea how you could have the windows in the new roof

---

[30] See Ps. 2:4, 9; Rev. 2:27.

[31] See p. 211, n. 35.

[32] I.e., King Ferdinand I, the archduke of Austria (Schiefer's native land), and the brother of Emperor Charles V. For the following see p. 219, n. 17.

[33] I.e., Pope Paul III.

[34] This quotation from Vergil *Aeneid* vii. 312 (used several times by Luther; see e.g., WA, Br 11, 12), is written in Latin.

[35] At least since the spring of 1539, Emperor Charles V (see LW 48, 175 f.) had been pursuing a policy toward the evangelicals which was a low-key attempt at reconciliation, or at least co-existence. Whether the Emperor's motivation was honest is another question. For details, see Lau-Bizer, pp. 141 ff.; Ranke 2[IV], 117 ff. On July 8 Melanchthon wrote to Bugenhagen about news which had arrived in Eisenach from Hagenau, according to which the Pope had sent a special envoy to Ferdinand in order to influence Ferdinand in such a way that the Colloquy of Hagenau would not get under way; C.R. 3, No. 1980.

[36] Ps. 110:1.

[37] Nicholas von Amsdorf (see LW 48, 218) had been called to Eisenach for consultation on the case of the Landgrave's bigamy. There was also the possibility that he might be sent to Hagenau. For documentation, see WA, Br 9, 174, n. 25.

[38] For the remodeling of the Luther house—the former Wittenberg Augustinian monastery (see LW 49, 59, n. 12)—undertaken by the Luther family in 1540, see E. Kroker, *Aufsätze zur Stadtgeschichte und Reformationsgeschichte: Aus Leipzigs Vergangenheit* 1 (Leipzig, 1929), 110; *Zeitschrift für die historische*

constructed, which I forgot to mention when I left.[39] Only two windows should be on the side toward the *Collegium*,[40] placed between the two firewalls;[41] in the upper part, the gable,[42] there should be none on the side toward the *Collegium*. On the side toward the kitchen[43] there should be only three little windows framed with upright bricks.[44] In the hall which leads to the dark chamber there should be the two [lower] half sections of the wall covered with mortar (so that one may pass by [unseen]), and the light should come from the roof. But I am afraid I am too late [with these suggestions].

Theologie 30 (1860), 484 ff.; H. Stein, *Geschichte des Lutherhauses* (Wittenberg, 1883), *passim*. Among other work done, a new roof was put on the house, and Luther was very pleased with the work of an out-of-town craftsman; see *Luther. Vierteljahrschrift der Luthergesellschaft* 11 (1929), 118.

[39] Literally: "for I forgot it [i.e., to mention 'my idea'] when I left."

[40] I.e., the first main building of the University which consisted of two buildings placed parallel to each other on an east–west axis and connected by a courtyard; it was located "a few hundred yards west" of the Luther house (Schwiebert, p. 232). Since the Luther house was also on an east–west axis, its small side and gable faced the gables of the *Collegium*.

[41] Whether these were "firewalls" in the present day sense of the word (i.e., heavier walls than the ones generally used; see also note 44), or walls enclosing or covering a chimney, could not be established.

[42] Luther wrote *first*, i.e., literally "ridge [of the roof]." The context makes clear that Luther meant gable.

[43] I.e., the east gable of the house, which faced the attached kitchen.

[44] Or: "windows the size of a brick placed upright." This last statement is unclear; so is the following sentence, which had to be translated freely in some cases because of some technical terms. It is clear that the hall to the "dark chamber" (was this a toilet?) was to receive light from a "skylight" and, perhaps, also from two windows placed in the upper sections of a wall of which the lower sections were to be closed, so that one could pass through the hall without being seen. It seems that this wall (made of wood boards, intertwined twigs, and clay; see *WA*, Br 9, 174, n. 29) was an inside wall, for the outside of the building was of solid stone. Apparently the changes were intended to facilitate the flow of traffic.

292

To Mrs. Martin Luther
[Eisenach,][1] July 16, 1540

Luther informs his wife of some everyday events: He is healthy and happy and enjoying his food and drink; Melanchthon also is healthy again; von Amsdorf is still in Eisenach; the delegation that went to Hagenau had a good time on the way and made a short trip from Hagenau to Strassburg; it is unbearably hot in Eisenach. Luther asks his wife to tell Schiefer a rumor that King Ferdinand is seeking the friendship of the Turks. He also asks her to write to him whether she has received all that he sent, especially the money. In closing, he extends von Amsdorf's greetings to Katie.

Text in German: WA, Br 9, 174–175.[2]

To my gracious maid, Catherine Luther von Bora and Zölsdorf,[3] at Wittenberg, my beloved

Grace and peace! My dear Maid and Lady Katie! Your Grace should know that we are chipper and healthy here (God be praised), eat like the Bohemians (yet not much) and drink like the Germans (yet not much).[4] We are happy indeed, for our gracious lord of Magdeburg, Bishop[5] Amsdorf,[6] is our table companion. Otherwise we have no news, except that[7] Doctor Caspar,[8] Myconius,[9] and Menius[10] have let themselves be pampered on the

---

[1] See letter No. 290, Introduction.

[2] The letter was extant as autograph which was deposited in Königsberg.

[3] For "Luther," see p. 48, n. 9; for "Zölsdorf," see p. 208, n. 13.

[4] See also p. 208.

[5] See *LW* 49, 87, n. 5.

[6] See p. 216.

[7] The following is news about the theologians of the Electoral Saxon delegation who went to Hagenau in place of Melanchthon; see letter No. 290, Introduction.

[8] I.e., Caspar Cruciger.

[9] Frederick Myconius.

[10] Justus Menius (1449–1558) of Fulda had studied in Erfurt (1514) and Wittenberg (1519), became a pastor at Erfurt in 1525, and the superintendent of the district of Eisenach in 1529. He is known for his translation of some of Luther's Latin writings into German and for his gifts in matters of ecclesiastical organization. Even though he strongly opposed the *Interim* of 1548 (see *O.D.C.C.*, p. 105), he was basically of a conciliatory nature and had strong

way[11] and made a leisurely trip[12] from Hagenau to Strassburg[13] to serve and honor John of Jena.[14] Also, Master Philip has again been totally restored.[15] God be praised. Tell my dear Doctor Schiefer[16] that his King Ferdinand is being talked about as if he intends to seek the friendship of the Turks against the evangelical sovereigns.[17] I hope this is not true for it would be too hard.

---

leanings toward the Melanchthonian wing of Lutheranism; this in turn caused the Gnesio-Lutherans to be hostile toward him. On Justus Menius, see *Die Religion in Geschichte und Gegenwart*, K. Galling *et al.* (eds.) 4 (3rd ed.; Tübingen, 1960), 854.

[11] Nothing could be established about the background of this statement.

[12] Literally: "they have walked [as one takes a walk, e.g., on a Sunday afternoon]."

[13] On this visit, see also *WA*, Br 9, 175, n. 3.

[14] I.e., for no special purpose. For the expression "John of Jena," see p. 129, n. 42.

[15] See also pp. 208 f.

[16] See p. 211, n. 35.

[17] Or: "friendship of the Turks as opposed to [the friendship of] the evangelical sovereigns." (For the phrase, "to seek the friendship of the Turks," Luther used: *zu gevatter[n] bitten*; for *Gevatter*, see *LW* 48, 201, n. 2.) A literal translation of the first portion of the sentence would read: "Tell my . . . that his King Ferdinand will get a rumor as if." Neither Enders (*Briefwechsel* 13, 111, 113) nor Rückert (*LB*, pp. 416, 418), nor *WA* Br (9, 172, 175; 13, 288; 14, xxxiv) tries to identify the circumstances behind this passage. Whether Luther based his statement on his knowledge of the political moves of King Ferdinand (of which he might have known through news from Hagenau or from the Electoral court), or on his personal distrust of the policies of Ferdinand (and the Emperor), or simply on pessimistic anticipation could not be established. In any event, Luther is speaking of a rumor. The source and extent of this rumor could not be established; perhaps the Weimar archive might produce some answers to these problems.—For the fact that the Emperor pursued a policy of reconciliation and that the papacy opposed this, see p. 216, n. 35; Jedin, pp. 370 ff.; Ranke 2[IV], 103 ff. Nothing could be established that would seem to justify Luther's fear (see p. 216) that the papacy was trying to agitate the Turks into attacking the Empire. Yet Luther had great sensitivity for papal diplomacy. As Ranke has pointed out (2[IV], 104 f.), ever since the Frankfurt Truce the papacy had ignored the Turkish threat. The papacy had even gone so far as to approve of the negotiations between Venice and the Turks which eventually led to a truce. The papacy's main concern was to bring about a rapprochement between Charles V and France which would effectively free the Imperial forces for subduing the Protestant heretics; see Ranke 2[IV], 106; Jedin, pp. 372 f. —Luther's low opinion of Ferdinand (see also p. 216) appears unjustified. According to Brandi (1, 365), the situation in Hungary was very much on Ferdinand's mind at that time, since in view of the pro-Ferdinand and the anti-Ferdinand parties in Hungary an intervention on the part of the Turks was a serious possibility. Luther's loss of hope regarding Ferdinand probably had its basis in the way in which Ferdinand and the papal theologians around him (esp. John Faber; see *LW* 49, 41, n. 35) handled the colloquy at Hagenau; see Jedin, pp. 372 ff.; Brandi 1, 365 f.; Lau-Bizer, pp. 161 ff. They operated on the presuppositions that the Pope was not to be party to, but judge of, the

[At least] write and let me know whether you have received all the things that I sent, such as the ninety gulden[18] that I sent recently with Wolf the driver, etc.[19] With this I commend you to God. Amen. Have the children pray. Here there is such a heat and drought[20] that it is beyond words and unbearable [day] and night. Come [O Last] Day. Amen.

July 16, 1540. The Bishop of Magdeburg[21] sends kind greetings.

Your loving[22]

MARTIN LUTHER

---

colloquy; that the validity of the Bull *Exsurge, Domine* and of the *Edict of Worms* (see *LW* 48, 176, 210) be accepted as a foregone conclusion; and finally, that the colloquy take as point of departure the compromise articles which had been worked out in Augsburg in 1530 (see *LW* 49, 403 ff.), rather than Scripture or the *Augsburg Confession.* "For the fiasco Ferdinand's many mistakes in the conduct of the meeting were largely responsible." So Jedin, p. 374. On July 16, the day on which Luther wrote the present letter to his wife, Ferdinand "had no alternative but to declare . . . that it had proved impossible to reach agreement on a *modus conciliandi.*" So Lau-Bizer, p. 162. Luther's statements above are, then, a combination of rumors, facts, and pessimism.

[18] I.e., forty-two *Taler* (or fifty gulden) and forty gulden for the account of George Schnell; see pp. 213 f.

[19] What "etc." refers to is not clear; see also p. 213, n. 7. One may perhaps think of the "silver apple" which Luther had sent on July 2 or 3 with Paul Eber (see pp. 210 f.). While it seems that on July 10 Luther had a letter from Katie in hand (see p. 215, n. 22), in terms of the time necessary for Eber to return to Wittenberg and a letter from Katie to reach Luther in Eisenach, it seems highly improbable that on July 10 Luther was referring to a letter written by Katie *after* Eber had delivered the "silver apple." In the letter to which Luther referred on July 10 Katie reported some dramatic events (executions) that took place in Wittenberg on June 29, and Katie would hardly have waited a long time—i.e., until *after* Eber's return to Wittenberg—to write about them if she intended to write about them at all. Further, on July 10, Luther apparently had already had this letter from Katie (reporting the executions) for some time since, except for the allusion to the events in Wittenberg (and perhaps a response to Katie's report about the construction at the house), Luther did not deal with this letter from Katie when he wrote to her on that day. Katie apparently had written the letter in which she reported the executions in response to one of Luther's letters (perhaps the third one) mentioned on p. 210. It seems, then, that by July 10 Luther had not yet received any confirmation about Katie's receipt of the "silver apple," and it is quite possible that "etc." refers to this present.

[20] According to *WA*, Br 9, 175, n. 8, 205, n. 8, there were solar eclipses in 1539 and 1540 which were followed by heat-waves, which in turn caused forest fires and the drying-up of wells; see also p. 222, n. 12.

[21] See note 5, 6.

[22] Or: "[The man] whom you love."

293

To Mrs. Martin Luther
[Eisenach,][1] July 26, 1540

Although Luther is unsure just where his wife is as he writes this letter to her, he asks that some beer be ready for him on his return to Wittenberg, which he hopes will be soon. He comments briefly on the outcome of the Colloquy of Hagenau, on Melanchthon's recovery, and on fires in the Thuringian Forest. He encourages his family to pray and commends all of them to God.
Text in German: WA, Br 9, 205.[2]

To the wealthy lady at Zölsdorf[3], Mrs. Doctor Catherine Luther,[4] residing in the flesh at Wittenberg and living in the spirit at Zölsdorf, to my beloved: *Personal*

If she is absent, then Doctor Pomer,[5] the pastor, is to break [the seal] and read [the letter]

. . . Please[6] see to it that you have a good glass[7] of beer waiting for us. God willing, we shall leave tomorrow, Tuesday, for Wittenberg.[8]

Nothing was accomplished at the Diet of Hagenau;[9] effort and

---

[1] See letter No. 290, Introduction.
[2] The slightly damaged autograph (see also note 6) of this letter was extant, having been preserved by Luther's daughter, Margaret.
[3] See p. 208, n. 13.
[4] For "Luther," see p. 208, n. 11.
[5] I.e., John Bugenhagen; see *LW* 48, 303, n. 44. Luther wanted to be sure that the Wittenbergers knew of his pending departure from Eisenach.
[6] De Wette (*Dr. Martin Luthers Briefe* 5 [Berlin, 1828], 299) had the autograph specially copied for his text. He states that approximately one line of text is missing at the beginning of the letter.
[7] Literally: "a good drink of beer."
[8] The Luther party indeed left Eisenach on Tuesday, July 27 (see *C.R.* 3, 1067), and returned via Weimar and Naumburg (see *WA*, Br 9, 176, n. 1) to Wittenberg.
[9] Literally: "With the Diet of Hagenau it is dirt." "Diet" is sarcastic, for the colloquy at Hagenau was not a diet in the literal sense (see *LW* 48, 70, n. 1), but rather a conference of the Imperial Estates called by the Emperor for the purpose of discussing theological discrepancies in order to arrive at unity. For the outcome of the Hagenau colloquy, see also p. 219, n. 17.

labor are lost, and expenses have been incurred for nothing. Yet even if we accomplished nothing else, we fetched Master Philip from hell, and shall cheerfully bring him home from the grave,[10] God willing and by his grace. Amen.

The devil is on the loose, himself possessed by new, [more] evil devils,[11] burning and doing damage which is terrible.[12] In the Thuringian Forest more than one thousand *Acker*[13] of my Most Gracious Lord's[14] trees have been burned to the ground, and are still burning; in addition, today the news is that the forest near Werdau[15] and in many other places also has started to burn. No fire-fighting does any good. This will make wood expensive.

Pray, and have [the children] pray against that horrible Satan who most violently attacks us not only in soul and body but also in property and honor. May Christ our Lord come down from heaven and also start a little fire[16] for the devil and his companions which the devil would be unable to extinguish. Amen.

I am not sure whether this letter[17] will find you at Wittenberg or Zölsdorf;[18] otherwise I would like to write about more things.

---

[10] See pp. 208 f.

[11] See Matt. 12:45.

[12] In an October 10, 1540, letter to Duke Albrecht of Prussia, Luther reported (on the basis of confessions supposedly made by the criminals involved in these cases of arson) that Henry of Brunswick, a bitter foe of the evangelicals, was to be held responsible for the many fires which were plaguing central Germany at that time; Luther added: "It is impossible that such arson which often proves fatal [*Mordbrennen*] does not originate in high circles, for there is enough money there; the Pope, supposedly, has given 80,000 ducats (see LW 49, 286, n. 36) for this, etc." WA, Br 9, 242. See also Melanchthon's September 19 letter to Duke George of Anhalt (*C.R.* 3, No. 2011), the material presented in WA, Br 9, 243, nn. 7, 8, and the references from Luther's Table Talks listed in Rückert, LB, p. 416, n. 9. See, however, also p. 220, n. 20.

[13] How reliable Luther's figure is, or how literally it is to be taken cannot be established. According to one metric equivalent (one used esp. in Thuringia) almost 3000 square kilometers had burned to the ground. According to another equivalent (one used in Saxony in general) approximately 550 square kilometers had burned to the ground; this figure seems to be the more natural one.

[14] Elector John Frederick; see LW 48, 181 f.

[15] Werdau is located west of Zwickau. According to WA, Br 9, 205, n. 8, this information cannot be verified.

[16] See Gen. 19:24; II Kings 1:10; Ezek. 21:31; Luke 9:54.

[17] Literally: "I have not been sure whether these letters [i.e., the present letter and at least one other no-longer extant letter] would find you."

[18] In a no-longer extant letter, Katie apparently had informed her husband that she would go to Zölsdorf, or was eager to go (hence Luther's statement in the address).

With this I commend you to God. Amen. Greetings to our children, the boarders,[19] and all, etc.

July 26, 1540   Your loving[20]

MARTIN LUTHER, DOCTOR

294

To Mrs. Martin Luther
[Wittenberg,] September 18, 1541

Luther hurriedly wrote[1] *this short note to his wife (who apparently was at Zölsdorf)*[2] *so that she would not be frightened if she heard rumors about the Turks, and because he himself was worried about his wife, having received no letters from her. He tells Katie to make the necessary arrangements and come home; as he views the present situation, there is danger at hand, and God will punish "our" sins.*

Text in German: WA, Br 9, 518–519.[3]

---

[19] See p. 126, n. 17.

[20] Or: "[The man] whom you love."

[1] How hurriedly the letter was written can be seen from the fact that Luther folded the sheet of paper for sealing while the ink of his signature was still wet so that the signature is mirror-printed on one of the fold-ins; see note 3. Also, if one compares this rather sober letter with others written by Luther to his wife, esp. the way in which Luther addresses his wife in this present letter and in others, it becomes clear that Luther was indeed in a great hurry.

[2] It is not as certain as Clemen and others make it sound (see WA, Br 9, 509, n. 9) that Katie was at Zölsdorf—Enders (*Briefwechsel* 14, 65, n. 3) and Rückert (*LB* 419, n. 2) are less positive than Clemen—though some observations, thus far omitted, make it probable that Katie was at Zölsdorf. In the present letter Luther states that Katie should sell and arrange whatever she can. This indeed suggests that Katie was at the "estate" in Zölsdorf during September to supervise the harvesting and the sale of farm products, and to make the necessary arrangements for winter. Also, the reference to the nobility of Meissen (if one may place any weight on this reference; see note 11) might suggest that Katie was at Zölsdorf, i.e., in the area south of Leipzig where many of the nobility of Meissen had their estates.

[3] The letter was extant as autograph which is now lost; see WA, Br 9, No. 3670, Introduction, and 13, 298, addition to *loc. cit.* A facsimile of the letter, which clearly shows the circumstances pertaining to the signature mentioned in note 1, can be found in W. Goetz, *et al.*, *Das Zeitalter der religiösen Umwälzung: Reformation und Gegenreformation, 1500–1660. Propyläen-Weltgeschichte 5* (Berlin, 1930), following p. 160.

LETTERS

To my dear mistress of the house, Katie Ludern[4] von Bora:
Personal

Grace and peace. Dear Katie! I am letting Urban[5] run to you with this letter, so that you should not be frightened if rumors[6] about the Turks[7] reach you. Also, it seems strange to me that you write or send absolutely nothing to us even though you certainly know that we are concerned about you because Mainz,[8] Henry,[9] and many of the nobility in Meissen[10] are very hostile toward us.[11] Sell and

---

[4] Why Luther suddenly used this form of his name again (see *LW* 48, 19) cannot be explained.

[5] This person cannot be identified. In Luther's correspondence a messenger with the name Urban is mentioned on April 15, 1518 (*WA*, Br 1, 166); for details about this man and his possible identity, see Enders, *Briefwechsel* 1, 185, n. 5; *WA*, Br 13, 13, addition to *WA*, Br 1, 167, n. 6. Another possible translation of this portion of the sentence would be: "Herewith [i.e., by the act of writing, sealing, and dispatching the letter, and paying the messenger] I am letting Urban run."

[6] Literally: "noise [or: wailing]."

[7] In 1541 the Turks successfully intervened in the confused situation in Hungary by supporting the anti-Ferdinand party, by conquering large areas of the central Hungarian plains, and finally, in August, by storming Budapest. (On approximately September 8 the Elector informed Luther officially of the fall of Budapest and requested that Luther order the preachers in the territory to admonish the people from the pulpit to pray for God's help against the Turkish danger; see *WA*, Br 9, No. 3666. Soon thereafter Luther published his *Appeal for Prayer Against the Turks*; *WA* 51, 585 ff.; *LW* 43, 219 ff.) This time the Turks were determined to retain their conquest; therefore they established a military administration. To offset the victory of the Turks, Emperor Charles undertook a military expedition against the Turks in Algeria in the autumn of 1541; it ended disastrously; see Ranke 2[IV], 142 ff.; Brandi 1, 377 ff. According to *WA* 51, 577, the conquest of Budapest at once raised fears of a new Turkish invasion of the Empire.

[8] I.e., Luther's old foe, Archbishop Albrecht of Mainz (see *LW* 48, 44 f.). Luther expected trouble from him because in the spring of 1541 the Reformation movement had been victorious in Halle, one of the favorite towns of the archbishop; see *LW* 48, 344 ff.; Köstlin-Kawerau 2, 549 f.

[9] I.e., Duke Henry the Younger of Brunswick-Wolfenbüttel (1489–1568; see *NDB* 8, 351 f.). Since 1525 he had been a bitter political opponent of the Reformation, not only for religious reasons, but also (and predominantly) for dynastic, geographic, and economic reasons. In 1538 the hostility between the Duke and the evangelicals grew more intense, erupting in a pamphlet war in 1539. In spring of 1541 Luther published his *Against Hanswurst* which was written against the Duke (*WA* 51, 469 ff.; *LW* 41, 185 ff.). Finally in the spring of 1542 outright war between the Duke and the leaders of the Smalcaldic League (Landgrave Philip of Hesse and Elector John Frederick of Saxony) broke out. For details, see Ranke 2[IV], 170 ff.; Köstlin-Kawerau 2, 557 ff.; Lau-Bizer, pp. 175 f.

[10] Some of the nobility of Meissen were angry with the Elector of Saxony and

224

arrange what you are able to, and come home.[12] For it appears to me that a storm is brewing[13] and that God will punish our sins with the rods of his wrath.

With this I commend you to God. Amen.

September 18, 1541   MARTIN LUTHER

295

To Justus Jonas
[Wittenberg,] February 16, 1542

At the time Luther wrote this letter, Jonas was in Halle to organize and supervise the evangelical church there. Luther asks Jonas to see to it that his messengers (who would bring letters to Wittenberg) wait for a reply if Jonas expects to get a reply at all. Then Luther mentions that Kilian Goldstein, the carrier of the present letter, was a most welcome visitor, and would have been even more welcome had he stayed for dinner. As an afterthought, Luther responds to a no-longer extant letter of Jonas by stating that he, too, wishes to

---

Luther because they prevented Julius von Pflug (see *O.D.C.C.*, p. 1059), an Erasmian reform Catholic and a member of an old, highly respected Meissen family, from ascending to the episcopal see of Naumburg, and instead managed to have Nicholas von Amsdorf (see *LW* 48, 218) become bishop of Naumburg. For details, see *WA*, Br 12, 314 ff.; Lau-Bizer, pp. 176 ff.; P. Brunner, *Nikolaus von Amsdorf als Bischof von Naumburg. Schriften des Vereins für Reformationsgeschichte* 67, No. 179 (Gütersloh, 1961).

[11] Apparently Luther feared that harm might be done to his wife by one of the aforementioned parties. How serious Luther was, and how much weight one may place on this statement has to remain an open question, esp. in view of the following statement made by Luther on September 25: "As I see, you have heard all the sad news about the Turks. You are correct in stating that we are now enduring the absolutely unbearable Turks, Henrys, men of Mainz, usurers, and big shots." *WA*, Br 9, 521. It seems that Luther and the addressee of the letter here quoted lumped together all the anti-evangelical forces, which were raging at that moment, considering them dangerous and intolerable, but not actually *personally* dangerous.

[12] Since in the September 25 letter, cited in note 11, Luther extends the greetings of his wife to the addressee, one may assume that by that time Katie had returned to Wittenberg.

[13] Literally: "that it will rain dirt." I.e., the situation is as dangerous and foreboding as if it would rain dirt. Luther used this expression several times; see *WA* 51, 647, No. 71, 673, No. 71; *WA*, TR 4, 642; 5, No. 5296.

know whether Karlstadt passed away with a repentant heart and by
announcing the pending arrival of Karlstadt's widow in Wittenberg.
In a lengthy postscript Luther communicates news: Bucer's wife,
his daughters, and a son have perished in the plague; a ghost dis-
turbs Karlstadt's grave and house; the Sultan intends to invade the
Empire, and the Sultan's oldest son is revolting against his father;
the Hungarian stories have been printed in Wittenberg; and finally,
Eck has published a book about the Diet and Colloquy of Regens-
burg.

On Justus Jonas, see LW 48, 275, n. 3.

Text in Latin: WA, Br 9, 621–622.[1]

To the illustrious man, Mr. Justus Jonas, Doctor of Theology,
the provost[2] at Wittenberg, a faithful ambassador of Christ[3]
at Halle, my superior[4] to be revered in the Lord.

Grace and peace! I have told[5] that excellent man, Doctor Kilian,
your syndic,[6] the same thing that I am communicating to you
[now] by means of this pen, dipped in ink and filling up the
paper, namely, that you should not continue to request an answer
from me[7] unless you have first coaxed the messengers or letter

---

[1] The letter is extant in manuscript copies (of which one, by John Aurifaber, is now deposited in Wolfenbüttel), and in the common editions of Luther's works; see WA, Br 9, No. 3714; 14, 160, No. 360. See also below note 15.

[2] I.e., provost of the All Saints' Chapter at Wittenberg's Castle Church. See Schwiebert, pp. 235 ff., 259 f.

[3] See II Cor. 5:20.

[4] Or: "Elder."

[5] Literally: "I have ordered with [my] mouth."

[6] This was Kilian Goldstein (1499–1568) from Kitzingen in Franconia. He matriculated at Leipzig University in 1515 and at Wittenberg in 1521, and became a member of the Wittenberg Arts Faculty in 1528; he also studied law in Wittenberg. In 1530 he completed his legal training, in 1533 became a member of the Saxon judiciary system, and in 1541 was granted a leave of absence to function as syndic (see LW 49, 97, n. 6, 284, n. 22) for the city of Halle. He spent the remaining years of his life in the service of the city of Halle. On Kilian Goldstein, see NDB 6, 622 f. The background for Goldstein's visit to Wittenberg could not be clarified.

[7] The background of this and the following statements could not be clarified; see also note 10. Luther's previous extant letter to Jonas is dated January 16, 1542; WA, Br. 9, No. 3705. In a February 6 letter to Nicholas von Amsdorf (see LW 48, 218), in which Luther makes the identical request of von Amsdorf regarding the letter carriers, Luther writes that Jonas pesters him for answers but does not instruct the messengers to take these answers along as return mail; see WA, Br 9, 611 f.

carriers to do a small service—that is, at least to return after they have delivered a letter, and pick up[8] an answer. For they deliver your letters to me as if they were forced to take care of other things after they have dropped off your letters, or to turn them over to the first person they meet, or in the meantime to kill a Turk. Well, if you do not take care of this, then have no doubt that I am unable to answer. For (as you know) I am too poor[9] to be able to send letters to you by my own messengers; further, I am too occupied to be able to look around for someone who might perhaps go or move from here to Halle. This is in reply to your four letters, or perhaps even more.[10]

By the way, Doctor Kilian was a most welcome visitor, and would have been even more welcome had he stayed for dinner. But he said that he had to hurry, so I urged him in vain to stay. Be that as it may, the agreement of souls is a sufficiently large and happy banquet, however far apart their bodies are, according to the saying: the church is the fellowship of saints.

Farewell, and pray for me. The Lord be with you. Amen.

Greet your highly respected wife, the fruitful one who is blessed with children, on behalf of all of us. Concerning Karlstadt's death,[11] I too[12] wish to know whether he passed away with a repentant heart.[13] His wife will be here about Easter,[14] and from her we shall find out everything.

Again farewell.

February 16, 1542.[15]

---

[8] Or: "search for [or: request] an answer."

[9] On Luther's financial situation, see Schwiebert, pp. 262 ff.; WA, Br 12, 415 ff., 423 ff.

[10] Unfortunately none of these letters is extant.

[11] Karlstadt (see LW 48, 79, n. 12) had died in Basel on December 24, 1541, after an attack of the plague. For the events concerning the ghost, mentioned below, see H. Barge, *Andreas Bodenstein von Karlstadt* 2 (Leipzig, 1905); reprint: Nieuwkoop, 1968), 511 ff.

[12] In one of the no-longer extant letters mentioned above Jonas must have made a statement to the effect that he was wondering whether in the hour of death Karlstadt had confessed his sins and repented of them.

[13] Literally: "passed away as a penitent one."

[14] In 1542, Easter fell on April 9. Nothing about the background of this statement concerning Anne of Mochau could be established; see also Barge, *op. cit.*, 515 ff.

[15] Clemen (WA, Br 9, No. 3714, Introduction) argues that the following postscript belongs most probably to a no-longer extant letter written by Luther to

Bucer's[16] wife has perished in the plague; also all his daughters and a son. Many learned men have died,[17] as I think you know.

A friend writes from Basel that Karlstadt has died and adds a fantastic story; he insists that some ghost comes to Karlstadt's grave and moves around in his house, making all kinds of noise by throwing stones and gravel.[18] According to Attic Law[19] one may not speak evil of the dead;[20] therefore I shall add nothing.

We have seen to it that the Hungarian stories have been printed.[21] The Poles say that the Turkish tyrant aims for the domi-

---

Jonas a few days earlier. He supports his argument with the following observations: (a) The statement regarding Karlstadt's death which Luther makes in the postscript presupposes that Luther assumes that Jonas does not yet know that Karlstadt had died, while the statement which Luther makes regarding Karlstadt's death in the last paragraph of the letter clearly indicates that Luther is reacting to Jonas' knowledge about Karlstadt's death and to Jonas' comments on this event. (b) All the news that Luther communicates in the postscript was available to Luther prior to February 16, the date of the present letter to which the text tradition, beginning with the Aurifaber copy (see note 1), has added this postscript. Both supporting arguments are convincing, and Clemen's view makes good sense. The form of the letter seems strange, though counterarguments to Clemen's view could be raised.

[16] See LW 48, 247, n. 13; Bucer's wife's name was Elisabeth, née Pallas.

[17] Among them were Capito (see LW 48, 305, n. 2) and Grynaeus. On the plague in general, see LW 49, 175, n. 26; on the plague which raged in the second half of 1541 in southwestern Germany, see WA, Br 9, 622, nn. 8, 9.

[18] This news came to Wittenberg via Camerarius (see LW 49, 81, n. 22) from the printer John Oporin (see Benzig, op. cit. [see p. 185, n. 1], p. 36, No. 27) in Basel; see WA, Br 9, 623, n. 10; C.R. 4, No. 2453.

[19]Erasmus in his Adagia (III: 10, 69; Clericus 2, 943E) records the saying that the dead are not to be slandered and illustrates it with a quotation from Homer Odyssey xxii. 412. So WA, Br 9, 623, n. 11. What Luther meant with the term "Attic Law" is unclear. In citing what amounts to the classical maxim, "Nil nisi bonum de mortuis" ("Nothing but praise for the dead"), and considering it a part of Attic Law, Luther could have had the following circumstances in mind: This maxim was a free translation of a saying attributed to the Spartan statesman Chilon (see O.C.D., p. 186) and recorded in Diogenes Laertius Lives i. 70 (Chilon). Plutarch Lives: Solon xxi. 1, attributed a slightly different version (one which was closer to the Homeric passage cited by Erasmus than to the traditional form) to Solon (see O.C.D., pp. 847 f.), the Athenian statesman, lawgiver (see Plutarch Lives: Solon i. 1; Aristotle Athen. respublica vi–xii), and poet. Both Chilon and Solon were counted among the Seven Sages, "men of practical wisdom, statesmen, lawgivers and philosophers" (so Oxford Companion, op. cit. [see p. 156, n. 19], p. 391). If indeed Luther had these circumstances in mind—and he could very well have since Plutarch's Lives and Laertius' Lives had been published in the fifteenth century (1470/71, 1475)—then "Attic Law" would be an allusion to the legal pronouncements of Solon, or of the Seven Sages in general.

[20] This phrase is written in Greek.

[21] What Luther was thinking of is not clear. In January of 1542 Hans Lufft

nation of Europe, and that there is no doubt that the Turks intend to invade Germany and demand free passage from the Poles. The Poles promise to fight, provided that they will get help from the Germans. But if at this Diet of Speyer, just as at the others, there is quarreling back and forth in a Sophist-like way,[22] then the events will speak [louder], and Germany will be beset by some doom. I sustain myself with this one consolation, that is, I know that God cares for the church.

From Hungary comes the news that the oldest son of the Turkish tyrant has revolted against his father and intends to make war in Syria because, it is said, the father intends to turn over the empire to the youngest son.[23]

---

published a booklet in Wittenberg, entitled: *True News about the Turks* (for bibliographical information, see *WA*, Br 9, 623, n. 12), and it is possible that Luther had this title in mind. The source and circumstances of the following information received from Poland could not be established. This information documents the general feeling of the time. Since the fall of Budapest to the Turks, the possibility of a Turkish invasion of the Empire hung like a dark cloud over the people. In October of 1541 the sovereigns of Brandenburg, Hesse, and Saxony met and discussed defense plans for use if the Turks conquered Bohemia; see Ranke 2^{IV}, 147, n. 1; Lenz, *BPB* 3, 151 ff. On November 16 a diet was summoned to meet in Speyer (see note 22) in order to discuss the defense of the Empire against the Turks. On the other hand, the Sultan had long since returned to Constantinople, and it was not until summer of 1543 that the Turks engaged in another major campaign in Hungary. See Enders, *Briefwechsel* 14, 183, n. 10; *C.R.* 4, 774; Elton p. 524.

22 On November 16, 1541, the diet was summoned to meet on January 14, 1542, in Speyer, but it was not officially opened there until February 9; see Enders, *Briefwechsel* 14, 183, n. 9. Apparently this delay, not unusually long, caused Luther to be pessimistic about this diet. While the diet was indeed filled with the usual bickering among the Estates, and with the signs and effects of the political division of the Empire along religious lines, the diet nevertheless approved a rather substantial army for the purpose of driving the Turks out of Hungary—this to the utter surprise of the Venetian ambassador in the Empire. See Ranke 2^{IV}, 147 ff.

23 The source must have been letters received by the Wittenbergers from Hungarian friends. On February 3 Melanchthon reported the same news to Veit Dietrich (see *LW* 49, 282, n. 13), saying that "our Hungarians" almost swear that the rebellious older son of the Sultan has entered into an alliance with the Persians; *C.R.* 4, 774. Further documentation of this rumor is not available. From reports of an Imperial envoy at the court in Constantinople we know, however, that at least by 1545 the Sultan's oldest son, Mustafa, was strongly opposed by the current favorite of the Sultan, Khurrem, who tried to promote the political careers of her own offspring (Ranke 2^{IV}, 228; Elton, pp. 527 f.). Mustafa tried to gain political and military strength to offset Khurrem's maneuvers. Mustafa's ambitions finally cost him his life: in 1553, with the consent of his father, Sultan Suleiman, he was executed as a traitor; see Elton, p. 528. The news from Hungary, mentioned by Luther, could not be verified in the standard

Eck[24] has published a most rabid treatise about the events at Regensburg; in tearing Bucer apart Eck proves to be more biting than Archilochus, though he also directs his attacks against others.

Yours,

MARTIN LUTHER

296

To Marcus Crodel
[Wittenberg,] August 26, 1542

In 1542 Luther sent his son John to Torgau, where John was to stay with Marcus Crodel, the headmaster of the Torgau Latin school. In the present letter Luther asks Crodel to add John to the class of boys who would be trained in grammar and music, to keep an eye on John's conduct, and to send a progress report on the boy's studies, along with an evaluation of the boy's potential. Luther also sends along Florian von Bora who, Luther says, will need a firm hand; Luther hopes that Crodel might perhaps place him with a citizen in Torgau. Luther points out that he considers education through the example set by classmates better than private tutoring. He assures Crodel that if the arrangement with John works out,

---

secondary literature. Therefore, this news could have been wishful thinking on the part of the Hungarian source, the result of intimate, otherwise unknown information, simply a rumor, or a combination of all these.

[24] John Eck (see *LW* 48, 80, n. 13) and Martin Bucer (see note 16) were among the participants in the Colloquy of Regensburg (April 21–May 31, 1541) in which an attempt was made to find a theological compromise between evangelicals and papists. On this colloquy, see Lau-Bizer, pp. 165 ff.; Kidd, Nos. 136–140; Ranke 3[VI], 133 ff. After Bucer had published his interpretation of the events, Eck put out a rejoinder. See R. Stupperich, *Bibliographia Bucerana,* in *Schriften des Vereins für Reformationsgeschichte* 58, Heft 2, No. 169 (Gütersloh, 1952), 55, No. 69; *Corpus Catholicum: Werke Katholischer Schriftsteller im Zeitalter der Glaubensspaltung,* 16 (1930), cxxx, No. 95. Archilochus (?753–716 B.C.) was an iambic and elegiac poet of Paros who was known for his verbal assaults on Lycambes, whose daughter Archilochus was trying to marry (Horace *Epistolae* i. 19. 23 ff.), and for his supposed authorship of a hymn sung by the victors at Olympia. See *O.C.D.*, p. 82. Citing Cicero *Ad Atticum* ii. 20, 21, Erasmus in his *Adagia* (II: 2, 57; Clericus 2, 467D) defines "Archilochian pronouncements" as pronouncements full of abuse and stench, and refers to Archilochus' attacks on Lycambes.

then his other two sons would also come to Torgau for further schooling. Luther praises Crodel as a teacher, particularly for his diligence and his strictness. In conclusion Luther extends greetings to John Walther, who would be the one to take care of John's musical training, and to Gabriel Zwilling and his family.

Marcus Crodel of Weimar (1487?–1549) was graduated as Bachelor of Arts from Wittenberg University in 1521 and, except for a short period of service in the office of the Electoral chamberlain, taught on the secondary level for the remainder of his life. In 1529 he became a teacher at the Torgau Latin school, and in 1539 head-master (Rector) of that school. He is described as a learned man who even knew some Hebrew, and he is known for a Latin textbook which he published in 1541. Under his guidance the Torgau Latin school developed into one of the leading institutions of Humanism, organized around the liberal arts with emphasis on rhetoric and music. Luther and Melanchthon held Crodel in high regard and presented him with copies of many of their writings. Crodel was several times a guest in Luther's house.

On Marcus Crodel, see Enders, Briefwechsel *14, 323, n. 1; ZKG 52 (1933), 339; WA, Br 10, No. 3783, Introduction; WA 48, 60, 256; on the Latin school in Torgau, see also LJB 15 (1933), 39 ff.*

Text in Latin: WA, Br 10, 134.[1]

To the excellent man, Marcus Crodel, a most faithful
and upright teacher of the young people at Torgau,
my most beloved friend in the Lord

Grace and peace! As you and I have agreed,[2] my Marcus, I am sending my son John[3] to you so that you may add him to the boys who are to be drilled in grammar and music.[4] Also, keep an eye on

---

[1] The letter is extant in one manuscript copy, and in the common editions of Luther's works.
[2] Nothing could be established about the background of this statement.
[3] On John Luther, see LW 49, 152, n. 7.
[4] Enders, *Briefwechsel* 14, 323, n. 2, suggests that this sentence is to be under-stood to mean that John Luther (who by this time was sixteen years old and had already received a bachelor's degree) was to be a "teaching assistant," help-ing Crodel in drilling the pupils. WA, Br 11, 323, addition to WA Br 10, 134, n. 1, presents material which could strengthen this interpretation. On the other hand, the whole tone of the letter suggests beyond a doubt that John was to

his conduct and correct it, for in the Lord I have great confidence in you. I shall liberally pay for your expenses, and you will please inform me how much he has progressed in [a certain] time, and how much one might expect of him.[5] I have added the boy Florian,[6] especially since I see that these boys need the example set by a crowd of many boys; this seems to me to accomplish more than individual, private education. But be very strict with this one, and if you can place him with a citizen,[7] do it; otherwise send him back. May God prosper what has been begun.

If I see success with this son, then soon, if I live, you will also have my other two sons.[8] For I think that after you there will be no teachers as diligent as you, especially in grammar and in strictness so far as conduct is concerned. Therefore "make use of the moment, for time races with a swift foot,"[9] and diligent teachers disappear even faster. Thereafter the boys will return here for higher studies for which they will then be better equipped.[10]

Farewell in the Lord, and tell John Walther[11] that I pray for his well-being, and that I commend my son to him for learning music. For I, of course, produce theologians, but I also would like

---

receive further training (as Clemen suggests in *WA*, Br 10, 134, n. 1) away from home, though the possibility of a work-study arrangement also exists. See also note 7. Obviously Luther felt that John's schooling was insufficient, notwithstanding the fact that John had already received a bachelor's degree.

[5] Literally: "and how far one is to proceed with him."

[6] Florian von Bora was a son of an otherwise unknown brother of Catherine Luther; see also *WA*, Br 8, 215, n. 3. This brother died in 1542, and the Luthers took care of the boy who apparently was difficult to handle. After Luther's death Catherine continued to look after the boy; his studies apparently did not progress as expected so that Catherine felt compelled to turn to her brother John for help. On Florian von Bora see de Wette, *Dr. Martin Luthers Briefe* 6, ed. J. K. Seidemann (Berlin, 1856), 647 ff.

[7] This could mean that Crodel was to find lodging for Florian, or was to find for Florian some kind of work in return for room and board. If one adopts the latter possibility then it would seem that Luther hoped that Florian, and perhaps also John, would do some work while studying at the Torgau Latin school. Enders' suggestion, mentioned in note 4, would then be more probable.

[8] I.e., Martin (born on November 7, 1531) and Paul (see Letter No. 254).

[9] Ovid *De arte amandi* iii. 65.

[10] Literally: "will more successfully [or: blessedly] return here for higher studies."

[11] John Walther (1496–1570) was the well-known *Kantor* of Torgau who cooperated with Luther on many musical projects (e.g., *German Mass*), in addition to making significant contributions to the evangelical hymnal. On John Walther, see E. Blom (ed.), *Grove's Dictionary of Music and Musicians*, 9 (5th ed.; New York, 1955), 155 f.; F. Blume (ed.), *Die Musik in Geschichte und Gegenwart*, 14 (Kassel, 1968), 192 ff.

to produce grammarians and musicians.[12] Again farewell, and also greet Gabriel and his family.[13] Farewell for the third time and for eternity!

August 26, 1542   Yours,

                                                         MARTIN LUTHER

297

To Marcus Crodel
[Wittenberg,] August 28, 1542

Luther asks Crodel to punish Florian von Bora for having stolen a knife.

On Marcus Crodel, see p. 231.

Text in German: WA, Br 10, 136–137.[1]

To the excellent man, Marcus Crodel, a devout and
faithful teacher of the young people at Torgau,
my dearest friend in the Lord[2]

Grace and peace! Dear Marcus! I shall be the first to file a complaint against that scoundrel Florian[3] whom I have sent to you along with John.[4] I ask you to have a severe thrashing[5] administered to him daily, on three consecutive days, without any pity as a welcome present.[6] He thinks he has escaped the whip, but the whip shall be his reception committee.[7]

---

[12] I.e., by sending "my own boys" to Torgau for training in grammar and music.
[13] On Gabriel Zwilling, who was superintendent in Torgau, see *LW* 48, 39, n. 3.
[1] The letter is extant in one manuscript copy, and in the common editions of Luther's works.
[2] The address is written in Latin.
[3] Florian von Bora.
[4] See letter No. 296.
[5] Literally: "a good fat shilling." Throughout the letter Luther uses this technical term for a thrashing; see *WA*, Br 10, 137, n. 4.
[6] The text reads *bene veneris;* according to *WA*, Br 10, 137, n. 2, this was the technical term sometimes used for the thrashing given to a prisoner upon his arrival at jail for the purpose of subduing him from the very beginning.
[7] Literally: "He thinks he has run away from the whip but it is to await him."

He should receive the first thrashing because on the way [to Torgau] he brazenly took away the knife or dagger[8] from my [son] Paul;[9] the second, because he lied and said that I presented the knife to him[10] (because of the lie this thrashing should draw blood); the third, because without my knowledge and consent he has thus taken away and stolen the knife from me.[11] This thrashing should be the best one. Or send the scoundrel back here. John should take the knife and look after it. If that rascal were still here I would teach him [what it means] to lie and steal. He did not do it previously.

With this I commend you to God. Amen.

August 28, 1542   MARTIN LUTHER

298

To Marcus Crodel
[Wittenberg,] September 6,[1] 1542.

In September of 1542 Luther's daughter Magdalen became so seriously ill that she was expected to die.[2] Lenchen, as she was called (the second of Luther's living children), was especially close to her older brother John and desired to see him. Consequently Luther dispatched a carriage to Torgau (where John was studying with

---

[8] All texts have an ellipsis for "dagger." In the extant manuscript copy the ellipsis was filled in afterwards, using different ink. The word added was obviously unknown to the writer and consequently garbled; see Enders, *Briefwechsel*, 14, 326, n. b. According to WA, Br 13, 309, addition to WA, Br 10, 137, line 8, the word that was used is to be translated as "long knife."

[9] I.e., Paul Luther who had accompanied his brother John and Florian for some distance on the way to Torgau, and then upon his return apparently reported the incident to his father.

[10] And on that pretense Florian simply took the knife from the nine year old Paul Luther.

[11] "From me," i.e., from "my" son Paul to whom "I" had given the knife.

[1] See note 5.

[2] See LW 49, 218. On the basis of the available material the nature of the illness could not be established. On Magdalen's illness and death (she died in her father's arms), and on the effects these events had on Luther, see pp. 238, 246, n. 18; see further E. Kroker, *Katharina von Bora* (Zwickau, 1925), pp. 144 ff.; WA, TR 5, Nos. 5490–5502; LW 54, 428 ff.; LCC 18, 50 f.

Marcus Crodel)[3] *in order to bring John home to the bedside of his ailing sister. In the following letter Luther informs Marcus Crodel of Magdalen's illness and asks that John be sent home at once. Crodel is to make some pretense for the trip but is not to tell John the real reason for the sudden trip to Wittenberg. John will return to Torgau soon, says Luther, either when Magdalen has recuperated, or fallen asleep in the Lord.*

On Marcus Crodel, see p. 231.

Text in Latin: WA, Br 10, 147.[4]

Grace and peace!

My Marcus Crodel! I ask you to be quiet to my son about what I am writing to you: my daughter Magdalen is ill and almost in her last hour; in a short while she might depart to the true Father in heaven, unless God has decreed otherwise. She herself longs so much to see her brother that I feel compelled to send a carriage [for him]. They loved each other so much; perhaps his arrival could bring her some relief. I am doing what I can so that later the knowledge of having left something undone does not torture me. Therefore without giving John any reason, order him to fly back in this carriage; he will return soon, when Magdalen either has fallen asleep in the Lord, or has recuperated. Farewell in the Lord! Tell John that something is the matter which is to be entrusted to him in secret. Otherwise everything is fine.

September 6, 1542[5]   Yours,

                                        MARTIN LUTHER

---

[3] See letter No. 296.

[4] The letter is extant in a manuscript copy, and in the common editions of Luther's works. Even though the address is missing in all witnesses, the content of the letter makes clear to whom Luther was writing.

[5] According to the official death announcement (WA, Br 12, No. 4291), Magdalen died on September 20. Luther says above that his daughter is almost in her last hour. Since there was no prior mention of Magdalen's illness in September, and since Luther and others made a quick trip to Dessau on September 8 (see Buchwald, LK p. 145), it has been suggested that the traditional date for this letter, September 6, has to be considered a mistake by the copyist, and that the actual date of the letter is September 16. On the other hand, according to all available evidence, esp. the death announcement, it is certain that Magdalen's illness stretched over a longer period of time, so that Luther's statement above and the trip to Dessau would not necessarily demand a change of date.

299

To Justus Jonas
[Wittenberg,] September 23, 1542

In the first portion of this letter Luther comments on the negotia-
tions between the Elector of Saxony and the Archbishop of Mainz
concerning the possible sale of the lordship connected with the
castle at Halle. The Archbishop, Luther points out, will never spend
the money to acquire this lordship, and he most certainly will not
do so under the condition that the gospel must continue to be
preached in Halle. The Archbishop sees in the negotiations, says
Luther, only an opportunity to make the Elector look ridiculous and
a chance to have his fun worrying the people in Halle that this
lordship might be sold. Then Luther informs Jonas about a serious
talk he has had with Jonas' oldest son, whom he strictly admonished
to show obedience to and appreciation of his father, and whom he
urged to be grateful to God for having a father who could guide
him during the years of growing up. In the last paragraph Luther
talks about the death of his daughter Magdalen. He knows that he
and his wife should be grateful for the blessed departure of their
daughter. Yet his love for her and the memory of this child make it
difficult for him to be grateful just now; therefore Luther asks Jonas
to give thanks to God in his stead for Magdalen's blessed end.
On Justus Jonas, see LW 48, 275, n. 3.
Text in Latin: WA, Br 10, 149–150.[1]

To the illustrious man, Mr. Justus Jonas, Doctor
of Theology, the provost at Wittenberg,[2] Christ's
ambassador[3] in Halle/Saxony,[4] my elder[5] in the Lord

Grace and peace in the Lord! I still think, my Jonas, that it will

---

[1] The letter is extant as autograph, which is deposited in the Wolfenbüttel Library.
[2] See p. 226, n. 2.
[3] See p. 226.
[4] See p. 225.
[5] Or: "superior."

never happen that the Satan at Mainz[6] will buy[7] the lordship co·· - nected with the castle at Halle, especially not for such a high price and on the condition that he is to let the gospel have its free course. All that that cursed son of perdition[8] does or says is a lie and hypocrisy. You will remember that I used to say that not even the sun has seen anything more sly than this[9] fellow.[10] He only wants to make a laughing stock of our Sovereign,[11] as he does of all people. Therefore I think that you people at Halle have been disturbed for no reason, or terrified by a tempest in a teapot.[12] This, of course, has been most welcome to that monster who, as the most demonic devil, lives precisely for such a thing, that is, to see the tragedy of wretched people, or, in case the woe is not real, to rejoice that nevertheless they are terrified by an imagined calamity.

As[13] you had requested, I admonished your son in a strict and

---

[6] I.e., Cardinal Albrecht, archbishop of Mainz; see *LW*, 48, 44 f. The elector of Saxony held the title of *Burggraf* (count of the castle) of Magdeburg. This title gave him certain rights in the city of Halle which, from a territorial point of view, belonged to Albrecht, the archbishop of Mainz, who was also bishop of Magdeburg. When the church of the Reformation was organized in Halle, Elector John Frederick intended to send troops into Halle in order to prevent the Archbishop from interfering with this development, but abandoned this plan upon Luther's advice on August 21, 1542 (*WA*, Br 10, No. 3780). In order to eliminate the legal basis for any possible action on the Elector's part, the Archbishop tried to buy the title of *Burggraf* from the Elector, and the Elector was willing to sell for a substantial sum and on the condition that the evangelicals would not be harassed. This in turn badly upset the people of Halle, who through Jonas and Luther approached the Elector with the offer to pay the Elector a yearly sum provided he would retain the title and exercise the protectorate over the city. See *WA*, Br 10, 140, and Nos. 3788–3790. Upon Luther's urging (*WA*, Br 10, No. 3796), the Elector finally accepted this proposal. For details, see W. Delius, *Die Reformationsgeschichte der Stadt Halle a. S.* (Berlin, 1953), pp. 92 f. Luther's opinion ("I still think") mentioned above refers either to Luther's letter to Jonas of May 22, 1541 (*WA*, Br 9, No. 3621), or to any of the letters exchanged between Luther and the Elector and his officials (see the previous *WA*, Br references), of which Jonas could have known.
[7] By mistake Luther used the equivalent of "sell."
[8] Literally: "that son of malediction and perdition." See John 17:12; II Thess. 2:3.
[9] The translation is based on the correction of the text made by Clemen in *WA*, Br 10, 150, n. 3.
[10] Literally: "genius [or: brain; or: head]."
[11] I.e., Elector John Frederick; see *LW* 48, 181 f.
[12] Literally: "or terrified by a [bolt of] lightning [coming] out of a basin." Erasmus records this saying in his *Adagia* (II: 7, 90; Clericus 2, 634F).
[13] The following paragraph has been freely translated. Luther is referring here to a no-longer extant letter of Jonas which had been delivered to him by Justus Jonas Jr. on (or shortly after) September 3 and to which he had replied on

serious talk. I exhorted him to be appreciatively obedient to his father—on top of it, such a father—and to remember that God has blessed him so abundantly that this father is still alive and around him in the years of his puberty.[14] [I further pointed out] what help this father's advice and aid can be in guiding such an impressionable age and controlling [the effects of] original sin in a world which is so full of evil and the fury of the devil. He has promised to be obedient and to heed your advice and that of his teachers.

I[15] believe the report has reached you that my dearest daughter Magdalen has been reborn in Christ's eternal kingdom. I and my wife should only joyfully give thanks for such a felicitous departure and blessed end by which Magdalen has escaped the power of the flesh, the world, the Turk, and the devil; yet the force of [our] natural love[16] is so great that we are unable to do this without crying and grieving in [our] hearts, or even without experiencing death ourselves. For the features, the words, and the movement of the living and dying daughter who was so very obedient and respectful remain engraved deep in the heart; even the death of Christ (and what is the dying of all people in comparison with Christ's death?) is unable totally to take all this away as it should. You, therefore, please give thanks to God in our stead! For indeed God did a great work of grace to us when he glorified our flesh in this way. Magdalen had (as you know) a mild and lovely disposition and was loved by all. Praised be the Lord Jesus Christ who has called, elected, and made her glorious. God grant me, and all my [loved] ones, and all our friends such a death—or rather, such a life. This alone I ask of God, the Father of all comfort and mercies.[17] In him, farewell to you and your whole family. Amen.

September 23, 1542   Yours,

MARTIN LUTHER

September 5; *WA*, Br 10, No. 3791. This son of Jonas (see *LW* 49, 175, n. 27), who later caused much grief to his father, was traveling back and forth between Halle and Wittenberg at this time; see *WA*, Br 9, 508, n. 8. He must have been quite arrogant at that time already, for he supposedly said at one time that he ought to be the son of a great king rather than of a theologian; see Enders, *Briefwechsel* 14, 339, n. 3.

[14] Justus Jonas Jr. was born on December 3, 1525.
[15] For the following, see p. 234, n. 2.
[16] Luther used the Greek word *storgē*.
[17] See II Cor. 1:3.

300

To Marcus Crodel
[Wittenberg,] December 26, 1542

After John Luther had returned to Torgau from Wittenberg, where he had been on the occasion of his sister Magdalen's illness and death,[1] he became homesick and, misunderstanding a statement made by his mother at his departure from Wittenberg (see letter No. 301), wanted to come home. In this situation Luther approaches John's teacher in Torgau, Marcus Crodel, and, mentioning the good rapport that (according to John) exists between John and the Crodels, asks Crodel to help John overcome "that childlike weakness." Under the present circumstances Luther does not want his boy to return home, but Luther does ask Crodel to inform him should John get sick.

On Marcus Crodel, see p. 231.

Text in Latin: WA, Br 10, 228–229.[2]

Grace and peace!

I readily believe, my Marcus, that my son turned soft through the words of his mother, in addition to mourning over his sister's death. Talk seriously with him.[3] For when he was here he certainly praised you and your wife, saying how well he is treated by you there, even better than by us here. Order him, therefore, to curb that womanish feeling, to get accustomed to enduring evil, and not to indulge in that childlike weakness. For this is the reason that he has been sent away, namely, that he learn something and become hardened. I do not wish him to return if there is no other reason. Should another illness come to him, however, please inform me. In the meantime he should be diligent in fulfilling that for which he has been sent away, and [thus] obey his parents.

---

1 See letter No. 298. When John returned to Torgau could not be established.
2 The letter is extant in one manuscript copy, and in the common editions of Luther's works.
3 Literally: "But you are to admonish him strongly."

We here are fine and healthy by God's grace. Farewell!
December 26, 1542   Yours,

MARTIN LUTHER

301

To John Luther[1]
[Wittenberg,] December 27, 1542

Luther assures his son John that the family is fine, and then encourages him to master "those tears." He suggests that obedient dedication to his studies will help him forget "that softness." Then Luther clarifies a statement made by his wife: when she had said that John should return home if he feels poorly, she was thinking of an illness. In closing Luther also tells John that his mother wishes him to put aside his mourning over Magdalen's death so that he can study in a peaceful frame of mind.

On John Luther, see LW, 49, 152, n. 7.

Text in Latin: WA, Br 10, 229.[2]

To John Luther, my dearest son, at Torgau

Grace and peace in the Lord! My son John: I and your Mother, along with the whole house, are fine. You see to it that you overcome those tears like a man, so that you do not cause your Mother additional pain and worry, for she worries easily and becomes anxious. Be obedient to God who through us has ordered you to be educated there, and you will [more] easily forget that softness. Mother was unable to write, and also thought it unnecessary. She

---

[1] See also letter No. 300.

[2] The letter is extant in one manuscript copy, and in the common editions of Luther's works. The letter apparently was written as an afterthought—hence it was written on December 27, the day after letter No. 300 was written—and in an attempt to soften the blow when Crodel would tell John that he was to stay in Torgau. One may further suggest that Luther wrote the letter because letter No. 300 had not yet been sent, and that both letters were dispatched by the same messenger on or after December 27.

TO WENCESLAS LINK, JUNE 20, 1543

says all that she said to you (that you should return if by chance you feel poorly) was meant to refer to an illness, so that you would inform us at once if you got sick.[3] In addition she wishes you to put aside this mourning so that you may study in a happy and peaceful frame of mind.

With this farewell in the Lord!

December 27, 1542   Your father,
                                               MARTIN LUTHER

302

To Wenceslas Link
[Wittenberg,] June 20, 1543

Luther announces that a preface he had to write has finally been written and is being sent along with this letter. As reasons for the delay Luther mentions his physical condition and his work load, as well as the fact that he is not the right man for writing prefaces. Then Luther makes certain observations: He is tired and longs for a peaceful departure from this world; his work is done, and "our congregations" are in good shape; the arrogant people of Zürich and Switzerland condemn themselves; he is praying against the Turks, about whom "we" hear monstrous things, but the German sovereigns behave every bit as badly as the Turks; all the godlessness in the world is a sure sign that the world is working its way toward its end. Luther ends the letter with greetings to Link's family and friends in Nürnberg.

On Wenceslas Link, see LW 48, 169 f.

Text in Latin: WA, Br 10, 335.[1]

To the distinguished and excellent man, Mr. Wenceslas Link, a true Doctor of Theology, a most faithful minister of Christ in the church[2] at Nürnberg, my dearest friend in the Lord

---

[3] I.e., and at such time a decision would be made about John's possible return.
[1] The letter is extant in one manuscript copy, and in the common editions of Luther's works.
[2] See *LW* 49, 61, n. 9.

LETTERS

Grace and peace in the Lord! My preface comes to you rather late,[3] my Wenceslas, and the reason for this is that your thoughts are different from my thoughts.[4] You think that I am healthy and have little to do, and, what is even less the case, that I am the right man to write decent prefaces. I think quite differently: I am more dead than alive,[5] yet I am overwhelmed with writing letters and books; the theological lecture,[6] the stone[7] and much else[8] weigh me down. Consequently I am very seldom free to read or say my prayers, which is enough of a problem for me. But, anyway, here you have the preface, however it turned out. If you do not like it, you can either change it if you wish, or throw it out.

For myself I desire a good hour of passing on to God. I am content, I am tired, and nothing more is in me. Yet see to it that you pray earnestly for me, that the Lord takes my soul in peace. I do not leave our congregations in poor shape;[9] they flourish in pure and sound teaching, and they grow day by day through [the ministry of] many excellent and most sincere pastors.

The people of Switzerland and Zürich are bent on condemning themselves, as Paul says,[10] through their haughtiness and madness.[11] May the Lord enlighten and convert their hearts. Amen.

---

[3] Link had written a commentary on the Pentateuch and he asked Luther for a preface. On July 25, 1542, Luther promised to write this preface "promptly"; WA, Br 10, 111. Yet time passed and Luther did not send the preface. Consequently in a no-longer extant letter Link must have put pressure on Luther, who finally sent the preface almost a year later; WA. 54, 1 ff. Link's commentary was published with Luther's preface in Strassburg in 1543.
[4] See Isa. 55:8.
[5] Literally: "I am a cadaver."
[6] From June 3, 1535, to November 17, 1545, Luther lectured, with interruptions, on Genesis. See WA 42–44, 48, 358–364; LW 1–8.
[7] On August 20, 1543, Melanchthon mentioned that Luther had had an attack of the (kidney?) stone "last night"; C.R. 5, 165.
[8] From 1536 to 1546 Luther was dean of the Theological Faculty.
[9] Literally: "I do not leave behind a sad face of our congregations, but one which flourishes."
[10] See Titus 3:11.
[11] This statement could simply be a general reference to the way in which the Swiss continued to maintain Zwingli's interpretation of the Lord's Supper. The statement could also be the result of a November 26, 1542, letter written to Luther by the evangelicals of Venice (WA, Br 10, No. 3817), as Enders, Briefwechsel 15, 173, n. 3, suggests. The Venetian evangelicals complained about the lack of unity among the Protestants because of the controversy on the Lord's Supper, which was now also disturbing the evangelicals of northern Italy. On June 13, 1543, Luther finally found a trustworthy messenger for a

242

About the Turk we hear monstrous things.[12] I am praying against him, but I am uncertain against which Turks [God] will hurl my prayer. For if our Rephaim, Nephilim, Zamzumim, Emim, and Anakim continue to act as they do, then we will be ruled by them no less tyrannically than by the Turk.[13] They rage furiously, according to their lusts. Now is the time which was predicted to come after the fall of Antichrist,[14] when people will be Epicureans[15] and atheists,[16] so that the word of Christ might be fulfilled:

---

reply (WA, Br 10, No. 3885) in which he was highly critical of the people of Zürich, who had rejected the Wittenberg Concord. The statement above could very well reflect the contents of this letter to Italy.

12 Literally: "grandiose things." Luther apparently had heard of the pompous departure of Sultan Suleiman from Adrianople in April of 1543, and of the powerful army which had accompanied the Sultan. The Sultan's goal was to secure his hold on Hungary by pushing beyond Budapest and conquering Esztergom (Gran). As always, the rumor that the Turks would attack Vienna began to circulate. The Turks were allies of Francis I of France, who had been engaged in his fourth war (1542–1544) against Emperor Charles V. In addition to their activities in Hungary, the Turks harassed the Emperor in the Mediterranean Sea. Shortly after Luther made the statement above, Esztergom fell to the Turks (August 10), and a combined Turkish-French fleet and army conquered Nice (August 20). See Ranke 2^{IV}, 153, 177; Elton, p. 524.

13 This list of names from the Old Testament has to be reduced to "Rephaim" and "Nephilim," for "Emim," "Anakim," and "Zamzumim" were only different names for the Rephaim; whether the Rephaim and the Nephilim were identical has to remain open. The Rephaim and the tribes called by the synonyms for Rephaim were "a people great and many," and of great height; see Deut. 2:10 f., 20 f. In Isa. 14:9, "Rephaim" is translated in the RSV as "leaders of the earth." According to Die Religion in Geschichte und Gegenwart, K. Galling et al., (eds.), 6 (3rd ed. Tübingen, 1962), 912, the Rephaim were a mythological tribe of giants living in Canaan. Some of the tribes inhabiting Palestine descended from these Rephaim, but in Abraham's and Moses' times new names had come into usage for these tribes. The Nephilim, "the mighty men of old" (Ezek. 32:27), "the men of renown" (Gen. 6:4), "the men of great stature," "the sons of Anak" (in comparison with whom the spies that Moses sent into Canaan felt like "grasshoppers"; Num. 13:32 f.), have their origin in the sexual relations between "the sons of God" and "the daughters of men," mentioned in Gen. 6:4. The Vulgate translated "Nephilim" and "Rephaim" with the equivalent of "giants" (Gen. 6:4; Deut. 2:11, 20; Isa. 14:9), or of "monsters conceived by giants" (Num. 13:34). Luther, who several times applied the name Nephilim to the German sovereigns (see e.g., WA, Br 9, 521 [September 25, 1541], 548 [November 10, 1541]; WA 51, 623; LW 43, 240; Enders, Briefwechsel 15, 173, nn. 4, 5), intended to say that "our giant monsters" ("big shots") behave in such a way that, if they continue to do so, they will rule just as tyrannically as the Turks do. It has to remain open whether such disenchantment with the ruling class was triggered by specific incidents (as seems to have been the case in the two passages from the letters of the year 1541, cited above), or whether it was simply an expression of pessimism and a general indictment.

14 See I John 2:18 ff.; see also LW 48, 114, n. 16.

15 On Epicurus and his school of thought, see O.C.D., pp. 324 f. Luther con-

"As it was in the days of Noah and Lot, so will it be on the day of the arrival of the Son of man."[17]

Farewell in the Lord to you and your family! I greet your friends reverently.

June 20, 1543
Yours,
MARTIN LUTHER

303

To James Propst
[Wittenberg,] December 5,[1] 1544

Luther is tired and sluggish, and feels like an old useless man for whom nothing remains but to die. He believes his end is near, and perhaps the end of the world as well. So he asks for Propst's prayer that his death may be pleasing to God and salutary for himself. Having made these sober observations, Luther sends thanks from his daughter Margaret to her godfather Propst for a gift he had sent her; Luther adds that she has been seriously ill for the last ten weeks. Continuing in the somber mood of the first part of the letter, Luther says he would not feel angry with God if Margaret were to be taken from this satanic world. In closing Luther extends greetings from his wife and all their friends, and asks for Propst's prayer in their behalf.

On James Propst, see LW 48, 233, n. 34.

Text in Latin: WA, Br 10, 554.[2]

Grace and Peace in the Lord!

I am writing very briefly, my James, so that I do not avoid writing

---

sidered, e.g., Erasmus to be an Epicurean; see WA, TR 1, Nos. 432, 466; *LW* 54, 69, 77 f.

[16] See II Tim. 3:1 ff.

[17] Luke 17:26.

[1] For the address and the date, see note 20.

[2] The letter is extant in one manuscript copy, which originates with John Aurifaber (see WA, Br 14, 160, No. 360), and in the common editions of Luther's works.

altogether and thus give you the impression that I have either forgotten you or that I would neglect you.[3] Yes, I am sluggish, tired, cold—that is, I am an old and useless man.[4] I have finished my race;[5] it remains only that the Lord call me to my fathers,[6] and that my body be handed over to decomposition and the worms. I have lived enough, if one may call it living.[7] Please pray for me that the hour of my passing will be pleasing to God and a blessing for me.

I care nothing for the Emperor[8] and the whole Empire except that I commend them to God in my prayers. It looks to me as if the world, too, has come to the hour of its passing,[9] and has become an old wornout coat (as the Psalm says),[10] which soon has to be changed. Amen.

There is nothing of heroic virtue left in the sovereigns, but only hatred and discord, avarice and selfish lusts which cannot be healed.[11] So the commonweal has no men, and the third chapter of Isaiah[12] runs [toward us] head-on. Nothing good can be expected, therefore, except that the day of glory of the great God of our salvation may be revealed.[13]

---

[3] Luther's last prior extant letter to Propst is dated October 9, 1542; WA, Br 10, No. 3797. See also note 18.
[4] For a similar statement, see p. 242, and WA, Br 10, 548 (March 30, 1544).
[5] II Tim. 4:7.
[6] See I Kings 19:4; II Sam. 7:12.
[7] See Horace Satires i. 1. 117 ff.
[8] Emperor Charles V; see LW 48, 175 f. Apparently Luther was thinking of the military preparations made by the Emperor during the 1544 Diet of Speyer for the purpose of striking a decisive blow against the French with whom he had been engaged in a fourth war since 1542. In September, 1544, this war was ended, however, when a peace document was signed at Crespy. Among other conditions, France agreed to aid the Emperor in a war against the Turks. See Ranke 2[IV], 177, 184 ff., 194 ff. See also WA, Br 10, 553 (April 17, 1544). In this connection a secret agreement between the Emperor and the French King was signed on September 19, according to which France agreed that the assistance to be provided against the Turks might be used against the German Protestants. See Lau-Bizer, pp. 186 f.
[9] For a similar statement, see p. 243, and WA, Br 10, 553 (April 17, 1544).
[10] Ps. 102:26.
[11] See also p. 243.
[12] See Isa. 3:1 ff., a passage in which judgment over Judah and Jerusalem is prophesied. According to Clemen (WA, Br 10, 554, n. 5), Luther's statement that the commonweal has no men corresponds to the statement in Isa. 3:1 ff., that the Lord is taking away from Jerusalem and Judah "stay and staff, . . . the mighty man . . ."
[13] See Eph. 4:30; Luke 21:27 f. For a similar statement, see WA, Br 10, 553 (April 17, 1544).

My daughter Margaret thanks you for your gift.[14] Along with all her brothers[15] she was sick with the measles.[16] Although they have long ago recuperated, she has caught a very high and persistent fever which has lasted now for almost ten weeks; she still hangs between life and death, and the outcome is uncertain.[17] I shall not be angry with the Lord, if he takes her out of this satanic age and world[18] from which I, too, desire quickly to be taken, together with all my loved ones. For I long for that day and for the end of the raging of Satan and his followers.

Farewell in the Lord Jesus Christ! Greetings to your flesh,[19] and also to you, in behalf of my Katie and all our friends. Pray for us!

December 5,[20] *1544*   Yours,

MARTIN LUTHER, DOCTOR

---

[14] See also p. 210, n. 28, and *WA*, Br 10, 24 (March 26, 1542), a letter in which Luther thanked Propst on behalf of his daughter for a gift of money.
[15] I.e., John (who, if he is to be counted among "all" of Margaret's brothers, must have returned from Torgau; see p. 230), Martin, and Paul.
[16] The text reads *morbillos.*
[17] The last portion of this sentence (from "she still hangs") has been quite freely translated. Nothing could be established about this incident, except that on April 17, 1544, Luther informs Jonas that the measles *have* ruled in Wittenberg, that all his children *have* suffered from them, and that Margaret has caught a fever from which she is still suffering; *WA*, Br 10, 553.
[18] On October 9, 1542, Luther wrote to Propst: "My most beloved daughter Magdalen has departed from me and gone to the heavenly Father; she passed away having total faith in Christ. I have overcome the emotional shock typical of a father, but [only] with a certain threatening murmur against death; by means of this disdain I have tamed my tears. I loved her so very much." *WA*, Br 10, 156. From this information about Magdalen's passing and the impact it had on Luther it becomes clear that Luther felt rebellious (see also p. 238). A different outlook on death is set forth above, when Luther informs Propst about the possibility of Margaret's death. If one is willing to grant that when telling Propst of this possibility Luther remembered his 1542 letter, then one could paraphrase the passage above as follows: I shall not be angry with the Lord if he calls Margaret to himself, as I was rebellious about Magdalen's death when I wrote to you in my [last] letter.
[19] See Gen. 2:23.
[20] This is the date given to the letter in the Aurifaber manuscript copy (see note 2). This date has been questioned by Enders (*Briefwechsel* 16, 121, n. 1) and Clemen (*WA*, Br 10, No. 3983, Introduction). Aurifaber's source is unknown to us. It is possible the letter was undated in this source, and Aurifaber gave it a date on the basis of reasons which can no longer be established; or the letter could have been dated, and Aurifaber changed it for unknown reasons; or Aurifaber misread the date. In any case, on the basis of the similar statements (see notes 4, 8, 9, 13, 17)—in some cases the statements are almost identically phrased—which Luther made in his April 17, 1544, letter to Jonas (*WA*, Br

246

304

To Justus Jonas
[Wittenberg,] January 26, 1545

Urged by Jonas' son, Luther writes this letter though he feels that he has nothing to say. Luther mentions two items, however, which he thinks might be news for Jonas, and briefly comments on them: The Pope has issued a brief in which he chastises Emperor Charles for engaging in religious colloquies with the evangelicals; at the pending diet the Emperor intends to propose a reform of the church. Luther concludes his letter by asking for Jonas' prayers in his behalf.

On Justus Jonas, see LW 48, 275, n. 3.

Text in Latin: WA, Br 11, 29–30.[1]

To the most illustrious man, Mr. Justus Jonas (the Elder),
Doctor of Theology,
the true and faithful bishop of the church at Halle,[2]
my elder[3] in the Lord

Grace and peace in the Lord, and a most happy [new] year. Amen. Your son, Justus Jonas,[4] who, of course, is not [yet] a *magister noster*, but rather one of our Masters [of Arts],[5] has

---

10, No. 3982) and his March 30, 1544, letter to Sybille, wife of Elector John Frederick (*ibid.*, No. 3978), it is clear that this present letter has to be placed in proximity to these two letters, i.e., into March or April of 1544. Clemen dates the letter "about April 17, 1544." This date is too specific, however, since the letter could very well have been written prior to the letter of April 17 to Jonas, or even shortly prior to the letter written to the wife of the Elector on March 30. Except for the facts that James Propst is the addressee established for this letter in the tradition, that Luther speaks to a James in the letter, and that Luther's daughter Margaret, mentioned in the letter, was Propst's godchild, there is no material available to establish the addressee.

[1] The letter is extant in manuscript copies, and in the common editions of Luther's works. According to a notation on one of the manuscript copies, Jonas received the letter on February 21; see Enders, *Briefwechsel* 16, 181.

[2] For "bishop" and "church," see LW 49, 61, n. 9, 87, n. 5; for "Halle," see p. 225.

[3] Or: "superior."

[4] See p. 237.

[5] Literally: "*magister noster*, but rather our *magister*." While the title *magister noster* designated the highest academic degree in the Arts Faculty (i.e., the

[nevertheless] admonished me to write to you, my Jonas; indeed, he said that you desire a letter, and that you would welcome one. Therefore I am writing now, though I have nothing important to write about, since you are always faster in writing about news [than I am]. Yet perhaps you do not know the following: A letter[6] of the Pope is circulating which the brethren have sent to Veit Dietrich from Venice; it is written in an absolutely arrogant and violent tone, and is addressed to Emperor Charles V. In this letter the Pope, with great and typically Italian arrogance,[7] demands to know from the Emperor why the Emperor dares to permit and promise colloquies about religion since it is not the Emperor's place to teach but rather to listen to and learn from Mother Church and the teacher of faith. (These are words well known to you as an apostate jurist.)[8] Many question whether this is a serious affair or the joke of a libeler; yet it certainly appears to me to be something.

In addition there is much ado about the fact that at the pending diet[9] Charles intends to propose a reform in accordance with the

---

Master of Arts), it was also sometimes used as a synonym for the title of doctor, esp. the title of Doctor of Theology. Luther sometimes called his Scholastic opponents at Cologne, Louvain, and Paris *magister noster*. Justus Jonas, Jr. was graduated as Master of Arts on September 4, 1544, and became a member of the Arts Faculty sometime prior to April 7, 1545. For documentation, see WA, Br 11, 30, n. 2.

[6] The following is a reference to a papal brief which had been issued on August 24, 1544. The evangelicals in Venice sent a copy of this brief to Veit Dietrich in Nürnberg (see LW 49, 282, n. 13), who forwarded it to Wittenberg. The Venetian copy was also mentioned by Melanchthon on December 13, 1544 (C.R. 5, 547). For this brief, see NB. 1. Abt. 7, 579 ff.; ZKG 44 (1925), 399 ff.; Jedin, pp. 497 ff. The brief was the result of the peace policy pursued by Emperor Charles V (see p. 219, n. 17) toward the Protestants in an attempt to gain their help against France and the Turks, and in an attempt to make them feel safe while he himself was preparing for a military solution to the whole Reformation issue in the Empire. See also p. 245, n. 8. On June 10, 1544, the Diet of Speyer had passed a resolution which prompted Pope Paul's brief. In this resolution the Emperor "held out the prospect of another Diet in the autumn or winter at which the religious question would be discussed anew. At that Diet 'devout, learned and peace-loving men' would submit a plan for a 'Christian reformation.'" So Jedin, p. 496. See also Ranke 2^{IV}, 184 ff. It is academic to ask whether in the following statements about the pope Luther was always thinking of the incumbent pope, Paul III, or was speaking in general terms.

[7] Literally: "with much and great and openly Italian arrogance."

[8] Jonas was called to Wittenberg as professor of Canon Law, i.e., as a "jurist," but refused to teach the (ungodly) Canon Law, and instead taught theology; see also LW 48, 275.

[9] For "pending diet," see p. 250, n. 8.

example set by the church at the time of the Council of Nicaea. What a lively reformation that will be! If this is true, then the pope's goose is really cooked.[10] If it is a trap set up in order to coax us to an agreement (as I rather assume), then the pope, the one who [only] makes promises,[11] really will ridicule us who fell into the trap. For to believe the promises of the pope is the same as to believe the father of lies[12] (whose real son the pope is). Yet I do wish that the pope would be forced to abide by the ways of the church at the time of the Council of Nicaea. Good God, where would this leave your Coadjutor—your torturer—your[13] Cardinal?[14] Let us pray earnestly while they play and make a mockery of God and all his creation. For it will be that they cease to play; then they will really weep in hell.[15]

Now you have what I was able to write, for I wanted to write something.

Farewell, and pray for me!

January 26, 1545   Yours,

                                      MARTIN LUTHER, DOCTOR

---

[10] The text reads: *res Papae ad restim redierit*. The phrase, *ad restim res redit*, was used by the Roman playwright Terence in his *Phormio* (iv. 4. 5), was recorded by Erasmus in his *Adagia* (I: 4, 21; Clericus 2, 1898B), and was interpreted to designate the highest despair concerning a matter. Luther meant to say that if a diet (see *LW* 48, 70, n. 1) indeed engaged in the task of reforming the church, such a diet would be dealing with purely ecclesiastical matters—a fact totally contrary to Canon Law—and would function in place of a church council. Luther anticipated that a "national council" of this sort would enact such far-reaching reforms that it would bring about the end of papal authority in Germany.

[11] I.e., while the Emperor acts. This is obviously an allusion to the past papal maneuvers about the council. On November 19, 1544, the Pope had again issued a bull in which a council was summoned for March 15, 1545; see Jedin, pp. 504 f.

[12] John 8:44.

[13] The tradition presents an unclear text at this point, and the translation is based on a conjecture suggested in *St. L.* 21b, 3068, n. 2.

[14] This is a reference to Cardinal Albrecht, the archbishop of Mainz, and his efforts to stop the spread of the Reformation in Halle. "Coadjutor" is a reference to an official of the Cardinal who, residing in Magdeburg and holding ecclesiastical responsibility for Halle, played a major role in the Cardinal's efforts.

[15] See Matt. 8:12.

305

To King Christian of Denmark
[Wittenberg,] April 14, 1545

On a date unknown to us King Christian III of Denmark pledged to send annually a certain amount of butter and herring to Luther, Melanchthon, and Bugenhagen.[1] *Since it proved difficult to keep this promise,*[2] *on January 6, 1545,*[3] *the King changed this pledge into an annual stipend of fifty Taler*[4] *for each of the three Wittenberg theologians.*[5] *In letter No. 305 Luther first of all thanks the King for this stipend. Then he briefly mentions that the Diet of Worms is getting off to a slow start, that the council "behaves like a crab," that Emperor Charles suffers from arthritis, and that he himself has no news about the Turks. In closing Luther recommends Tobern Anden, who has been one of his boarders.*

On Christian III, see p. 147, n. 18.

Text in German: WA, Br 11, 70.[6]

Grace and peace in the Lord, and my humble *Pater noster!*[7]

Mighty, Most Illustrious, Noble, Most Gracious Sir [and] King! I most humbly thank Your Royal Majesty for such a gracious pledge which I do not deserve. May our dear Lord God abundantly grant his Holy Spirit to Your Royal Majesty to govern blessedly, and to fulfill his divine, good will. Amen.

The diet is getting under way slowly,[8] the council behaves like

---

[1] See J. Luther, *Martin Luthers Auslegung des 90. Psalms* (Berlin, 1920), p. 40, n. 38.

[2] See Christian's letter to Luther, dated January 29, 1544 (*WA*, Br 10, No. 3964), and the material presented in *WA*, Br 11, No. 4064, Introduction.

[3] See *WA*, Br 11, No. 4064.

[4] See the postscript to Luther's November 26, 1545, letter to the King; *WA*, Br 12, No. 4297. On the *Taler*, see p. 94, n. 8.

[5] See the material presented in *WA*, Br 11, No. 4090, Introduction. Luther's widow continued to receive this pension; see WA, Br 11, No. 4064, Introduction. For the whole matter, see also *WA*, Br 12, 423 f.

[6] The letter is extant as autograph. The background of the letter and the additional letters by Bugenhagen, cited in *WA*, Br 11, No. 4090, establish the addressee.

[7] See p. 69, n. 4.

[8] The sources of this and the following news could not be established. Emperor Charles (see *LW* 48, 175 f.) had summoned the diet to Worms for March,

a crab,[9] His Imperial Majesty is in the Netherlands and is supposedly suffering severely from arthritis, and the sophists[10] boldly rage against God. We do not know what the Turk is doing.[11] May God the Almighty help [us] so that all turns out well—which certainly will not happen unless the Last Day comes soon. Amen.[12]

1545, in an attempt to pursue the policy which he had initiated in Speyer in 1544 (see p. 248, n. 6). The situation, however, had changed radically. While the Emperor and his brother Ferdinand were trying to discuss the reform of the church, Pope Paul III, in an attempt to block any further meddling in ecclesiastical affairs on the Emperor's part, had summoned a council to Trent, and this time neither Pope nor Emperor attempted to seek the consent of the evangelicals for the council, or to invite the evangelicals to the council. This was a clear signal to the evangelicals that they were to be excluded from the council and thus to be treated as already condemned people. Therefore in the opening days of the Diet of Worms there was a bitter tug-of-war between the evangelicals and Ferdinand, who acted for his still absent brother; this was apparently the point of reference for Luther's statement. Before the evangelicals would agree to participate in any further diet discussions they demanded an unconditional guarantee for peace, regardless of any council decisions. No agreement could be worked out on this issue, however, because Ferdinand felt that the Emperor himself should participate in these negotiations. After the Emperor had arrived in Worms on May 16, the negotiations were begun again. The Emperor was determined to have the evangelicals accept the council and its decisions unconditionally; if necessary he was ready to use military force (and he prepared to do so; see pp. 245, n. 8, 265, n. 4; Jedin 1, 521). Yet he also continued to promote the idea of a religious colloquy between evangelicals and papists, and of ecclesiastical reforms (or of a "free council") in order to lull the evangelicals into security. (See Luther's statement about the "trap" on p. 249.) Since the evangelicals continued to hold fast to their position, however, a crisis rapidly developed; it was avoided only because of the delaying tactics on the part of the Emperor and the political blindness on the part of Elector John Frederick. See Ranke 2[IV], 215 ff.; Brandi 1, 425 ff.; Jedin, pp. 506 ff.; 515 f., 527 f.

[9] Literally: "the council behaves as if it intends to walk the walk of a crab." I.e., just as a crab walks backwards, or makes a sidestep, esp. when confronted with danger, so the council makes no headway. Luther used this phrase several times; see WA 51, 653, No. 226, 696, No. 226. The council was supposed to be convened on March 15, 1545, yet all through the first months of 1545 the Curia did little to prepare for it. On March 13 the official representatives of Pope Paul III arrived in Trent where, except for one bishop, "there was as yet not a single prelate from any other place" (Jedin, pp. 510 f.). Finally at the end of the month a number of prelates and envoys of secular powers arrived in Trent. All through spring and summer the alliance negotiations between Pope and Emperor and the secret preparations for war against the German Protestants delayed the opening of the council, so that by September 12 the council was in danger of fading away. Finally on December 13, 1545, the council was officially opened. See Jedin, pp. 508 ff.

[10] I.e., the papists; this could very well be an allusion to the theologians of Louvian (see p. 255), as Clemen suggests in WA, Br 11, 71 n. 5.

[11] See pp. 243, n. 12, 245, n. 8, 253, n. 3.

[12] The following paragraph has been rather freely translated.

Master Tomvernus,[13] who for some time has been my companion at my table and my boarder, is now returning home to Your Royal Majesty. I humbly recommend him to Your Royal Majesty. He is a godly and learned man, and I am confident that God intends to accomplish much good through him; for this I pray with all my heart.

With this I commend Your Royal Majesty to the dear God. Amen.

April 14, 1545   Your Royal Majesty's dedicated
                                    MARTIN LUTHER, DOCTOR

306

To Duke Albrecht of Prussia
[Wittenberg,] May 2, 1545

Luther gives as reasons for writing this letter the request for a recommendation made by Christopher Albert von Kunheim, and his own knowledge that Duke Albrecht would patiently accept his letter. Luther disposes of the request in one short sentence at the end of the letter. In the remaining portions of the letter Luther communicates news: Nothing certain is known about the movement of the Turks; no one in the Empire is prepared for the possibility of a Turkish attack; the Emperor persecutes the gospel in the Netherlands; the Archbishop of Cologne remains steadfast in his support of the cause of the gospel, and "this Easter" the Elector of the Palatinate has publicly affirmed the gospel; the Pope continues to play games with the council, of which the opening date has been postponed.

On Duke Albrecht of Prussia, see LW 49, 60.

Text in German: WA, Br 11, 83–84.[1]

---

[13] I.e., Tobern Anden, who had studied in Wittenberg since 1542 in order to prepare himself for the position of superintendent of Trondheim in Norway; in 1546 he was installed there as the first evangelical bishop. See Enders, *Briefwechsel* 16, 205, n. 1; WA, Br 11, No. 4090, Introduction.
[1] The letter is extant as autograph which at one time was deposited in Königsberg and is now deposited in Göttingen; see WA, Br 13, 341, addition to WA, Br 11, 84.

TO DUKE ALBRECHT OF PRUSSIA, MAY 2, 1545

Grace and peace in the Lord!

Illustrious, Noble, Gracious Sir! The bearer of this letter, Christopher Albert von Kunheim,[2] has asked me for it and urged me [to write it], though I have no special reason for writing. Yet his desire to be recommended to Your Sovereign Grace by me and to bring my [letter of] testimony [to Your Sovereign Grace], and in addition my knowledge that Your Sovereign Grace would endure my writing with gracious patience—these were sufficient reasons for me [to write this letter].

We have no news. One says the Turk is coming, the other says he is staying away.[3] It is certain, however, that neither Emperor,[4] nor King,[5] nor sovereigns are preparing for war.[6] The Emperor is beginning to persecute the gospel severely in the Netherlands.[7] May God prevent it. Amen.

By God's grace, the [Arch]bishop of Cologne still stands

---

[2] Literally: "This present, Christopher von Kunheim, has asked me for this letter and admonished me." Christopher was the oldest son of George von Kunheim, one of the officials of Duke Albrecht. Since George von Kunheim was dead by this time, and since Christopher was a godchild of Duke Albrecht (see WA, Br 11, 107), the Duke felt responsible for Christopher. Christopher was a brother of George von Kunheim who in 1555 married Luther's daughter Margaret. Christopher had matriculated at Wittenberg University in 1536, and at Tübingen University in 1540; WA, Br 10, 73, n. 1. Apparently he returned home and then went once more to Wittenberg, for on June 13, 1542, a son of George von Kunheim was mentioned as having arrived at Wittenberg shortly prior to this date; see WA, Br 10, No. 3757, Introduction. Clemen suggests (loc. cit.) that this son could have been either Christopher or his brother Erhard. In any case, in May of 1545 Christopher returned to Prussia after he had spent some time in Wittenberg; he obviously was the carrier of the present letter, and most probably also of an April 26 letter of Melanchthon to Duke Albrecht (C.R. 5, No. 3181).
[3] Source for and background of this statement could not be identified. Throughout 1544 and early 1545 the Turks harassed the Austrian-Hungarian borderlands; see Ranke 2[IV], 228; Elton, p. 524. See further p. 269, n. 12.
[4] Charles V; see LW 48, 175 f.
[5] Ferdinand of Austria.
[6] This statement has to be considered either the product of Luther's growing disenchantment with the rulers of Germany (see, e.g., pp. 243, 245), or of a growing lack of interest in and knowledge about political affairs (see also p. 245). The 1544 Diet of Speyer had made preparations for war against France and the Turks (see Ranke 2[IV], 185 ff.; Brandi 1, 426 f.), and the Diet of Worms was not yet closed, though up to the time that Luther was writing the present letter the Turkish question had not been a major one in Worms, in spite of having been a part of the agenda;. see Brandi 2, 355 ff.
[7] Luther mentions here what was in reality a single incident, i.e., the execution of a noble woman and her two daughters in the Belgian areas of the Netherlands.

firm.[8] Further, Count-Palatine Frederick, the elector, and his wife
have accepted the gospel.[9] This Easter they publicly took the sacrament in both kinds and [thus] affirmed [the gospel]. God be
praised and honored; may he strengthen them.[10] Amen. The
Roman abomination[11] continues to mock the Emperor and the
Empire with his council;[12] he has postponed it from Laetare Sunday to [St.] Michael's Day.[13] In Ferrara it is said that it is a long
time till then.[14] For once this is at least a word of truth coming
from this lying mouth,[15] since for all eternity the papists are unable
to endure a council.[16]

With this I commend [Your Sovereign Grace] to the dear

Judging by the references found in the correspondence of the evangelicals (see
WA, Br 11, 73, n. 17), this incident disturbed them greatly. In view of this
single incident Luther's statement seems to be an exaggeration.

[8] This is a reference to the efforts of Hermann von Wied, archbishop and
elector of Cologne (see O.D.C.C., p. 629), to organize the Reformation in his
territory with help from Bucer and Melanchthon. Had the Electoral vote of
Cologne been joined to those of Saxony, Brandenburg, and the Palatinate in
support of the Reformation the balance in the Electoral college with its seven
votes would have been upset; had the Cologne territory become evangelical it
would have been a severe loss for the papal church in terms of souls, territory,
and resources. In addition to these considerations, it should also be noted that
von Wied's efforts were destined to find imitators among other prince-bishops,
and that the territory of Cologne was close to the Netherlands, the Emperor's
homeland. Consequently prior to, during, and after the 1545 Diet of Worms the
Emperor did everything in his power, short of using force, to undo von Wied's
accomplishments or at least to obstruct von Wied's efforts. For details, see Ranke
2[IV], 203 ff., 221 ff.; Lau-Bizer, pp. 187 ff.

[9] While the Elector of the Palatinate, Louis V (1508–1544), had an unclear
position on political matters related to the religious issues of the day and liked
to play the mediator between the Protestants and the Emperor, his successor,
Frederick II (1544–1556), openly affirmed the Reformation; see ADB 7, 603 ff.
Together with his wife Dorothy (a former Danish princess), Frederick received communion in both kinds (see LW 48, 143 f., 342 f.) on Easter (April
5, 1545). For more details, see WA, Br 11, 84, n. 4.

[10] I.e., Elector Frederick and his wife.

[11] I.e., Pope Paul III.

[12] See p. 249, n. 11.

[13] I.e., from "mid-Lent Sunday" (so literally), or Laetare Sunday, i.e., March
15, 1546, to September 29. In the spring of 1545 no one in Germany, including
the Emperor, believed that the council would be opened on time, if it would
be opened at all; see Jedin, pp. 507, n. 6, 508 ff.; WA, Br 11, 88. "St. Michael's
Day" (September 29) as a possible date for opening the council could not be
established.

[14] Source and background of this statement could not be established.

[15] I.e., the Pope's.

[16] This is an allusion to the papacy's hesitation to call a council which might
enact reforms, a hesitation which dates back to the days of fifteenth century
conciliarism.

God. Amen. I also commend this Kunheim[17] to Your Sovereign
Grace, for he is a good chap who behaved very well here.

May 2, 1545   Your Sovereign Grace's willing servant,
                     MARTIN LUTHER, DOCTOR

307

To Elector John Frederick
[Wittenberg,] May 7, 1545

*Luther sends some material pertaining to articles issued by the
Theological Faculty of Louvain and deplores the fact that the Emperor has affirmed these articles. Luther also comments on news
and rumors about the Council of Trent; he considers such news to
be gossip spread by the papists, who he thinks will do everything
possible to forestall the opening of the council for they fear that a
council would endanger them. Should there be a council anyhow,
says Luther, it would accomplish nothing but nonsense.*

On Elector John Frederick, see LW 48, 181 f.

Text in German: WA, Br 11, 88.[1]

To the Most Illustrious, Noble Sovereign and Lord, Sir
John Frederick, duke in Saxony, archmarshal and elector
of the Holy Roman Empire, landgrave in Thuringia,
margrave in Meissen, and count of the castle in Magdeburg,
my Most Gracious Lord

Grace and peace in the Lord, and my poor *Pater noster!*[2] Most
Illustrious, Noble Sovereign, Most Gracious Lord! I am sending to
Your Electoral Grace my answer to the articles issued at Louvain,

---

[17] See note 2.
[1] The letter is extant as autograph. There is a notation on the autograph to the
effect that Luther is sending what he has written *against* the Louvain articles,
and that Luther considers the news pertaining to the Council of Trent to be
"empty" news. See also Excursus.
[2] See p. 69, n. 4.

for about eight days ago we also received them in print.[3] It is very good that these miserable people betray and destroy themselves in this way. In the Emperor's letter they are called his, that is, the emperor's daughter.[4] O unfortunate emperor who must be the father of such a great, disgraceful, abominable whore! All right, the pope[5] is mad and foolish from the top of his head to his heels, so that his followers do not know what they are doing or saying. There is no doubt that, should a council be opened, the papists would produce similar wisdom, and even worse, in this council. But I think they certainly are clever enough—especially their holy spirit, [the man from] Mainz[6]—to let the council remain out in the field like unripe barley,[7] even though they cannot stop prating about it.

The other item—the news[8] about the council at Trent and

---

[3] Or: "I am returning to Your Electoral Grace the articles issued." So according to Clemen (*WA*, Br 11, No. 4103, Introduction). See Excursus.

[4] On March 14, 1545, Emperor Charles V (see *LW* 48, 175 f.) issued a letter in Brussels in which he approved of the articles issued by the professors "of our University at Louvain, our daughter," ordered them to be distributed to all ecclesiastical dignitaries, and to be affirmed by all engaged in "religious education." *WA* 54, 417.

[5] It is not clear whether Luther was thinking of Pope Paul III, or whether he was thinking of the papacy and the papists in general. If Luther was thinking of the incumbent pope, then the circumstances which Luther had in mind are unknown to this editor, and the reasons for the sudden switch from the Louvain articles to Pope Paul and the council are unclear. It seems to this editor, however, that Luther was not thinking of any specific action of Pope Paul III, but of the papacy in general. For the purpose of the Louvain articles was to set forth the true articles of faith (see Köstlin-Kawerau 2, 609), i.e., to do exactly what the pending council was to accomplish. Consequently the council would no longer be necessary, even though there was much talk about it (see the last sentence of the paragraph). But even if a council were to come about—which was highly dubious—it would arrive only at nonsense, i.e., "wisdom" similar to that set forth in the Louvain articles, because "they" (so the literal translation for "his followers," i.e., the papists in general and the Louvian theologians in particular) did not know what they were doing, or about what they were talking; no wonder, since the head whom they follow, i.e., the pope, is both mad and foolish.

[6] I.e., Cardinal Albrecht, the archbishop of Mainz; see *LW* 48, 44 f. No special reason could be established for Luther's sudden mention of his old foe. Luther talks here in general terms, just as in the following paragraph when he mentions the men at Rome and Mainz and obviously holds Pope Paul and the Archbishop responsible for the spread of the gossip.

[7] Literally: "they will let the council remain like unripe barley stuck in the stack." Luther intends to say that as a wise farmer will not bring home the unripe barley (or hay), which he has stacked in the field for ripening (or drying), so the papists will be "clever" enough not to open the council because they are well aware of the danger into which a council could bring them.

[8] Source and circumstances of this news could not be identified.

those who supposedly are present there—I consider to be gossip and nonsense spread by the men at Rome and Mainz,[9] [and] they certainly will have to regret it, should it come true.[10] God does not want them and they do not want him either. So let it be; all will turn out well.

With this I commend Your Electoral Grace to the dear God who, for the sake of putting his gracious and perfect will into operation, is to rule and protect Your Electoral Grace. Amen.

May 7, 1545   Your Electoral Grace's dedicated

MARTIN LUTHER, DOCTOR

---

[9] Literally: "I consider Roman and Mainzian gossip and nonsense." It was rumored that many important clerics were assembled in Trent; it was hoped that this rumor would heighten the prestige of the council, and thus counter the generally waning confidence of the public in the possibility that the council would ever really convene.

[10] I.e., that the council would indeed get under way.

EXCURSUS

In the opening sentence of letter No. 307 Luther referred to thirty-two theses issued in December of 1544 by the Theological Faculty of the University of Louvain, in which the teachings of the evangelicals were summarized, briefly explained, and refuted (text of theses: WA 54, 417 ff.; LW 34, 346 ff.). At the end of April/beginning of May, Luther and Melanchthon had these theses in hand; they had received a printed copy of the theses from a "certain friend." See the statement above, p. 256, and p. 251, n. 10; WA, Br 11, 85 (May 2); C.R. 5, 753 (May 1); Kawerau, Jonas Briefwechsel 2, 161. Shortly thereafter the Elector also sent a copy of these theses to Luther, which the Elector had received from Landgrave Philip of Hesse (see LW 49, 124 n. 8). On June 6 (not May 10 as is stated in WA 54, 414) the Elector returned this copy to the Landgrave, saying that Luther had returned the copy to him and enclosing a copy of Luther's "writing"; see C. G. Neudecker (ed.), Merkwürdige Aktenstücke aus dem Zeitalter der Reformation 1 (Nürnberg, 1838), 450 f. It is commonly assumed (Neudecker, loc. cit.; Clemen, see p. 256, n. 3) that the enclosed copy of Luther's "writing" was a copy of letter No. 307, and that letter No. 307 was the covering letter with which Luther returned the Elector's—i.e., the Landgrave's—copy; Luther had no use for this copy since about eight days earlier he had already received a copy of the articles (see p. 256), and since he was requested to return this copy (see Neudecker, loc. cit.). Consequently one would have to translate Luther's statement as: "I am returning . . . the articles, issued at Louvain," as Clemen argues (see p. 256, n. 3). That Luther did indeed return the articles to the Elector is obvious from the fact that the Elector returned the articles to the Landgrave; and it is almost certain that Letter No. 307 was the covering letter.

In light of the notation on the autograph of letter No. 307 (see p. 255, n. 1), however, the situation is more complex than it seems to be at first glance, and the translation "I am returning" is problematic, a fact overlooked by Clemen. The notation clearly states that, along with this letter, Luther is sending something which he *has written against* the theologians of Louvain. This suggests that as early as May 7 Luther's refutation of the Louvain articles was completed, at least the manuscript of it, and that on May 7 Luther not only returned the Landgrave's copy to the Elector, but also sent a copy of his own refutation to the Elector. He was able to work on this refutation because he had received a copy of the Louvain articles almost eight days ago. If this were indeed so then one wonders why it took so long (from the beginning of May to the end of August/beginning of September,) to have this refutation (in the form of theses; WA, 54, 425 ff.; LW 34, 354 ff.) of six pages in quarto published. One may want to get around this difficulty by arguing that the notation was made *after* the refutation had been published and found its way to the Electoral court, i.e., some time in September, or that the notation was made even later than that date at a time when the clerk or whoever made the notation no longer knew the precise circumstances. These arguments are weak, for if the "writing" of Luther, of which the Elector sent a copy to the Landgrave on June 6, was indeed letter No. 307 then this letter must have been in the chancellery by June 6 for the purpose of being copied; it is extremely awkward to assume that the notation was not made at that time, i.e., at the time of receipt of the original, but later on.

A closer examination of the text further makes clear that Clemen's interpretation and the alternate translation, presented on p. 256, n. 3, are not as definite as they appear to be. Luther wrote: *Ich Schicke Ekfg* [to your Electoral Grace] *wider die Artickel zu Loüen gestellet.* The problem is caused by the word *wider.* Clemen assumes that *wider* (in the sense of the present-day German *wieder,* i.e., "again, anew, afresh") is to be connected with *schicke* to mean "I am sending again," or "I am returning." This meaning is supported by the circumstances surrounding this copy (Luther had received it from the Elector, did not need it, returned it to the Elector who, in turn, returned it to the Landgrave). But this adverbial usage of *wider* is not the only meaning which Luther used, in fact it is not even the predominant one. (For details, see J. Erben, *Grundzüge einer Syntax der Sprache Luthers* [Berlin, 1954], *s.v.* wider.) *Wider* in the sense of the present-day German *wider* or "against" can be connected with *gestellet* so that one would have to translate: "I am sending [what I have put together] against the articles issued at Louvain." In this case *wider* would be understood as a preposition which has its object in "the articles issued at Louvain." And the whole prepositional phrase would be the object of *ich schicke.* Since the text and context do not help us to establish which meaning Luther had in mind one has to rely on the surrounding circumstances, i.e., the notation on the autograph. Certainly the clerk or whoever made this notation understood Luther to say that he, Luther, was sending his refutation of the Louvain articles. Or should one have to suggest that the clerk totally misunderstood Luther, or that the notation was made at a time so far removed from the event that no one knew any longer what actually happened? This is of course possible, but is it probable?

If one adopts the prepositional meaning of *wider* then one would have to suppose that on May 7 Luther sent to the Elector a manuscript of his refutation of the Louvain articles; he also returned the copy of the Louvain articles which he had received from the Elector, though he did not specially mention it because he considered them a part of his refutation. Since Luther had been in possession of the articles for approximately eight days, he had had time to work on his reply; since the reply was in the form of theses, rather than a pamphlet or book, Luther could easily have "dashed it off" in this short time, esp. since at the conclusion of the theses Luther "promised" to say more on the subject soon (*WA*

54, 430; *LW* 34, 360). Thus Luther's *Against the Thirty-two Articles of the Louvain Theologists* would have been written in the first week of May, 1545, and not some time during the summer of 1545 (as one has to assume on the basis of *WA* 54, 422).

(That Luther's refutation was completed by May 7 can be also seen from the following observations: On April 14 Luther informed von Amsdorf that he had not yet decided whether he would respond to the latest attack of the Zwinglians; if he would respond at all then it would be only briefly. See *WA*, Br 11, 71. On May 8, i.e., one day after Luther [supposedly] sent a copy of his refutation of the Louvain articles to the Elector, Luther informed von Amsdorf that he has decided not to reply to the Zwinglians, except for a brief indirect remark, and that he has more to do than read the writings of the Zwinglians who never come to terms with the issues anyhow; *WA*, Br 11, 95. Luther arrived at this decision because he could consider his brief remarks made in the refutation of the Louvain articles [see Luther's theses, Latin text, Nos. XV, XXVII] sufficient, at least for the time being. By June 15 Luther had changed his mind, for on that day he informed von Amsdorf that he was in the process of planning a short book against the sacramentarians, but that a sudden stone attack "last night" interrupted his work; *WA*, Br 11, 120 f.)

If Luther's refutation of the 1544 articles of the Louvain theologians had indeed been completed by May 7 why did Luther send a manuscript copy of this refutation to the Elector, and why did it take so long (i.e., from the beginning of May to the end of August/beginning of September) to have the refutation published? The answer to the first question can be derived from the nature of the Louvain articles. Because of the Emperor's approval of the articles (see p. 256, n. 4), they were not only a theological "slander" of the evangelicals, but also a political and legal document which could have major consequences; therefore Luther felt it necessary to inform his territorial lord of his own position on the articles at the earliest possible moment. The second question cannot be exactly answered but the following observations may help to understand the situation. At the time that Luther became acquainted with the Louvain articles he was occupied with the question whether to write something against the Zwinglians (see above; April 14, May 8, June 15). He was also occupied with planning and was actually working on another book against the papacy; *WA*, Br 11, 72 (April 14), 91 (May 7), 120 (June 15), 177 (September 23). Further, Luther's health was poor (see p. 267, n. 14); in July and August Luther was away from Wittenberg (see pp. 273 ff.), and Melanchthon had ideas about a response to the articles (*C.R.* 5, 758; May 22). And finally, the printers might have been busy. In view of these circumstances it is not quite as strange as it appears at first glance for Luther to have put his refutation aside for a while— perhaps even until after he returned to Wittenberg in the middle of

August—esp. if one considers the fact that Luther could have felt at ease about the matter since his position on the articles had been made known to the Elector. In any case, Luther considered his refutation, once it was printed, insufficient—was this because he had "dashed it off" in the first week of May?—and at once prepared a book against the theologians of Louvain (WA, Br 11, 177 [September 23]; C.R. 5, 848 [September 9]) and started to work on it (see p. 317).

308

To Nicholas von Amsdorf
[Wittenberg,] June 3, 1545

Luther replies to von Amsdorf's inquiry about a "monstrosity" per-
taining to foxes, and admits that he and the hunters with whom he
has talked about this incident have no way of explaining it, except
perhaps that it might be an omen of the end of the world. Then
Luther makes a pessimistic statement about the Diet of Worms and
the pending council, and reports that the people of Nürnberg have
captured a nobleman whose freedom they hope to exchange for the
freedom of one of their citizens, Jerome Baumgartner, currently
being held by a relative of the nobleman they captured. He also
comments briefly on a picture of the Pope. In a postscript Luther
mentions that the Emperor has ordered the people of Augsburg to
accept their newly appointed bishop, and that the people of Augs-
burg plan to resist this order.

On Nicholas von Amsdorf, see LW 48, 218.

Text in Latin: WA, Br 11, 115.[1]

To the Most Reverend Father in the Lord, Sir Nicholas,
bishop of the true and holy church at Naumburg,[2] a sincere
minister of Christ, my esteemed superior[3]

Grace and peace in the Lord! Most Reverend Father in the Lord: I
have presented your question about that monstrosity pertaining to
the foxes[4] to people who are experienced in and who practice the

---

[1] The letter is extant as autograph.
[2] For "bishop," "church," and "Naumburg," see LW 49, 61, n. 6, 87, n. 5, and
above, p. 224, n. 10.
[3] Or: "elder."
[4] The following statements could not be clarified since the letter to Luther in
which von Amsdorf reported the incident is no longer extant. On the basis of
Luther's statements it is certain that at least a portion of the "monstrosity" was
the fact that the foxes hunted near their dens. But the "monstrosity" seems to
have included more than this fact, for von Amsdorf would hardly have bothered
to think about this fact, to communicate it to Luther, and to ask Luther for an
opinion about the meaning of the "monstrosity" if the "monstrosity" were nothing
more than foxes preying in the neighborhood of their dens. According to
Clemen (WA, Br 11, 116, n. 1), the reference to the foxes in the city moat of
Köthen contributes little to the reconstruction of the "monstrosity."

art and occupation of hunting, and who really are masters of this art. At first they said what I had told them could not be true. Then, when I had shown them your letter, they were amazed beyond all measure. Unanimously they declared that a fox is too cunning to prey where he has his den. The case of Köthen was cited, where foxes have dens in the (so-called) city moat but do not harm anyone there.[5] I do not know what this is supposed to mean except, perhaps, that a change of all things is pending,[6] for which we pray and which we await. Amen.

I do not care about diets and councils, I do not believe anything about them, I do not expect anything from them, I do not worry about them. Vanity of vanities.[7] The people of Nürnberg have captured a certain nobleman in the hope that in return for his freedom they might free their Baumgartner.[8] Unless God intervenes, this incident might well be the spark of some future fire[9] [which might come] as a punishment on Germany; but may God take us and those who belong to us from this misery prior to that. There is no justice, no central authority, and the Empire is without power. This is the end and finish of the Empire.[10]

---

[5] Köthen is located in the territory of Anhalt, approximately twenty-two kilometers southwest of Dessau. For a description of the fortifications of Köthen, see O. Hartung, *Geschichte der Stadt Cöthen* (Cöthen, 1900), pp. 220 ff.

[6] For a similar statement, see p. 245.

[7] Eccles. 1:2.

[8] Luther here reports an incident which is often mentioned by him and his friends. See *WA*, Br 10, Nos. 4009, 4048; 11, Nos. 4076, 4079, 4156. Jerome Baumgartner (see *NDB* 1, 664, f.) was an alternate delegate of the Nürnberg city government to the 1544 Diet of Speyer. When he returned from Speyer, he was kidnapped by the Franconian knight Albrecht von Rosenberg on May 31, 1544. Negotiations for Baumgartner's release accomplished nothing because of Albrecht's high ransom demand. Finally Nürnberg went to war against Albrecht, intending to lay siege to one of his castles in the hope that Baumgartner was being held captive there. Albrecht, however, had found out about the plans of the Nürnbergers and, prior to the beginning of the bombardment of the castle by the forces of Nürnberg, moved Baumgartner somewhere else. When the Nürnberg authorities were able to get their hands on one of Albrecht's relatives, negotiations for Baumgartner's release were renewed, and on August 4, 1545, Baumgartner finally was returned to Nürnberg. Luther's source was the correspondence between Veit Dietrich in Nürnberg (see *LW* 49, 282, n. 13) and Melanchthon in *C.R.* 5. For the documents and the secondary literature related to this incident, see Klaus, pp. 228 ff.; *WA*, Br 11, 116, n. 3.

[9] The *WA*, Br text is typographically corrupted here; the translation is based on Enders, *Briefwechsel* 16, 245, and *WA*, Br 13, 343, addition to *WA*, Br 11, 115, line 14.

[10] Literally: "that is, the dregs and the end of the Empire." Luther intends to

Your nephew George[11] has shown me the picture of the Pope,[12] but Master[13] Lucas is a rough painter. He could have spared the female sex for the sake of God's creation and of our mothers. He could have painted other images suitable to the pope, that is, more devilish ones. But you will judge for yourself.
Farewell in the Lord, farewell in Christ!

Yours,

MARTIN LUTHER

The Emperor has commanded the people of Augsburg to receive the Cardinal, that is, their bishop, along with the clergy and the papal ceremonies. But the people are getting ready to protect themselves by means of arms.[14] The priests do not wish to have peace or possess what is theirs in peace—so let what they seek happen.

309

To Nicholas von Amsdorf
[Wittenberg,] July 9, 1545

Even though Luther thinks that von Amsdorf is better informed about "all things" than he himself is, he reports two news items and

---

say that in view of the general conditions within the Empire, as illustrated by the Baumgartner incident, the dregs of society are ruling, and this fact means that the Empire is nearing its end.

[11] For some information on this George, who was a son of a deceased brother of Nicholas von Amsdorf and a student in Wittenberg, see WA, Br 10, 2, n. 11, 601, n. 9.

[12] See WA 54, 346 ff., 357 f.

[13] From "Master" (i.e., Master Craftsman Lucas Cranach; see LW 48, 201) to the end of the sentence, Luther used German.

[14] In April of 1543 Christopher Stadion, the humanistically oriented bishop of Augsburg (see LW 49, 350, n. 16, 416), died. The cathedral clergy elected Otto Truchsess von Waldburg (see NCE 14, 322), a stern supporter of the papal church, who promised to undo the Reformation in Augsburg, and who in December, 1544, was made a cardinal. The reference to Emperor Charles V (see LW 48, 175 f.), and to the possible use of force by the citizens of Augsburg could not be verified. According to S. Roth, *Augsburgs Reformationsgeschichte* 3 (Munich, 1907), 215 ff., Luther's statements apparently were based on rumors.

comments on them: The Emperor demands that the evangelicals consent to the council, even though the Pope has declared the evangelicals to be heretics who are not to participate in the council. Luther sees in this situation a trap laid by the papists for the evangelicals, who will be caught regardless of their response to the Emperor's demand. Therefore, Luther argues, the evangelicals must continue to reject the council as long as the Pope insists on being superior to the council. The second item Luther reports is that the Emperor is trying to make peace with the Turks and that this fact raises the possibility that, having finally established this peace, the Emperor might turn his force against the evangelicals. In closing Luther mentions a severe stone attack he has had recently and says that he would prefer death to the pain caused by such an attack.

On Nicholas von Amsdorf, see LW 48, 218.

Text in Latin: WA, Br 11, 131–132.[1]

To the Reverend Father and Lord in Christ, Sir
Nicholas, true bishop of the church at Naumburg,[2] my
superior[3] venerably to be esteemed in the Lord

Grace and peace in the Lord. If I had something to write, I would write, Reverend Father in Christ. But I suppose that all things are better known to you than to us.

From the diet they write[4] that the Emperor strongly insists

---

[1] The letter is extant as autograph, in several manuscript copies, and in the common editions of Luther's works.

[2] See p. 262, n. 10.

[3] Or: "Elder."

[4] Literally: "one writes." The source of the following news from the Diet of Worms could not be identified; it might not be wrong, however, to suggest that Luther became acquainted with the developments in Worms via the Electoral Saxon court. Luther's statements reflect the developments of the day. Up to the middle of March, 1545, Pope Paul III was strongly opposed to the policy of Emperor Charles V (see *LW* 48, 175 f.) toward the Protestants (see e.g., p. 248). The Council of Trent was to block all further negotiations between the Emperor and the evangelicals, negotiations to which the Emperor had been committed since the days of the Diet of Speyer. Then the Pope received news from Cardinal Truchsess and others to the effect that the Emperor was pursuing a two-track policy: the Emperor was trying to gain the good will of the Protestants; and he was determined to seek a solution to the whole Reformation issue by means of military force unless the Protestants subordinated themselves to the council and its decrees. (See also p. 245, n. 8; Lau-Bizer, p. 190, esp. n. 6.) As a result of this news, the Pope dispatched his secretary of state, Cardinal

that our party consent to the council. Since our friends do not wish to do this he is angry, so they say. What kind of a monstrosity this is, I do not understand: the Pope shouts that we are heretics and that we must not have a place in the council; the Emperor wants us to consent to the council and its decrees. Perhaps God is making fools out of them;[5] indeed Satan reigns, [and] all of them are so totally mad that they condemn us and at the same time ask for our consent. But this seems to be their raging wisdom; since thus far they were unable to scare us with their very evil cause by using the authority and power of the pope, the church, the Emperor, [and] the diets, they are now thinking of operating with the authority of the council; thus they could be in a position of publicly decrying us as incorrigible people who are willing to listen neither to the pope, nor the church, nor the Emperor, nor the empire, and now not even to the council, which we ourselves have so often requested. Look at this wisdom of Satan in contrast to that foolish God![6] How will that God be able to escape such clever plans? But it is the Lord who will ridicule the mockers.[7] If we now have to consent to such a council, why did we not twenty-five years ago agree with the lord of the councils, the pope, and his bulls? Let the pope first acknowledge

---

Alessandro Farnese (see NCE 5, 840 f.), to Worms. The Cardinal arrived in Worms on May 18, and began at once to enter into discussions with the Emperor. When on June 2 the Cardinal returned to Trent, the tug-of-war between the Emperor and the papacy had gone in favor of the Emperor and his plans: The Pope was willing to postpone the opening of the council so that the Emperor could continue to negotiate with the Protestants as if he were seeking a peaceful solution to the whole situation by means of a colloquy; and a secret military alliance between the Emperor and the Pope, directed against the German Protestants, was established shortly after June 8. See Jedin, pp. 517 ff.; Ranke 2[IV], 232 ff. Meanwhile in Worms the Emperor put pressure on the Protestants to accept the council and its decrees unconditionally (see the statement above), while at the same time he continued to hold out to the evangelicals the possibility of a colloquy on the religious issues; in fact, the resolution of the diet issued on August 4 fixed November 30 as the date for the beginning of a colloquy in Regensburg (Jedin, p. 535). The Protestants rejected the council because they were not even invited and thus they realized that the council could not be a "free" council (ibid., pp. 527 f.). Luther's statement that the Pope shouts that "we" are heretics is either a general statement (based, perhaps, on the bull summoning the council; see p. 249, n. 11), or it is a reference to a special incident which this editor was unable to identify. See also Lau-Bizer, pp. 190 ff.
[5] I.e., either the Pope and the Emperor together, or the papists in general.
[6] See I Cor. 1:18 ff., esp. 1:25, and Luther's Heidelberg Disputation of 1518 (LW 31, 39 ff.; WA 1, 350 ff.).
[7] See Ps. 2:4, 37:13, 59:8.

that the council is superior to him,[8] and let him listen to the council [even] if it speaks against him—just as his conscience testifies against him—[and] then we shall discuss the whole matter. They are insane and stupid.[9] Thanks be to God.

The Emperor, Ferdinand, and the Frenchman are trying to make peace with the Turk,[10] and some think that the Emperor might turn his weapons against us.[11] But David says: "Yet I was praying."[12] "May the Lord's will be done."[13]

Farewell in the Lord, my Reverend Father! Both of us are old; perhaps in a short while we will have to be buried. My torturer, the stone, would have killed me on St. John's Day, had God not decided differently.[14] I prefer death to such a tyrant.

Again farewell!

July 9, 1545   Your Reverend Lordship's dedicated

MARTIN LUTHER

---

[8] This is, perhaps, an allusion to the Bull *Execrabilis* (see *NCE* 1, 703) issued by Pope Pius II on January 18, 1460, in which any appeal from a papal verdict to a council was forbidden; thus the "lordship" of the pope over the council was established. Churchly custom went one step further and ascribed to the pope the exclusive right of calling a council and confirming its decrees; at least this was Sylvester Prierias' (see *LW* 48, Index, *s.v.*) argument against Luther. Luther had dealt with this problem in his *To the Christian Nobility* of 1520 (*LW* 44, 115 ff.; *WA* 6, 381 ff.).

[9] Luther wrote this sentence in German.

[10] See pp. 269 f.

[11] It could not be established whether this statement is based on a feeling on Luther's part—if so he was more than correct; see note 4—or on factual knowledge. In any case, prior to and during the Diet of Worms the Protestants became increasingly tense about the possibility that the Emperor might use force against them, perhaps as a means of executing a conciliar decision; see Ranke 2^{IV}, 220 f., 240.

[12] Ps. 109:4 (Vulgate; Luther Bible).

[13] This is an allusion to the Third Petition of the Lord's Prayer. See also Ps. 109:20 (Vulgate; Luther Bible).

[14] On June 15 Luther wrote to von Amsdorf that in the past night he had suffered a kidney stone attack which caused him such pain that he wanted to die, and that as yet he had not passed a stone; *WA*, Br 11, 120. On St. John's Day (June 24) Luther suffered another kidney stone attack, as he now (on July 9) tells von Amsdorf, in words which are similar to the ones he had used to inform von Amsdorf about the June 15 attack.

310

To Justus Jonas
[Wittenberg,] July 16, 1545

Luther hopes that Jonas has recuperated from the stone (gall stone?) which had troubled him, and suggests that by avoiding certain foods further problems might perhaps be eliminated. Then Luther communicates some news: The Archbishop of Mainz has sent "ridiculous delegates" to the Council of Trent; God will disperse the council; on June 21 a legation of the Emperor and others left Venice in order to establish peace with the Turks; the envoys dressed themselves in Turkish clothing so as not to be despised by the Turks. In this pragmatic action on the Emperor's part Luther sees a sign of capitulation of those who previously have decried and fought the Turks as enemies of Christendom. Luther underscores the ridiculousness of the situation by pointing out the financial manipulations of the popes in connection with the wars against the Turk, this enemy of Christendom, with whom one now is trying to make peace. For Luther all this is a sign that the end of the world is near.

On Justus Jonas, see LW 48, 275, n. 3.

Text in Latin: WA, Br 11, 142.[1]

To the reverend man, distinguished by godliness
and virtue, Mr. Justus Jonas, Doctor of Theology,
my dearest brother

Grace and peace. I pray God to give you something better than what you write about your stone,[2] my Jonas. Why do you not give up your *Faliscum*[3] and similar things[4] so that they do not, as one says, make you imagine such horrible things?[5] May God have mercy upon us.

---

[1] The letter, or portions of it, is extant in several manuscript copies, and in the common editions of Luther's works. Whether the available form of the letter was the original one is open to question.
[2] This letter is not extant.
[3] So in all witnesses.
[4] Or: "persons."
[5] This sentence is unclear, chiefly because *Faliscum* cannot be precisely de-

The man of Mainz has sent some ridiculous delegates to the council,[6] but that monster laughs at the same time about us and the pope. The council is really *Tridentum*, that is, in German, torn apart,[7] split up, and dissolved,[8] for God disperses it and will disperse it together with all its delegates. I absolutely believe that they do not know what they are doing[9] or are supposed to do. God has cursed their plans, as is written: Cursed is the man who trusts in man and makes flesh his arm.[10]

I believe you have heard (it[11] is true) that on June 21[12] a splendid legation of the Emperor, the Frenchman, the Pope, [and]

---

fined. *St.L.* 21b, 3119, suggests that *Faliscus* (?) is an Italian wine, while Clemen (*WA*, Br 11, 143, n. 1) suggests that it could be a heavy sausage, or a person who (to modify a present day phrase) was giving Jonas "stomach aches"; hence the alternate translation suggested in note 4. It seems most natural to assume, however, that Luther intended to say Jonas should stick to a diet.

6 See pp. 271 f.

7 The text uses the German word *zertrennet* (i.e., torn apart) in which Luther sees an allusion to *Trient*, the German version of Trent, the city in which the council was to be in session.

8 It is difficult to evaluate Luther's statement. It would be easiest simply to see here Luther's negative attitude toward the council and the much discussed "pessimism" of his old age. On the other hand, as the statement about "the man of Mainz" and the other statements in the letter demonstrate, Luther and his friends (see the correspondence of Jonas and of Melanchthon) were quite well informed about general events, esp. about the situation pertaining to the council, both as to facts and rumors. (Jedin's argument [p. 528] to the effect that the German Protestants were poorly informed about "the happenings at Trent" seems to be shaky.) Luther could very well have been aware of the "atmosphere of uncertainty and hesitation" regarding the future of the council (*ibid.*, p. 526) that existed in June and July among the small number of assembled delegates in Trent. As late as September even Cochlaeus (see *O.D.C.C.*, p. 305) was highly skeptical about the fate of the council (Jedin, p. 528). This awareness, combined with Luther's "pessimism," might have led Luther to imply that the very name of the city in which the council was to meet suggested that nothing would come of the council.

9 Luke 23:34.

10 Jer. 17:5.

11 Literally: "for it is."

12 The source of the following news was a letter from Venice which arrived in Wittenberg on July 13, and about which Melanchthon reported on July 14 to John Lang (see *LW* 48, 14); *C.R.* 5, No. 3218; see also *WA*, Br 11, 143, n. 7. When on July 9 Luther reported to von Amsdorf that the Emperor and others were trying to establish peace with the Turks, then either Luther was reporting a rumor only, or his source cannot be identified. Following the Peace of Crespy a joint action of Western Christendom against the Turks was expected. Yet in order to have a free hand against the German Protestants, Emperor Charles (see *LW* 48, 175 f.) used the services of the Portuguese, and of the French king, Francis I (the former ally of the Turks), to initiate negotiations with the Turks while at the same time he proposed to the Diet of Worms a discussion of the means necessary for a war against the Turks. The Emperor's envoy, Gerhard

Ferdinand, loaded down with precious gifts, left Venice for the Turks in order to seek peace. What is most honorable and worthy of eternal remembrance is the fact that all of the envoys have laid aside their native clothing and have decked themselves out in Turkish clothing, that is, in a longer [tunic], so that the Turks should not despise them.[13] This is the way in which they conduct the war against him whom for so many years they have decried as the enemy of the Christian name, [and] against whom the Roman satan, by means of indulgences, annates,[14] and endless rapacity has wrung so much money from the people. Can you see the downfall of the Empire? Can you see that the day of our salvation is at hand?[15] We shall be happy, glad, and rejoice; the end of the world is here. Praise and glory be to God through all eternity. Amen.

July 16, 1545   Yours,

                              MARTIN LUTHER

311

To Nicholas von Amsdorf
[Wittenberg,] July 17, 1545

Replying to a no-longer extant letter of von Amsdorf, Luther states that he is not disturbed by the news which von Amsdorf has written to him. Luther also mentions that it is no wonder that a wooden statue of Elector John Frederick toppled over, since it was poorly

---

Veltwyck, accompanied by the French envoy Blaise de Monluc, went from Venice via Ragusa to Constantinople, while an envoy of Ferdinand of Austria went there via Hungary and Bosnia. In October an eighteen month truce was signed between the Emperor and the Turks, which guaranteed the *status quo* in Hungary upon the annual payment of ten thousand ducats (see LW 49, 286, n. 36) by Ferdinand. See Ranke 2^{IV}, 227 ff.; Brandi 1, 438; 2, 354; Lenz *BPB* 2, 347 n. 8. This editor was unable to verify any participation of an envoy of Pope Paul III in this peace mission.

[13] Luther's source states *only* that the envoys wore long reddish tunics; see WA, Br 11, 143, n. 7.
[14] I.e., a certain sum of money to be paid to the pope by clergymen upon their appointment to certain benefices. For details, see W. E. Lunt, *Papal Revenues in the Middle Ages* (New York, 1934), 1, 93 ff., 315 ff.; 2, 315 ff.
[15] See Joel 2:1; Rom. 13:12; II Cor. 6:2; Eph. 4:30.

set up. Then Luther reports the presence of twenty-three bishops and three cardinals in Trent, and comments briefly on the unimpressive delegation sent by the Archbishop of Mainz to the council. In the remaining portion of the letter Luther tells von Amsdorf about the legation sent by the Emperor and others to the Turks for the purpose of reaching a peace agreement, and comments on this event.

On Nicholas von Amsdorf, see LW 48, 218.

Text in Latin: WA, Br 11, 143–144.[1]

To the Reverend Father and Lord in Christ, Sir Nicholas,
true and faithful bishop of the church at Naumburg,[2]
my superior[3] in the Lord, etc.

Grace and peace in the Lord! I am not disturbed by the events about which you write,[4] Reverend Father in Christ. Do not worry about dreams, says [Cato].[5] Scripture teaches the same thing, "unless someone is a prophet," as is stated in Numbers 12 [:6]. But that sexton is no prophet. Further,[6] that statue of the Sovereign[7] which was erected in Torgau was made of wood. I saw it in Luke's[8] house before it was painted. No wonder that this statue fell down; it's a miracle that it stood so long. Everyone has said that it could fall by itself any day now, even without any wind, so poorly had it been set up. May these things pass away.

From Trent comes news[9] that twenty-three bishops and three cardinals are present, and that they wile away their time and do not

---

[1] The letter is extant as autograph.

[2] See p. 262, n. 2.

[3] Or: "elder."

[4] Since von Amsdorf's letter is not extant the circumstances of this statement could not be clarified.

[5] Cato *Disticha* ii. 31.

[6] It is not clear whether the following still belongs to the events pertaining to the sexton, or is a new subject.

[7] I.e., Elector John Frederick; see *LW* 48, 181 f. Nothing could be established about this statue.

[8] I.e., Lucas Cranach the Elder; see *LW* 48, 201.

[9] The source of this news could not be identified. Was it the special messenger mentioned by Jonas on July 16 (Kawerau, *Jonas Briefwechsel* 2, 165; see also Jedin, p. 528), as is suggested by Clemen in *WA*, Br 11, 144, n. 5? But according to Jonas' statement that messenger reported only the presence of twenty-three bishops. On the arrival of the official delegates in Trent, see Jedin, pp. 510 ff.

know what they are supposed to do or what they will be doing. The [Arch]bishop of Mainz,[10] or rather that scoundrel of all scoundrels, has sent envoys there, one suffragan bishop and a Franciscan. I do not know whether he intends to mock them[11] or us with this ridiculous delegation—that such an important man sends such envoys to such important men. But the council will be worthy of such [representatives]. May they have a bad time, as the wrath of God moves them.

Listen to something else if you do not know it already:[12] the Pope, the Emperor, the Frenchman, and Ferdinand have dispatched a very splendid legation, loaded down with precious gifts, to the Turks for the purpose of establishing peace. The nicest thing about this is the fact that in order not to offend the eyes of the Turks, all of the envoys have laid aside their native clothing and have decked themselves out in long tunics, according to the custom of the Turks. It is said that they departed from Venice on June 21. These are the people who until now have decried the Turk as the enemy of the Christian name, and using this pretext have wrung money from the people and agitated the inhabitants of their territories against the Turks. In order to make war against the Turks, the Roman satan has bled the world of its money by means of indulgences, annates, and endless sly thievery. What Christians, or rather hellish idols of the devil [!] I hope that these are very cheerful signs of the nearness of the end of all things. Therefore, while they[13] worship the Turk, let us shout to the true God who will listen to us, and who through the splendor of his future arrival will humiliate even the Turk, along with them.[14] Amen.

July 17, 1545   Your Lordship's dedicated
                                   MARTIN LUTHER, DOCTOR

---

[10] I.e., Cardinal Albrecht; see *LW* 48, 44 f. As his representative Albrecht sent to Trent the Mainz coadjutor Michael Helding, along with a Dominican by the name of Konrad Necrosius (not a Franciscan as stated by both Luther and Jonas [Kawerau, *Jonas Briefwechsel* 2, 165]), and a legal consultant by the name of Kauf; see Jedin, p. 529.

[11] I.e., the papists in general and the delegates assembled in Trent in particular.

[12] For the following, see pp. 267, 269 f.

[13]I.e., those who have dispatched the splendid legation to the Turk, the enemy of Christianity.

[14] See note 13.

312

To Mrs. Martin Luther
[Zeitz,][1] July 28, 1545

On July 25 Luther, his son John,[2] and one of his boarders, Ferdi-nand von Maugis,[3] joined Caspar Cruciger[4] on a trip to Zeitz, where Cruciger was to try to settle a bitter controversy between some pastors who stood under the jurisdiction of Nicholas von Amsdorf, the evangelical bishop of Naumburg.[5] Luther was in Zeitz on July 27,[6] and on July 28 he wrote the following letter to his wife.

In this letter Luther tells Katie first that John will report details about the trip, and that they all received much hospitality on the way. Then Luther informs Katie that he is disgusted with moral conditions in Wittenberg and would like to arrange matters so that he would not have to return to Wittenberg. He feels that the people of Wittenberg would make difficulties for his family anyhow, once he had died; and so he suggests that Katie now dispose of their properties in Wittenberg and move to Zölsdorf. He hopes that the Elector will continue to pay his salary for this year, which he feels might well be the last year of his life, and that this salary would enable him to improve the estate in Zölsdorf. Luther tells his wife

---

[1] For the place from which Luther wrote this letter, and for Luther's itinerary, see note 6.

[2] See *LW* 49, 152, n. 7.

[3] For some material pertaining to this student from Austria, see *WA*, Br 11, 150, n. 2, and 13, 345, addition to *loc. cit.*

[4] See *LW* 49, 104, n. 12.

[5] On the controversy, see *WA*, Br 10, Nos. 3860, 3866, 3870; 11, Nos. 4135, 4159. Why Luther joined Cruciger and what part Luther played in this settlement are not clear. Clemen argues without documentation (*WA*, Br 11, 148) that von Amsdorf requested Luther's presence, while Köstlin-Kawerau (2, 606, 608) interprets Luther's journey as a pleasure trip. See also note 54.

[6] Luther's itinerary can be reconstructed on the basis of the following facts: The present letter was written on July 28 (see also *WA*, Br 11, 148); the opening sentence makes clear that Cruciger was about to return to Wittenberg; the negotiations in Zeitz took place on July 27 (see *WA* Br 11, 196, and 13, 348, addition to *loc. cit.*); Luther mentioned a second stopover in Leipzig which is documented for July 26 (see note 33), following a first stopover in Löbnitz (which is about ten kilometers west of Düben and less than a day's journey south of Wittenberg). This brings Luther's departure from Wittenberg to July 25. See also *C.R.* 5, 800, 801.

that "the day after tomorrow" he will drive to Merseburg to visit George of Anhalt. In closing, Luther leaves it up to his wife to decide whether to inform Melanchthon and Bugenhagen of his intention not to return to Wittenberg; if his wife does tell them, then she is to ask Bugenhagen to inform the congregation of Luther's decision, and to say farewell to the congregation in Luther's name. Luther had considered leaving Wittenberg in protest before[7] he wrote the present letter. But the determination with which Luther spoke in the present letter was a considerable shock for the University and the town. Luther's colleagues immediately conjectured that Luther wanted to leave Wittenberg because of doctrinal differences which existed between Luther and "one" of Luther's colleagues.[8] On August 1 the University wrote to Elector John Frederick, enclosing a copy of the present letter,[9] and informing the Elector that the University would deputize Bugenhagen and "some

---

[7] See Köstlin-Kawerau 2, 573.

[8] See the official letter of the University to Elector John Frederick (see LW 48, 181 f.) dated August 1: St. L. 21b, 3126 ff. It was esp. Melanchthon (see LW 48, 77, n. 3) who in his conference (see note 9) with Brück (see LW 49, 51 f.) hinted at reasons for Luther's decision other than the ones Luther gave; see Brück's report about this conference to the Elector in Analecta Lutherana, op. cit. (see p. 172, n. 7), p. 416; St. L. 21b, 3131 f; WA, Br 11, 161. Was Melanchthon esp. touchy because of the differences which existed between him and Luther on the interpretation of the Lord's Supper? He seems to have had some reason for this, for it looks as if Luther had left Wittenberg without Melanchthon's even knowing his itinerary; see C.R. 5, 800. Or was Melanchthon thinking of Luther's controversy with the members of the Law Faculty? On July 14, 1545, Luther mentioned this controversy and said that he would have left Wittenberg had the decision in the controversy gone against him; WA, Br 11, 139. On this controversy, see H. Dörries, Wort und Stunde, 3: Beiträge zum Verständnis Luthers (Göttingen, 1970), 271 ff.

[9] See notes 8, 25. Melanchthon delivered the University's letter to the court in Torgau, and while there had a conference with Brück about which Brück reported to the Elector on August 3; see note 8. From Torgau Melanchthon, who was to be accompanied by Bugenhagen (see LW 48, 303, n. 44) and Major, was to continue his journey and meet with Luther in Merseburg. It is not clear whether in Torgau Melanchthon changed his plan to see Luther (so Clemen, WA, Br 11, 161; see however also ibid., n. 9), or continued his journey. At this point we can reconstruct Melanchthon's itinerary as follows: He left Wittenberg on August 2 and arrived in Torgau late that day; on August 3 he searched for the Elector in the morning, and then had lunch with Brück. Whatever Melanchthon's plans were after that, Brück did not mention them in his report to the Elector. It is important to note, however, that the Elector assumed that Melanchthon, Bugenhagen, and Major were with Luther in Zeitz when he wrote to Luther and issued his instructions for Ratzeberger (see notes 11, 12). This suggests that Melanchthon left Brück, and through him the Elector, with the impression that he would continue his journey to see Luther.

others" to negotiate with Luther for his return. The University requested the Elector to summon Luther and try to influence him to change his mind.

As a result of this request, the Elector deputized his personal physician, Matthias Ratzeberger,[10] to deal with Luther; Ratzeberger was to confer with Melanchthon first, however.[11] Ratzeberger was to give Luther the Elector's personal letter[12] (a masterpiece of psychological diplomacy) and, along with von Amsdorf, Melanchthon, Bugenhagen, and Major, to persuade Luther to change his mind.

Meanwhile Luther had gone from Zeitz to Merseburg,[13] where he met with Ratzeberger on or after August 6.[14] It becomes difficult to reconstruct Luther's activities for the days after August 6. On

---

[10] On Matthias Ratzeberger, see ADB 27, 372 ff.

[11] Only the Elector's special instructions for Ratzeberger are extant; they are printed in Enders, Briefwechsel 16, 281, n. 3, and WA, Br 11, 163 f. To strengthen his argument that, while in Torgau, Melanchthon abandoned his plan to visit Luther (see note 9), Clemen argues that according to these special instructions Ratzeberger was to confer with Melanchthon in Wittenberg. Thus Clemen presupposes that Melanchthon returned from Torgau to Wittenberg. The text presented by Clemen and Enders does not support Clemen's reconstruction of Melanchthon's activities. To the contrary, the instructions presupposed that Melanchthon, Bugenhagen, Major, von Amsdorf, and Ratzeberger were together—and this could only have been the case in Zeitz, not in Wittenberg (see esp. the suggestion that all the Wittenbergers depart together from Zeitz for Torgau); further, the instructions ordered Ratzeberger to confer with Melanchthon at a "special place," unknown to Luther—again this could only have been the case in Zeitz. Since Melanchthon was in Merseburg on August 4 (see note 54), one would have to assume (were one to accept Clemen's reconstruction) that Melanchthon traveled from Torgau to Wittenberg and from Wittenberg to Merseburg in the period from the afternoon of August 3 through August 4, which seems technically impossible. Contrary to Clemen, one has to assume that Melanchthon continued his trip from Torgau to meet with Luther. More problematic is the fact that in his August 5 letter to Luther (see note 12), as well as in his instructions for Ratzeberger, the Elector assumed Luther to be in Zeitz, even though from Luther's letter to his wife it must have been common knowledge in Wittenberg, and also in Torgau, that by that time Luther had moved on, at least to Merseburg.

[12] WA, Br 11, No. 4143, dated August 5, 1545.

[13] Luther went to Merseburg on July 30 (see note 52), stayed there until August 5, when he accompanied Jonas to Halle (preaching there on August 5) and then returned to Merseburg on August 6. Luther's activities in these first days of August can be reconstructed on the basis of the extant sermons which he preached; see Buchwald, LK, p. 156.

[14] Since the Elector's letter to Luther was dated August 5, the earliest date that Ratzeberger could have met with Luther in Merseburg (see ZKG 22 [1901], 623 f.) was August 6, the day on which Luther was again in Merseburg; see note 13.

August 7 or 8 Luther left Merseburg;[15] *we find him next in Leipzig, where he preached on August 12. On August 16 he was at the Electoral court in Torgau.*[16] *He left there on August 17 and was in Wittenberg again shortly after midnight on the same day, tired and suffering from a recurrence of his stone problem.*[17]

Contrary to Melanchthon's assumption[18] *that Luther's decision to leave Wittenberg had something to do with doctrinal matters, it is clear, on the basis of a letter written by Ratzeberger,*[19] *that Luther's decision was based on his disappointment with and anger about the conditions in Wittenberg; the decision was apparently actually made (on the spur of the moment) under the impact of some stories about Wittenberg which Luther heard in the countryside.*[20] *The Elector and Brück had a much more realistic view of the situation than Melanchthon had.*[21] *The Elector simply talked about those complaints Luther had which he felt could be settled. And Brück argued that one should not make so much ado about it all, saying that, thank God, it would not be as easy to dispose of the property as Luther thought it would be; while Brück was well aware that Luther might be stubborn and remain "sitting on his head," he also realized that in view of the problems which would arise in connection with the sale of Luther's property, the last word on this matter had not yet been spoken.*

How serious Luther was about his decision to leave Wittenberg could not be ascertained. His continued absence from Wittenberg without any given reason seems to indicate that Luther was indeed serious. On the other hand, while in Merseburg, Luther supposedly was promised "in the name of the church and the state" that the poor moral conditions in Wittenberg would be corrected;[22] *according to Köstlin-Kawerau,*[23] *after Luther's return to Wittenberg, the city council and the University did indeed draft (upon the Elector's*

---

[15] See *C.R.* 5, 830.
[16] Enders, *Briefwechsel* 16, 284.
[17] *ARG* 25 (1928), 23 f.; *WA*, Br 11, 168.
[18] See note 8.
[19] See *ZKG* 22 (1901), 623 f.
[20] See below.
[21] See the Elector's letter to Luther (note 12), his special instructions for Ratzeberger (note 11), and Brück's report to the Elector (note 8).
[22] So according to Ratzeberger's letter, *ZKG* 22 (1901), 623.
[23] 2, 608.

orders) ordinances directed against the poor public behavior which supposedly had caused Luther's anger. Since Luther left Merseburg on August 7 or 8, the issues must have been well on the way to being settled by that time. In any case, Luther did eventually return to Wittenberg, and Ratzeberger and Melanchthon[24] had accomplished their missions. While obviously the promises made to Luther at Merseburg and the "arm-twisting" by his friends played some part in Luther's change of heart, the fact that Luther may in any event have had second thoughts about his decision to leave Wittenberg must not be discounted.

Text in German: WA, Br 11, 149–150.[25]

To my kind and dear mistress of the house, Luther's
Catherine von Bora, a preacher, a brewer, a gardener,[26]
and whatever else she is capable of doing[27]

Grace and peace! Dear Katie! John[28] surely will tell you everything pertaining to our journey; I am not yet certain whether he should stay with me, but Doctor Caspar Cruciger[29] and Ferdinand,[30] of

---

24 See also note 54.

25 The autograph of the letter is no longer extant. What Clemen (*WA*, Br 11, No. 4139, Introduction) and others have considered to be the autograph has been identified in *WA*, Br 13, 345, addition to *loc.cit.*, as a copy written by Caspar Cruciger and added to the official letter which the University sent to the Elector (see note 8); since Cruciger obviously took along the present letter from Zeitz (see also note 31), and since the business was important, it may safely be assumed that Cruciger used extreme care in writing this text; it may further be assumed that Cruciger copied from the autograph, and that Cruciger's copy presents a text as close to the autograph as is humanly speaking possible. The *WA*, Br text reproduces this Cruciger copy, except for the address; see note 27.

26For "brewer" and "gardener," see pp. 81, n. 12, 108, n. 17, 208, n. 12.

27 The address, which is missing in the Cruciger manuscript copy (see note 25), is supplied from a manuscript copy which is deposited in Zwickau. This copy is a part of a collection of *Lutherana* put together by Stephen Tucher (and an unknown scribe) who had been a member of the Wittenberg Arts Faculty since the winter semester of 1544/45. Since Enders, *Briefwechsel* 16, 271, does not reproduce any variant readings from this Tucher copy, one has to assume that Tucher's text agrees with Cruciger's text. Perhaps it is not wrong to assume that Tucher copied from the autograph at the time that Cruciger did. That the address was indeed phrased as Tucher transmits it may be seen from the typically Luther flavor of this text. On Tucher and his work, see *WA*, Br 14, 173 (No. 390), 327.

28 See note 2.

29 See note 4.

30 See note 3.

course, will tell you.[31] Ernst von Schönfeld has treated us graciously at Löbnitz,[32] and Heintz Scherle at Leipzig even more so.[33]

I would like to arrange matters in such a way that I do not have to return to Wittenberg. My heart has become cold, so that I do not like to be there any longer. I wish you would sell the garden and field, house and all.[34] Also I would like to return the big house[35] to my Most Gracious Lord.[36] It would be best for you to move to Zölsdorf[37] as long as I am still living and able to help you to improve the little property with my salary.[38] For I hope that my Most Gracious Lord would let my salary be continued at least for one [year], that is, the last year of my life.[39] After my death the four elements[40] at Wittenberg certainly will not tolerate you [there]. Therefore it would be better to do while I am alive what certainly would have to be done then. As things are run in Witten-

---

[31] Because Luther is certain that Cruciger and von Maugis will return to Wittenberg, he takes advantage of this opportunity to send the present letter along. While it cannot be documented, John seems to have gone with Cruciger and von Maugis. Nothing can be established about John's continuing to accompany his father.

[32] According to WA, Br 13, 345, addition to WA, Br 11, 149, line 5, Ernst von Schönfeld was a brother of Ave and Margarete von Schönfeld, two of the nuns who left the nunnery in Nimbschen with Catherine von Bora; see LW 49, 115, n. 1; 105, n. 21. Luther spent the night from July 25 to 26 in Löbnitz; see also note 6.

[33] On July 26 Luther was in Leipzig, where the city council presented him with some wine (see WA, Br 11, 152, n. 5), and where he was guest of honor in the house of one of its wealthiest citizens, Heintz Scherle. On Scherle, and on Luther's visit to Leipzig, see the detailed material presented in WA, Br 5, 252; 11, 150, n. 4.

[34] The text reads: Haus und Hof, i.e., literally "house and yard." The term Hof can be used as a synonym for farm, and the phrase "Haus und Hof" often designates all the property a person owns. For more details on Luther's property, see note 26, and WA, Br 9, 575 ff.; 12, 415 ff.

[35] I.e., the main building of the former Wittenberg Augustinian monastery which had been presented to Luther as a wedding gift by Elector John; see LW 49, 59, n. 12.

[36] Elector John Frederick; see LW 48, 181 f.; see also LW 49, 58, n. 8.

[37] See p. 208, n. 13.

[38] See pp. 212 f.

[39] Literally: "at least one year of my last life [or: living]."

[40] I.e., fire, air, water, and earth. Luther intends to say that all things will cooperate to drive his family from Wittenberg, once he is dead. Luther envisioned that after his death the Wittenbergers would, e.g., demand payment for services and favors which had been freely granted Luther. In this connection materials drawn up by Luther in approximately 1542 are very instructive; see WA, Br 9, 579 ff.

berg, perhaps the people there will acquire[41] not only the dance of St. Vitus[42] or St. John,[43] but the dance of the beggars or the dance of Beelzebub, since they have started to bare women and maidens in front and back,[44] and there is no one who punishes or objects.[45] In addition the Word of God is being mocked [there]. Away from this Sodom![46] If Lecks Bachscheisse,[47] our other Rosina,[48] and [her] seducer[49] are not yet imprisoned, then help as much as you

---

41 Literally: "Perhaps Wittenberg, as it goes with its government, will acquire."

42 The help of St. Vitus (a martyr of the late third or early fourth century; see *O.D.C.C.*, pp. 1427 f.) was called upon by people who suffered from a disorder of the nervous system (convulsions, jerking, etc.) which was sometimes called St. Vitus' Dance. The German term, *Veits Tanz*, designates not only this physiological disorder but could also designate any weird, strange movements or behavior of a person.

43 I.e., the dances around the St. John's fires which were lighted on June 24.

44 This is a reference to a kind of dance which rapidly became popular in the first half of the sixteenth century. In this dance a man would spin his female partner around, and the partners would pirouette either jointly or separately. In the process the lady's skirt could fly up (i.e., the lady could be "bared" in front and back). This dance was considered by many to be highly immoral. As early as 1511, the city council of Leipzig, e.g., prohibited this dance; so did Wittenberg University in 1540, and Luther and others preached against it; see Enders, *Briefwechsel* 18, 124, n. 11.

45 See *WA*, TR 5, No. 6406.

46 Literally: "Only away and from this Sodom."

47 Luther made up this name, intending it as an insulting epithet. On the basis of note 48 it is clear that the person in question had been a maid in Luther's house who had been seduced. Nothing further could be established.

48 This is a reference to events which occurred in 1541, and which had repercussions as late as January 1544. For references, see *WA*, Br 9, 505; 10, 176, 519 ff.; *WA*, TR 5, No. 6165. One day a woman appeared at the Luther house and asked for help, saying that she was a former nun of noble birth by the name of Rosina von Truchsess. The Luthers took Rosina in, and Rosina became chief maid. Soon Luther found out that Rosina had lied, that she was in fact the daughter of a Franconian citizen who had been executed in the aftermath of the Peasants' War. Confronted with the truth, Rosina confessed, asked for forgiveness, and was forgiven. Yet her remorse was shortlived. She stole and cheated, but was always able to get away with it. As Luther said later on, she was also highly promiscuous, though she was able to keep up a pretense. Her game came to an end, however, when she became pregnant, and when, apparently, one of Luther's maids refused to perform an abortion on her. Luther fired her (this is mentioned for the first time on August 30, 1541: *WA*, Br 9, 505). Rosina took up the life of a vagabond, and again, apparently, tried to make capital from her old story. In 1544 Luther supposed her to be in Leipzig. Then she disappeared from Luther's correspondence. Luther was inclined to assume that Rosina was planted into his house by the papists in order to ruin him. "Who knows what else she had in mind [in addition to stealing and cheating] since I entrusted my chambers and children to her?" *WA*, Br 10, 520.

49 The text uses a Latin word here.

can to see that this scoundrel loses what he has gained.[50] While in the country I have heard more than I find out while in Wittenberg.[51] Consequently I am tired of this city and do not wish to return. May God help me with this.

The day after tomorrow[52] I shall drive to Merseburg, for Sovereign George[53] has very urgently asked that I do so.[54] Thus I shall be on the move, and will rather eat the bread of a beggar than

---

[50] Literally: "this scoundrel must cheat himself." For "cheat" a four-letter word is used.

[51] The text does not make clear whether this sentence refers to "Lecks Bachscheisse" or to the general situation in Wittenberg.

[52] I.e., July 30. That Luther actually did travel on July 30 from Zeitz to Merseburg cannot be established, though there is no material available that would force one to assume that Luther's plans were changed.

[53] George III of Anhalt; see NDB 6, 197.

[54] In the spring of 1545 Duke August of the Albertine family of Saxony (see LW 48, 110, n. 20, and above, p. 185) took over the secular administration of the diocese of Merseburg, and George III of Anhalt was placed in charge of the spiritual affairs of the diocese, i.e., he became bishop. He wanted to be ordained to this office. He therefore asked Matthias von Jagow, the bishop of Brandenburg (who in 1539 had renounced the papacy and turned evangelical; see ADB 20, 654 ff.), to perform this service; since in the meantime Bishop Jagow died, George asked Luther (in a way and on a date unknown to us) to perform this service. On August 2 Luther, with Jonas and others, performed this ordination in the cathedral at Merseburg. For details, see the materials cited in WA, Br 11, No. 4141, Introduction, and WA 48, 228 f. When Luther informs his wife that he will go to Merseburg because George of Anhalt has urged him to do so, and then goes on to say that he would rather move around than return home, Luther leaves the impression that the trip to Merseburg was an afterthought, and that Katie did not know of the pending ordination of George of Anhalt. This is, of course, possible but not probable. The ordination was an extremely important event which was carefully prepared by George. A liturgy had to be devised. (Luther's long letter to George of Anhalt, dated July 10, 1545 [WA, Br 11, No. 4133], which dealt with ceremonies and which was Luther's reply to a no-longer extant letter of George, may very well have had something to do with George's preparation of this liturgy.) Luther and the assistants had to be invited; other arrangements had to be made. While it is peculiar that in the extant material in WA, Br, Kawerau, Jonas Briefwechsel, and C.R. the preparation for the ordination is not mentioned, and that as late as August 5 the Elector was of the opinion that Luther was in Zeitz and therefore was apparently not aware of this ordination (see note 11), it would be even more peculiar to suggest that the ordination was a spur of the moment affair, and that George asked Luther for this service for the first time on July 27 or 28 just because he heard that Luther was in Zeitz, i.e., in the neighborhood. It is more natural to assume that Luther's trip had two purposes from the beginning, namely, the negotiations in Zeitz (see note 5), and George's ordination. Luther's statement above would then simply have to be understood as an attempt on Luther's part to keep his wife informed. For Luther's stay in Merseburg, see note 13. Prior to Luther's and Jonas' departure for Halle, i.e., on or prior to August 5, Melanchthon arrived in Merseburg, for he drafted the ordination certificate for George of Anhalt. This draft was signed by Luther, Jonas, and others. August 4/5 were the latest dates that Jonas could have

torture and upset my poor old [age] and final days with the filth at Wittenberg which destroys my hard and faithful work.[55] You might inform Doctor Pomer[56] and Master[57] Philip[58] of this (if you wish), and [you might ask] if Doctor Pomer would wish to say farewell to Wittenberg in my behalf. For I am unable any longer to endure my anger [about] and dislike [of this city].

With this I commend you to God. Amen.

July 28, 1545   MARTIN LUTHER, DOCTOR

313

To Count Albrecht of Mansfeld
[Wittenberg,] December 6, 1545

In 1420[1] the Grafschaft Mansfeld, which Luther often called his fatherland or his native land, had been divided between the two sons of the then ruling count, and in 1501 it was once more divided into three parts, whereby Count Albrecht III received the area around Eisleben, the town in which Luther had been born. Notwithstanding these divisions, the rich mining business of the territory (as well as other business matters) was jointly administered by the whole ruling family. This proved a constant source of irritation to the various members of the three branches of the Mansfeld dynasty especially since, much to the dismay of the other counts,

---

signed this draft; therefore Melanchthon must have been in Merseburg by that time. He had been in Torgau on August 3 (see note 9) and left there, probably in the afternoon, and arrived in Merseburg on August 4. The final form of the ordination certificate was predated to August 2, the date of the ordination; *WA*, Br 11, No. 4141. It was written by Paul Eber, shows a notation in Melanchthon's handwriting, and was signed by Luther, Jonas, and others; consequently Eber must have finished writing the document prior to Luther's and Jonas' departure from Merseburg on August 5. Melanchthon stayed in Merseburg while Luther went to Halle; the time when he and Luther talked about Luther's decision not to return to Wittenberg could not be established; but there can be no doubt that they discussed the matter.

55 Or: "I shall be on the move . . . Wittenberg at the expense of the loss [i.e., because I move around I lose the reward] of my hard and faithful work."

56 John Bugenhagen, the pastor of the City Church; see *LW* 48, 303, n. 44.

57 I.e., Master of Arts.

58 Philip Melanchthon; see *LW* 48, 77, n. 3.

1 The material presented in the following paragraph is taken from *WA*, Br 12, 364 f., where further details and documentation can be found.

Albrecht (the most capable ruler among the counts) operated with farsighted, innovative, perhaps even ruthless administrative policies. In addition Albrecht supposedly usurped the rights and property of one of the members of another branch of the family, founded a new town for the miners outside Eisleben (which the other counts thoroughly disliked), and jeopardized the law of patronage of one of the wealthy churches in Eisleben. Real and imagined rights and privileges were violated by Albrecht, real and imagined advantages were gained by him. Notwithstanding constant negotiations, mediations, and partial compromises, there was ever increasing bitterness dividing the ruling family of Mansfeld. The situation was right for one of those private, local feuds which were typical of Germany at that time.

Luther was genuinely distressed by these developments.[2] After 1540 he became increasingly involved in these matters, first by way of the personal affairs of relatives and friends "back home,"[3] and then officially, because of the patronage law of the church in Eisleben[4]—and apparently also because Count Albrecht wanted him as mediator. At the beginning of October, 1545, Luther, Melanchthon, and Jonas were, therefore, in Mansfeld, but accomplished nothing since some of the counts were absent.[5] In a pleading letter[6] Luther urged Counts Philip and John George to make peace with Albrecht, who in turn, so Luther assured the counts, would also be willing to come to terms. Luther also offered his further services to help bring the quarreling parties together.

In the following letter Luther informs Count Albrecht of the willingness of Counts Philip and John George to make peace, and tells of their request that he, Luther, set the date for a meeting. As a

---

[2] See, e.g., WA, Br 11, 189 f.

[3] See WA, Br 9, No. 3481; 10, Nos. 3723, 3724, 3755; 11, p. 191.

[4] See WA, Br 10, No. 3760.

[5] According to Buchwald, LK, p. 157, Luther was absent from Wittenberg from October 3 to approximately October 12. The reason for Luther's trip to Mansfeld is not clear. Luther could have gone there in response to Albrecht's request; see also note 9. On the other hand, on the basis of all available sources it seems that someone in Mansfeld (a relative?) asked Luther for help, and that Luther was eager to go there; see WA, Br 11, 191, n. 1. In any case, while he was in Mansfeld Luther was able to discuss the situation only with Count Albrecht (see WA, Br 11, 189), since the other counts were involved in a military expedition of the Smalcaldic League against Duke Henry of Brunswick; see WA, Br 11, 191, n. 1; Ranke 2^{IV}, 170 ff., 225 f.

[6] WA, Br 11, No. 4157, dated October 7.

result of this request, Luther says, he is changing his plans to go to Eisleben now and then on to Mansfeld for Christmas. He promises to come to Eisleben after January 1 in order to get the mediation negotiations started in spite of other pressing tasks. He expresses his confidence that Count Albrecht will stand by his offer to negotiate, and thus demonstrate his good will toward ending this quarrel.

On Count Albrecht, see LW 49, 103, n. 6.

Text in German: WA, Br 11, 225–226.[7]

To the Magnanimous, Noble Lord, Sir Albrecht,

count and lord at Mansfeld,

my gracious and dear lord of my [native] land

Before all else, grace and peace in the Lord, and my poor *Pater noster!*[8] Gracious Lord: I was willing to be with Your Grace once again[9] this coming Monday,[10] as I had offered. Yet today, at this hour, a letter[11] from my gracious lords, Count Philip and Count John George,[12] arrived in which they give me a very gracious answer to my previous letter;[13] I am extremely pleased with this. The

---

[7] The letter is extant in a manuscript copy, and in the common editions of Luther's works.

[8] See p. 69, n. 4.

[9] The meaning of this phrase is unclear. Luther could have meant to say that once again he was ready to go to Mansfeld to mediate the affair in response to Albrecht's request, as was the case in October (see also note 5). Nothing could be established about Luther's intention to go to Mansfeld or Eisleben in December. Had this date been discussed with Albrecht in October? Or did Luther simply want to accomplish two things, a Christmas visit in Mansfeld (see below) and the mediation of the quarrel?

[10] December 6, 1545, the day on which Luther wrote this letter, was a Sunday. "This coming Monday" can only be December 14, not only (as Clemen [WA, Br 11, 226, n. 2] suggests) because Luther would probably have written "tomorrow" had he meant December 7, but also in view of Luther's plans. To spend Christmas in Mansfeld (see below) Luther would hardly have had to leave Wittenberg on December 7, even if he intended to visit with Albrecht and engage in the mediation either in Mansfeld itself or in Eisleben. Further, it would have been very difficult, if not impossible, for Luther to be in Mansfeld on December 7, i.e., in the midst of a very severe winter (see WA, Br 11, 277, n. 12) to have made a journey of approximately ninety kilometers (as the crow flies) in a day. At some time and under circumstances unknown to us (see note 9) Luther had decided to be with Count Albrecht on December 14 (either at Eisleben or Mansfeld), to try then to negotiate a settlement of the issues dividing the counts of Mansfeld, and thereafter to spend Christmas in Mansfeld, obviously with relatives—his brother James lived there (see LW 49, 268, n. 4), as did friends.

[11] This letter is no longer extant.

[12] They were members of one of the branches of the ruling Mansfeld family (see WA, Br 12, 366) and the chief opponents of Count Albrecht.

[13] See note 6.

counts very kindly offer to participate in negotiations with Your Grace. They indicate that I am to name a [meeting] day after the upcoming Leipzig Fair.[14] Therefore, once again I have to remain here, though I had made up my mind to spend this Christmas at Mansfeld. Since the counts demonstrate such kindness toward Your Grace and such graciousness toward me, I shall appear in Mansfeld soon after the close of the Leipzig Fair; I shall let you, the two parties, yourselves name a day, and shall summon whomever you wish to appear or have present. I am ready to give up eight days, one way or the other, for this matter—though I have very much to do—so that I may lie down in my coffin with joy, having previously been able to reconcile the dear lords of my native land and having seen unity of hearts established.[15] I have no doubt that Your Grace will comply with Your Grace's [previous] offer,[16] and that [Your Grace] would like to see this quarrel settled.

With this I commend Your Grace to the dear God.

December 6, 1545[17]   Your Grace's willing [servant],

MARTIN LUTHER, DOCTOR

314

To Mrs. Martin Luther
Halle, January 25, 1546

"I am writing, my James, as an old man, decrepit, sluggish, tired, cold, and now also one-eyed,[1] *and as a man who now that he has*

---

[14] I.e., shortly after January 1.

[15] The last portion of this sentence (from "and having seen") has been freely translated.

[16] This offer was the result of Luther's October visit to Mansfeld; see Introduction.

[17] Notwithstanding this letter, according to which Luther intended to delay his next visit to the counts of Mansfeld until after January 1, Luther and Melanchthon left Wittenberg on December 22 and traveled via Halle to Mansfeld, where they arrived in the evening of December 24; they returned to Wittenberg on January 7, with Melanchthon deathly ill. See Buchwald, *LK*, p. 158; *WA*, Br 11, No. 4184, Introduction. Thus Luther fulfilled his original intention to spend Christmas in Mansfeld. During this visit preparations were made for further discussions, which were to begin on January 25, 1546.

[1] Except for the reference to the weakness of one eye, Luther had used similar terms to describe his condition in other letters to Propst; see p. 245 (March/April 1544), and *WA*, Br 10, 23 (March 1542). Apparently during the last years

died would be given the highly deserved rest (as it seems to me) he was hoping for. [But] as if I had never worked, written, said, or done anything, so I am now overloaded with matters on which I have to write, speak, negotiate, and act. Yet Christ is all in all; he is capable of doing all things, and he does them; blessed be he in eternity. Amen." So wrote Luther to James Propst, his friend of many years, on January 17, 1546.[2] *Approximately a week later, on January 23, Luther embarked on yet another journey to the counts of Mansfeld to mediate their controversy,*[3] *that "pig business" as Gregory Brück called it.*[4] *And three weeks later, while in his native town of Eisleben, Luther passed away in the early hours of February 18, having successfully accomplished his mission.*[5]

It is one of the ironies of history that the man who for approximately one half of his life had stood at the center of controversy, and who in the words of the Edict of Worms of 1521 was "like a

---

of Luther's life the sight (see also LW 49, 314) in one of his eyes rapidly deteriorated. According to WA, Br 11, 264, n. 2 (a reference which has to be compared with the material cited in WA, Br 13, 351, addition to *loc. cit.*) there is available a picture of Luther from the year 1543 in which one can detect a weakness in the left eye.

[2] WA, Br 11, 263 f. On James Propst, see LW 48, 233, n. 34.

[3] See pp. 281 f. On this journey to Eisleben, see Buchwald, *LK*, p. 159; WA 54, 478 f.; Strieder, *passim*; Schubart, *passim*. The winter of 1545–46 was a severe one (see WA, Br 11, 277, n. 12). Luther left Wittenberg on January 23 (C.R. 6, 19), spent the first night in Bitterfeld, and arrived in Halle before noon on January 24, where he stayed with Jonas; WA 54, 487. Luther was accompanied by his three sons, John, Martin, and Paul (see WA 54, 487), and also by John Aurifaber; at least Aurifaber was with Luther in Eisleben. In Halle, Jonas joined the Luther party which, after an unsuccessful attempt to depart from town on January 25, finally left Halle on January 28 and arrived in Eisleben the same day in the late afternoon. Luther stayed in the house of the city clerk, John Albrecht, which belonged to the city council and was used as quarters for official guests; see WA, Br 11, 280, n. 7. On January 29 the mediation negotiations began in which, in addition to Luther and Jonas, legal experts and members of the neighboring nobility participated; among them was Count John Henry of Schwarzburg with whom Luther had corresponded as early as 1522; see LW 49, 19. As the following letters indicate, the negotiations dragged on and sorely tried Luther's patience. Luther finally sat in on the daily negotiations only for short periods of time; see Kawerau, *Jonas Briefwechsel* 2, 177. It was Luther's sheer presence and the force of his personality which brought the negotiations to a successful conclusion on February 16 and 17.

[4] C.R. 6, 12.

[5] For the eyewitness reports of Luther's last hours, see Strieder, *passim*; Schubart, *passim*; *The Last Days of Luther by Justus Jonas, Michael Coelius and Others*, trans. and ed. M. Ebon, introduction by T. G. Tappert (Garden City, N.Y., 1970); for general information, see Köstlin-Kawerau 2, 622 ff.; Schwiebert, pp. 747 ff.; for the medical circumstances, see the title cited on p. 165, n. 3.

madman plotting the manifest destruction of the holy church," who
"writes nothing which does not arouse and promote sedition, dis-
cord, war, murder, robbery and arson"[6] was to spend his declining
physical strength in efforts to bring about peace among the ruling
family of his native land.

Letters Nos. 314 through 325 are all of the extant letters which
Luther wrote during these final weeks of his life while he was away
from Wittenberg.[7] In letter No. 314, written from Halle two days
after Luther had left Wittenberg, Luther informs his wife that he is
unable to continue his journey because a flood and the drifting of
the ice on the Saale River make the crossing of this river too dangerous. Jokingly he mentions that under these circumstances Katie
would certainly have suggested not going on; by not continuing the
journey, Luther gently teases, Katie could see that he at least once
followed her advice.

Text in German: WA, Br 11, 269.[8]

To my kind and dear Katie Luther,[9] a brewer and a judge[10]
at the pig market[11] at Wittenberg: *Personal*

Grace and Peace in the Lord! Dear Katie! Today at eight we drove
away from Halle, yet did not get to Eisleben, but returned to Halle
again by nine. For a huge female Anabaptist met us with waves of
water and great floating pieces of ice; she threatened to baptize us
again, and has covered the [whole] countryside.[12] But we are also

---

[6] Hillerbrand, pp. 95, 98.

[7] In fact, together with the materials discussed on pp. 317 f., these letters are
the last materials extant from Luther's pen.

[8] The *WA*, Br text is based on a manuscript copy which was made in the
eighteenth century, supposedly from the autograph. In comparison with this
text, the many other witnesses which in part give different readings are of
secondary importance, since the variant readings demonstrate efforts to improve
or even explain the text and content of the letter.

[9] See p. 48, n. 9.

[10] The text uses for both nouns the German female form so that one would
have to translate literally: "a brewress and a she-judge". For "brewer," see
pp. 81, 95. "Judge" could very well be a jovial allusion to Catherine Luther's
domestic ability and "government" (so Clemen in *WA*, Br 11, 269, n. 1), esp.
if one considers that in front of friends Luther liked to play the henpecked
husband (see *ibid.*, 270, n. 9).

[11] See p. 208, n. 12.

[12] I.e., a sudden thaw (see also p. 292) broke the ice in the Saale river and
caused the river to go over the banks.

unable to return because of the Mulde [River] at Bitterfeld,[13] and are forced to stay captive here at Halle between the waters—not that we are thirsty to drink of them.[14] Instead we take good beer from Torgau and good wine from the Rhine, with which we refresh and comfort ourselves in the meantime, hoping that the rage of the Saale [River] may wear itself out today. For since the ferryman and the people themselves were of little courage [to try to cross], we did not want to go into the water[15] and tempt God. For the devil is angry at us, and he lives in the water.[16] Foresight is better than hindsight, and there is no need for us to prepare a fool's delight for the pope and his hangers-on.[17] I did not think that the Saale could create such a flood[18] and rumble over the stones[19] and everything in such a way.

No more for now. You people pray for us, and be good. I am sure that, if you were here, you too would have advised us to proceed in this way; [so,] you see, at least once we are following your advice. With this I commend you to God. Amen.

On the day of the conversion of St. Paul,[20] when we too turned away from the Saale and returned to Halle.[21] 1546[22]

MARTIN LUTHER, DOCTOR

---

13 I.e., return to Wittenberg, because to do so Luther would have to cross the Mulde.

14 The translation follows the interpunctuation given in the WA, Br text. According to the interpunctuation given in Rückert, LB, p. 425, one would have to translate: ". . . between the waters. Not that . . . them; instead we take . . ."

15 I.e., cross the river by ferry.

16 See also WA, TR 3, No. 3841, 6, No. 6562.

17 The text reads Schupen, i.e., scales, e.g., of a fish, or plates in an armored suit. Luther used the Latin equivalent, squama, quite often in connection with Antichrist, or the pope, to designate their followers. See, e.g. LW 48, 321, where the phrase has been translated as "Antichrist and his armor." See also WA, RN 48, 101, No. 134.

18 Literally: "bath".

19 I.e., the cobblestones of the street(s) paralleling the river.

20 I.e., January 25.

21 In the German phrasing this sentence is a pun and would have to be translated literally: "On the day of the turning around of St. Paul on which we too turned around [i.e., away] from the Saale toward Halle".

22 As Melanchthon informed Luther on January 31, the present letter was most welcome to Catherine Luther, who had been deeply worried about her husband since she had heard of the flooding; see WA, Br 11, 274.

315

To George of Anhalt
Eisleben,[1] January 29, 1546

Luther arrived in Eisleben on January 28. The next day he wrote the following letter to George of Anhalt, confirming the receipt of a letter from him. Luther also tells George that Melanchthon stayed in Wittenberg because he was sick. Then Luther assures George that he remembers well his promise to visit George, that he cannot keep this promise at the moment, since he is an official guest of the counts of Mansfeld, but that he intends to fulfill it in the spring; he hopes George will understand this. Luther mentions that the Council of Trent has been officially opened, but adds that he has little hope that it will accomplish anything positive.

On George of Anhalt, see p. 280, n. 53.

Text in Latin: WA, Br 11, 273.[2]

To the Most Reverend Father and Lord in Christ, Sir George,
most worthy bishop[3] of the church[4] of Merseburg,[5]
most illustrious sovereign of Anhalt,
noble count of Ascania, and famous lord of Bernburg,
my Lord to be venerably esteemed

Grace and peace in the Lord! Most Illustrious Sovereign, I have received Your Lordship's letter[6] addressed to Master[7] Philip[8] and me. Because of illness, Master Philip has stayed at home.[9] Only I

---

[1] See p. 285, n. 3.

[2] The letter is extant as autograph.

[3] See *LW* 49, 87, n. 5.

[4] See *LW* 49, 61, n. 9.

[5] See p. 280, n. 54.

[6] Or: "letters". Whether George wrote one letter addressed jointly to Luther and Melanchthon, or two letters, addressed to them separately, cannot be established. In any case, the communication was sent to Eisleben; see note 11.

[7] I.e., Master of Arts.

[8] Philip Melanchthon; see *LW* 48, 77, n. 3.

[9] Melanchthon, who had returned from the December journey to Mansfeld severely ill (see p. 284, n. 17), and who was disgusted with the affairs of the counts of Mansfeld anyhow, stayed home this time, contrary to the expectations of George. How seriously Melanchthon's illness was taken by Luther and his friends can be seen from the fact that Melanchthon was not sent to the Colloquy of Regensburg; see *WA*, Br 11, No. 4184.

am here, along with Doctor Justus Jonas.[10] I remember well the promise I made and have not yet fulfilled,[11] but carriage and horsemen are not at my disposal. The counts of Mansfeld have summoned and conducted me [to this town] with many horsemen[12] with whom I have to travel using a route they themselves[13] determined. Yet I shall do all in my power to fulfill my promise sometime this coming spring. For I hope that then everything will be safer. Therefore in the meantime I ask Your Highness to accept this delay with good grace.

I have no news, for I assume that Your Highness has heard that the council has been opened (as they call it) by the Pope; that is, it has begun.[14] But the middle will be slow [in coming], and the end will be nothing,[15] [except] that the Roman Sirens[16] will vex the people, as is the custom, style, nature, and age-old wickedness in that Babylon.[17] May the Lord arise[18] and scatter his enemies.[19] Amen. Amen. Amen. In him farewell to Your Highness, to whom I commend myself with devout prayer.

From Eisleben, January 29, 1546

Your Highness' dedicated

MARTIN LUTHER, DOCTOR

---

10 See *LW* 48, 275, n. 3.

11 On the basis of an excuse made by Luther in a December 25, 1545, letter written to George of Anhalt from Mansfeld (*WA*, Br 11, 242 f.), to the effect that in view of Melanchthon's illness he, Luther, could not keep his promise and visit George now, it is safe to suggest that on a date unknown to us Luther promised to visit George in Merseburg. Since George heard that Luther (and he thought also Melanchthon) was on his way to Eisleben, he sent a no-longer extant letter (or letters) to Eisleben reminding his friends of the promised visit (as he had also done in December by sending a no-longer extant letter to Mansfeld).

12 At the border of the *Grafschaft*, when he finally crossed the Saale river on January 28 (see p. 285, n. 3), Luther was received by an honor guard of sixty horsemen; see *WA*, Br 11, 274, n. 4 (other sources give different numbers).

13 I.e., either the counts of Mansfeld or the members of the honor guard.

14 On December 13, 1545, the Council of Trent was solemnly opened by a representative of Pope Paul III; see Jedin, pp. 574 ff.

15 See also *LW* 49, 367.

16 The Sirens, mythological creatures (half woman, half bird), known esp. from Homer's *Odyssey*, tried to lure innocent people to their destruction with their "beautiful" songs. See *O.C.D.*, p. 842.

17 See Rev. 18.

18 This may be an allusion to the opening words of *Exsurge, Domine* (*Arise, O Lord*), the papal bull of June 15, 1520, in which Luther was threatened with excommunication unless he would recant within sixty days; see *LW* 48, 179, n. 1.

19 See Num. 10:35.

316

To Mrs. Martin Luther
[Eisleben,]¹ February 1, 1546

In Luther's last years he became even more firmly set against those who he felt were enemies of Christ; these included not only the enthusiasts and the papists, but also—on the basis of their religion —the Jews.² In the following letter Luther informs his wife that on the journey to Eisleben he had become dizzy, that this had been due to his own carelessness, but that she would probably have said it was the fault of the Jews. He mentions that he passed through a village in which "many" Jews are living, that more than fifty Jews are living in Eisleben, that Count Albrecht has outlawed them, and that he would have to deal with this problem. Luther assures his wife that he is well again and that the beer of Naumburg agrees with him and even provides him with a laxative. He also tells his wife that their sons have gone to Mansfeld. Luther closes by extending greetings to the whole house.

Text in German: WA, Br 11, 275–276.³

To my dearly beloved mistress of the house, Catherine Luther,⁴
a doctor, the lady of Zölsdorf [and] of the pig market,⁵
and whatever else she is capable of being

Before all else, grace and peace in Christ, and my old, poor, and, as Your Grace knows, powerless love. Dear Katie. Yes, on the way, shortly before Eisleben, I became dizzy.⁶ That was my fault. Had you been here, however, you would have said that it was the fault

---

¹ See p. 285, n. 3.
² On Luther and the Jews, see *LW* 47, 57 ff.; see also G. Rupp, *Martin Luther and the Jews* (London, 1972).
³ The letter is extant in manuscript copies, and in the common editions of Luther's works.
⁴ See p. 48, n. 9.
⁵ For "doctor," see *LW* 49, 236, n. 10, 401, n. 7; for "Zölsdorf," see p. 208, n. 13.; for "pig market," see p. 208, n. 12.
⁶ The text reads: *Ich bin ia schwach gewesen.* The *ia* (i.e., yes, or of course) suggests that Luther was replying to a no-longer extant letter of his wife in which she inquired about his health.

of the Jews or their god. For shortly before Eisleben we had to travel through a village[7] in which many Jews are living, [and] perhaps they have attacked me so painfully.[8] At this time over fifty Jews reside here in the city of Eisleben.[9] It is true that when I passed by the village such a cold wind blew from behind into the carriage and on my head through the beret, [that it seemed] as if it intended to turn my brain to ice. This might have helped me somewhat to become dizzy. But thank God now I am well, except for the fact that beautiful women tempt me so much that I neither care nor worry about becoming unchaste.[10]

After the main issues[11] have been settled, I have to start expelling the Jews.[12] Count Albrecht[13] is hostile to them and has already outlawed them.[14] But no one harms them as yet. If God grants it I shall aid Count Albrecht from the pulpit, and outlaw them too.[15]

I am drinking beer from Naumburg which tastes to me almost like the beer from Mansfeld which you praised to me. It agrees with me well and gives me about three bowel movements in three hours in the morning. The day before yesterday your little sons[16]

---

[7] I.e., Rissdorf, east of Eisleben; see WA, Br 11, 276, n. 4, and 13, 352, addition to loc. cit.

[8] In the following letter to Melanchthon, Luther explains the circumstances slightly differently. According to the "official report" (see p. 285, n. 5) about Luther's death, written by Jonas and the Eisleben pastor Michael Coelius (see LW 49, 320, n. 5), Luther said in the carriage, as he began to feel ill: "The devil does this to me every time I intend and ought to undertake something important—he first tempts me in this way and attacks me with such a tentatio [i.e., Anfechtung; see LW 48, 28, n. 10]." WA 54, 487 f.

[9] When the Jews had been expelled from the Magdeburg territory by the archbishop of Magdeburg, they found refuge in the Grafschaft Mansfeld. For details, see K. Krumhaar, Die Grafschaft Mansfeld im Reformationszeitalter (Eisleben, 1855), p. 288.

[10] Luther is probably needling Katie with these remarks. An alternate and rather different translation, which is also a possibility, is: "except for the fact that beautiful women do not bother me, so that I neither care for nor am afraid of any kind of unchastity."

[11] I.e., among the counts; see pp. 281 f.

[12] See p. 303, n. 19.

[13] See LW 49, 103, n. 6.

[14] Nothing could be established about this event.

[15] See also p. 317.

[16] I.e., John, Martin, and Paul, who had accompanied their father to Eisleben (see p. 285, n. 3), had gone to Mansfeld, obviously to visit relatives.

drove to Mansfeld because John of Jena[17] so humbly begged them to do so. I do not know what they are doing there. If it were cold they could join the people who are freezing; however, since it is warm they certainly could do or endure anything else, as they are pleased.

With this I commend you and the whole house to God; give my greetings to all the table companions.

February 1, 1546

Your loving

MARTIN LUTHER, who has grown old[18]

317

To Philip Melanchthon
Eisleben,[1] February 1, 1546

Luther thanks Melanchthon for his prayers and urges him to continue them. He points out that he himself is old now and ought to be retired. But notwithstanding his age, Luther continues, he is now being drawn into a struggle, and he wishes Melanchthon could be with him, were this not harmful to the health of his friend. Then Luther informs Melanchthon about recent developments: "Today" the most difficult issue in the controversy among the counts of Mansfeld has been settled; from now on the battle should be less severe, though Luther does expect that Wolf Pucher, a wealthy citizen and official of Eisleben, might still cause problems; he admits that with his criticism of legal sophistry he himself has deeply offended one of the jurists; on his journey to Eisleben he had been ill because he carelessly overexerted himself. Throughout the letter Luther asks repeatedly for Melanchthon's prayers. He closes with greetings to his co-workers in Wittenburg and thanks them for their prayers.

---

[17] See p. 129, n. 42. I.e., boredom or general curiosity made the sons go to Mansfeld.
[18] Or: "Martin Luther, your old one whom you love."
[1] See p. 285, n. 3.

On Philip Melanchthon, see LW, 48, 77, n. 3.
Text in Latin: WA, Br 11, 277–278.[2]

To the man of outstanding learning, Mr. Philip Melanchthon,
Master [of Arts],[3] theologian and servant of God,
my dearest brother in the Lord

Grace and peace in the Lord! I do thank you,[4] my Philip, for your prayers for me, and I ask you to continue to pray. You know that I am an old man, and a man who ought to be retired.[5] [But] now I am being drawn into a struggle[6] which is troublesome to my studies, totally incompatible with my disposition, and quite bothersome to my old age; consequently I certainly wish you were here, were it not that consideration for your health forces me instead to think it is good that we left you at home.[7] With God's help we have slain today the most bristly of all porcupines, the case concerning Newtown[8]—though not without a great fight. We hope that finally the battles will be less pitched if it pleases God.

I have deeply offended Doctor Melchior[9] (as I see) since I really growled at the rigidity or bristles of the law—even though he himself had offended me first by the tremendously rude loudmouth-

---

[2] The letter is extant as autograph. The translation is based on the WA, Br text (which is taken from a manuscript copy made of the autograph) which for this translation has been clarified on the basis of some of the more correct readings of the autograph provided in WA, Br 13, 352, addition to WA, Br 11, No. 4196, even though this is not specifically stated in each case.
[3] Literally: "Mr. Master Philip Melanchthon."
[4] Or: "I, too, thank you." In this case it could not be established who else was grateful for Melanchthon's prayers. Had Luther received a letter from his wife (see also p. 290, n. 6), in which he was informed how grateful she was for Melanchthon's prayers on Luther's behalf? If one adopts the translation given above, then it seems that Luther responded to a letter from Melanchthon.
[5] Literally: "someone who must be presented with a thin staff also in my professional work." "To present a thin staff" is a technical phrase used by classical writers and recorded by Erasmus (*Adagia* I: 9, 24; Clericus 2, 343B/C). A thin staff was given, e.g., to a gladiator who could no longer perform his duties.
[6] I.e., the quarrel among the counts of Mansfeld; see pp. 281 f.
[7] See p. 288.
[8] "The case concerning Newtown [i.e., the town founded by Count Albrecht outside of Eisleben; see p. 282]" is written in German. As it turned out, Luther was too optimistic at this point.
[9] On Melchior King (or Kling), a member of Wittenberg's Law Faculty, see *ADB* 16, 185 f.; Friedensburg, *GUW*, pp. 201 ff.

edness[10] with which, even prior to the battle, he bragged about gloriously exaggerated victories. The jurists[11] are fooling themselves with their little bits of knowledge of the law, while in my opinion they all together have not the slightest idea of the usage of the law. Like hired pettifoggers they behave without any honor; they care nothing about peace, the commonweal, or religion. As usual, however, these are the things we are concerned about.

During the trip[12] both a loss of consciousness[13] and that illness which you usually call *humor ventriculi*[14] caught me. For I went on foot, but this was beyond my strength, so that I perspired. Afterwards in the carriage when my shirt also had gotten cold from the sweat, the cold grabbed a muscle in my left arm. From this came that tightness of the heart and something like shortness of breath.[15] It is my own stupid fault. But now I am quite well again; how long—well that, of course, I do not know, since one cannot trust old age, in view of the fact that youth . . .[16]

---

[10] Luther wrote *vultuositas*, i.e., a noun which he himself created (see WA, Br 11, 278, n. 4) from the Latin adjective *vultuosus,-a,-um*; according to Lewis and Short, *s.v.*, this means "of an expressive countenance, full of expression, full of airs or grimaces, grimacing, affected." While the translation is obviously free, the context seems to justify it.

[11] On Luther's negative attitude toward the jurists, see the title cited on p. 274, n. 8.

[12] For the following see also pp. 290 f.

[13] Luther used *syncope*.

[14] *Ventriculus* designates in a particular sense the stomach and in a wider sense any cavity of the body. In connection with the heart it designates the chamber(s) of the heart. On the basis of the following statement it is clear that Luther was thinking of the heart. The word *humor* is not a misspelling of *rumor*, i.e., murmur, for Melanchthon used the same word when he announced Luther's death to the students in Wittenberg on February 19; see Strieder, p. 11. On that occasion Melanchthon said that Luther had suffered from an oppression of the *humores* in the orifice of the *ventriculum*. *Umor* designates anything liquid which in connection with the heart would obviously be the blood. *Humor ventriculi* would then designate the circulatory system and conveys the idea that Luther experienced an impediment of the flow of blood to the heart. The resulting condition ("tightness of the heart," "shortness of breath") seems to suggest that Luther suffered an attack of *angina pectoris*. See also ZKG 46 (1928), 407 ff.

[15] According to the Jonas-Coelius report (see p. 285, n. 5), Luther had been very weak, so that one feared for his life; WA 54, 487. In Jonas' personal report to Elector John Frederick (see LW 48, 181 f.) written on February 18 at 5:00 A.M., the incident is described in a less dramatic way; Strieder, p. 1.

[16] Due to a fold in the paper the remaining words of this sentence cannot be deciphered.

Thus far God has at least granted that all the counts,[17] together and individually toward one another, are demonstrating extraordinary good will. Pray that God may continue and increase this. Now that we have defeated Enceladus and Typhoeus[18] we shall tomorrow pursue the remaining [monsters], among whom we suspect that Pucher will give us something to do.[19] But God lives, and he is to retain the victory.[20] Amen.

Farewell in the Lord, my Philip, and greet all—especially the Doctor Pastor[21] [and] Doctor Cruciger[22]—for whose prayers we are thankful, surely trusting that God will hear them.[23]

Eisleben, February 1, 1546   MARTIN LUTHER, DOCTOR

318

To Philip Melanchthon
[Eisleben,][1] February 3, 1546

Luther tells Melanchthon that, contrary to statements made in the letter of February 1, the most important issue in the controversy among the counts of Mansfeld has not yet been settled. He thinks that an ill fate is harassing the Grafschaft, *that the devil has a hand*

---

[17] See pp. 281 f.

[18] Enceladus and Typhoeus were giants, those people of Greek mythology who possessed monstrous size and strength. They rebelled against the gods and, in an attempt to expel the gods from Mount Olympus, stormed the mountain. The gods, with the help of Heracles, fought back and killed all of the giants, who were buried under the volcanoes of the Mediterranean world. See *O.C.D.*, p. 387. Luther intended to say that the most important task of the mediation negotiations, namely, the case concerning Newton, had been settled; see also note 8. For other passages where Luther used this picture, see *WA* 30^{III}, 532; *WA*, Br 5, 418.

[19] Wolf Pucher was one of the mining businessmen in the *Grafschaft* Mansfeld, and was *Stadtvogt* (bailiff) in the city of Eisleben. He and Count Albrecht were not seeing eye to eye because of the Count's economic policies regarding the mines. See Krumhaar, *op. cit.* (see p. 291, n. 9), pp. 252, 272, and *passim*.

[20] See Ps. 118:15 (Luther Bible).

[21] I.e., John Bugenhagen; see *LW* 48, 303, n. 44.

[22] See *LW* 49, 104, n. 12. This last paragraph also suggests (see note 4) that Luther was responding to a no-longer extant letter from Melanchthon.

[23] The last portion of the sentence (from "surely trusting") is translated freely.

[1] See p. 285, n. 3.

in all this, and that the ruin of the Grafschaft *might be followed by the ruin of Germany. Then Luther tells of a fire he had in the chimney of his quarters, and asks Melanchthon to see to it that this event does not give rise to any rumors. He informs Melanchthon that Justus Jonas will write the news concerning political develop-ments and, in closing, asks for Melanchthon's prayer that he might soon return home.*

On Philip Melanchthon, see LW 48, 77, n. 3.
Text in Latin: WA, Br 11, 279–280.[2]

To the distinguished man, Mr. Philip Melanchthon,
a faithful servant of Christ, my dearest brother

Grace and peace in the Lord. I wrote to you the day before yester-day, my Philip, that we had slain the porcupine.[3] But this was really rejoicing before the victory,[4] [for] this territory is indeed harassed by a certain ill fate, whoever might be to blame. I fear that the ruin of Germany also will follow, once this territory has passed away. Until now I have played the role of the sick goat,[5] almost in despair concerning the successful outcome of this tragedy or com-edy. Satan lets loose all his forces. Thus far we have resisted him by prayer. Yesterday after my sermon[6] the chimney of my quarters was set on fire,[7] no doubt by Satan himself who has very much frightened my poor hosts.[8] I suspect Satan of ridiculing our efforts, or of threatening [us with] something else. You see to it that no one interprets this event as being worse [than it really is], and that the rumormongers at Leipzig[9] do not blow it out of proportion and

---

[2] The letter is extant in one manuscript copy, and in Enders, *Briefwechsel* 17, 70–71.
[3] See pp. 293, 298.
[4] See Erasmus, *Adagia* I: 7, 55; Clericus 2, 283D.
[5] A "sick," i.e., stubborn, goat makes difficulty for the goatherd. In Luther's time a story was circulating in which St. Peter was trying to shepherd a goat which caused him great difficulty; for details, see *WA*, Br 11, 280, n. 4; *LW* 54, 450.
[6] For Luther's sermon of Tuesday, February 2, see *WA* 51, 163 ff.
[7] See also pp. 302, 305.
[8] See p. 285, n. 3.
[9] The translation is based on a suggestion made in Enders, *Briefwechsel* 17, 71, n. 7.

spread rumors they themselves have invented. Doctor Jonas[10] will write you about the news we recently received concerning the Emperor and the Pope, and their war plans.[11]

Pray for me that the Lord may bring me back [home] before I am killed by these battles of the wills![12] Farewell in the Lord!

February 3, 1546   Yours,

MARTIN LUTHER, DOCTOR

319

To Philip Melanchthon
[Eisleben,][1] February 6, 1546

Luther informs Melanchthon about the lack of progress in the nego-tiations among the counts of Mansfeld,[2] and asks that Melanchthon and Brück try to see to it that Elector John Frederick recall him. Luther hopes to use such an order as a means of pressuring the parties into coming to terms, "for I feel they could not tolerate my departure without the affair having been settled." Luther also men-tions that he now sees a possible way of reaching an agreement, and that some progress is being made in the affairs of Newtown. He blames the slowness in the negotiations on the jurists, the "plagues of the human race," and their "ambiguities, sophistries, and chi-caneries," which are poisoning the climate of the negotiations and which make clear that some of the people partaking in the negotia-tions lack good will and faith.

On Philip Melanchthon, see LW 48, 77, n. 3.

Text in Latin: WA, Br 11, 285–286.[3]

---

[10] Justus Jonas; see *LW* 48, 275, n. 3, and above, p. 285, n. 3.

[11] This letter is not extant. See pp. 265, n. 4, 312, n. 30.

[12] I.e., the wills of the counts of Mansfeld; see pp. 281 f.

[1] See p. 285, n. 3.

[2] See *ibid.*

[3] The letter is extant as autograph which is deposited in Nürnberg. In Enders, *Briefwechsel* 17, and *WA*, Br 11, the February 6 letter to Katie (No. 320) precedes this present February 6 letter to Melanchthon. This fact suggests that Luther wrote first to his wife and then to Melanchthon. In the letter to his wife Luther says that the messenger was in a great hurry. This would mean—were

To the most distinguished man, Mr. Philip Melanchthon,
a faithful servant of God, my dearest brother

Grace and peace! We are sitting and lying around here, idle and busy, my Philip; idle, because we accomplish nothing, busy because we are enduring endless torture since Satan harasses us with his wickedness. Among so many ways we finally found one which showed hope; [but] Satan blocked that one again. Then we turned into another way where we thought that all problems were already settled; [but] Satan blocked that one too. Now we have picked a third route which looks as if it is absolutely safe and as if it cannot fail; but the end of the road will show the result.[4]

I would like—and I am asking you for this—you and Doctor Brück[5] to negotiate with the Sovereign[6] so that he will call me home with a letter for some necessary business; perhaps in this way I can force them[7] to speed up the settlement. For I feel that they could not tolerate my departure without the affair having been settled. Therefore I shall give them this one week, and thereafter I intend to threaten them with [this] letter of the sovereign.

Today is about the tenth day[8] that we have started to regulate [the affairs of] Newtown[9] properly. I think it was much easier to establish Newtown than it is for us to regulate its affairs. Mistrust

---

one to adopt the sequence of letters established in Enders and WA, Br—either that the messenger suddenly had enough time for Luther to write the present, rather long, letter to Melanchthon, or that the two letters were sent with different messengers. Both possibilities seem forced if one considers the content of the letters. In the letter to Melanchthon, Luther reports on the situation of the negotiations. He also asks that Melanchthon and Brück get the Elector to recall him. This was an important decision that Luther had reached on February 6, and obviously was the reason for Luther's letter to Wittenberg, a letter for which a messenger was available. The letter to Melanchthon having been written, and thus the important business having been taken care of, Luther quickly wrote the note to his wife (No. 320) while the messenger was getting ready to leave. Thus, the sequence of letters written by Luther on February 6 to Wittenberg seems to be exactly the reverse of that suggested by Enders and in WA, Br 11. See also p. 300, n. 4.
[4] On the basis of the material available to this editor (esp. Krumhaar, *op. cit.* [see p. 291, n. 9]), the exact development of the negotiations and the point they had reached on February 6 could not be established.
[5] Gregory Brück, the Electoral Saxon chancellor emeritus; see LW 49, 51 f.
[6] Elector John Frederick; see LW 48, 181 f.
[7] I.e., the counts of Mansfeld and their negotiators; see p. 285, n. 3.
[8] I.e., counting from January 29, the day on which the negotiations began.
[9] See pp. 281 f., 293, 296.

on both sides is so great that they suspect poison is being served to them in each syllable. You may say this [whole business] is a word-war or a word-insanity, a pleasure one owes to the jurists.[10] They have taught the whole world so many ambiguities, sophistries, and chicaneries—and are still doing so—that [their] jargon is certainly more confusing than all the tongues of Babylon. For as no one there was able to understand the other,[11] so here no one is willing to understand the other. Woe to those parasites, woe to those sophists, those plagues of the human race. I am writing in anger; I do not know whether I would speak more appropriately if I were more composed. But the wrath of God looks at our sins. The Lord will judge his people, but may he have more compassion on his servants.[12] If this is the art of the jurists, then there is no reason for jurists to be as proud as they all are.[13] Isaiah 3 [:1] declares: "The Lord is taking away from Judah and Jerusalem the man," etc.

Farewell, and pray for me!

February 6, 1546   Martin Luther, Doctor

320

To Mrs. Martin Luther
[Eisleben,][1] February 6, 1546

In this hastily written note Luther informs his wife that he will not be able to come home for the next eight days, that their sons are still in Mansfeld, and that he himself could have a good time in Eisleben were it not for the negotiations among the counts. This affair both disgusts and tortures him, says Luther, but pastoral considerations compel him to stay. He also suggests that his wife tell Melanchthon to correct the interpretation of Luke 8:14 in the Postil.

Text in German: WA, Br 11, 284.[2]

---

[10] For the translation, the interpunctuation has been slightly changed at this point. For Luther's relationship with the jurists at this time, see p. 274, n. 8.

[11] Gen. 11:7 (Luther Bible).

[12] See Ps. 135:14.

[13] This sentence is written in German.

[1] See p. 285, n. 3.

[2] The autograph of this letter was at one time deposited in Königsberg, but can now no longer be traced.

To the highly-learned woman, Catherine Lüther,[3]
my gracious mistress at the house at Wittenberg

Grace and peace! Dear Katie! We are sitting here allowing ourselves to be tortured. Though we want to leave, it will not be possible for us to do so for eight days (as it looks to me).[4] You might tell Master[5] Philip[6] to correct his *Postil*, for he has not understood why in the gospel the Lord calls riches "thorns."[7] Here[8] is the school where one learns to understand this. But I am horrified that everywhere in Scripture the thorns are threatened with fire.[9] Therefore I am even more patient that with God's help I might accomplish something worthwhile. Your little sons are still at Mansfeld.[10] Except [for this, nothing is new]; we have enough to eat and drink,[11] and could have a good time, were it not for this disgusting business. It looks to me as if the devil mocks us; may God mock him in return.[12] Amen. Pray for us. The messenger was in a great hurry.

    February 6, 1546   MARTIN LUTHER, DOCTOR

---

[3] For "Lüther," see p. 48, n. 9. Why Luther used this form of spelling could not be established.

[4] I.e.. because Luther had already decided, as he had stated in the letter he had just written to Melanchthon, to allow the negotiations one more week of grace.

[5] I.e., Master of Arts.

[6] Philip Melanchthon; see *LW* 48, 77, n. 3.

[7] In his 1544 *Annotations to the Gospel Lessons* (*C.R.* 14, 161 ff.) Melanchthon had explained Luke 8:14 (*op. cit.*, 220 ff.) in a way which, in light of recent experiences, no longer seemed adequate to Luther. See also *C.R.* 24, 405 ff.

[8] I.e., in the negotiations which were supposed to settle the quarrels among the counts of Mansfeld (see pp. 281 f.), since many of these quarrels were about "riches," e.g., the revenue from the mines.

[9] See, e.g., Ps. 118:12; Isa. 9:18, 10:17, 27:4, 33:12.

[10] See pp. 291 f.

[11] For "eat" and "drink" Luther used earthy words, in the sense of overeat and overdrink like a pig.

[12] This may be an allusion to Ps. 2:4.

321

To Mrs. Martin Luther
[Eisleben,][1] February 7, 1546

Luther, realizing his wife is worried about him, tries to give her some comfort by urging her to read the writings of St. John and the Small Catechism. He tells her to stop worrying about him since he has Jesus Christ, who can care for him better than she and all the angels. Then Luther muses about the situation in which he finds himself: All the devils seem to have congregated at Eisleben; many Jews are living in Eisleben and Rissdorf, and though they have been outlawed, no one does any harm to them; "today" Luther voiced his opinion on the Jews bluntly; he was angry enough that he almost left for home today; he has become a jurist, and intends to attack vigorously the haughtiness that the jurists demonstrate in the present negotiations; though busy (so that he is unable to write to Melanchthon, a fact which Luther hopes Melanchthon will take in good spirit), Luther is living well, and the beer and wine agree with him (though he thinks that the beer from Naumburg congests his chest). In closing Luther assures his wife that all her letters, and those of Melanchthon, have reached him.

Text in German: WA, Br 11, 286–287.[2]

To my dear mistress of the house, Catherine Ludher, a doctor, the
lady of the pig market[3] at Wittenberg—placed into the
hands of, and at the feet of, my gracious lady[4]

---

[1] See p. 285, n. 3.

[2] The letter was extant as autograph which was deposited in Breslau and which, since 1945, can no longer be traced. The autograph text on which the text of the common editions is based (Enders, *WA*, Br, de Wette) has been preserved in a facsimile in an early edition of Köstlin's *Leben Luthers* (1888). Enders, *Briefwechsel* 17, 30, gives textual material pertaining to the autograph; some of this material has been reproduced below for the purpose of giving an insight into the mind of the writer.

[3] For "Ludher," see p. 48, n. 9. Why Luther used this spelling of his family name could not be established; for "doctor," see p. 290, n. 5; for "pig market," see p. 208, n. 12.

[4] The German equivalent of the phrase, "into the hands," is the technical phrase which has to be translated with *"Personal"* (or: Private), as is done throughout this edition of Luther's letters. For the sake of a more smooth reading of the

Grace and peace in the Lord! You, dear Katie, read John[5] and the *Small*[6] *Catechism*, about which you once said: Everything in this book has been said about me. For you prefer to worry about me instead of letting God worry, as if he were not almighty and could not create ten Doctor Martins, should[7] the old one[8] drown in the Saale,[9] or burn in the oven,[10] or perish in Wolfgang's bird trap.[11] Free me from your worries. I have a caretaker who is better than you and all the angels; he lies in the cradle and rests on a virgin's bosom, and yet, nevertheless, he sits at the right hand of God, the almighty Father. Therefore be at peace. Amen.

I think that hell and the whole world must now be empty of all devils, who, perhaps for my sake, have congregated here at Eisleben, so hard has this affair[12] run aground. There are also Jews here, about fifty in one house,[13] as I have written to you previously.[14] Now it is said that in Rissdorf—close to Eisleben, where I became ill during my journey[15]—there are supposedly about four hundred Jews living and working.[16] Count Albrecht, who owns all the area around Eisleben, has declared that the Jews who are caught on his property are outlaws.[17] But as yet no one wants to do them any harm. The Countess of Mansfeld, the widow of Solms,[18] is consid-

---

whole phrase and to allow the particular flavor of the phrase to come through, a more literal translation has been used in preference to the technical term this time.

[5] Exactly what Luther was thinking of could not be established. According to material presented in *WA*, Br 11, 287, n. 2, "John" could be a reference to Luther's sermons on John; see *WA* 28, 31 ff., 39, No. 2; *LW* 24.

[6] Luther added the equivalent of "Small" in the margin.

[7] Originally Luther wrote "should die for you," but then he crossed out the equivalent of "for you."

[8] Luther added the equivalent of "old" between the lines.

[9] See pp. 286 f.

[10] See pp. 296, 305.

[11] This is a reference to Wolfgang Seberger and his efforts to trap birds in the backyard of the Luther house in Wittenberg; see *LW* 49, 158, n. 7.

[12] I.e., the negotiations among the counts of Mansfeld; see p. 285, n. 3.

[13] Luther wrote the equivalent of "in one house" in the margin. What Luther meant here could not be established.

[14] See p. 291.

[15] Literally: "became ill during the drive here." See pp. 290 f., 294.

[16] Literally: "riding in and out, and go by."

[17] See p. 291.

[18] This is a reference to Countess Dorothy of Solms, the widow of Count Ernest II, the father of Counts Philip and John George; see *WA*, Br 12, 366; 10, No. 3905, Introduction.

ered to be the protector of the Jews. I do not know whether this is true. Today I made my opinion known in a sufficiently blunt way if anyone wishes to pay attention to it.[19] Otherwise it might not do any good at all. You people pray, pray, pray, and help us that we do all things properly, for today in my anger I had made up my mind to grease the carriage. But the misery of my fatherland, which came to my mind, has stopped me.[20]

I have also now become a jurist,[21] but this will not be to their[22] advantage. It would have been better had they let me remain a theologian, for if I meddle with them, should I live, I will turn out to be a goblin who by God's grace will attack vigorously[23] their haughtiness. They behave as if they were God; certainly they had better abandon this attitude soon, before their god turns into a demon,[24] as happened to Lucifer, who because of his haughtiness simply was unable to remain in heaven. Well, God's will be done.

Please let Master[25] Philip[26] read this letter, for I have no time to write to him. [Instead I wrote to you, however,] so that you could comfort yourself with the knowledge that I would love you if

---

[19] In Luther's sermon of February 7, 1546 (*WA* 51, 173 ff.) no "blunt" statements against the Jews can be found. This sermon has been preserved in notes and was published later. At the end of this first edition the *Admonition Against the Jews* (*WA* 51, 195 f.), which has been ascribed to Luther, was added; this writing seems to fit the description Luther outlines above—though this judgment may be debated—but it does not fit the one made on p. 291, since Luther does not "outlaw" or "expel" the Jews in this document. It is, of course, possible (as is suggested in *WA*, Br 11, 288, n. 15) that the editor of the sermon and of the *Admonition* "polished" the text somewhat and perhaps eliminated passages that sounded too harsh. Even though there is some evidence that the *Admonition* could have been a part of Luther's last sermon preached in Eisleben and thus would be dated February 14/15, the arguments and the material presented in Rückert, *LB*, p. 429, n. 9, are sufficiently strong to suggest the *Admonition* was a part of Luther's February 7 sermon.

[20] I.e., from having the carriage readied for the journey home. A different translation would be: "has kept me here."

[21] See also p. 274, n. 8.

[22] I.e. here and throughout this paragraph, the reference is to jurists in general and the legal experts at the negotiations in Eisleben in particular.

[23] Literally: "comb."

[24] The translation does not totally reproduce what Luther intends to say. For "God" and "demon" Luther used *Gottheit* and *Teufelheit* (a word which Luther perhaps created). Luther intends to say that the jurists should abandon their claim to be divine like God, lest, like Lucifer, they fall from divinity and become demonic.

[25] I.e. here and throughout the letter, Master of Arts.

[26] Philip Melanchthon; see *LW* 48, 77, n. 3.

I could, as you know, and as Melanchthon perhaps also knows as far as his wife is concerned, and as he well understands.

We are living well here; for each meal the city council gives me one half *Stübig*[27] of Italian wine[28] which is very good.[29] Sometimes I drink it with my companions. The native wine is also good, and the beer of Naumburg is very good, except I think that because of its pitch[30] it congests my chest. In all the world the devil has spoiled the beer for us with pitch, and among you people [he has spoiled] the wine with sulphur.[31] But here the wine is pure, if one disregards the particular quality of the native wine.

So that you do not get confused, you should know that all the letters[32] you had written have arrived here; today those have arrived which you wrote last Friday[33] and sent along with Master Philip's letters.[34]

February 7, 1546   Your loving[35]

MARTIN LUTHER, DOCTOR

---

[27] I.e., either one-half liter or 1–2 liters.

[28] I.e., *Vinum Rifolium*, an Italian wine which was in high demand at Luther's time; see *WA*, Br 11, 288, n. 22.

[29] Luther added the equivalent of "which is very good" in the margin.

[30] Luther wrote *pech*.

[31] In the material available to this editor the references to "pitch" and "sulphur" are not explained. "Pitch' could be a reference to the material used to seal beer barrels which might give the beer a peculiar taste, or to a thickish by-product of the brewing process which may sometimes not have been completely eliminated. "Sulphur" might be a reference to a material sometimes used to clean out barrels by "smoking them" in an attempt to "sterilize" them and make them free from odor and residue of taste.

[32] None of these letters is extant. Certainly they were written in response to the news which arrived in Wittenberg about Luther's trip to Eisleben; see pp. 290 f., 294, 307 f.

[33] I.e., February 5.

[34] There is extant a letter from Melanchthon which can be dated February 5 with some certainty; *WA*, Br 11, No. 4198. This letter, too, speaks of Katie's worries and fears about her husband's health and general well-being.

[35] Or: "[The man] whom you love, Martin Luther, Doctor."

322

To Mrs. Martin Luther
[Eisleben,][1] February 10, 1546

Luther writes with both gravity and humor in this letter. He thanks his wife for her great concern on his behalf and tells her that her worries have almost resulted in his death. Since she has begun to worry he has almost been burned to death and struck by a large stone that could have squashed him, had the angels not protected him! Citing Psalm 55:22, Luther admonishes his wife to put into practice what she has learned from the Catechism. Then Luther informs his wife that he is healthy, that Jonas had a slight accident, and that he is eager to come home, if this be God's will.

Text in German: WA, Br 11, 291.[2]

To the holy lady, full of worries, Mrs. Catherine Luther,
doctor, the lady of Zölsdorf,[3] at Wittenberg,
my gracious, dear mistress of the house

Grace and peace in Christ! Most holy Mrs. Doctor! I thank you very kindly for your great worry which robs you of sleep.[4] Since the date that you [started to] worry about me, the fire in my quarters, right outside the door of my room, tried to devour me;[5] and yesterday, no doubt because of the strength of your worries, a stone almost fell on my head and nearly squashed me as in a mouse trap. For in our secret chamber[6] mortar has been falling down for about two days;[7]

---

[1] See p. 285, n. 3.
[2] This letter is extant in several manuscript copies, and in the common editions of Luther's works.
[3] For "Luther," see p. 48, n. 9; for "doctor," see p. 290, n. 5; for "Zölsdorf," see p. 208, n. 13.
[4] See Excursus.
[5] This event occurred on February 2; see p. 296. As Luther knew on the basis of the letters which he answered on February 7 (see Excursus), Katie was extremely anxious about him because of the flood, his health, and the cold weather. Picking up the casual reference to the fire made in the February 7 letter—obviously because Katie talked about this incident in her latest letter— Luther elaborated on it, and then added the most recent incident about which Katie did not even know.
[6] I.e., the toilet.
[7] Literally: "for in our secret chamber lime and clay drizzled [from] above our head for about two days."

we called in some people who [merely] touched the stone with two fingers and it fell down. The stone was as big as a long pillow and as wide as a large hand; it intended to repay you for your holy worries, had the dear angels not protected [me]. [Now] I worry that if you do not stop worrying the earth will finally swallow us up and all the elements[8] will chase us. Is this the way you learned the *Catechism* and the faith?[9] Pray, and let God worry. You have certainly not been commanded to worry about me or about yourself.[10] "Cast your burden on the Lord, and he will sustain you," as is written in Psalm 55[:22] and many more passages.

We are chipper and healthy, praise be to God, except that the affair[11] is disgusting to us and that Jonas[12] would also like to have a bad calf;[13] and so he accidentally bumped into a chest. So great is human envy that he did not want me to have a bad calf all by myself.[14]

With this I commend you to God. We would gladly be free [of the matter] now[15] and drive home, if God would will it. Amen.

February 10, 1546 Your Holiness' willing servant,

MARTIN LUTHER

---

[8] See p. 278.

[9] Enders, *Briefwechsel* 17, 32 and *WA*, Br 11, 291, give *Glauben*, the German equivalent for "faith," with a lower case "g." On the other hand, Rückert, *LB*, p. 431, gives it with an upper case "g"; this would suggest that Luther was thinking of the *Creed*. Were one to adopt Rückert's reading, Luther would say: Is this the way you learned the *Catechism* and the *Creed?* This makes little sense, since the *Creed* is a part of the *Catechism*. It seems rather that Luther intends to say: Is this the way you learned the *Catechism*, and is this the way you practice the faith which is expounded in the *Catechism?*

[10] This sentence is missing in some witnesses.

[11] I.e., the negotiations to bring about peace among the counts of Mansfeld; see p. 285, n. 3.

[12] Justus Jonas.

[13] The text reads *Schenckel*, which could designate either the thigh (so commonly) or the calf. It was a "bad calf," as is established in the material cited in *WA*, Br 10, 374, n. 4.

[14] Luther is referring here to one of those treatments which he underwent from time to time. From at least the summer of 1543 (see *WA*, Br 10, 374 f.), and upon the advice of Matthias Ratzeberger, Luther had used an acid, abrasive stone (see p. 314) to make and keep a cut (*fontanella*) in his left calf (see note 13), which by oozing was supposed to give relief from all kinds of ailments, esp. headaches and high blood pressure. For documentation, see *WA*, Br 10, 374, n. 4. Dorothy, the countess of Mansfeld, advised Luther to let this wound heal, and to try a sneezing powder instead; *WA*, Br 10, 374.

[15] See note 11.

Luther's statement in his letter of February 10 (No. 322) that his wife worried so much that she was unable to sleep suggests that Luther had in hand a letter in which his wife made a statement to this effect. This was the latest in a series of letters sent by Katie to her husband, letters which reflected Katie's increasing fears over the welfare of her husband. Luther had left Wittenberg in the midst of a bitterly cold winter; see WA, Br 11, 277, n. 12. Then a sudden thaw occurred; p. 292. Rumors about the breakup of the ice and the flooding of the Mulde and Saale rivers, which Luther had to cross, reached Katie and she started to worry about her husband. Luther's letter of January 25 (No. 314) arrived in Wittenberg on or shortly prior to January 31 (see p. 287, n. 22); in it the rumors about the breakup of the ice and flooding were confirmed, but more importantly, Katie was assured that her husband and her sons were in good condition, and that her husband had been sensible enough to wait out the bad weather in Halle. In the meantime, not at all at ease, Katie had apparently written to her husband in Eisleben (see p. 290, n. 6) asking him how he was, and pleading with him to take care of himself. Perhaps Melanchthon, too, wrote a similar letter (see p. 295, n. 22). By February 1 Luther had these letters in hand, and on that day he answered both Katie and Melanchthon (Nos. 316, 317). Quite matter-of-factly he informed his wife and Melanchthon of his illness; but he also assured them that he was now totally well again. Thus Luther apparently thought that he had dissolved his wife's fears, and in the following letters (Nos. 318, 319, 320) Luther concentrated on day-by-day affairs. When the February 1 letters arrived in Wittenberg cannot be established. But the news about the cold wind which made Luther's brain turn almost to ice (see p. 291) did not put the Wittenbergers at ease, notwithstanding Luther's assurance that he was now well. Thus the letter which Melanchthon supposedly wrote on February 5 (see p. 304, n. 34) reflected some worry over Luther's health in view of the climate; WA, Br 11, 281. Simultaneously Katie wrote several times to Luther voicing her anxieties (see p. 302) which were heightened when she received Luther's February 1 letter telling her of his illness. How many letters Katie sent cannot be established. It is safe to suggest that Katie sent some medicine with one of these letters (see Strieder, p. 1). Katie wrote for the last time on February 5; Luther had all these letters in hand on February 7 and answered them on that day. In his long letter, No. 321, Luther tried to put things in the proper perspective for his wife and comfort her, not realizing that in the meantime his wife's worries on his behalf had been substantially increased because she found out that there had been a fire in the chimney of Luther's room. Luther mentioned this incident for the first time in his February 3 letter to Melanchthon. This letter was not in Melanchthon's hands by February 5 when Melanchthon and Katie wrote to Luther. While the argument based on silence is always a dangerous one, it is nevertheless significant that in his February 5(?) letter Melanchthon did not mention this incident; he dealt only with those threats to Luther's well-being which the Wittenbergers knew about from Luther's January 25 (No. 314) and February 1 (Nos. 316, 317) letters. That Luther mentioned the fire in his February 7 letter need not have been in response to a possible statement made by Katie about this incident in her February 5 letter; the casual reference to the fire could have been made simply because Luther realized that by the time Katie received this February 7 letter she also would have heard from Melanchthon about the fire. Before this long letter of comfort (No. 321) reached Katie, she wrote another letter in which she confessed her fright for him, saying that she worried so much that she could not sleep. The date on which Katie wrote this letter cannot be established, but it is safe to suggest that she wrote it after she had found out from Melanchthon about the fire incident, i.e., shortly after February 5. In any case, Luther received the letter after he had dispatched his February 7 letter, so that he felt it necessary to write letter No. 322.

323

To George of Anhalt
[Eisleben,][1] February 10, 1546

Luther returns a document which deals with questions pertaining to matrimonial matters and on which he has briefly noted his opinion; he promises to elaborate further on these problems when he has more time. Luther underscores the fact that something must be done regarding these matters in order to avoid scandals lest conditions similar to those described in Genesis 6:2 develop. He points out that dispensations from the law can cause serious problems for a person's conscience, as can clearly be seen in the case of Henry VIII of England.

On George of Anhalt, see p. 280, n. 53.

Text in Latin: WA, Br 11, 292.[2]

To the most Reverend Father and Illustrious Sovereign and Lord, Sir George, bishop of the church at Merseburg[3] and prior of the church at Magdeburg, sovereign of Anhalt, count of Ascania, lord at Bernburg, most illustrious and famous lord

Grace and peace! Most Reverend Father in Christ and Most Illustrious Sovereign! As briefly as I was able I have noted my opinion in the margin. I am ready to elaborate further on the matter at some other time and when I have more leisure, though in view of Your Highness' very great wisdom further material is not necessary. Certainly one has to meet head-on the scandals into which the thoughtless and wild ones plunge themselves, as if one must live without

---

[1] See p. 285, n. 3.

[2] The autograph of the letter is extant. At one time the original of the document sent by George with the short marginal replies Luther made in his own handwriting was also extant; it is published in WA, Br 11, 293 ff. According to WA, Br 13, 354, addition to *loc. cit.*, this original document can now no longer be traced.—It is quite possible that George wanted to discuss these problems pertaining to matrimonial law with Luther in person and that, tired of waiting for Luther to come (see p. 289), he finally put the problems on paper and asked for Luther's opinion in writing.

[3] For "bishop," "church," and "Merseburg," see LW 49, 61, n. 9, 87, n. 5, and above, p. 280, n. 54.

any laws. Otherwise that which Moses tells us[4] happened prior to the flood will happen again, namely, that they took for wives whomever they desired,[5] even sisters, mothers, and those whom they stole from their husbands. I hear that some similar events are definitely occurring in secret. May God prevent them[6] from ruling in broad daylight, as one has seen in the cases of Herod[7] and the kings of Egypt,[8] etc. The King of England was an unhappy husband; his example always should be avoided, for although he was granted a dispensation, in the end his conscience was not calmed by it. People are able to get a bad conscience unnecessarily, even in affairs which are correctly handled, a fact which by itself causes us enough of a problem; doesn't it? More at some other time, God willing; in him farewell to Your Illustrious Highness.

February 10, 1546   Your Illustrious Highness' dedicated
MARTIN LUTHER

324

To Mrs. Martin Luther
Eisleben,[1] February 14, 1546

Luther informs his wife that he hopes to return this week, that practically all the issues have been settled, and that today he will undertake the personal reconciliation of the counts. There is much joy and laughter among the children of the counts, Luther says, and Countess Anna (who gave some trout to Luther which he is sending on to Katie) rejoices about the accord which has been reached. Luther tells his wife that their sons are still at Mansfeld, that although he is healthy and well taken care of, Jonas' leg is not doing well. Luther also reports some rumors: he supposedly has been "led

---

[4] Gen. 6:2.
[5] Or: "chose."
[6] I.e., the people who try to nullify certain laws, esp. concerning the degrees of relationship between marriage partners.
[7] Matt. 14:3 f.
[8] This is a reference to the custom according to which the Egyptian kings sometimes married their sisters.
[1] See p. 285, n. 3.

*away," the Emperor is "nearby," the King of France and the Land-
grave are hiring mercenaries.*
Text in German: WA, Br 11, 300.[2]

To my kind, dear mistress of the house, Mrs. Catherine Luther[3]
von Bora, at Wittenberg: *Personal*

Grace and peace in the Lord! Dear Katie! We hope to return home
again this week,[4] God willing. Here God has demonstrated great
grace, for through their councilors the lords have settled almost
everything[5] except two or three issues, among which is the reconciliation of the two brothers, Count Gebhard and Count Albrecht,[6]
which I am to bring about today. I shall ask them to be my guests
so that they may talk with each other. For until now they have been
silent, and in [their] writings have shown much bitterness toward
each other.[7] Otherwise the young lords[8] are happy, and ride
around together in sleighs decorated with fools bells,[9] as do the
young ladies; they all visit each other in carnival masks,[10] and are
of good cheer, even Count Gebhard's son.[11] Therefore one is forced
to grasp the fact that God is the "listener to prayers."[12]

---

[2] The letter is extant in manuscript copies, one of which was written by George
Rörer, and in the common editions of Luther's works. See *WA*, Br 11, No. 4207,
Introduction; 13, 354, addition to *loc. cit.*; 14, 232.
[3] For "Luther," see p. 48, n. 9.
[4] In 1546, February 14 was a Sunday.
[5] See pp. 317 f.
[6] Count Gebhard, the brother of Count Albrecht, felt esp. bitter toward Count
Albrecht since the latter had managed to acquire rights and properties belonging
to Gebhard because of the large debts incurred by Gebhard due to mismanage-
ment. See also pp. 281 f.
[7] Literally: "they have severely embittered themselves in writings." To what
"writings" refers is not clear. Luther could have been thinking, e.g., of the
written material that was a part of the suit filed with Emperor Maximilian by
one of the counts against Albrecht (see *WA*, Br 12, 364), or of the various
settlements signed by the counts prior to 1546 which in reality were not settlements at all but only instruments which merely further complicated the situation.
[8] I.e., the many offspring of the counts; see *WA*, Br 12, 366.
[9] I.e., bells similar to those on a fool's cap and mounted on the harnesses of the
horses.
[10] Literally: "they bring carnival things to one another."
[11] It is not clear why Luther singles out one of Count Gebhard's sons. Was this
son esp. embittered? Of which son was Luther thinking? One son of Count Gebhard, George II, died in July of 1546; perhaps he was ill at the time that
Luther made the statement above. In any case, Katie must have known whom
Luther meant, a fact which suggests that she knew about the situation in detail.
[12] This phrase is written in Latin. See I Sam. 7:9 (Vulgate, Luther Bible); Ps.
91:15 (Vulgate, Luther Bible), 118:5 (Vulgate, Luther Bible).

I am sending to you the trout which Albrecht's Countess[13] has presented to me; she rejoices from her heart about the accord.

Your little sons are still at Mansfeld,[14] [and] James[15] will take care of them well. We have plenty[16] to eat and drink, [and live] like lords. We are well cared for, even too well, so that we might easily forget about you people in Wittenberg. Also the stone[17] does not bother me, praise be to God.[18] But Doctor Jonas' leg really turned out to be bad because of the holes in the shin.[19] But God will also help [in this]. You might tell all this to Master[20] Philip,[21] Doctor Pomer,[22] and Doctor Cruciger.[23]

The rumor has arrived here that Doctor Martin has been led away;[24] they are saying the same thing at Leipzig and Magdeburg. It is the wisenheimers, your fellow countrymen, who are dreaming up these stories.[25] Some say the Emperor[26] is thirty miles[27] away from here, near Soest in Westphalia;[28] some say that the Frenchman[29] is hiring mercenaries and that the Landgrave[30] is doing the

---

13 I.e., Anna, wife of Count Albrecht.
14 See pp. 291 f. They returned before February 17—at least Paul and Martin did; they are the only sons consistently mentioned in the accounts of Luther's death as having been present in the final hours of the Reformer's life; see Strieder, pp. 4, 14, 26, 27.
15 See LW 49, 268, n. 4.
16 In the Rörer manuscript copy this word has been added between the lines; see Enders, Briefwechsel 17, 49, n. g.
17 See also pp. 165 ff.
18 This phrase has been added between the lines only in the Rörer manuscript. See Enders, loc. cit., n. i.
19 See p. 306.
20 I.e., Master of Arts.
21 Philip Melanchthon; see LW 48, 77, n. 3.
22 I.e., John Bugenhagen; see LW 48, 303, n. 44.
23 Caspar Cruciger; see LW 49, 104, n. 12.
24 I.e., kidnapped.
25 This is a reference to the people of Meissen (Katie's native land), whom Luther suspected of being his bitter enemies—and he did have some good reason to think so; see also p. 224; WA, Br 10, 402.
26 Charles V; see LW 48, 175 f.
27 I.e., approximately 205 kilometers.
28 Soest in Westphalia is about 230 kilometers west from Eisleben as the crow flies.
29 I.e., Francis I, king of France.
30 Landgrave Philip of Hesse; see LW 49, 124, n. 18. The rumors reported by Luther foreshadow coming events. Since the winter of 1545 the rumors of mobilization and war (see also p. 267) had been hanging over Germany like those dark clouds which Titian painted into the background of his famous 1548 picture of Charles V (now in the Prado in Madrid), portraying the Emperor as general, and all the statements of the Emperor to the contrary accomplished

same. But let them say and sing [what they wish]; we shall wait for what God will do. With this I commend you to God. Amen.

Eisleben, February 14, 1546   MARTIN LUTHER, DOCTOR

325

To Philip Melanchthon
[Eisleben,]¹ February 14, 1546

Luther informs Melanchthon that he has received a letter from Elector John Frederick in which he is being called home; since he is

little in dispelling the rumors. Following the establishment of the alliance between Pope Paul III and Charles V in June of 1545 (see p. 265, n. 4), the Emperor continued his policy of attempting to reconcile the evangelicals with the Roman church through negotiations. But his determination to stop the further spread of the Reformation and to subjugate the evangelicals to the authority of the Roman See became increasingly clear. The 1545 Diet of Worms arranged a colloquy scheduled for Regensburg; once more evangelicals and papists were to try to find a peaceful solution to the problems, though the representatives of the Roman church, old diehards handpicked by the Emperor, gave little room for hope. Even to the most hopeful of the evangelicals and to those most willing to attempt compromises it became increasingly obvious that the moment of crisis had arrived. The delegates to the colloquy were slow in arriving in Regensburg, and after several postponements the colloquy was finally officially opened on January 27. At the beginning of March the futility of any further discussion had become evident to all parties, and by the end of March the colloquy had faded away. On this colloquy, see Lau-Bizer, pp. 194 f. Contrary to the rumor (reported by Luther to his wife) that Charles V was in Soest, the Emperor was in fact still in the Netherlands, moving slowly toward a diet which he had summoned to Regensburg. At a meeting in Maastricht in February of 1546 the Emperor assured a delegation of the Electors that the rumors of a planned war against the Protestants were without the slightest foundation. At the end of March, in Speyer, the Emperor assured Landgrave Philip of Hesse that all the negotiations with France and all the military preparations were directed against the Turks and not against the Protestants. On April 10 the Emperor arrived in Regensburg, and on June 5 the diet was officially opened. During this diet, Elector John Frederick and Landgrave Philip of Hesse were, without due process, outlawed by the Emperor as rebels, and on July 9 the first shots of the Smalcaldic War were fired. See Ranke 2ᴵⱽ, 234 ff.; Brandi, 1, 445 ff.; L. Theobald, *Die Reformationsgeschichte der Reichsstadt Regensburg*, 2 (Nürnberg, 1951), 84 ff. It cannot be documented that in February of 1545 either the Emperor or Francis I or Landgrave Philip of Hesse were mobilizing—the Emperor's actual order of mobilization was not issued until June 9, 1545, and the Smalcaldic League officially mobilized on July 4. Yet the speed with which the Imperial army and that of the Smalcaldic League were ready to march suggests that while the actual content of the rumor may not have been true, nevertheless preparations for war were being made on both sides.
¹ See p. 285, n. 3.

*disgusted with the negotiations among the counts of Mansfeld, he
will hurry to leave Eisleben. He also asks that some medication be
sent to him. Then Luther tells Melanchthon of the death of Pope
Paul III, and of a pending meeting between the Archbishop of
Cologne and the counts of Mansfeld.*

On Philip Melanchthon, see LW 48, 77, n. 3.

Text in Latin: WA, Br 11, 301–302.[2]

To Philip Melanchthon, a most worthy brother in Christ

Grace and Peace! Today I have received the most welcome letter
from the Sovereign[3] calling me home, my Philip, and I hurry to
leave, since I am sick and tired of this affair.[4] Notwithstanding this,
I am asking you to see to it that, if I should perhaps already be on
the way, a messenger would at least meet me and bring some of
that caustic with which my calf is usually kept open.[5] For the
wound which was opened at Wittenberg is almost completely
healed, and you know how dangerous this might be.[6] And they do
not have any of this caustic here. My Katie knows where in my
room[7] this kind of caustic is, which is so necessary [for me].

---

[2] The letter is extant in manuscript copies, and in the common editions of Luther's
works. The many variant readings reproduced in Enders, *Briefwechsel* 17, 50,
are of no major significance for the meaning of the text, though they demonstrate
that the tradition of the letter is unclear.

[3] See p. 298. This letter of Elector John Frederick (see *LW* 48, 181 f.) is no
longer extant. Apparently it was written prior to February 10, for on that day
the Elector wrote to Luther about some other matter (*WA*, Br 11, No. 4206);
he addressed Luther as being in Wittenberg, perhaps because he assumed that
by the time the letter reached the addressee, Luther would be back again from
Eisleben.

[4] I.e., the negotiations among the counts of Mansfeld; see p. 285, n. 3.

[5] See p. 306, n. 14.

[6] Ratzeberger argued that the healing of this *fontanella* could have contributed
to Luther's death; see *WA*, Br 11, 291, n. 10.

[7] The text uses *hypocaustum*, i.e., a sweating-chamber, a bath room, or any
small room that can be heated. Luther used the same term in his letter of about
November 10, 1527, to Jonas, where the term has been translated as "my bedroom"; see *LW* 49, 174. This may not be the best translation, and perhaps "my
personal room," or even "my study" would be a more appropriate translation.
Whether this room was identical with the famous Tower Room, as is suggested
in *WA*, Br 11, 302, n. 2, has to remain open. *Hypocaustum* need not necessarily
refer only to Luther's private room (i.e., the Tower Room), for the same term
is used in a January 26, 1544, letter, to describe a living room which, in addition to a bedroom, could be made available to a visitor; see *WA*, Br 10, 519.

Pope Paul III died on January 3[8] and has been buried; this was written to us as true news. The [Arch]bishop of Cologne has written a letter to Count Albrecht inviting him to Nordhausen for a meeting of counts on March 1, in order to discuss there with them matters which concern them.[9] For he thinks that the counts will be excluded from the diocese of Cologne by N.N.[10] Other things shortly in person, God willing, for I want to tear myself away [from here].

Farewell in the Lord!

February 14, 1546   Yours, MARTIN LUTHER

---

[8] This news was false, for Pope Paul III died on November 10, 1549. However, this "news" was quite widespread; see *WA*, Br 11, 302, n. 3.

[9] The background and circumstances of this sentence could not be clarified. Hermann von Wied, the archbishop of Cologne, who was in serious trouble with the Emperor at that time, apparently tried to gain the support of the counts of Mansfeld and of other counts.

[10] In the original the person's name was given, perhaps with a pseudonym or a cipher. Was it the Emperor?

Epilogue

On February 14 Luther wrote two letters to Wittenberg, one to his wife (No. 324), and one to Melanchthon (No. 325). In Enders, *Briefwechsel*, and in *WA, Br* 11, the letter to Luther's wife precedes the one to Melanchthon; this fact suggests that Luther wrote first to his wife and then to Melanchthon. Internal criteria tend to substantiate this suggestion. Luther reported to his wife details about the situation pertaining to the negotiations among the counts of Mansfeld and informed her that he expected to come home "this week," i.e., any time between February 14 and 20; see p. 311. He also told her that she could inform Melanchthon and others accordingly. There was, then, no need for a letter to Melanchthon, unless after the letter to Katie had been sealed, and perhaps also dispatched, "new business" arose. This was exactly the case when Luther received the Elector's letter, a fact about which Melanchthon had to be informed since he had been asked to procure this letter (see pp. 298, 314), and when Luther remembered that he needed the medication. Luther could and should have asked his wife for this medication; he obviously had forgotten to do so. It seems, then, that the letter to Melanchthon was indeed an afterthought. To corroborate this suggestion, one could ask if Luther would not have informed Melanchthon about the successful developments in the negotiations, had he written first to Melanchthon. On the other hand, *St. L.* 21b and de Wette (*Dr. Martin Luthers Briefe* 5 [Berlin, 1828]) place the letter to Melanchthon before the letter to Katie; this would suggest that Luther wrote first to Melanchthon, and then to his wife, a suggestion which is somewhat romantic since thus Luther's last extant letter would be addressed to his wife. The letters do provide some basis also for such a sequence. Luther said to Melanchthon that he would hurry to leave Eisleben, that he wanted to tear himself away from there, and that he was sick and tired of the affair; see pp. 314, 315. Would Luther have spoken in this way if he already knew that almost everything had been settled? (See p. 311). One is tempted to answer negatively. But then one would be forced to demonstrate (*a*) that on February 14 a breakthrough in the negotiations did indeed occur; and (*b*) the role the Elector's letter did or did not play in this breakthrough. The breakthrough would have had to be so sudden that between the time of writing the letter to Melanchthon and the one to Katie all those things occurred of which Luther spoke in the first paragraph of his letter to Katie. This is, of course, possible—but is it probable? As long as no exact record of the negotiations is available, so that one would be in a position to say that on February 14 a breakthrough in the negotiations occurred, it is dangerous to toy with the idea (as does K. Aland, *Luther Deutsch* 10 [Stuttgart, 1959], 394) that the arrival of the Elector's letter influenced the negotiations in such a way that Luther (perhaps in the afternoon of February 14) could quite precisely tell his wife that he expected to be home "this week," after he had told Melanchthon (perhaps in the morning of February 14) that the Elector's letter had (just) arrived and then quite vaguely added that he, Luther, would hurry to leave Eisleben. On the basis of the presently available material the sequence of the February 14 letters cannot be precisely established. Since the tone of the letter to Melanchthon leaves one with the feeling that this letter was an afterthought the sequence of letters established in Enders and WA, Br has been retained.

The letters of February 14 are the last extant letters Luther wrote. They are a part of the very last materials extant from Luther's pen. While Luther was away from Wittenberg he preached, to our knowledge, five times: once in Halle on January 26, and then four times in Eisleben (January 31, February 2, 7, and 14 or 15, though February 15 seems to be the more probable date). It can no longer be established who recorded these sermons (except in the case of the January 26 sermon) but they were printed in 1546, soon after Luther's death. See WA 51, xii, xiv ff., 135 ff.; LW 51, 381 ff. These posthumous editions of Luther's sermons are of secondary value compared with the other material extant from these days, since it can no longer be determined whether and to what degree the editors used editorial license in their work. Similar care would have to be taken with the dedicatory sentences or paragraphs which Luther inscribed in books during these days. They have been preserved for posterity in the 1547 editions by John Aurifaber and by George Rörer, as well as in a manuscript written by Rörer. In some cases the text and date of these dedications can be exactly verified, in other cases questions remain which cannot be answered. See Enders, *Briefwechsel* 14, No. 3086, Introduction; 17, No. 3628; WA 48, ix-297, and WA, RN to *loc. cit.*

Of more primary value is the material that is extant from Luther's own pen, or at least in reliable copies.

Luther took along to Eisleben an unfinished manuscript of a work "against the asses of Paris and Louvain." He had started this work in September of 1545 (see p. 261), but in view of his involvement with the counts of Mansfeld and his declining health, he did not get far; and so he started over again in January of 1546. While in Eisleben, he supposedly kept the manuscript in the chest into which Jonas accidentally bumped (see p. 306), and he continued to work on it. He did not finish the manuscript, however, and the portion of it which he had completed disappeared; it was finally discovered in the nineteenth century, and is published in WA 54, 447 ff. See WA, Br 11, 177, 264, 265 f.; Strieder, pp. 34 f.

While in Eisleben, Luther planned to write something against the Jews (see p. 291). This plan was apparently not carried out, unless one wishes to see in the *Admonition* (see p. 303, n. 19) the result of this plan.

Some time during his stay in Eisleben Luther and Jonas drafted a brief on the ecclesiastical situation of the old and new town of Eisleben, esp. the various institutions, their relationships to one another, and the duties and privileges of the counts, the clergy, and the teachers. This was one of the sore areas in the relationship among the counts of Mansfeld, and in this brief Luther and Jonas made precise suggestions for a settlement of the problems. This brief became a part of the first document (WA, Br 12, No. 4300) in which the quarrels among the counts were settled. Luther had written this document, and he and Jonas signed it on February 16. On the same day also the very last of Luther's extant written statements was put on paper. This is a short paragraph which deals with the understanding of Holy Scripture, and in which the last line reads: "We are beggars. That is true." See LW 54, 476. (For this translation one should also see the text provided by Aurifaber [he stated that he had copied directly from the autograph; WA, TR 5, No. 5468], and the material provided in WA 48, 241 and WA, RN to loc. cit.)

By February 16 Luther's strength was at an end. During his last sermon, he had suffered an attack of dizziness so that he had to end the sermon prematurely; see WA 51, 194; LW 51, 392. He pulled himself together for the negotiations on February 16, which must have exhausted him, for his friends urged him not to attend the session on February 17 (see Strieder, pp. 1, 7, 13, 26); on that day the long, second document (WA, Br 12, No. 4301) was finally adopted in which the many details which had been controversial among the counts were settled. In contrast to the document of February 16, this document of February 17 was formulated without Luther's assistance, though it is sealed with Luther's seal. Whether the Reformer personally signed the document could not be established.

With the letters of February 14, and the document and the short paragraph on the understanding of Scripture, both of February 16, Luther's own literary productivity ended. On February 17 (for the following, see the references cited on p. 285, n. 5) Luther's health fluctuated, with a steady downward tendency, and in the early morning hours of February 18, between two and three o'clock, Luther passed away. He was in pain physically, but contrary to all the wild stories which soon circulated, he was mentally alert, spiritually composed, and steadfastly confessing the faith he had come to embrace. Funeral services were held in Eisleben, and even though the counts of Mansfeld tried hard to have Luther's remains buried in Eisleben, Elector John Frederick insisted that the remains be interred in Wittenberg (WA, 54, 493). The funeral procession reached Wittenberg in the morning of February 22 and proceeded to the Castle Church. After Bugenhagen's sermon and Melanchthon's eulogy, interment took place near the pulpit, where, again contrary to all the wild stories, Luther's earthly remains have rested throughout the centuries, "sown in dishonor in order to be raised on that day in eternal glory," as Jonas and Coelius, quoting I Cor. 15:43, state in the "official" report of the events (WA 54, 496).

INDEXES

INDEX OF NAMES AND SUBJECTS

[References to biographical sketches are in boldface type.]

INDEX

Joachim II, elector of Brandenburg, 68 ff., **69 n. 2,** 110 n. 6, 149 n. 7, 228 n. 21
John, 175 n. 2
John of Anhalt, 175
John, elector of Saxony, 3 ff., 22, 23 ff., 41 ff., 41 n. 7, 43 n. 12, 47, 48, 50, 56 ff., 160 n. 20, 278 n. 35
John of Jena, 129, 219, 292
John, margrave of Brandenburg-Küstrin-Neumark, 149 n. 7
John of Salisbury, xv
John Frederick, elector of Saxony, 42, 45 n. 18, 57, 80 n. 10, 87, 93 n. 3, 97 n. 3, 99 n. 12, 139 n. 3, 144 n. 1, 186, 197, 205, 214, 214 n. 10, 215, 222, 224 nn. 9, 10, 228 n. 21, 237, 237 n. 6, 255, 271, 274, 274 nn. 8, 9, 275 n. 25, 280 n. 54, 294 n. 15
and the council (*see* Smalcaldic League, and the council)
and Emperor Charles V (*see* Charles V, and the Protestants)
and England (*see* Smalcaldic League, and England)
and Ferdinand I, 104 n. 18, 108 n. 7, 112 nn. 21, 25
and France, 88 ff.
official contacts with Luther, 41 n. 1, 46 n. 19, 57, 81 ff., 89, 100 ff., 105, 114, 117 ff., 119 n. 16, 121 n. 35, 132 ff., 139, 140, 153 f., 156, 157 ff., 185 ff., 192 ff., 195 f., 197 ff., 203, 207, 224 n. 7, 255 ff., 258 ff., 278, 297 n. 3, 298, 314, 314 n. 3, 316
personal contacts with Luther, 94 n. 8, 95 n. 14, 122, 130 n. 2, 135, 156, 167 f., 204 ff., 210 f., 246 n. 20, 275, 276, 278, 318

John George, count of Mansfeld, 282 f., 302 n. 18
John Henry, count of Schwarzburg, 285 n. 3
Jonas, Justus, xix n. 26, 47 n. 5, 144 n. 1, 154, 154 nn. 5, 7, 159 n. 13, 207 nn. 5, 8, 225 ff., 236 ff., 269 n. 8, 271 n. 9
and Luther, 47, 80 nn. 6, 8, 87 nn. 7, 8, 14, 93 ff., 94 n. 8, 95 n. 18, 107 ff., 109 ff., 144 ff., 153 ff., 163 n. 43, 168 n. 21, 207 n. 5, 210 n. 26, 225 ff., 236 ff., 237 n. 6, 246 nn. 17, 20, 247 ff., 268 ff., 275 n. 13, 280 n. 54, 285 nn. 3, 5, 289, 291 n. 8, 294 n. 15, 297, 306, 312, 317, 318
and Wittenberg University, 56, 63, 67, 93 f., 102, 144 n. 1, 204, 248 n. 8.
Jonas, Justus, Jr., 237 f., 247 f.
Jüterbog, 115, 209 n. 21
Julius II, pope, 32 n., 35, 121 n. 39
Jurists, 11 f., 105, 248, 274 n. 8, 293 f., 299, 303
Justification by faith, 20, 67, 108, 131 n. 6, 202, 204, 209 n. 20

Kaliningrad (*see* Königsberg)
Kantor, 232 n. 11
Karl Marx Stadt (*see* Chemnitz)
Karlstadt, Andrew, 55, 55nn. 14, 15, 131, 227, 228
Karlstadt, Anne, 227 n. 14
Kassel, 194 n. 11
Kauf, 272 n. 10
Kaufmann family, 128
Kaufmann, Magdalen, 168 n. 21, 209 n. 21
Keller, Michael, 173, n. 14
Khurrem, 229 n. 23
King, Melchior, 293
Kitzingen, 210 n. 30, 226 n. 6

331

Lower Saxon Circuit, 68, 69
Lucifer, 303
Lübeck, 29, 30, 31, 199 n. 30
Lufft, Hans, 185 n. 4, 186 n. 8,
    228 n. 21
Luther, Catherine, xv, 21, 47 ff.,
    72 f., 74, 79 ff., 100, 109,
    112 f., 117, 124, 147, 153,
    165 ff., 168 n. 22, 170, 174,
    176, 180, 184, 207 ff., 209,
    212 ff., 215 n. 22, 218 ff.,
    221 ff., 223 ff., 225 n. 12, 232
    n. 6, 239, 240, 246, 250 n. 5,
    273 ff., 278 n. 32, 280 n. 54,
    284 ff., 287 n. 22, 290 ff., 293
    n. 4, 297 n. 3, 299 f., 300,
    301 ff., 305 f., 307 f., 310 ff.,
    314, 316 f.
  manages the Luther household,
    49, 81, 94 f., 108 f., 110 n. 2,
    113, 126, 167 n. 13, 212,
    213 ff., 216 f., 220, 221, 222
    n. 18, 223 n. 2, 224 f., 278,
    286 n. 10, 312
Luther, Elizabeth, 73 n. 1
Luther, James, 18, 128, 283 n. 10,
    312
Luther, John, 50, 73 n. 1, 93 n. 2,
    129, 151 ff., 210 nn. 27, 28,
    231 f., 234, 239, 240, 246 n.
    15, 273, 277, 285 n. 3, 291 n.
    16, 300, 312
Luther, Magdalen, 50, 73 n. 1,
    234 f., 238, 239, 246 n. 18
Luther, Margaret, 79 n. 1, 184, 208
    n. 9, 210 n. 28, 218 n. 2, 221
    n. 2, 246, 246 nn. 17, 18, 20,
    253 n. 2, 299 n. 2
Luther, Martin, xiv, 73 n. 4, 84 n.
    16, 110 n. 2, 128, 224 n. 4,
    269 n. 8, 281, 285 f., 300 n. 3,
    301 n. 3, 303, 312
  and John Bugenhagen (see
    Bugenhagen, John, Luther's
    friend and pastor)
  and the council, 157 ff. (see also

John Frederick, elector of Sax-
    ony, official contacts with Lu-
    ther; Smalcaldic League, and
    the council)
  and Elector John Frederick (see
    John Frederick, elector of Sax-
    ony, official contacts with Lu-
    ther; John Frederick, elector
    of Saxony, personal contacts
    with Luther)
  and England (see England, cause
    of the gospel in; Luther, Mar-
    tin, works: Opinion on the di-
    vorce of Henry VIII)
  and France (see Melanchthon,
    and France)
  and Justus Jonas (see Jonas,
    Justus, and Luther)
  and the Turks, 9, 46, 54, 55,
    69 ff., 69 n. 2, 72, 155, 164 f.,
    219, 224, 224 n. 7, 225 n. 11,
    227, 228 f., 238, 243, 251,
    270, 272 (see also Charles V,
    and the Turks; Ferdinand I,
    and the Turks; Turks)
  and Wittenberg University (see
    Wittenberg University, Faculty
    of Theology)
  enjoys food and drink, 48, 81, 87,
    208, 218, 221, 287, 291, 300,
    304, 312
  evaluates himself and his work,
    129 f., 137 f., 242 (see also
    Luther, Martin, feels frus-
    trated, old, tired, and useless)
  expects to die and longs for
    death, 184, 238, 242, 245, 246,
    267, 278, 281, 284 f.
  family of, 26 f., 50, 151 n. 1, 156,
    167, 210 f., 222, 223, 231 f.,
    246, 287, 291 f., 300, 312
    (see also Luther, Catherine)
  feels frustrated, old, tired, and
    useless, 79, 110, 182, 188, 245,
    267, 281, 284 f., 290, 293,
    294, 298, 300, 302 (see also

177, 192, 193 f., 195 n. 17, 196, 198 n. 25, 199 n. 30, 205 n. 5
Mount Olympus, 295 n. 18
Mühlpfort, Hermann, 50
Müller, Caspar, 124 ff.
Mulde River, 287, 307
Murder, 123 n. 4 (*see also* Arson)
Music, musician, 231, 232, 233
Mustafa, 229 n. 23
Myconius, Frederick, 178, 190 n. 17, 195, 218
Mylius, Kraft, 189 n. 12, 191 n. 18

Nassau, territory of, 199 n. 30
Naumburg, city of, city government of, 144 n. 1, 207 n. 8, 221 n. 8, 291, 304
evangelical bishop of (*see* Amsdorf, Nicholas von)
Necrosius, Konrad, 272 n. 10
Neobulus, Joducus, 172 n. 7, 173 n. 14, 174 n. 19
Nephilim, 243
Netherlands, 251, 253, 254 n. 8, 312 n. 30
Neunburg/Upper Palatinate, 78
Newtown (*see* Eisleben)
Nicaea, council of (325), 249
Nice, 243 n. 12
Nice Truce (1538), 183 n. 16
Nicholson, John (*see* Lambert, John)
Nimbschen, nunnery at, 278 n. 32
Nobility of Germany, 98, 224 f., 225 n. 11, 243, 243 n. 13, 245, 253 (*see also* Meissen, nobility of)
Nordhausen, 315
Nürnberg, city of, city government of, 9 f., 11 n. 18, 14 n. 10, 17 n. 1, 54, 54 nn. 4, 5, 56, f., 58 n. 13, 61 ff., 75 ff., 77 n. 13, 119, 209 n. 20, 248 n. 6, 263, 297 n. 3

evangelical church in, 13 ff., 61 ff., 65 n. 23, 75 ff., 241
Nürnberg League (1538), 189 n. 5, 190 n. 16
Nürnberg Truce (1532), xiv, 54, 54 nn. 5, 7, 82 n. 4, 155 n. 14
Nuncio, 145 n. 13 (*see also* Legate)

Oecolampadius, John, 3, 4, 5, 7
Olympia, 230 n. 24
Oporin, John, 228 n. 18
Orator, 127, 160
Ordination, 280 n. 54
Orestes, 156 n. 21
Osiander, Andrew, 13, 13 n. 8, 16 n. 21, 67, 67 n. 31, 75 ff., 77 n. 13
Ovid, *De arte amandi*, 232 n. 9

Pack, Otto von, 72
Padua, 83 n. 8
Palatinate, 78, 147 n. 19, 254 (*see also* Elector, of the Palatinate)
Papacy, papal church, papal intrigues, papists, papistical abomination, error, foolishness, and tyranny, xiii, 9, 20, 40, 60, 82, 84, 98 n. 10, 104, 114 n. 5, 115, 116, 144, 145, 158 ff., 160 ff., 165, 176, 184, 188 n. 4, 189, 190 n. 16, 200 f., 209 nn. 19, 24, 219 n. 17, 247 n. 5, 254, 256, 256 n. 5, 257, 270, 272, 279 n. 48, 280 n. 54, 289, 312 n. 30, (*see also* Antichrist; Paul III, pope; Sophists, sophistry)
Paris, 190 n. 17
University of, 247 n. 5
Paros, 230 n. 24
Pastoral counseling, 17 ff., 47 n. 5, 50 ff., 68 ff., 76 n. 10, 79
Patentaler, 74 n. 10
Pater noster, 69, 71, 84, 100, 119, 127, 186, 205, 250, 255, 283

INDEX TO SCRIPTURE PASSAGES

DATE DUE

7 25			
NO 24 82			
GAYLORD			PRINTED IN U.S.A.